HARVARD STUDIES IN CULTURAL ANTHROPOLOGY, 1

General Editors
David Maybury-Lewis
Stanley J. Tambiah
Evon Z. Vogt, Jr.
Nur Yalman

The Harvard Studies in Cultural Anthropology is founded in the belief that answers to general questions about the human condition may be discovered through the intensive study of other cultures. The series will publish books which elucidate and interpret cultural systems in order to contribute to comparative understanding.

Dialectical Societies
The Gê and Bororo of Central Brazil

Edited by David Maybury-Lewis

Contributors
Joan Bamberger
J. Christopher Crocker
Roberto da Matta
Jean Lave
David Maybury-Lewis
Julio Cezar Melatti
Terence S. Turner

Harvard University Press
Cambridge, Massachusetts
and London, England
1979

Library of Congress Cataloging in Publication Data

Main entry under title:

Dialectical societies.

   (Harvard studies in cultural anthropology ; 1)
    1.   Tapuya Indians—Addresses, essays, lectures.
2. Bororo Indians—Addresses, essays, lectures.
I. Maybury-Lewis, David. II. Bamberger, Joan.
III. Series.
F2520.1.T3D5   981'.004'98   79-10689
ISBN 0-674-20285-6

This book is dedicated to Curt Nimuendajú in memory of his pioneering studies in ethnology and his deep affection for the Indians of Brazil

Acknowledgments

This volume brings together some of the results of research carried out by seven anthropologists over more than a decade. It would be difficult to list all those people and institutions who have helped each one of us during that time and impossible to acknowledge their help in any adequate fashion. Fieldwork in Central Brazil posed logistic and personal problems which could never have been surmounted without the generous assistance we all received. We would, therefore, like to acknowledge our dependence on and express, however inadequately, our gratitude to our friends and sponsors in Brazil. Above all, we are grateful to the Museu Nacional of the Federal University of Rio de Janeiro, which sponsored all of our fieldwork, and to Roberto Cardoso de Oliveira who, as director of its Department of Anthropology, acted for many years as godfather to the Harvard–Central Brazil research project.

Our work has been financed from various sources over the years, but we are particularly grateful to the National Institute of Mental Health, whose grant during the period 1962–1967 provided the major funding for the field research carried out under the project.

We would also like to thank the Southwest Museum in Los Angeles for permission to reproduce figure 1 in chapter 7 from Nimuendajú, *The Šerente,* and the Clarendon Press of Oxford University for permission to reproduce figure 3 in chapter 7 from David Maybury-Lewis, *Akwẽ-Shavante Society.*

Finally the editor wishes to thank Judy Bevis for her work in preparing the manuscript for publication and Joan Bamberger, Jason Clay, Pia Maybury-Lewis, and Biorn Maybury-Lewis for cheerfully carrying out the tedious task of reading the proofs.

Contents

Foreword

Charles Wagley

THE ETHNOGRAPHIC PICTURE of the vast lowlands of South America is just now coming into focus. In the late 1930s, when I began to study South American ethnology, Clark Wissler's *The American Indian* (New York, 1917) was still the standard survey work on the Indians of both hemispheres. In that book, Wissler included all of the tribes of tropical lowland South America in one vague area which he called the "Manioc Area." He did distinguish between the so-called Tapuya of the inland steppes and the Arawak, Carib, and Tupian groups of the tropical forest. The basic ethnographic data on lowland South American Indians were written in German, Swedish, Spanish, Italian, and Portuguese. Mainly, they consisted of reports by early chroniclers, naturalists, explorers, or anthropologists who undertook expeditions that yielded fragmentary data on several tribes. Most often there was more information on bows and arrows, pottery, basketry, or body paint than on the social organization or ideology of any specific tribe. Monographs on a single tribe providing analysis of its society and culture were few in number. To study South American ethnology was like trying to put together a jigsaw puzzle with many of the pieces missing. The major justification for undertaking the monumental *Handbook of South American Indians* (Smithsonian Institution, Bureau of American Ethnology, Bulletin 143, 7 vols.), which began publication in 1946, was to attempt to draw together and to organize into some sort of a coherent framework the very diverse sources of data on this ethnographically "least known continent."

Since 1950, however, an increasing number of skilled and well-trained anthropologists have conducted research in the South American lowlands. Several of them are Europeans or North

Americans, but perhaps for the first time much of the research is now being done by South American anthropologists, some trained abroad but others trained in universities in their own countries. There is an inevitable gap between actual field research and the appearance of research reports, but in the last decade the scientific "payoff" has begun to appear. Since about 1960, a series of excellent book-length studies and numerous specialized articles on lowland South American cultures have been published. In recent years, numerous papers and symposia have been presented at the annual meetings of the American Anthropological Association and at the biannual meetings of the International Congress of Americanists. If this growing body of research (much of it still unpublished) is any indication of the future, this once neglected and poorly understood ethnographic area will by the end of this decade be one of the better known regions of the ethnographic world.

The publication of this volume by David Maybury-Lewis and his associates is an important event in the continued development of South American anthropology. It is particularly significant because it helps to resolve a puzzling anomaly in the South American ethnographic scene, namely, the rather specialized adaptation and the highly complex social structure of the Gê-speaking peoples of central Brazil. This book demystifies Gê social structure and at the same time modifies and reinterprets some of our traditional ideas, about kinship, affiliation, and descent. The apparent anomaly surrounding the Gê-speaking tribes first came to light with the publication of two articles in 1937 and 1938 by Robert H. Lowie and Curt Nimuendajú, both of which are cited frequently in this volume. These articles, like Nimuendajú's detailed monographs on the Apinayé (1939), the Sherente (1942), and Eastern Timbira (1946), were based upon long-term, detailed, and concentrated field research among these tribal societies. It might almost be said that Curt Nimuendajú initiated a new era in lowland South American social and cultural anthropology and that his research "turned on end" some of the previously held views regarding the ethnography of this part of the world.

Who was this man who, almost singlehandedly, changed the face of lowland South American ethnography and to whom this book is dedicated? He was born in Jena, Germany, in 1883, as Curt Unkel. Little is known about his early education and how and when he acquired his early interest in South American Indians. At twenty years of age, he moved to Brazil, becoming a Brazilian citizen only in 1922, when he was thirty-nine years old. In Brazil he lived for several years among the Guaraní Indians of southern Mato Grosso, São Paulo, and Paraná. He seems to have learned to speak Guaraní and he lived among the Guaraní as if he were a member of their society. It was from the Guaraní that he acquired his Indian surname, Nimuendajú, which he adopted formally. His first two publications in the *Zeitschrift für Ethnologie* in 1914 and 1915 were signed Curt Nimuendajú Unkel, but afterwards he dropped his German surname and used his Indian name legally and on all his subsequent publications. In 1910, he became an employee of the newly created Indian Protection Service (SPI), which made use of his thorough knowledge of the Indians of southern Brazil and subsidized his research for several years. In fact, when I met him in 1941 in Belém (state of Pará), he told me that he was able to write his first important monograph, *Die Sagen von der Erschaffung und Vernichtung der Welt als Grundlage der Religion der Apapocuva-Guaraní (Zeitschrift für Ethnologie,* vol. 46, pp. 284–403, 1914), as a neglected and unnoticed employee of the SPI in Rio de Janeiro. In 1913, he moved to Belém, where he was rather vaguely connected with the Museu Paraense Emilio Goeldi for many years. During those years he traveled and lived among the Indians of the Brazilian Amazon, supporting himself by making ethnographic collections for European museums and by undertaking occasional activities for the Indian Protection Service, such as the expedition of 1921–1923, where he led the group which pacified the hostile Parintintin on the Madeira River. By the early 1930s, he had entered into correspondence with Robert H. Lowie, and their long-distance collaboration had begun. Lowie became his scientific adviser, translator (from German into English), and his editor. Lowie seems to have been able to find some limited financial support for Nimuendajú's fieldwork from the Carnegie Institute of Washington and from the University of California at Berkeley.

By then, Nimuendajú had settled upon the Gê tribes of central Brazil as his principal focus of field research. From 1930 until 1940, there was hardly a year that he did not work with one or another of these groups—Apinayé, Sherente, Krahó, Kayapó, and Canela (the local Brazilian term for the Ramkokamekra and Apaniekra of the Eastern Timbira). It was thus during the late 1930s that his major monographs appeared on the Apinayé and the Sherente, and not until 1946 that his most detailed study, *The Eastern Timbira,* was published.

Nimuendajú was not an academically trained anthropologist; in fact, he was almost self taught in both ethnography and anthropological theory. To my knowledge, he never traveled abroad after arriving in Brazil and never attended scientific meetings. If the chronological list of his fieldwork published by Herbert Baldus in his obituary is correct, there was not a year from 1905 until 1942 that he did not undertake fieldwork of some kind with Brazilian Indians (see *American Anthropologist,* vol. 48, no. 2, pp. 238–243). Yet he carried on a lively correspondence with European and North American anthropologists, particularly with Robert H. Lowie. He must have been rather widely read, at least in North and South American ethnology. When I visited him in 1941 in his simple home in Belém, one large room was filled with books in Portuguese, Spanish, German, French, and English. Although he always corresponded with Lowie in German, he showed me books in English which Lowie had sent him. Yet he was a humble man, professing to know little in his field, and he plied me with questions about Franz Boas, Robert Lowie, A. L. Kroeber, Paul Radin, Ruth Benedict, Ruth Bunzel, and other American anthropologists whose work he seemed to have read. He seemed pleased that a young anthropologist from Columbia University would make a special trip to Belém to visit him. Since I was about to begin research among the Guajajara-Tenetehara, he made for me a copy of the kinship terms of this tribe, which he had collected among them many years before. He was a superb cartographer, and for several hours he showed me ethnographic maps of Brazil which he had prepared (some of them appeared in the *Handbook of South American Indians*). Basically, however, Nimuendajú was an ethnographer of the older German tradition—closer to the nineteenth-century naturalists than to the twentieth-century social scientists. He was always a passionate *Indigenista,* fighting as he knew best for the rights of the Brazilian Indian against the "Neo-Brazilians," as he called the modern Brazilians in his writings. It was in keeping with this life long interest that he died, probably of a heart attack, while doing fieldwork among the Tukuna Indians on the Solimões River in the upper Amazon.

Nimuendajú's field reports opened up a series of questions for students of lowland South American cultures. How could these Gê tribes living on the Brazilian steppe or savannah (better designated by the Portuguese term, *cerrado* [bush land]) support villages of eight hundred, a thousand and even more people, as the historical data seem to indicate? Although by Nimuendajú's time they were already reduced in numbers, these villages were larger than those of the tropical forest societies. These Gê-speaking tribes with an exceedingly simple technology, who lacked pottery, boats, hammocks, perhaps any elaborate domestic house forms, who depended marginally upon horticulture in the narrow gallery forests, and wandered part of each year almost like hunting and gathering nomads, were suddenly revealed as societies with complex social systems and a very elaborate ceremonial life. They were an anomaly in lowland South American ethnography. They were similar in material traits to the marginal tribes of the southern pampas and Tierra del Fuego, but more complex in social structure and ceremonial life than the peoples of the Amazonian tropical forest. This contradiction was hardly resolved by the editor of the *Handbook of South American Indians,* who consigned them with certain caveats to volume 2 in company with the simple marginal tribes of the extreme southern portion of the hemisphere. Others attempted to explain their apparent technological simplicity combined with sociological and ideological complexity by interpreting them as "degenerate remnants of higher South American civilizations" or as peoples driven out of the tropical forest by more aggressive groups (see the Introduction to this book). Neither explanation seemed tenable historically, ethnographically, or functionally. Thus, when well-trained sociocultural anthropologists were able to do field research in Brazil, many turned to further work with the Gê-speaking tribes.

One of the earlier restudies of the Gê tribes is the longitudinal study of the Eastern Timbira (Ramkokamekra and Apaniekra) being carried out by William H. Crocker of the Smithsonian Institution, which began in 1957 and still continues. A long series of articles, many of which are cited in this book, have been published and two monographs are near completion. Crocker has corrected many of Nimuendajú's earlier observations and has provided new data and new interpretations on the culture of these important Gê-speaking tribes.

The second research program, after Nimuendajú's time, on these Gê groups and the Bororo (a tribe with only a distantly related language but many Gê-like features in its social structure) was the Harvard Central Brazil Project, which was carried out between 1962 and 1967 under the direction of David Maybury-Lewis. This program was a cooperative endeavor in which methodology, concepts, and theoretical interpretations were shared and a series of independent field research projects were undertaken by the individual participants. This was the first time in the history of lowland South American ethnology that a planned comparative research program had been carried out among the lowland peoples of South America. (Almost simultaneously, a program involving some of the same anthropologists on Areas of Interethnic Friction was being carried out under the leadership of Roberto Cardoso de Oliveira, then of the Museu Nacional of Rio de Janeiro, now of the University of Brasília). The participants in the Harvard program were both Brazilian and North American, as is noted in the following Introduction. As a result of this research, a long series of articles (citations may be found in the references for the individual papers) , a large number of doctoral theses (most of them still unpublished) , and books by David Maybury-Lewis on the Akwẽ-Shavante, by Julio Cezar Melatti on the Krahó, and by Roberto da Matta on the Apinayé have appeared.

The present book, *Dialectical Societies,* is an important result of this seminal research program. Although the editor denies that the primary aim of this book is "to set the ethnographic record straight," it did just that for this reader. And it also taught me much more about Brazilian social anthropology and the general theory of social structure. This book combines exciting ethnographic data with new theoretical interpretations. It shows clearly that the social systems of the Gê (and Bororo) tribes are based upon uxorilocal domiciles which are cross-cut and segmented by ceremonial moieties, age-sets, and other social categories or classifications. It shows affiliation in several groups to be intimately intertwined with a complex system of transmission of names and associated rights. And, above all, the authors of this book explain how ideology (the natives' theories of their own culture) helped them to understand the logic of these intricate social systems and the meaning and use of kinship within these systems. But let us allow the book to speak for itself. There is much that is new and fresh both for students of lowland South American social anthropology and anthropological theory in general.

University of Florida, Gainesville
October 1978

Dialectical Societies

We have, throughout this volume, followed the convention of designating kinship terms by their first letter (M for mother), except Z for sister to distinguish it from S for son.

Introduction

David Maybury-Lewis

THE INDIANS of Central Brazil have always been something of a mystery. In colonial times they were little known, feared and despised alike by the peoples of the coast and by the Portuguese, who were quick to explore but slow to settle the interior. Reports dating back to the seventeenth century (Barlaeus 1647, Marcgrav 1648, Baro 1651) speak of the hinterland as being peopled with wild Tapuya, nomads who lived by hunting and gathering and enjoyed running races with tree trunks on their shoulders. These tribes were probably related to but not the direct ancestors of the Gê and the Bororo who are described in this volume.[1] It was not until the mid-nineteenth century that von Martius (1867) drew up a preliminary classification of the languages and peoples of Central Brazil and named the Gê family. The first reasonably full accounts of the Gê-speaking peoples and the Bororo came much later. It was Curt Nimuendajú, writing on the Apinayé (1939), the Sherente (1942), and the Eastern Timbira (1946), as well as the Salesian fathers Colbacchini and Albisetti with their monograph on the Bororo (1942), who established the existence of highly complex social systems among peoples who had hitherto been classified as "marginal."

The marginal peoples of South America were a residual category defined in terms of cultural traits which they were reported to lack, such as agriculture, tobacco, alcohol, boats, pottery, hammocks, and so on (Steward 1946). The writings of Nimuendajú and the Salesians, therefore, merely deepened the mystery. How could peoples whose technical ability appeared to be so rudimentary have developed such cultural complexities? Had we underestimated their technology, or perhaps been overimpressed by their social institutions? Perhaps the anomaly could be explained

1

by claiming that the Gê and Bororo were degenerate remnants of a higher South American civilization (Lévi-Strauss 1944) or at the very least by assuming that they were peripheral barbarians who had acquired, let us say, the cultural panoply of the Incas, without the economic and social substratum necessary to re-create the whole civilization (Haeckel 1939).

Such learned speculations seem, to the writers of this volume, somewhat strained. We have been engaged on research into the culture of the Gê and the Bororo for the past decade and this book is, in effect, a tribute to the people we studied. Their view of the world and of their place in it, their social theory and social organization, are of a complexity and sophistication which have proved daunting. To us, who elected to try and understand them and to communicate this understanding, it has seemed as if each analytical advance was like scaling a foothill. It presented us with views of more important peaks which were yet to be climbed. We do not claim to have arrived even now at the Everest of our research. Yet we believe that the essays in this book provide an adequate preliminary analysis of these intriguing systems and at least point to some of the comparative implications of our inquiry.

The present series of investigations started in the mid-1950s, when Professor Herbert Baldus, who was my teacher at the Escola de Sociologia e Política of the University of São Paulo, urged me to take up the study of the Gê-speaking peoples once again. He pointed out that the rich materials already provided by Nimuendajú and the Salesians raised a host of interesting analytical questions which could only be resolved by further fieldwork. I decided to undertake the task.

Like my predecessors, I was intrigued by the social systems of the Central Brazilian peoples and, above all, by their dual organization. Their interlocking systems of exogamous moieties and agamous moieties, with all their overlapping social fields and attendant complications, were a model maker's delight; but how did they actually work on a day-to-day basis? What did they mean to the people who ordered their lives by them? I felt that if I could answer such questions, then we would be in a better position to understand the meaning and function of dual organization the world over. But in order to answer these questions, I had to find a dualistic society, going about its business with a minimum of interference from the outside world, and to study its workings.

This was not going to be too easy. Nimuendajú had stressed that dual organization was the key to the understanding of the Gê-speaking peoples; yet there were disquieting hints in his monographs that the system was breaking down when he had studied it,

that the Indians themselves no longer lived by their own rules—
and Nimuendajú was describing it as he had seen it in the 1930s.
Where, then, was I to find a fully functioning system of dual organization in Central Brazil twenty years later? The answer
seemed to be among the Shavante.

The problem with the Shavante was that they were hostile. Attempts were being made to establish peaceful contact with them,
but these had not so far been successful. In any case, they could be
expected to be monolingual, so that fieldwork among them would
require me to learn their language somehow. I therefore went off
to study the Sherente in 1955–56. The Sherente were reputed to
have been one people with the Shavante in the distant past and
therefore presumably spoke a similar or perhaps even identical
language. They were also settled and comparatively accessible,
and they spoke Portuguese as well as their own language.

I returned to the field in 1958–59. By this time it was possible
to work with the recently contacted Shavante. I discovered that
they and the Sherente spoke dialects of a common language, Akwẽ.
The result was that I could communicate with the Shavante when
I got into the field, although they found my Sherente version of
Akwẽ hilariously funny.

My work with the Sherente had already taught me that Nimuendajú's forebodings about the imminent collapse of their culture
and the demise of their dualistic system twenty years previously
had been premature. They had certainly adapted to changing circumstances and learned to live very much like the poor backwoodsmen of that part of Brazil; but they spoke their own language and maintained a living culture of their own, including the
traditional dualism. It seemed, then, that it was not too late to
undertake a comparative study of the social institutions of the Gê-
speaking peoples. I therefore launched the Harvard Central Brazil
Project in an effort to solve some of the puzzles of Central Brazilian ethnology to which I have already alluded.

My collaborators and I resolved to try and study the societies
of Central Brazil through controlled comparison. We would carry
out an all but simultaneous investigation of the Gê-speaking peoples, focusing on the dual organization which they were all reputed to have. Since these peoples all spoke closely related languages, it was reasonable to suppose that they had had quite close
historical connections and had thus developed similar institutions.
We hoped that our investigations would be able to elucidate the
themes and variations in these institutional arrangements.

The Bororo presented a difficulty. Linguists could not decide
whether their language could be classed as belonging to the Gê

family or not. If not, it was at least a not too distant relative. It was clear that the Bororo had lived cheek by jowl with the Gê speakers for a long time. Their culture presented fascinating analogues with, and equally interesting divergences from more conventional Gê patterns. If they were not quite Gê, it seemed that they were not quite non-Gê either. Would it not, therefore, be both fruitful and methodologically defensible to try to fôcus on a Gê-Bororo cultural complex? This was the line of inquiry that we resolved to pursue.

The Nambikwara case was more difficult. The Nambikwara were reported to have dual organization and a two-section system of kinship terminology. They lived on the fringes of the lands traditionally occupied by the Gê and Bororo speakers, but their language was quite different from that of the former. We scheduled a study of the Nambikwara in our initial plans for the project, feeling that the data would be instructive, if only for purposes of contrast. As the research proceeded, however, we decided to focus on our controlled comparison of the Gê and the Bororo and to treat the Nambikwara as a separate case.

The interrelationships between the various peoples who speak languages belonging to the Gê family are set out in Table 1. At the minimum level of differentiation, the languages or dialects

TABLE 1. Linguistic affinities of Gê- and Bororo-speaking peoples

Northern Gê
  Eastern Timbira
    Apaniekra
    Ramkokamekra
    Krīkatí
    Krahó
  Western Timbira
    Apinayé
  Kayapó
    Gorotire
    Xikrin
  Suya
Central Gê
  Sherente
  Shavante
Bororo
Southern Gê
  Kaingang
  Shokleng

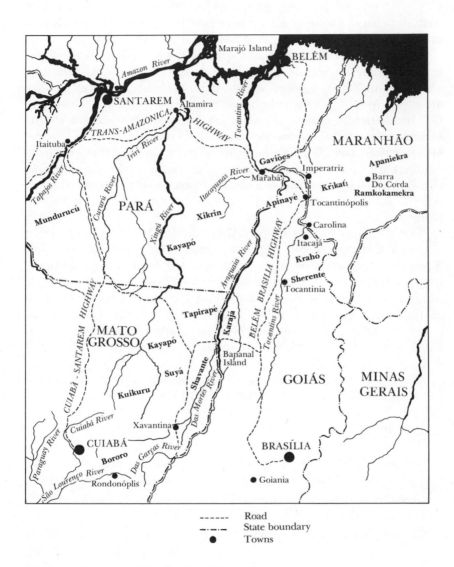

MAP 1. Location of Central Brazilian tribes

are mutually intelligible. The Krĩkatí have no difficulty understanding the Krahó, the Sherente the Shavante, the Kaingang the
Shokleng, and so on. People speaking languages from different
Northern Gê groups (for example, the Eastern Timbira and the
Kayapó) may understand something of each other's speech, but
with difficulty. There is no mutual intelligibility between Northern Gê, Central Gê, Bororo, and Southern Gê, respectively.

These Gê- and Bororo-speaking peoples have lived on the Central Brazilian highlands for as long as we have any information
about them. Their modern descendants are scattered over a huge
area (see Map I). From the most northeasterly of the Northern
Gê (the Apaniekra and the Ramkokamekra) to the most south-
westerly (the Suya), these peoples are found spread over a wide
arc on a diameter of about eight hundred miles. Further south, it
is about six hundred miles from the Sherente in the northeast to
the Bororo, who live just beyond the Shavante to the southwest.
And it is about a thousand miles from the Apaniekra to the
Bororo.

The Southern Gê are even farther afield. They live in the state
of Santa Catarina about eight hundred miles south of Brasília.
They are not shown on Map 1. Indeed, we did not include them
in our original research plan because we thought, erroneously, I
am happy to say, that they had died out, or at least that their way
of life was extinct. Recent research by Silvio Coelho dos Santos
(1973) and Gregory Urban (1978) has shown, however, that the
Kaingang and the Shokleng are still living in recognizably Gê
style.

The following investigations were actually carried out under
the auspices of the Harvard Central Brazil Project:

Joan Bamberger Terence Turner	Kayapó	(research started in 1962)
Roberto da Matta	Apinayé	(research started in 1962)
Julio Cezar Melatti	Krahó	(research started in 1962)
Jean Carter Lave Dolores Newton	Krĩkatí	(research started in 1963)
Christopher Crocker	Bororo	(research started in 1964)
Cecil Cook	Nambikwara	(research started in 1966)

Since the time when these research projects were completed and
the initial dissertations based on them written, the group of Central Brazilianists has been widely scattered in various universities
on two continents. It has thus been very hard to produce a joint

volume. The administrative difficulties were heightened by intellectual ones. It has been genuinely difficult to reach the point where we felt we had a reasonable comparative understanding of the Gê and the Bororo. We would meet as a group to discuss these societies, as we did at Harvard in 1968, at Oxford and Stuttgart (during the Congress of Americanists) in 1968, and again at Harvard in 1971, and each time the euphoria of the meeting would soon give way to solitary analytical doubts about each others' suggestions and interpretations. During this period of cogitation we have also benefited from other people's collaboration. Pierre and Elli Maranda spent a summer analyzing Gê myths and contributed their conclusions to our discussions. William Crocker, from the Smithsonian Institution, who had done extensive fieldwork among the Apaniekra, was such a frequent contributor to our discussions and meetings that we have come to regard him as a classificatory member of the project itself.

The members of this group are now so busy with other activities, including the preparation of their own books on the Gê and Bororo, that it has taken much editorial pressure to get this volume ready for press. Synchronization of the submissions has thus been very difficult. In order to avoid an endless process of revision in the light of the latest paper submitted, I have summarily decided at various moments that certain papers were ready and held them for the volume. Thus the papers by Melatti and da Matta have been ready for some years now. Crocker, Lave, and Maybury-Lewis completed their contributions next. The Kayapó materials, by Bamberger and Turner, are the most recent. With their submission, the volume was ready to go to press.

The papers on the Northern Gê peoples are presented first. Then there is a single paper on the Central Gê, followed by a paper on the Bororo. The concluding paper of the volume is a summary one, which comments on the results of our research as a whole.

There are brief notes at the beginning of most papers on the present situation of each people discussed. These notes are for convenient and summary reference only. The current problems that these societies face in their dealings with outsiders, particularly Brazilians, are being treated in other publications. It should be explained, however, that the agency of the federal government of Brazil responsible for Indian affairs used to be the SPI, or Serviço de Proteção aos Índios. It is referred to throughout this volume as the Indian Protection Service. The SPI was disbanded in 1967, after a governmental inquiry into scandals within its administration, and supplanted by the FUNAI, or Fundação Nacional do

Índio. This is referred to in this volume as the National Indian Foundation. It is important to remember that the FUNAI often carries on administering the old SPI posts. When we write of an Indian Protection Service post, (or simply of an Indian Service post), we refer to a post founded by the Indian Protection Service and now operated by the National Indian Foundation.

While the names of these government agencies should present little difficulty, there is a problem as to how to distinguish verbally between Indians and non-Indians. In Central Brazil the difficulty of defining an Indian is not serious. For the most part, Indians are those very few people who live in Indian villages. There is a negligible number of people living close to, but not in, the villages whose status is ambiguous. The rest are not Indian. The non-Indians are usually referred to by local people, including the Indians themselves, as *Cristãos* (Christians) or *civilizados* (civilized people). This is interesting in itself, but we did not wish to adopt that ethnocentric usage in this volume. The use of the term "whites" to refer to non-Indians is much rarer in Central Brazil, for obvious reasons. In the population as a whole, skin color varies from light to dark tan, and the Indians are not always noticeably darker or redder than their non-Indian neighbors. We also felt that Nimuendajú's scrupulous designation of non-Indians as neo-Brazilians, leaving the term "Brazilian" to be applied (if at all) to the only "true" Brazilians, the Indians themselves, was a little precious. The whole concept of Brazil and Brazilians is, after all, an idea introduced by the settler society and one which was quite foreign to the Indians themselves. We have therefore chosen the terms "Indian" and "Brazilian" as being the least objectionable ones through which to express the opposition between Indians and the rest.

Our research has led to a substantial revision of Central Brazilian ethnography and, we believe, to a deeper understanding of the cultures of the Gê- and Bororo-speaking peoples. Yet it must be stressed that it is not the primary aim of our book to set the ethnographic record straight. This is being done elsewhere.[2] We have thus faced a difficult problem of exposition. We could not assume that our readers were familiar with the data we were discussing, yet we wished to present a series of arguments, not a collection of miniature ethnographies. We have accordingly tried to provide just the amount of ethnographic information needed to follow the arguments.

These arguments have been profoundly affected by the comparative nature of our project. The interpretation of each individual society has been deepened and modified by a consideration of the data on the others. It would be difficult to reconstitute the stages in this process of understanding, and they would in any case be of little consequence. Yet something needs to be said at the outset concerning our common approach.

Initially, we devoted special attention to problems of social organization, for it was here that the data were especially puzzling. The descent system reported for the Apinayé was anomalous (Maybury-Lewis 1960). The Northern Gê were reportedly matrilineal, the Central Gê patrilineal, and the Bororo matrilineal again. Since these societies were so closely related to each other, we wondered why they differed in such a fundamental fashion. Nor was it clear how these descent systems worked or how they were articulated with other institutions such as age-sets, ceremonial organizations, and moieties, both agamous and exogamous. Above all, how was all this related to dual organization? Was the latter merely a matter of moieties or did it go deeper than that? Was it a philosophical idea or an institution that ordered people's daily lives? Or was it both?

We therefore undertook a comprehensive investigation of the cultural categories of each society. We wanted to understand what their social theories were, how these were reflected in their institutional arrangements, and how all this related to their everyday behavior. We soon discovered that the features of the Gê-Bororo complex were somewhat different from what had hitherto been supposed. All of these societies traditionally inhabited circular or semicircular villages whose layouts reflected their view of the world and of themselves. They make a sharp distinction between the forum, or central, ceremonial sphere (which was conceptually a male place) and the houses, the peripheral, domestic sphere (which was conceptually female). Their rule of postmarital residence was thus everywhere uxorilocal. On this common base, each society had constructed its own peculiar set of institutional arrangements. The Eastern Timbira and the Apinayé attached great importance to ceremonial moieties to which people were affiliated through their names. Kayapó life was focused more on age-grades and men's associations. These were also important among the Central Gê, who had invested them with ceremonial functions, in contrast to their politically oriented descent groups. Finally, the Bororo appeared to have the most thoroughgoing dual organization of them all, with exogamous matrilineal moieties and name-based clans engaged in a constant series of exchanges.

The varying emphases of the papers in this volume reflect, to some extent, the differences between the societies with which they deal. There are also differences of opinion regarding the theoretical conclusions which can be drawn from our exercise in comparison, and these will be noted as they occur.

Jean Carter Lave, for example, focuses on naming among the Krĩkatí. The issue of names, naming, and the affiliation to social groups through one's name runs through all the discussions of the Gê and Bororo, but it is nowhere so salient as among the Krĩkatí. Lave discovered that it was impossible to make a satisfactory analysis of Krĩkatí society or of the Krĩkatí kinship system without first understanding the overriding principles of their naming system. Her paper therefore focuses on Krĩkatí naming and suggests why this institution has come into such prominence among them.

Julio Melatti takes up the issue of naming too, but first insists that the relationship system of the Krahó cannot be understood until we have grasped the principles of the dualism which permeates their society. The Krahó distinguish between central, ritual activities, which concern the society as a whole and peripheral, instrumental ones, which are held to be of domestic concern. The former are performed by groups to which a person is affiliated through a name; the latter by groups whose members are held to be physically related to each other. This opposition, Melatti argues, is expressed through their relationship terminology.

Roberto da Matta takes up a similar theme in his analysis of Apinayé ideology. In his formulation, the Apinayé distinguish between two types of kinship relations—"given" relationships of common substance, which involve a person in domestic activities, and "constructed" relationships, in which names play a prominent part, and which involve a person in ceremonial activities. After showing how Nimuendajú was mistaken about their descent system and thus resolving the "Apinayé anomaly," da Matta goes on to show how the Apinayé relationship system, like that of the Krahó, articulates the various domains of Apinayé culture. He then considers the comparative implications of this, not only for Central Brazilian societies but for other societies whose kinship systems are reportedly of the Crow or Omaha type.

The Kayapó, whose social arrangements are outlined in the paper by Joan Bamberger, contrast with the Krĩkatí, Krahó, and Apinayé in that their age-grade system is still a vital part of their social organization. This gives Kayapó society a rather different cast and has markedly affected their own style of dual organization. This was ideally and traditionally a matter of the opposition between the two men's houses, which any properly constituted village was supposed to have. But in recent times no such village has actually existed, and this opposition has been transformed into a political clash between the age-grades of mature men (with children) and immature men (still childless). Bamberger focuses on Kayapó politics and discusses the fluidity and divisiveness of their communities in terms of Hirschman's concepts of exit, voice, and loyalty.

Two papers by Terence Turner follow. In the first, he outlines a general theory of dual organization which applies, *a fortiori,* to all the Central Brazilian peoples. He maintains that, throughout Central Brazil, men seek to control other men by retaining their own daughters after marriage and dominating their in-marrying sons-in-law. Uxorilocality is thus essentially a political instrument, but it is also part of a pattern which generates moiety and age-class systems. These serve both as models of and as regulating mechanisms for the passage of individuals from their natal to their affinal families. In his second paper, he applies this argument to the Kayapó, and shows how their society functions as a feedback system in which these institutions shape each other.

I myself take a different view, as my paper on the Central Gê and my concluding essay should make clear. I do not think that the elaborate and pervasive dualism to be found among the Gê and the Bororo is usefully regarded as being modeled on their means of detaching individuals from their natal families. Nor do I feel that uxorilocality is primarily a political matter. In fact, my paper on the Central Gê argues that for them, the only patrilineal societies in Central Brazil, uxorilocality is a distinct embarrassment. They practice it, I believe, for the same symbolic reasons that make it common to all the other societies of Central Brazil. My paper deals, therefore, with how the Central Gê blur the sharp distinction between the central forum and the peripheral domestic sphere by their patrilineal descent system, and then proceeds to a general discussion of dual organization in Central Brazil. I also take up the issue of whether the Sherente can usefully be said to practice patrilateral cross-cousin marriage of a prescriptive or any other kind and consider the implications of my data, and of the arguments of my fellow contributors, for the discussions surrounding the Crow and Omaha type of kinship systems.

Finally, Christopher Crocker's paper on the Bororo takes up virtually all of the issues discussed by the other contributors, for the Bororo appear to ring the changes on all the institutions of the Gê-Bororo complex. They too make a distinction between the physical and social aspects of the individual, one which affects their ideas about descent and consequently the nature of their descent groups. They too sharply distinguish between the male and the female sphere and build elaborate men's houses in the middle of their villages where the men spend most of their time. Crocker's paper explores their rationale for grouping men together in a curious sort of matriliny and then investigates the complicated dialectics of the relationship between moieties and their constituent clans.

It is clear that a major concern of all of these papers is the topic which anthropologists loosely refer to as "kinship." This is partly because the idiom of kinship is central to these peoples' own way of thinking about social relationships. Yet an investigation of kinship terminologies also proved to be a useful tool for getting at the thinking behind their social classifications. We would argue that the Gê and the Bororo belong to that large class of societies whose kinship terminologies cannot be elucidated except as social matrices and in relation to other systems of classification. It is in this sort of society that the study of kinship is most fruitful; but it is also in this sort of society that what we study as "kinship" is furthest removed from the ordinary or folk notions of kinship pertaining in the societies from which most anthropologists come. Hence the paradox which has bedeviled "kinship" studies: they are most fruitful when they deal with phenomena which are least like kinship.

In this book, we have treated "kinship" as a branch of cultural classification. Each contributor has made a systematic effort to understand how social and cultural domains relate to each other in the society under study. The idea is not altogether novel, and interestingly enough Mervyn Meggitt (1972) carried out an analysis along similar lines for the Australians, whose kinship systems have so often been compared with those of the Central Brazilians. Yet this sort of total analysis has for the most part been either fitfully or intuitively carried out in anthropology. We have tried here to show what a more systematic application of these ideas can achieve and believe that we have produced significant results. The reworking of Central Brazilian ethnology has already been mentioned, but the implications of our work go beyond Central Brazil. We have found many of the concepts and classifications used by students of "kinship" to be inadequate or misleading. It follows, if we are right, that our results should lead to the modification or discarding of these concepts and to major revisions in the theory of "kinship."

Finally, a word about the title of this volume. It was the dual organization of the Central Brazilian peoples which first caught the attention of anthropologists in general. It is to their dual organization that the contributors to this book return again and again. The Gê and the Bororo have a binary view of the universe.

They state quite explicitly that their societies are imbued with oppositions, because opposition is immanent in the nature of things. The essays in this volume show how each society strives to create a harmonious synthesis out of the antithetical ideas, categories, and institutions that constitute its way of life. Of course everyday life cannot be so easily or so neatly channeled. The dynamics of social action in Central Brazil put severe strains on the systems. In certain cases, these strains appear to be moving them out of their dualistic mode altogether. Yet the Gê and the Bororo as we knew them were still trying to live by their traditional philosophies. They were still trying to achieve the synthesis of opposites, to create balance and harmony by opposing institutions. In that sense, they were truly dialectical societies.

THE KRĨKATÍ

THE KRĨKATÍ (also known as Caracati) are located in the southwest of the state of Maranhão. They inhabit six small villages in
two clusters, one close to the town of Montes Altos and the other
around the town of Amarante. These in their turn lie to the east of
Imperatriz, through which the Belém-Brasília highway passes.

The Krĩkatí's precise history is difficult to trace since there has been
considerable fission and fusion among Eastern Timbira groups in the
last hundred years (see Nimuendajú 1946:13–36). In fact, Nimuendajú reported that the Krĩkatí were on the verge of extinction in 1930.
Yet they have succeeded in reconstituting themselves. In the sixties
they numbered between 350 and 400 individuals, but the population
has now increased to about 600. They claim to be an amalgam of
various Eastern Timbira peoples who were once separate, such as the
Ronhugati, the Pihugati, and the Pukobke.

The Krĩkatí have frequent contact with other Northern Gê peoples,
especially the Apaniekra, the Ramkokamekra, the Krahó, and the
Apinayé. They also have a great deal to do with the Guajajara, of
Tupian linguistic stock, who live intermingled with the local Brazilians, though sometimes retaining their identity as Indians. Above all,
the Krĩkatí are in uncomfortably close contact with the Brazilians
themselves. They are surrounded by Brazilian backwoodsmen. Small
"roads" carry traffic right past their villages and they are only about
forty kilometers from the Belém-Brasília highway.

It is this proximity rather than the efforts of missionaries or the
Indian Protection Service (which did not until recently maintain a post
for the tribe) which has been the major force for change in their lives.
Although they still maintain themselves by subsistence farming and
gathering the wild products of the region, a cash income is becoming
increasingly important to them. Yet they have few systematic means of
earning money. At the same time, their uneasy relations with the local
Brazilians are always threatening to erupt into conflict over land or
over the alleged killing of the Brazilians' cattle.

15

1 | Cycles and Trends in Krĩkatí Naming Practices

Jean Lave

Introduction

THE SOCIAL ORGANIZATION of the Krĩkatí Indians is unusual among the world's societies because of the kinds of relationships which are utilized in conveying social information about individuals and recruiting them to formal communitywide groups. Relationships of kinship and marriage organize most domestic group activities, but relationships based on the transmission of personal names are equally important. The latter are used to recruit members to three different moiety systems and numerous ceremonial societies. They are used to transmit ceremonial roles, to establish responsibility for ceremonial training, and even as the basis for establishing an additional system of ceremonial relationships, known as formal friendship relations. Both kinship and naming relationships help to maintain the continuity of Krĩkatí society over time. But the way in which the Krĩkatí represent this continuity to themselves is through the name-based transmission of social identities from name-givers to name-receivers. Neither bilateral kindreds nor the corporate moiety systems of the Krĩkatí are assigned these functions. Naming and kinship relationships organize different domains of social life: this division of kin-based and name-based organizational devices is itself a major feature of Krĩkatí social organization, and much of the organizational significance of each set of principles comes from the contrasts and complex interrelations between them.

Since the system is unusual, the first task to be undertaken here is to present the rules of name transmission and the ways in which they serve as important organizational devices for the Krĩkatí. That is, I will try to describe how the system works.

The second problem to be discussed is why the Krĩkatí attach greater importance to personal name transmission than do other

16

closely related Gê groups. The importance of name transmission diminishes, while that of kin-based lineages and clans increases, as we move from the Northern Gê groups south to the Central Gê and Bororo. It is also true that the Krīkatí place more organizational emphasis on name transmission than any other group among the Eastern Timbira. It seems likely that the extraordinary importance of naming for the Krīkatí is the result of social change over the last thirty years. The deterioration of the traditional age-set system appears to be a key change which led to increasing reliance on naming as the primary basis of ceremonial organization. The lapsing age-set system also may have led to the comparatively strong emphasis in the mid-sixties on domestic clusters as the focus of domestic and political activity. Evidence to support these propositions comes from a close comparison of field data collected among the Krīkatí in the mid-sixties with Curt Nimuendajú's data on the Eastern Timbira groups, which he gathered in the late thirties.

Krīkatí Naming Practices and Their Relations to Other Aspects of Social Organization

The Krīkatí relationship domain is called *mekwu*. At the most general level, *mekwu* contrasts the Krīkatí to strangers, spirits, and monsters *(kakrit)*. At a less inclusive level, *mekwu* applies to all residents of one's own village and the closest neighboring village (about two hundred people) as opposed to residents of other villages. This is the group within which all members are customarily referred to and addressed by relationship terms. At the level of interpersonal relations, the term *mekwu* may be used to refer to close kin in contrast to individuals or domestic groups with whom the speaker is quarreling.

Informants included as *mekwu* all two hundred residents of the local Krīkatí villages when asked specifically about each individual in turn. They also conformed to their own ideals by referring to almost all of the residents by relationship terms. Criteria reported by informants for assigning referential terms were quite varied, including many other relations in addition to genealogical ones: "I call X 'term Y' because she is my mother"; "X is the mother of Y"; "Y is my child"; but also, "X gave his names to Y"; "X gave meat to Y in the last ceremony and Y gave rice to X"; "I call X 'term Z' because X has to look out for Y but cannot speak to her— it's because of names"; "X's name-giver is married to Y." In addition to consanguineal and affinal kin relations, the domain includes relationships of formal friendship, ceremonial trading partnerships, and naming relationships.

Formal friend relationships are acquired through naming. Ego's formal friends are the formal friends of his or her name-giver. As the formal friends acquire new name-receivers, these, too, become ego's formal friends. Formal friends may be of either sex, but opposite-sex formal friendships are maintained more elaborately than same-sex formal friendships. Formal friends must refrain from using each other's names in reference or address and must not meet face to face or speak to each other. Sexual relations and marriage between formal friends are forbidden. Emphasis is placed on the obligation of adults to give ritual protection and help to their young formal friends whenever the latter are threatened with ceremonial violence. Parents pay their children's formal friends for this assistance. Adult formal friends have few obligations to each other except to protest and demand payment from anyone who kills an animal whose name a formal friend bears. These protests are today carried out in a rough joking manner and no payments are actually made.

Ceremonial trading partner relations are very narrowly defined, although trading partners refer to and address each other at all times only as trading partners, *kuwuure*. This terminology is established when a woman and a man exchange cooked garden produce for game in one specific yearly ceremony. It continues so long as they exchange each year. The relationship is transmitted from the woman to her daughters and, according to a rule of parallel transmission, from the man to his sons. Each daughter trades with a single son of the mother's trading partner. In contrast to ceremonial trading partner relations, transmission of personal names and the relationship established through name transmission are elaborate, complex, and of central importance in Krīkatí social organization. I will now describe these relationships in detail.

NAMES AND THE RULES OF NAME TRANSMISSION

The Krīkatí possess about eight hundred personal names. Each Krīkatí acquires at birth a set of two to fifteen names, which the individual has the right to use during his or her lifetime, and to transmit to certain others after reaching adulthood. Each person is customarily addressed and referred to by one of these names. Ideally, a name-set is permanent, unambiguous, and indivisible.

If asked to recite the name-set, a Krīkatí man or woman will check with an expert—the person who gave the names—to make sure the list is complete and correct. In practice, however, persons with the same name-set frequently report substantially different sets of names, even after consulting their name-givers. Such discrepancies arise in various ways. One or more names may be forgotten. A nickname may be included in one individual's name-set but not be added to the name-set of other individuals who have the same names. Contrary to the rules, two persons sometimes insist on giving their names to the same child, and the child eventually transmits a combination of names from both sets. And sometimes, again contrary to the rules, a name-set is split and the two parts transmitted separately.

In spite of flux in the content of name-sets, the Krīkatí persist in the belief that name-sets are immutable. It may be that the belief goes unchallenged partly because the act of name transmission is itself sufficient to produce precise transmission of particular ceremonial affiliations, rights, and responsibilities. The name-receiver is constrained to follow exactly in the name-giver's footsteps. Therefore, once the individual has names, the names themselves are irrelevant, except for their use in identifying individuals. Remembering all of one's names is not necessary as long as everyone realizes, through frequent ceremonial activity, with whom the names are shared.

There is no rationale for including names in name-sets on the basis of similarity of meaning. Although most names have meanings, frequently the names of animals and plants, I never encountered a situation in which someone tried to reconstruct one name in a name-set from the meaning of another name in that name-set. Connections between names seem to be inferred from known connections between people.

The apparent absence of semantic connections between names in a name-set is explainable in terms of the process by which new names are added to name-sets. New names are added to the system in the form of nicknames referring to unusual events, usually of a sexual or excretory nature. These nicknames start out as long, vividly detailed descriptive phrases, but within weeks are shortened to a few words. Over the next months or years the name will be shortened even further to a word, or a string of syllables formed from the end of one word and the beginning of the next. In this way, and also because people eventually forget the events or personal peculiarities the names memorialize, nicknames lose their specific meaning and are incorporated into the name-set.

Some names belong to men, some to women. A man's name-set is occasionally transmitted to a woman or vice versa, but this is considered to be only a holding operation, and the recipient is expected to pass the names to someone of appropriate sex at the earliest opportunity.

RELATIONS BETWEEN NAME-GIVERS AND NAME-RECEIVERS

The Krĩkatí say that they differ from wild animals and wild Indians because they have personal names. They are very much concerned that a newborn child should receive names immediately, and the ceremony is held just after the umbilical cord is cut. The child is provided with a social identity at approximately the same time he or she becomes a separate physical being.

The child acquires all of his or her names at once. The ideal name-giver for a girl is her father's sister and for a boy his mother's brother. Ideally, firstborn son and firstborn daughter are paired from birth as future name-set exchangers. Each is expected to name his or her partner's first child of the appropriate sex. Second-born siblings are similarly paired as potential name-exchangers, and so on. In addition to naming each other's children, sibling pairs give each other ceremonial services in return for gifts of food. The name-giver performs the ceremonial service and the name-receiver's parent pays for the service with food.

Name-givers, both men and women, act as mentors to their name-receivers, guide them in ceremonial performances, teach them lore and songs, and teach them to run well. A major responsibility is supervising the endurance training of boys so that they will be good log-carrying relay racers when they grow up. The name-giver's obligations end when the name-receiver marries.

A male name-giver goes hunting for his name-receiver and represents him or performs other services for him in ceremonies, and is repaid in meat pies. The name-giver must agree before a young man may marry. Unlike the father, who cannot formally contribute to family deliberations on the matter, the name-giver is formally consulted. It is only after marriage that the relationship between giver and receiver becomes relatively egalitarian.

A female name-giver takes her name-receiver to the stream to bathe early each morning until the child can walk. (A male name-giver finds a close kinswoman to perform this duty for his name-receiver.) Each day the child's mother gives the bather a small gift of food as payment for the service. To mark the end of the bathing sessions, the parents give the name-giver a very large meat pie.[1] Although a woman does not go hunting on behalf of her name-receiver, she performs special ceremonial services for the child and is repaid in meat pies. She prepares a cord girdle which the girl wears from the time she is about ten years old until her first pregnancy. It is not clear how much influence a woman has on her name-receiver's choice of marriage partner. The relationship between female name-giver and her name-receiver is probably never as severely asymmetrical as that between males.

The Krīkatí do not distinguish in speech between the formal mentor (the direct giver of the names) and the other older persons who hold the same name-set. All are "name-givers" to ego. But distinctions between principal and subsidiary name-givers are certainly made in action. While a serious name-giving mentor cannot refuse to carry out his or her ceremonial responsibilities to the name-receiver, peripheral name-givers may elect to ignore the naming tie by addressing the child by name and treating him or her like other children. In this way, a distant name-giver simply does not acknowledge what is at most not a very demanding relationship on either side. Also, while the Krīkatí are proud of having many name-receivers, "there are limits," they feel. It is acceptable, if one already has many name-receivers, to decide at the birth of a particular child not to treat him or her as a name-receiver.

No one can give names to more than one living child of any given person. Thus although each person has a name-exchanger arranged from early childhood (the opposite-sex sibling nearest in birth order), name-exchange relations with other siblings and distant relatives must be established in order to give names to more than one child and, reciprocally, in order to find names for one's own children. It is quite common for a person to give names to one child of each opposite-sex sibling. It follows that each member of a set of siblings receives names from a different sibling of his or her opposite-sex parent. Hence, the ceremonial affiliations of siblings are quite heterogeneous.

If one person changes his or her ceremonial affiliations, the change does not affect the ceremonial affiliations of siblings or any other close kin. While the affiliations within a group of siblings are unrelated, each set of female siblings should hold exactly the same inventory of name-sets and ceremonial affiliations as their father's sisters, taken as a set. And a set of male siblings should have the same inventory as their mother's brothers, taken as a set. This reproduction of sibling-set characteristics across generations rarely works out, for a variety of practical reasons. But the Krīkatí have a special terminology for labeling same-sex sibling sets and are explicitly aware that their naming rules logically should lead to cross-generation identity between sets of same-sex siblings.

NAMING RELATIONSHIP TERMINOLOGY

The social identity between name-giver and name-receiver is made additionally clear in naming relationship terminology (see

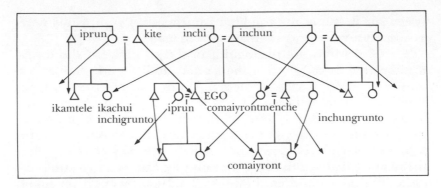

FIGURE 1a. Naming terminology for male ego

Figures 1a and 1b). It is possible to generate a set of rewrite rules underlying the structure of naming relations (cf. Lounsbury 1964). There are four rules, which are the same for men and women except for a difference in the order of application. Rules 1 and 2 are a merging rule and a half-sibling rule. Rules 3 and 4 are Crow III and Omaha III skewing rules, except that Crow III is applied before Omaha III for males and in reverse order for females (see Table 1). Egos of each sex use the rules which most accurately reflect the name-transmission relations in which they are involved. Whether Crow or Omaha, the rules reflect a single principle: that name-giver and name-receiver share a single social identity. Where the rules generate alternative usages (*ikachui/inchigrunto* and *ikamtele/inchungrunto*), the Krĩkatí express indifference as to which pair of reciprocals is chosen, and they occur in free variation. That is, ego can emphasize the equation of himself with his name-giver (his mother's brother) and hence refer to his mother's brother's daughter as *ikachui*, "daughter," or he can take the point of view that his mother's brother's daughter is

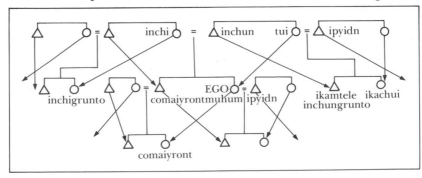

FIGURE 1b. Naming terminology for female ego

TABLE 1. Relationship terminology rules

1. Collateral merging rule
   ♀ZC → ♀C
   ♂BC → ♂C
2. Half-sibling rule
   FC → sibling
   MC → sibling
3. First skewing rule

Male ego: Crow rule III	Female ego: Omaha rule III
♀B . . . → ♀S . . .	♂Z . . . → ♂D . . .
Corollary: . . . ♂Z → . . . ♂M	Corollary: . . . ♀B → . . . ♀F

4. Second skewing rule

Male ego: Omaha rule III	Female ego: Crow rule III
♂Z . . . → ♂D . . .	♀B . . . → ♀S . . .
Corollary: . . . ♀B → . . . ♀F	Corollary: . . . ♂Z → . . . ♂M

his mother's name-receiver, socially identified with his mother, and refer to her as *inchigrunto,* "mother's name-receiver," or just *inchi,* "mother," for short. At the same time, from the mother's brother's daughter's point of view, the male is both her father's name-receiver, *inchungrunto,* and her name-giver's son, *ikamtele.*

When two Krīkatí are related by more than one type of relationship, naming relations take precedence over all but ceremonial trading partnerships and formal friendships as criteria for assigning customary terms of reference. Even close kin use naming terms in preference to kinship terms. Thus ego will refer to his sister as *tuire,* the same kin term he applies to his father's sister, if the father's sister named his sister. He keeps the two kinswomen separate, referentially, by appending their names to the term.

There is also a narrower, but more formal, usage involving name-sharers and their parents-in-law. A man and his father-in-law address and refer to each other's name-receivers by what is ordinarily an honorific suffix attached to in-law terms, *-ye.* This practice does not, however, extend to reciprocal use between the respective name-receivers.

Principles of name transmission are used as a vehicle for expanding the range of kin relations. Based on the social identity of name-giver and name-receiver and the broad interpretation of "giver" and "receiver" (which includes total strangers, if they have the same names), the rule is to call the kinsmen of one's name-sharer by the same terms one uses for one's kin and, reciprocally, to treat the name-sharers of one's kinsmen as kinsmen.

Naming terminology is preferred in cases where there is un-

certainty over whether a clearly specifiable relationship exists between two individuals. Two strangers or distantly related village
members may compare the names of their close relatives until they
find a correspondence and then treat each other accordingly. If a
stranger comes to live in the village, a Krĩkatí will transmit his
or her name-set to the newcomer. Strangers thus quickly acquire
names, and one relationship—that of name-giver/name-receiver.
They are in a position slowly to acquire naming and kin relationships. But the emphasis on the immediate naming of strangers,
and the practice of addressing and referring to them by name, is
an apt reflection of their marginal social position.

The use of names contrasts strongly with the use of naming terminology in reference and address. Naming terminology is used
to communicate the existence of relationships which have been
established on the basis of actual or putative bestowal of names.
Names are consistently used in reference and address to label positions which have not yet been combined into specific relationships. Therefore, they very often are applied to categories of
people who are marginal to the society.

The bestowal of names on strangers is one example. Another involves sexual relatedness. A person should marry or have sexual
relations only with persons referred to by name, that is, those with
whom no relationship exists. Ideally, sexual ties should not be
formed with those referred to by kin terms or naming terms. Since
there is also great emphasis on referring to all members of the
community by kin terms, to express a high degree of relatedness,
the two rules frequently come into conflict. To cope with the
problem, people often switch from kin terminology to the use of
personal names as a means of indicating sexual interest.

If two people have sexual relations, however, they are then
prohibited from addressing or referring to each other by name,
and only relational terms may be used. It is customary at this time
for the man and woman to adopt teknonymous designations for
each other. Each refers to the other as "parent of X," where X
stands for alter's name-exchanger, since that is the name which
will be given to the first child of each sex, should the two marry.[2]

NAME-HOLDING GROUPS

Since there is no formal term in the Krĩkatí language for a
group of people who share the same name-set, I have coined the
phrase "name-holding group." The members of such a group have
a great deal in common. They share the same names, sex, moiety
affiliations, formal friends, and ceremonial roles. But they do not
stand in uniform kin relationships with each other, since names

may be transmitted through two or more unrelated chains of kin. Indeed, members of a name-holding group need not even share tribal affiliation, since strangers are integrated into Krīkatí social life by acquiring Krīkatí names.

A member of a name-holding group is considered to be a name-giver to all those members who are younger than himself or herself. Conversely, he or she is treated as a name-receiver by all older members of the group. The Krīkatí say that whenever names are transmitted, all persons with those names take part in the giving. Whether each person is aware of the transaction at the time is irrelevant. The same principle is used to establish appropriate behavior and terminology between strangers who happen to have the same names. In these cases, it is appropriate for the elder of the two to take the role of name-giver and for the younger to adopt the role of name-receiver. No term exists for two people who share the same names and who are approximately equal in age and status. All relationships between holders of the same names are structured in terms of asymmetrical relations between a giver and a receiver.

There is one principle which results in the internal structuring of name-holding groups, and it too is concerned with seniority. Name-holding groups are split into older and younger halves. Which half a member belongs to depends on whether the individual has acquired at least one name-receiver. The younger half consists of those who have received but not yet transmitted names. Members of the older half have all transmitted their names at least once. The Krīkatí do not transmit their names until after they complete initiation. The notion of reciprocity between pairs of name-givers is so strong that people rarely bestow names on a child until they are starting their own family. It is after initiation and marriage, therefore, that the strong respect owed by young name-receivers to the older members of their name-holding group abates considerably, as young members begin to bestow their own names, and to bring new name-receivers into the name-holding group.

Certain major ceremonial roles are occupied successively by each member of a name-holding group. Most ceremonial roles may not be performed simultaneously by two members of the group, but must be performed by each in order, according to age. The parents of the name-receiver are supposed to sponsor the particular ceremony twice in order to dispatch the child's responsibility, once when the child is very young and a second time as she or he nears puberty. Decisions as to who will sponsor the ceremony in a given year involve discussions about which newborn name-holders have not had the ceremony performed for them yet, and whether there are children who are about to finish initiation and who thus must fulfill their ceremonial responsibilities in the near future.

A child who has completed both performances achieves the honorary title of "ripe," and one who fails to do so is "unripe." "Ripe" persons are felt to be dignified peace-makers of exceptional merit. Under ideal conditions the division of name-holding groups into ripe and unripe corresponds to the division between name-givers and those who have not yet transmitted their names.

Moiety Systems

Name-holding groups are the basic building blocks for three sets of moieties: Kuigatiye/Harungatiye, Kapi/Kaikula, and plaza moieties and their constituent plaza groups (Figure 2). The moiety affiliation of a name-holding group in one moiety system provides no clue to its affiliation in either of the others. Further, the rare Krĩkatí individuals who have changed moiety affiliations argue that switching their affiliation in one moiety set requires no comparable change in the other moiety sets.

These independent, permanent moiety systems have different characteristics, and are associated with different ceremonies.

1. Kuigatiye/Harungatiye moieties are former age moieties, no longer differentiated into age sets. These moieties are associated respectively with east and west, high and low, ostrich (a bird which stays on the ground and can scarcely fly) and turtle (an animal of both land and water). These moieties traditionally performed the marriage ceremonies, which are now obsolete, and they still perform ceremonies of mourning. It is this set of affiliations which the Krĩkatí think of first when they discuss moieties. Kuigatiye and Harungatiye each have chiefs, chosen by all of the men of the village. They serve as a pair, and when one of the two quits or dies, a new pair is chosen. The chiefs direct ceremonies, and harangue the village early in the morning about appropriate behavior and the day's activities. The job also involves providing hospitality for visitors to the village and adjudicating disputes between individuals or domestic clusters. (A domestic cluster is a group of houses located next to each other on the village circle, in which live the members of an uxorilocal extended family.)

2. Kapi/Kaikula moieties function during several ceremonies and also during fish-drugging expeditions. Behavior and personal likes and dislikes are felt to be influenced by this system. These moieties are associated with rainy season and dry season activities, respectively. The year is divided between the two moieties, which

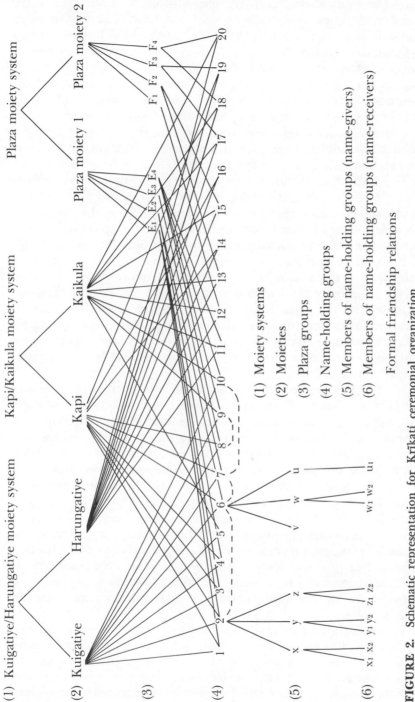

(1) Kuigatiye/Harungatiye moiety system   Kapi/Kaikula moiety system   Plaza moiety system

(2) Kuigatiye   Harungatiye   Kapi   Kaikula   Plaza moiety 1   Plaza moiety 2

(1) Moiety systems
(2) Moieties
(3) Plaza groups
(4) Name-holding groups
(5) Members of name-holding groups (name-givers)
(6) Members of name-holding groups (name-receivers)

Formal friendship relations

FIGURE 2. Schematic representation for Krĩkatí ceremonial organization

stand for rainy season and dry season, flood and drought, night and day, darkness and sunlight, cold and heat. The year is partitioned between times when there is plenty of food but relative social isolation (rainy season) and times of scarcity but heightened social interaction (dry season). The forest (cold, wet, dark) is opposed to the savannah (dry, warm, and sunny), and directions (east and up, versus west and down) are also opposed. The characteristics of the two moieties are associated with the diurnal cycle as well. Thus, Kaikula prefer cold, dark nights, and perform ceremonial activities at night, while Kapi prefer hot, sunny days and are ceremonially active during the day.

The Kapi chief is chosen from among the Kaikula men and vice versa. These chiefs are supposed to be overseers of the activities of the moiety which they govern. Each is appointed by the surviving chief when his opposite number dies. The Kapi chief governs during the day, the Kaikula chief at night. Kaikula, while being of the west, is also associated with the front of the body and the periphery of the village. Kapi is associated with the east and the back of the body, and with the plaza. The association of Kapi/Kaikula with the plaza/house circle opposition, or more generally with the center/periphery dichotomy found elsewhere among the Gê, is much attenuated. It does not have a major place in the symbolism associated with this moiety system, and is not expressed in ceremonial action.

3. Plaza groups and plaza-group moieties are restricted to males. While the plaza moieties are unnamed and practically inoperative, the eight plaza groups play a considerable role in ceremonies. They are paired across moieties for log-racing and paired in a different way for the exchange of meat pies (Figure 3). Each plaza group has a meeting place in the plaza, special paint insignia, a cry, and a leader. Plaza groups are active during the initiation ceremony and the *ponhupru* (maize) festival. Each group is headed by its eldest member, whose duties consist mostly of guiding ceremonial hunting expeditions. Like the other moiety systems, plaza-group moieties are composed of name-holding groups. But in this moiety system, the plaza groups constitute an additional level of organization, so that name-holding groups are aggregated into the eight plaza groups which in turn form the two moieties.

There are also two temporary moiety systems which function during specific ceremonies. In contrast to the permanent moieties, these systems are organized on principles other than naming. For the ceremony of *wu'tukrekre,* the population is divided into those who have more than one child (living or dead) and those with no

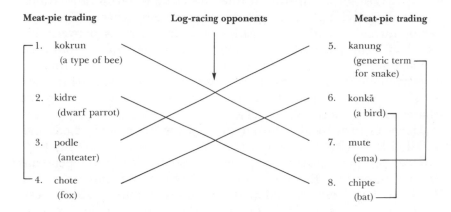

FIGURE 3. Pairing of plaza groups for ceremonies

children or only one child. For the *wu'tu* ceremony, the population is divided into *kloahugatiye* (water monsters, literally, *kloa-
buriti* palm *hu*-leaves, from which the water monster masks are
made) and *ropgatiye* (jaguars). The moieties are associated with
west and east, respectively, and subdivided into several named societies. Men enter the society of their choice at the beginning of
the festival. Women enter the female counterpart of the society
chosen by one of their formal friends and subsequently receive
payment for having "followed" the man.

The system of ceremonial organizations may appear confusingly
complicated. But in practice there is no ambiguity as to which
affiliation is governing an individual's activities at any given time
since no two moiety systems ever function simultaneously. The
segregation of ceremonial activities from domestic activities insures that a person's membership in a particular moiety does not
conflict with relationships outside the ceremonial context.

THE PUZZLE OF CORPORATE NAME-HOLDING GROUPS

Name-holding groups are sets of social positions. Each position
is labeled by a name from among the common set of names. At
the same time, the members of each name-holding group are
linked in ordered relations based on age and on a distinction between those who have given their names and those who have not.
In fact, they are corporate groups with a changing membership,
but with a continuous existence so long as the name-set survives.

The Krĩkatí, however, do not conceptualize name-holding groups as corporate entities. Rather, they talk in terms of relations between individual name-givers and name-receivers. They describe formal friend relationships in terms of links between individual name-givers and name-receivers, although it would be equally accurate to talk about a tie of formal friendship linking two name-holding groups. It is puzzling that the Krĩkatí do not make use of the corporate properties of name-holding groups in characterizing their own society.

However, this dyadic, rather than corporate, model of naming relationships makes better sense when viewed in the light of another problem: how to keep moiety systems clearly independent from one another, given that there is more than one moiety system in the society, and given that these moiety systems perform very similar manifest functions. The Krĩkatí have three moiety systems which recruit members through name transmission and which carry out primarily ceremonial functions. The actual integrity of name-holding groups across moieties (all members of a name-holding group have the same three moiety affiliations) dramatizes the interconnectedness of the three systems in ways that contradict more important messages of separateness encoded in the complex metasystem of three moiety systems. (See Lave 1976 for an analysis of relations among the three systems.) The message of continuity is much diluted if it is reduced to the level of special dyadic relations where an individual simply follows his or her name-giver into the three moieties with which that individual is affiliated. It is these considerations which have given shape to the local model of naming relationships among the Krĩkatí.

Naming As the Basis of Social Continuity through Time

The Krĩkatí are unusual in using naming relationships rather than kin ties as the basis for establishing social continuity through time. This is brought about by downplaying the long-term continuity of intergenerational kin ties while emphasizing these same features in intergenerational naming relationships.

Thus genealogical amnesia is encouraged and required by the Krĩkatí. Relations between the living and the dead are severed as quickly as possible. The living are enjoined to forget the dead. Talking or thinking about them is viewed as dangerous, leading to the possibility that the dead person will wish to continue the relationship with the living by bringing about his or her death. The constant reduction of genealogical information makes possible the useful fiction that domestic clusters consist of separate kin groups. This may be its major function. But it also eliminates the possibility of using genealogical ties to signify the broad ordering of time across generations.

In contrast, continuity is a major preoccupation in the transmission of names. Name-giver and name-receiver are felt to be a single social personage. The name-receiver is said to take the place of, to become, the name-giver. Indeed, the name-receiver steps into all the same ceremonial positions and roles as the name-giver, under the name-giver's tutelage. The term for name-receiver, *comaiyront*, can be roughly glossed as "shoots that grow up from a dying tree," and the Krĩkatí say that name-receivers grow up around the name-giver just like new shoots. Passing on one's social identity is so important that if an individual dies without living name-receivers, it is felt to be appropriate to break one of the basic rules of name transmission: that parents never name their own children. The names of the deceased will be given by adult siblings of the dead person to their *own* children in order to preserve the names and the "place" of the deceased.

This sense of urgency and concern about the transmission of names reflects the crucial function of naming in relating past, present, and future. It is conveyed in other ways as well. Pairing opposite-sex siblings as future name-exchangers establishes the next incumbents of a pair of social identities a generation before they physically arrive on the scene. The Krĩkatí do not depend on transmitting the social identity of someone long deceased, but rather, transmit identity from living adults to newborn babies. Name-givers are physically present when the transaction occurs and have substantial obligations during the years in which the name-receiver is becoming a full-fledged replacement. The individual transmits his or her social position to another almost immediately upon coming into full possession of it. This partially accounts for the Krĩkatí emphasis on the asymmetry of relations between name-giver and name-receiver, on who came first and who came after, for the distinction is crucial in maintaining continuity through time.

The contrast between naming and kin relationships has a number of implications. There is a clear opposition between physical reproduction of the body, involving parenthood, kin relations, and domestic group activities, and the reproduction of social identity, involving name transmission, name relations, and ceremonial activities. For the Krĩkatí, marriage is the last step in the process of initiation into adulthood. Men and woman cannot marry or transmit their names until they complete initiation. The end of initiation thus marks the point at which it becomes possible to marry and reproduce physically, on the one hand, and give names, thus bringing about social reproduction, on the other hand. It is marked by elaborate ritual, not only because it symbolizes crucial events in individual lives, but because it represents the point at which a new group of individuals are ready to transfer their names, thus insuring once again continuity through time for the community as a whole.

Initiation/marriage is also the point at which a man moves from his natal domestic group to join his wife in establishing a new domestic group within her natal domestic cluster. From the point of view of an individual, this is a one-directional move in the course of the life cycle. But from a sociocentric point of view, any individual is involved from birth onward in one primary set and one "shadow" set of relations, both of which continue simultaneously throughout life. This occurs because names and social identities alternate between domestic groups through the process of name transmission. Thus a child, as a name-receiver, acquires with his or her names a "spouse" and "children" (the name-giver's spouse and children). This is the reverse of the situation in ego's natal domestic group, where he or she is, of course, a child to his or her parents. When a man marries, he moves from his natal domestic cluster to reside in his wife's domestic cluster, taking his names with him. His sisters remain in their natal domestic cluster, establishing new nuclear families within it as they marry. Therefore, when a man transmits his names to his sister's son, the names, and his social identity, are returned to the domestic group from which they came. And when the woman transmits her names, they leave her domestic cluster, creating new ties outside her domestic group.

The Krîkatí way of maintaining continuity through time suggests an image to me of repeated short cycles, rather than some sort of linear progression. Within a lifetime a person matures and his or her name-set gradually shifts from belonging to a child, who is a name-receiver only, to belonging to an adult, who is capable of name-giving. Names are then transmitted, so that once again they belong to young children, and begin the cycle again. It is a short cycle in the sense that it goes only from birth to maturity. It is easy to imagine longer cycles in which names could be transmitted to a child from a person in old age, or soon after a death, or after a number of generations, but the Krîkatí do not use the system that way. Men's name-sets can be seen as cycling in space as well as in time; cycling, because they are taken to an affinal domestic cluster when the man marrys, but quickly returned to children of his natal domestic cluster. The cycles are short for men's names.

For women's names the spatial cycle is not so clear-cut; it is only in a general sense that women's names could be said to circulate among domestic clusters. But the cycling through time is not sex-linked, and applies to all Krīkatí.

The Loss of the Age-Set System

I believe that some of the importance of naming in Krīkatí social organization can be explained in terms of the loss of an age-set organization similar to that described for the Timbira in 1935 by Nimuendajú (1946). Since there is no description of the Krīkatí age-set system in 1935, I turn to Nimuendajú's description of the Timbira system as the closest approximation available.[3]

The Timbira age-set system in 1935 consisted of four active age-sets, divided equally between eastern and western moieties (Kuigatiye and Harungatiye). The surviving members of older age-sets were combined in a councilors' "set" that met in the center of the plaza, undifferentiated by moiety membership. The absence of both age-set and moiety distinctions within this group underscores that the councilors' position embodied concern for the welfare of the community as a whole.

The initiation period for an age-set spanned about ten years. New age-sets alternated between the eastern and western moieties, each moiety acquiring a new age-set every twenty years. Each new age-set usurped the meeting place in the plaza of the next older age-set in its moiety,[4] the oldest age-set being promoted to join the councilors in the center of the plaza.

The activities engaged in by the age-sets in 1935 were primarily ceremonial. But an age-set did build houses for those of its members heavily involved in public service, and the members helped each other in harvesting, especially the rice crop (Nimuendajú 1946:94). While Nimuendajú nowhere discusses the process of village fission, William Crocker (1966) says that among the Ramkokamekra in the 1960s factions crystallized around age-set leaders. Nimuendajú (1946:93) emphasizes the unusual authority of age-set leaders in the mid-thirties, although age-set activities were dwindling by that time:

It is they who actually govern the age classes, being possibly the only functionaries who literally issue orders among the Canella, a task for which they are trained from the beginning. Only they have the right to summon their class fellows, who are obliged to obey the call and may not assemble without their leaders. Anyone who has dealings with a class, including the chiefs, must turn to its *mamkyeti* (leader). These leaders are subject only to the council . . . Theoretically, the leaders are equals, but in practice, the abler of the two soon gains ascendancy without, however, completely eclipsing his colleague. In contrast to the chiefs, the *mamkyeti* exercise no authority whatever beyond their age class.

In former times the *mamkyeti* led their class in war and in the chase, though always aided by one or several older men. Since warfare belongs completely to the past and communal hunting has dwindled in importance the present significance of these officers is slight—apart from ceremonial.

Today the Krĩkatí have moieties called Kuigatiye and Harunga-tiye, the same names given by Nimuendajú for both age-set moieties and exogamous moieties. The Krĩkatí moieties have ceremonial functions, but are not divided into age-sets and do not participate in the organization of domestic activities. The Krĩkatí do not remember the names, meeting places, or members of age-sets, but there is one group of men in their late forties who agree that they were initiated together in a series of ceremonies. They are all Harungatiye. The probability is very small that all these men would belong to the same moiety if age had not been the principal recruiting mechanism for moiety membership. There is one younger group, men between the ages of thirty and forty, who went through at least one initiation ceremony together. They appear to be divided about evenly between Kuigatiye and Harunga-tiye. I would guess that it was some time during the period between the initiation of the thirty- to forty-year-old group and the forty- to fifty-year-old group that age-sets ceased to function and membership in Kuigatiye and Harungatiye moieties became name-based.

Ceremonies that among the Timbira in 1935 were connected with age-sets persisted among the Krĩkatí in 1965. One of these is an initiation ceremony. Krĩkatí children first enter seclusion for a two- to three-month period between the ages of eight and twelve, and may enter a second time, depending on their own inclinations and those of their parents. The ceremonies are held whenever there are two or more children whose parents wish to sponsor their initiation, and the whole community takes part. Each initiate has a companion, a special friend, who goes through the initiation at the same time, but large groups are no longer initiated together. The ceremony, *ikrere,* corresponds to the *pepye* age-set initiation ceremony described by Nimuendajú (1946:170–171, 179–201) and is identical in many details. As among the Timbira in 1935, children are beaten at ceremonial times and sent regularly to bathe at dawn. Krĩkatí men now in their thirties remember being hazed extensively until marriage. They entered seclusion in relatively large groups (six to ten). They also ended the seclusion period as a group and maintained various sex and food restrictions for some time afterward.

Differences in the ceremonial marking of life cycle events between 1935 and 1965 are mostly a matter of degree. The series of six or eight initiation ceremonies through which an age-set passed in 1935 has collapsed into a series of two, or at the most four, ceremonies, performed for one or more pairs of children. The informal aspects of initiation, including hazing and training for log-racing, continue in slightly attenuated form until marriage. As among the Timbira in 1935, the Kuigatiye and Harungatiye moiety system is the appropriate one for traditional marriage ceremonies among the Krĩkatí, on the rare occasions when they are performed. In the past, formal marriage ceremonies marked the end of the initiation ceremonies, but did not necessarily signal the beginning of actual coresidence and cohabitation. Today the marriage ceremony is, more often than not, simply a public announcement of actual coresidence and may occur some years after the initiation rites. Ceremonies for the dead are, however, carried out in consistent and elaborate style by the Kuigatiye/Harungatiye moieties, again corresponding to the Timbira practice in 1935.

As in 1935, the major ceremonial activity of the year occurs in May and October, at transition periods between the rainy and dry seasons, marking changes in the yearly cycle. Each ceremony is divided into two parts, a beginning and an end, both involving intensive ceremonial activity over a period of a few days. The two periods of a given ceremony involve quite similar, repetitive events. The time in between the opening and closing is relatively quiet, a sort of diffuse "holiday season" with little specific ceremonial activity. The closing festivities for one ceremony occur close together in time with the opening log race of the next ceremony, so that all the yearly cycle is given structure by the cycle of ceremonies.

The economic and political activities associated with age-sets among the Timbira of 1935 are organized by the Krĩkatí today according to domestic cluster affiliations. Planting and harvesting are coordinated among nuclear families within each domestic cluster. The ceremonies the Timbira performed in 1935 to open the corn harvest season officially are still performed among the Krĩkatí, but are not described as harvest ceremonies and do not affect harvesting. Ceremonial hunting trips are carried out by moieties—whichever pair is active for the particular ceremony. The men of each moiety, and their wives and children, travel together, make group decisions about which area to hunt in, and so on, although the game is not contributed to a common pot. Raiding, which among the Timbira in 1935 was conducted by age-sets, has not occurred among the Krĩkatí for many years. One of the oldest men in the community remembers a single raid when he was a young man. For the Krĩkatí, domestic clusters are the basic units in communitywide quarrels, and one or more domestic clusters may leave the village as a unit in the case of a community split.

There are no such strong leadership positions as Nimuendajú describes for the Timbira in Krĩkatí social organization today. The job of Kuigatiye or Harungatiye chief has onerous responsibilities and few rewards, and does not imply rights or powers to affect anybody's behavior except through moral persuasion. At least six living men have been chief at some time, and the Krĩkatí insist that they are happy to quit such a difficult and thankless job. Other "chiefs" have strictly ceremonial leadership roles, exercised during the ceremonial periods when their moiety system is in effect. Leadership today, for groups smaller than the community as a whole, resides informally with a few men and women with forceful personalities who have considerable influence in their domestic clusters.

Historical Trends: Organizational Changes Resulting from Loss of the Age-Set System

Evidence has just been presented to support the proposition that the Krĩkatí once had an age-set system and have lost it. The change was not an isolated one and much of the rest of the paper is concerned with tracing some of the implications of the loss of the age-set system.

First of all, as the age-set system became less important, individualization of age-based relationships increased. This came about through the increasing importance of name-transmission relations. Name transmission was not a new recruiting device for the Krĩkatí of 1965. Nor did it spring into existence only as the age-set system disappeared. Formerly, they coexisted. Among the Timbira in 1935, names were the basis for membership in plaza groups (and hence plaza-group moieties), rainy season/dry season moieties, and men's societies. Some formal friends were acquired through name transmission. However, membership in age-set moieties (Kuigatiye and Harungatiye) was based on age, membership in the *tamhuk* honorary organization was based on other principles, and formal friends could be acquired in ways other than naming. For the Krĩkatí today, essentially all ceremonial organization, including Kuigatiye/Harungatiye moiety membership and formal friendship relations, is based on naming. The only honorary positions (for example, ripe/unripe) are based on performance of special ceremonial roles, and the right to perform these roles derives only from possession of a particular name-set.

The referential terminology for name-transmission relationships does appear to be a recent development.[5] Not a single such term is reported by Nimuendajú (1946).[6] Nimuendajú would probably have reported such terms if they had been in use in the late thirties, for he would have heard them used constantly in address; and as a stranger being incorporated into the community, he would have been taught them when (1946:110) he received names and naming relatives.

To some extent, the change in relative importance of naming and age-set activities is a quantitative one. Between 1935 and 1965 there appears to have been a decrease in the amount of time spent in organized ceremonial activities. Where once log races and age-set meetings and other activities occurred every day, and there is daily involvement only just before, and during, periods of intense ceremonial activity.

Age was the primary organizing principle for the age-set system. Age continues to be an organizing principle. But the units organized according to relative age have undergone a drastic change. Name transmission and the organizations based on naming, especially name-holding groups, might be characterized as individualized versions of the age-set organization. A comparison of the major features of age-sets and name-holding groups will help to make the point clear.

In both the system of name-holding groups and the age-set system, a man changes status with age. Among the Timbira in 1935, an age-set shifted from initiate to mature-man status, then to councilor status, with accompanying changes in meeting places, and so on. The Krĩkatí in 1965 move from the status of name-receiver to that of name-giver. Both age-sets and name-holding groups have members of one sex only. Age-sets are ordered by age; individuals within a name-holding group are ordered by age. In both, the initiated are distinguished from the uninitiated—a distinction between sets in the one case and between individuals in the other. Initiation is a prerequisite for full participation in age-set activities, and completion of initiation confers the right to transmit names among the Krĩkatí today. A Krĩkatí child completes initiation with a special companion, and they aid and support each other for the rest of their lives, but they are not caught up with a set of peers in an extensive and absorbing set of group activities. Both age-sets and name-holding groups recruit members through initiation ceremonies, but initiation was carried out for an age-set in 1935 and for individuals in 1965.

In addition to individualization, there is a second consistent difference between 1935 and 1965 in the structure of interrelationships. It is partially an outcome of the individualization. Since 1935 there has been increasing participation of women in ceremonial activities, and the initiation of girls has become routine. Krĩkatí parents speak about sponsoring initiation ceremonies for their daughters with the same concern as for their sons. This contrasts with Nimuendajú's description of age-set initiation, in which only two representative girls were secluded with the boys. Krĩkatí women, as a group, now "own" ceremonies, including *wu'tu*, the most important ceremony of the Krĩkatí. Groups which perform in this ceremony are rather similar to the Timbira men's societies in 1935, but now there are both men's and women's societies, and societies of each sex have two opposite-sex associates. The ceremony for the dead is now performed by men for a deceased male and by women for a deceased female. When a man dies, the men of the community run with logs and the women sing and prepare a ceremonial meal. When a woman dies, women run while men sing and prepare food. None of these activities in which Krĩkatí women participate are reported for the Timbira of 1935 or for other groups of Gê.

Since both men and women received names, belonged to name-holding groups, and inherited ceremonial roles along with names in 1935, the increasing importance of names should have led to increasing involvement of women in ceremonial activities. No other principle of Timbira social organization exhibited this sexual symmetry. We can speculate about the processes which brought about this increasing involvement. Nimuendajú reports that Timbira women joined one age-set moiety or the other for occasional racing purposes. This connection could have been used as a new criterion for transmitting moiety membership along with names. Krĩkatí women have membership in Kuigatiye/Harungatiye today on the basis of their names. Similarly, women might have acquired ceremonial roles by serving as associates to men's ceremonial groups. Girls were chosen as *wu'tu* associates of the age-set moieties among the Timbira in 1935, and today *wu'tu* is a special girl's ceremonial role. When a girl had once acted a special ceremonial role, it would be consistent with the rules of name transmission for other women to gain access to the role along with a name-set. Another way in which ceremonial roles might have come to be more homogeneously distributed in the population is through the occasional transmission, on a temporary basis, of male names to females. Under some circumstances (the chances are increased by epidemics and general depopulation) , a girl might thus come to hold a special ceremonial role which once belonged exclusively to males. Today, for example, both males and females inherit the ceremonial role *ru'rut,* although their name-sets are said to be different from each other.

The third major historical change resulting from the end of age-sets was the strengthening of the political and economic position of the domestic cluster. At the present time, it is the heads of domestic clusters who provide leadership for village factions. In the past, quarrels severe enough to split the village appear to have crystallized around age-set leadership.

It is not at all clear what process has led to this long-term change in the organization of factions. But in the late thirties, there was almost certainly some complex interaction of kin ties and age-set ties which influenced individual and family decisions about whom to live with when village splits occurred. There must have been conflict for a man in deciding whether to move his family with his age-set, under its leader, or to follow the decision-makers of his wife's domestic cluster. In general, the stronger men's allegiances to their age-sets, the more likely that domestic clusters would split up in the case of factional division. Thus, a major implication of the demise of age-sets should be a strengthening of domestic clusters and, perhaps, sharper boundaries between them as they become the primary units in community disputes.

Nimuendajú did not seem impressed by the integration of Timbira domestic clusters in 1935 (1946:84, 161) :

> The members of a house community (domestic clusters) . . . are obviously closer to one another than to outsiders at large, but they fail to constitute a definite economic unit among the Timbira. The plantations of the residents are ordinarily in juxtaposition, but every married woman has her own plots and the house community as such has no property apart from the domicile.
>
> However, the entire group will safeguard the individual's rights against any injustice from outside . . . In this sense the safety of the individual rests on his affiliation with the major family . . .
>
> On the other hand, the house community plays not the slightest role in ceremonial.

And later: "The following legal principles emerge from the concrete instances: (1) Both the culprit and the aggrieved party are aided by the extended families; (2) the chiefs and councillors take pains to adjust quarrels as soon as possible; (3) for this purpose they use the services either of specially gifted persons or of the individuals linked by specially close ties to the parties involved."

While it is especially difficult to make comparative judgments when differences are a matter of degree, comparison of Nimuendajú's description with the data to be presented next seems to bear out the conclusion that Krīkatí domestic groups today are more integrated and solidary units than such groups were among the Timbira of 1935.

Nimuendajú's assessment of the Timbira is that in 1935 domestic clusters were rather trivial and unimportant social units. He reaches this conclusion on the basis of two lines of argument. First, Timbira house communities did not own property. Second, house communities took no part in ceremonial activity. But property ownership may not be necessary for strong group cohesion. Krīkatí domestic clusters achieve strong, economic cohesion through coordination of activities and exchange of goods, neither of which requires group ownership of property. Further, the fact that domestic clusters did not act as units in ceremonial activity in 1935 does not distinguish them from the Krīkatí today. But the reason why domestic clusters did not take part in ceremonies is precisely that they were domestic groups. It has much more to do with separating domestic from ritual occasions and activities than it does with the cohesion of domestic units.

Rather than measure the Krīkatí today against Nimuendajú's criteria, it may be useful to examine new evidence about the political and economic cohesion of Krīkatí domestic clusters in 1965. I will discuss first the economic activities of domestic clusters, then their political role. Finally, I will use patterns of kin-terminology usage to show the highly crystallized domestic cluster organization of Krīkatí villages.

Domestic clusters today are economic units of great importance. Economic solidarity is demonstrated in the coordination of daily activities and the exchange of food. Each of the major gardens of the Krīkatí is occupied by a single domestic cluster. Garden work parties change in purpose and composition throughout the growing cycle but always involve coordination of domestic cluster members' activities. Men cut the trees and undergrowth on the garden site. Each man (with the help of his unmarried sons) cuts his own plot. After the whole group fires the cleared area, he builds a portion of the common fence within the agreed-upon domestic cluster garden. The women clear the small brush and prepare the ground for planting. Clearing and planting work parties involve all of the women of a domestic cluster, who go to the garden early in the morning to work, each on her own plot, occasionally stopping to rest and gossip. Harvesting involves both men and women, using the same work pattern.

Coordination of daily activities within a domestic cluster applies to gathering and hunting expeditions, to the new forays to do wage work, and to traveling, as well as to gardening. Frequently a group of men within a domestic cluster go hunting together. Each man takes home what he has killed, to be cleaned, divided, and distributed by his wife. Women of a domestic cluster will set out together on a gathering expedition, each bringing home what she has personally collected.

There is essentially no coordination or cooperation *across* domestic cluster boundaries. Each cluster acts independently. People enter arcs of the house circle other than their own only when making specific visits to relatives. Similarly, no one enters the garden of any other cluster unless a member invites him or her.

Within the domestic cluster, nuclear families are linked in frequent and substantial exchanges of food, gossip, and other items. While productive activities are carried out through parallel, individual efforts of domestic cluster members, over half the food brought into the village by the person who labored to produce it is consumed by other members of the domestic cluster. Each house has a small path leading away from the village. This path probably minimizes the distance from the house to the nearest concealing cover. Even so, it is practically impossible for anyone to reach home carrying game or other food without being observed by other members of the domestic cluster. Immediately, a small child or other member appears from each nuclear family in the cluster to demand a share. The family is lucky to save enough for a single meal, but they have reciprocal rights to the fruits of their fellow residents' labors.

Domestic clusters do not "own" garden land or houses, but in both cases they have use rights. Nuclear families in a domestic cluster make their garden plots together and build adjacent houses. So long as they continue to use them, other people do not have the right to do so. If a garden is abandoned while still usable, other domestic cluster members have first rights to utilize it. When a garden is no longer plantable (after two years' use), it must lie fallow until regrowth has occurred (at least ten years), after which it is available to anyone who wishes to use it.

Use rights in houses are more complicated. A man builds a house and he and his wife and children live in it. Other nuclear families within the domestic cluster may join them after negotiating with the builder. If divorce or death removes the man from the house, the other residents continue to live there. If a house were to be abandoned by a family, other nuclear families in the same domestic cluster could move into it or utilize the house posts to build another; or (and this is the only way a nonmember of the domestic cluster could utilize the house) a relative of the deceased —his sister, for example—might appropriate the house posts to build a house in her own domestic cluster arc. Since a domestic cluster very rarely abandons use of a house, and there is never any reason why anyone would want to move into a village arc of which she or he was not a member, there do not exist situations which would provide proof that domestic clusters have use but not ownership rights to houses. I believe, however, that it is relationship and residence, rather than "ownership," that is involved.

Domestic clusters are also political units today. Factional splits occur along domestic cluster lines. The two domestic clusters of which São Gregorio was composed in 1964 had separated by 1967. One domestic cluster still lived in São Gregorio, while the other lived near its garden. In a similar village split in Governador in 1964, one domestic cluster moved to a new site. Manipulations of the residence rule contribute to the impression that domestic clusters are political units. But before describing variant uses of the rule, it will be helpful to present the normative rules of residence.

A cluster comes to occupy an arc of the village circle as daughters grow up and marry. When the parents' house becomes too crowded, young couples receive permission to build separate dwellings to the right of the parental house. The youngest daughter resides in the parental household indefinitely. When she and her husband have established a family, they request formal permission to build a separate dwelling. On this occasion, they take on the status of head of household regardless of the parents' reply to the request: either the young couple obtain permission to move out and build their own house, or permission is refused. In the latter case, the young couple remain and the parents turn management of the household over to them, becoming "children to their children," as the Krĩkatí say.

In practice, the residence rules are more complex. The Krĩkatí appear to arrange their houses where possible so that adult men who are heads of households live between their affinal and consanguineal domestic clusters. The houses of these men are transition points where two domestic clusters overlap, and members of both clusters are likely to treat the transition house as part of their domain.

The men who were in the position of living in proximity to both their natal and affinal domestic clusters in 1965 were all mature, with children approaching adulthood. Clearly, it is impossible for a majority of men to arrange their residence in such a conveniently ambiguous way. In general, a man has little choice when young but to follow the uxorilocal residence rule or to be divorced, but his options increase with age and with the development of his family of procreation. Older males seem to be able to place their households so as to align themselves with the politically strongest domestic cluster while maintaining ties to the other cluster as well. These individuals tend to play key roles as mediators in disputes between domestic clusters and to gain prestige from and the support of both. The fact that considerations of political advantage may be taken into account in locating houses on the village circle supports the notion that domestic clusters have become increasingly important as political units.

Other indications of the increased strength of the domestic cluster may perhaps be seen in the apparent decrease in the range of application of kin-relationship terminology and the absence of restriction to the domestic cluster of certain activities that among the Timbira were public events. It seems reasonable that as the domestic cluster becomes the basis for factions it becomes less appropriate for individuals to emphasize distant or uncertain kinship ties as a method for increasing the solidarity of their position in the community as a whole. The Krĩkatí comment frequently that young people today are rude and ignorant because they no longer refer to everyone in the village by a kin term. I have data from three men on their referential use of kin terms for all members of the community. Two of the men were in their thirties, one about fifteen years of age. The fifteen-year-old had completed initiation, was married, and like the thirty-year-olds was considered to be an adult by other members of the community. In many cases, the youngest man did not know how he ought to refer to people, while neither of the older men hesitated over the task at all. The two older men had no customary term of reference or address for two and eleven members of the community, respectively; the young man claimed no knowledge for sixty-nine.) The simplest explanation is that in the fifteen to twenty years separating him from the older men, the range of effective application has, in fact, shrunk.

Some activities which involved the Timbira age-sets in domestic affairs in 1935 are carried out exclusively within domestic clusters among the Krĩkatí of 1965. Marriage is such an occasion. Name-transmission ceremonies are also private now, while Nimuendajú describes public name-bestowing ceremonies for the Timbira of 1935. The Timbira rituals of public reentry into full social participation following childbirth, severe illness, mourning, and long journeys are all absent.

The age-set system integrated some ceremonial functions with some domestic ones. More important, it provided a strongly organized focus for men's activities which cut across domestic groups and made it nearly impossible for domestic group loyalties to serve as the basis for either communitywide factional disputes or, ultimately, the dispersion of the community. But the end of the age-set system did not lead to the disintegration of Krĩkatí society. Principles of organization which had played a minor role in earlier times were pressed into service, or perhaps expanded to fill an organizational vacuum, leading to a new version of the old system. That this organizational change involved a new balance between kin-based and name-based relations is in no way unique. In fact, the Gê societies all express different solutions to the problem of balancing interfamily relations in terms of the relative importance assigned to kin and naming relationships (see Chapter 5 and 6 and Lave, 1975, 1976).

The new integration, in which individual ties of naming replaced age-based, highly solidary groups, seems to me a weaker, more brittle system than the earlier form. It is unlikely, in the face of continued pressures from Brazilian settlers on the land, the resources, and the culture of the Indians, that they will be able to repeat again the feat of building a new integration out of the remains of the present system. But as this volume demonstrates, the possibilities for combining and recombining the structural features of Gê social organization are enormous. It is to be hoped that I, like Nimuendajú in the late thirties, am over pessimistic about the generative powers of Krĩkatí social organization.

THE KRAHÓ

THE KRAHÓ LIVE in the state of Goiás on a reservation with an area of almost 3,200 square kilometers near the small town of Itacajá. They have been in peaceful contact with the Brazilians since 1809. In this region, the settlers live by subsistence agriculture and cattle rearing. However, their very presence has cut down the supply of game animals, on which the Indians formerly relied. Consequently, Indians sometimes kill steers belonging to the local cattlemen, and this produces ill-feeling between them and the Brazilians. This was the issue that led the cattlemen to attack two Krahó villages in 1940 and kill at least twenty-three Indians. As a result the federal government adopted a series of measures for the protection of the Krahó. It punished the three ranchers responsible for the attack, demarcated a reservation for the tribe in 1944, and established an Indian Protection Service post on it.

In 1962–63 there were 519 Indians living in the villages on the reservation and 43 Indians (or people of Indian descent) living on the reservation but outside of the villages. By 1971 this population had increased to 586 in the villages and at least 49 on the reservation but outside the villages.

There are Indians living in the Krahó villages today who are descended from Sherente, Apaniekra, Apinayé, and Krenkateye. The sole Krenkateye village in the state of Maranhão was destroyed by settlers in 1913, and the survivors of the massacre scattered, some coming to live with the Krahó. The Krahó nowadays visit the villages of the Apinayé, Apaniekra, and Sherente. It seems that their contacts with other Timbira peoples tend to strengthen their Indian traditions, particularly as regards songs and rituals. By contrast, their contacts with the Sherente tend to influence them to adopt Brazilian ways.

Currently, the Krahó practice subsistence agriculture, but this is not sufficient to feed them all year round. They gather the wild fruits of the region and also gather fruit from trees planted at the Indian Protection Service post or from trees abandoned by ranchers in the region. Hunting was once very important but is now restricted to the killing of small game, since the larger animals are vanishing. Some Krahó are nowadays trying to rear cattle.

2 | The Relationship System of the Krahó

Julio Cezar Melatti

Translated from the Portuguese by David Maybury-Lewis

IN THIS PAPER I describe and analyze the relationship system of the Krahó using the data which I myself collected in the field.[1] I shall try to show that in order to understand this relationship system it is not enough to relate it to family organization, residential arrangements, or matrimonial choices. The system also shows a set of relationships which are ritual in nature, particularly the dualism which permeates most of Krahó institutions. This dualism is not limited to theories of oppositions between elements taken two at a time. One of its most notable features is that every opposition between two elements is opposed by another opposition which negates the first one. We thus find an opposition of oppositions.

Consequently, before proceeding to an examination of the relationship terminology and the behavior connected with it I must briefly describe Krahó domestic organization and the dualism in Krahó society and Krahó domestic organization. I give here only the minimum amount of information necessary for the reader to follow my argument.

Dualism

If we are to consider as examples of dual organization only those societies which are divided into exogamous moieties, then the Krahó cannot be numbered among them since they have no rule of cross-cousin marriage and none of their various pairs of moieties has the function of regulating marriage. But we give the term "dual organization" a broader connotation, using it to include those societies which have a substantial part of their institutions, their beliefs, and their symbolism organized in terms of oppositions that can be set out in a dyadic model (even though such a

46

model may be no more than a construct in the minds of members of those societies), then Krahó society can be considered an example of dual organization.[2] In fact, Krahó society is made up of a number of pairs of moieties with varying rules for membership in them.

First, there are the two moieties named Wakmẽye and Katamye. Each one has a set of personal names which belongs to it. Every individual of either sex belongs to one or the other of these moieties, depending on the personal name which he or she holds. There is a series of symbols associated with these moieties. The first one is associated with day, the dry season, the east, the cleared central space of the village, light-colored palm leaves used for ceremonial decorations, vertical stripes in body painting, and so on. The second moiety is associated with night, the wet season, the west, the outer circle of the village, with dark palm leaves used in ceremonial regalia, with horizontal stripes in body painting, and so on. The Krahó even classify the members of the animal and vegetable kingdoms as belonging to one or the other of these moieties. The moieties perform certain rituals. Moreover, each one of them supplies two men to direct the activities of the village. These "directors" function during the season which corresponds to their own moiety. These are the only moieties to which women belong on the same terms as men. Women are not primary members of any of the other pairs of moieties, but every woman belongs to her father's moiety before marriage and to her husband's moiety afterward.

Every man by virtue of his name belongs further to one of eight ritual groups that play an important role in the *ketwaye* (initiation) ceremony. These eight groups are divided into two moieties, four groups to each one.[3] The names of these moieties are Khoirumpekëtxë and Hararumpekëtxë, the former being stationed on the east side and the latter on the west side of the village plaza. The two pairs of moieties so far discussed are the only ones to which people belong by virtue of their personal names.

Krahó men also belong to age-sets, which are in turn grouped in the Khöikateye and Harãkateye moieties. Boys are allocated to age-sets by a man of the village with sufficient experience. The age moieties appear on the occasion of various ceremonies.

There are certain other pairs of moieties where an individual simply chooses which one he will belong to. Every male chooses the moiety he wishes to belong to before the ceremony in which the moieties have to take part. The next time that the same ceremony is performed the individual may choose, if he wishes, to join the opposite moiety from the one he joined the first time. Such pairs of moieties are, for example, those called Hëk and Krókrók or those called Tép and Teré.

The dual organization of the Krahó is made up not only of these various moiety systems but also of a series of other oppositions, such as the opposition between men and women. In the first place, men and women are contrasted by a strict division of labor. Men hunt, gather honey, cut down forests to clear the land for planting, and manufacture certain ritual objects. Women gather fruit, cook, and look after the children. There are some activities in which both sexes may take part, such as collecting firewood or planting certain crops. As far as rituals are concerned, only men go through initiation rites. Women are totally excluded from political life. Moreover, the chief of the village and the "directors" have to be men. This opposition between the sexes also comes out in the differences in body paint, in the stylized movements which the members of each sex make while singing and chanting, in exchanges of goods and services, in the ritual aggressions practiced between the sexes, and, above all, in those rituals where male and female behaviors are inverted so that each sex behaves in the ways appropriate to the other one.

The layout of Krahó villages expresses this dualism. The houses are built in a circle. A path leads from each house to the plaza, situated at the center of the circle. Thus the plaza, which is where the men have their meetings, where all ritual processions end, where people from other villages are formally received, and where unmarried boys and men sleep, is in clear opposition to the periphery of the village, where food is prepared, meals are eaten, and domestic life takes place. This opposition between the center (plaza) and the periphery (houses) translates into spatial terms other oppositions, such as the one mentioned between Wakmẽye and Katamye. It is also a representation of the opposition between man and woman or male and female, since men as a class meet in the plaza while women's work is done at the periphery in the houses to which women belong throughout their lives, since residence is uxorilocal. In times past, the dead were buried close to the houses (or even inside them), so that one might say that the opposition between center and periphery also reflects the opposition between the living and the dead.

There seems to be a certain correspondence between the oppositions Wakmẽye/Katamye, man/woman, and living/dead. The dead are beings who no longer participate in the activities of the living, while women are excluded from certain privileges and activities which are exclusively masculine, so that one might say that only the men participate fully in rituals and in public life.

The Katamye moiety is associated, among other things, with night and the rainy season, and the Krahó believe that during the night and on days which are rainy or overcast the souls of the dead enter the village. Furthermore, rain interferes with rituals and prevents meetings from being held in the plaza. One might therefore say that in the oppositions Wakmẽye/Katamye, man/woman, and living/dead the first element in each case corresponds to society and the second to nature.

A notable feature of Krahó dualism is that every opposition which states a difference between two elements is counterbalanced by another one which insists on the identity of those same elements. The two oppositions thus cancel each other out. Some examples will illustrate what I mean. Consider the opposition man/woman. We know that men are contrasted with women in the division of labor and in their participation in both political life and initiation rituals. Nevertheless, there are certain rituals where women do men's tasks and men do women's work; the wife of the village chief and the wives of the two "directors" are granted certain honorific attributes; during initiation rites, two girls always accompany the boys who are taking part in the ritual. Consequently, while Krahó custom insists that men are different from women, the series of institutionalized exceptions affirm the contrary: that men and women are equal.

The opposition living/dead shows a similar contradiction. Traditionally, the dead were buried either close to the houses or actually inside them. However, some people who had occupied important or honorific positions during their lives were buried in the central plaza. Thus, against the insistence that the dead are distinct from the living, these exceptions insisted that the living were similar to the dead.

A similar example can be cited for the society/nature opposition. There is a series of myths which describe how the Krahó learned their rituals, their songs, the use of fire, and their knowledge of agriculture. All these myths insist that the Indians acquired these various forms of knowledge from beings (animals, plants, stars, or monsters) who lived outside the village. These myths thus stress that those elements which today are characteristic of Krahó society were once part of the natural world. Yet at the same time, there are myths which describe how human beings in the past used to turn into animals and monsters. The symbolic statement that society is distinct from nature is thus counterbalanced by a statement to the effect that society and nature are equivalent.

I could cite further examples to illustrate the oppositions between oppositions, but the ones already adduced should be sufficient. As we shall see, a number of characteristics of the Krahó relationship system can be understood in terms of this principle of opposition between oppositions. At the same time it should be noted that, whenever a statement of difference between two elements is opposed by another affirmation of their identity, the first proposition carries more weight, for it represents the rule while the second indicates certain institutionalized exceptions to the rule. In other words, these exceptions act in such a way as to produce a double result: at the same time that they emphasize the rule, they also deprive it of its absolute character.

Domestic Organization

To understand Krahó domestic life, we have to consider the following groups: the elementary family, the domestic group, and the residential segment.

The elementary family is made up of father, mother, and children or adoptive children. Such a family rarely has its own household, but generally shares a house with other families. Of all the residential groups, it is the elementary family which most obviously acts together as a unit. The economic activities of the father and mother complement each other and are directed, above all else, to the support of their children. As far as subsistence is concerned, the elementary family is a self-sufficient unit. Each one cultivates its own plot of land for itself. Within the household it possesses its own more or less clearly defined space, though it may not necessarily have its own hearth. At mealtimes the elementary family eats separately as a group.

The domestic group generally consists of more than one elementary family within a single household. Since postmarital residence is uxorilocal, the wives in the various elementary families in the household are related to each other matrilineally. At the same time, there is a certain amount of collaboration between a father-in-law and his sons-in-law within the domestic group. It is the father-in-law who directs economic activities. When he becomes senile or dies, this leadership passes to one of his sons-in-law. It is not always clear where the leadership of a domestic group lies. The situation is usually clear enough when the household consists of a father-in-law and sons-in-law, but it is harder to identify the leader when the father-in-law has died and the household is given over to the husbands of a set of sisters. A house with more than one father-in-law is exceedingly rare. It seems that, when the third generation of a domestic group starts to marry, the couples of the second generation take their children and move into separate households. However, I have data on too few cases of this sort of rupture within domestic groups to be able to state with any certainty that this is the rule. The members of a domestic group usually cultivate adjoining gardens, although this is not obligatory. When a woman cooks food, all the members of her domestic group share in it, although they separate into small elementary family groups for the actual eating of it.

When a domestic group splits up, those who are leaving it build a house beside the original household. For this reason, one frequently finds a set of houses making up a segment, the women of which are all related matrilineally to each other. I shall provisionally call such sets of houses *residential segments*.[4] When the village is moved to a new site, the residential segments occupy the same part of the circumference of the village, with reference to the cardinal points, that they did at the previous site. When a domestic group moves from one village to another, its members construct their house at the same point on the circumference of the village as it was located in their village of origin. In this way, a single residential segment can be represented in more than one village. The members of a residential segment do not necessarily work together. They do not appear together as a unit in any single ritual. They are not distinguished by the common possession of a name. Residential segments are distinguished only by two characteristics: the fact that their members always occupy the same part of the circumference of the village and the fact that all the evidence points to their being exogamous. I know of only one case of sexual relations having taken place between the members of a single residential segment.

It is hard to define the locus of domestic authority among the Krahó. Roberto da Matta, in his analysis of the Aukhe myth, came to the conclusion that in this myth both the Canela and the Krahó were avoiding the definition of domestic authority. In those versions of the myth where the maternal grandfather and father of Aukhe are present, his maternal uncle is absent and vice versa (da Matta 1967:124–135). Is authority therefore held by the men who are born in the household or by the men who enter the household at marriage?

Since I have distinguished three types of kin grouping among the Krahó, we need now to consider who exercises authority in each one of these groups. It is also worth considering whether authority belongs to different individuals according to the various types of problems which the group has to resolve.

To take the elementary family first, is it possible to speak of authority within this group at all, and if so would the husband be considered the head of the elementary family? It seems that there is a high degree of economic collaboration within the elementary family based on the sexual division of labor. At the same time, it is difficult to find any evidence which would enable us to argue that one or the other spouse has authority. In spite of the fact that the elementary family is, in theory at least, an economically independent unit, it usually shares a house with other such families. Ritually, however, the woman depends on her husband. There are, as I have noted, various pairs of moieties which are preeminently masculine and to which women belong only by virtue of their husband's membership in them. When a man occupies certain positions, such as chief of the village or "director," his wife receives certain privileges as a result of this. The wife of a village chief even has a special name: *sadon*. Furthermore, a common way of honoring a man is to confer the title of *witï* on one of his children. A man can therefore be seen as mediating between his elementary family and the public life of the community. Nevertheless, this ritual precedence of the husband does not appear to bring him authority within his elementary family.

As far as the domestic group is concerned, the evidence indicates that authority is vested in that man who married into the household the longest time ago. This authority is most clearly evidenced when it resides in the father-in-law/son-in-law relationship. The authority of a father-in-law is noticeably exercised over young sons-in-law. It is the father-in-law who allocates the daily tasks to his sons-in-law. Older sons-in-law, however, themselves decide how to help their father-in-law without his having to tell them. Authority within the domestic group is thus more or less economic authority. It is limited to dividing up work among the married men of the household or organizing their efforts on a specific task.

It is hard to determine any clear locus of authority within the residential segment. Since one of the characteristics of such segments is exogamy, one might imagine that one of the attributes of authority within the residential segment might be the power to make decisions concerning marriages. However, after examining numerous cases of marriage and of disputes connected with affinal relationships, I was unable to isolate any single category of relationship which was said to have the last word on these matters.

It could be said, then, that the Krahó do not seem to have any clearly defined pattern of authority either in the elementary family or in the residential segment. Furthermore, although authority within the domestic group seems to be a little clearer, it has a limited scope, being confined to economic activities. The leader of the domestic group does not in the last analysis make decisions concerning the marriages of its members, nor does he represent its members in political or ritual activities.

This discussion of domestic authority leads to a paradoxical conclusion. Authority is more clearly defined in the domestic group and refers above all to economic matters. Nevertheless, the self-sufficient economic unit is the elementary family, and in this there is no clearly defined authority figure to regulate its internal activities, but rather a mediator who links it to the public life of the village, but only as regards political and ritual matters, not economic ones. But the paradox has a partial explanation. Since the economic activities of a man and his wife are complementary, they do not require any authority to organize them. The domestic group, however, is made up of a number of elementary families which are theoretically independent and self-sufficient, so that the interaction between them within the larger unit has to have some sort of coordination.

The Relationship System

TERMINOLOGY

Krahó relationship terminology, even if restricted as it is here to the terms of reference (the majority of which are also terms of address), is very rich in synonyms and nuances. This is not the place for an exhaustive examination of the terminology in all its details. I shall therefore pass over those aspects of it which seem to me to be of minor importance and shall present a set of the most commonly used terms.

These terms are the ones which are most inclusive, and upon occasion they have been chosen in preference to their synonyms in order to simplify the schematization of the system. The number preceding each term identifies it both in the text and in the accompanying tables.

1. *ïtxũ*: F, FB, FZS, FMB, MH, MZH . . .

This term designates all those men who have or who might have been permitted to have sexual relations with ego's mother. This term in its simple form is always applied to the genitor or the genitors of ego, since, according to the Krahó, a person may have more than one biological father. The other relationships mentioned may be denominated by this term as it stands or by the term followed by suffixes such as *ti* ("large"), *ré* ("small"), *prek* ("old") or *kuprï* ("young"), to mention only the most common ones. Note that this is not the only term whose radical denotes the kin types mentioned. There is another radical, seen in the form *apam,* which means "your father" (either biological or classificatory) . There is also another form, *hum,* which is only found in descriptive terms and in teknonymous use.

2. *ītxe*: M, MZ, FW, FBW . . .

This term designates all women who may have sexual relations with the genitor or genitors of ego. The term in its simple form is used to indicate ego's genetrix. When referring to the classificatory mothers, the term is usually extended by one of the suffixes mentioned above, namely, *prek* and *kuprï.* Another radical with the same connotation is found in the form *anã,* which means "your mother" (biological or classificatory) . The variation *ītxi* is found only in descriptive forms and in teknonymous usage.

3. *keti*: MB, MMB, MF, MFB, FF, FFB . . .

The term *keti* and the term *kederé* are variations of another term which may be written *ket,* but this latter never appears in its simple form. It is always used in conjunction with the suffixes *ti* and *ré.* I designate the first form quite arbitrarily to represent all its variations. The term *ikrãtum* is less frequently used and its connotations appear to be identical with those of *keti.*

4. *tïi*: FZ, FZD, FZDD, FM, FMZ, MM, MMZ . . .

The most common variations on this term are *tïre, tïikuprï,* and *tïiprek.* The term is also found in the composite word *atïktïi,* which means "your *tïi.*"

5. *itõ*: B, MS, FS, MZS, FBS . . .

This term designates all sons of those people whom ego refers to by terms 1 and 2 above. There is a less-used term which includes all the reference of this term and its corresponding feminine term (number 6 below) , namely, *inõ.* A female speaker often calls those people who would normally be referred to by this term, number 5, *ipantuhum,* which means "father of my *ipantu.*" The term *ipantu* refers to people younger than ego who have received the same personal name as ego. All individuals referred to by this term *itõ* can be distinguished according to their relative age. Those older than ego are called *ihë.* Those younger than ego are referred to as *yapuré* or *yoheïket.*

6. *itoï*: Z, MD, FD, MZD, FBD . . .

This term designates all the daughters of people whom ego designates by terms 1 and 2 above. A male speaker will often refer to women to whom this term might otherwise be applied as *ipan-tumẽtxi,* which means "mother of my *ipantu*" (see the presentation of term 5 above). All individuals designated by term 6 can also be distinguished according to their relative age. Those older than ego are referred to as *itoĩkhë* or *mamkhë* (this latter appears to be reserved for distant relatives of ego). Those younger than ego are referred to as *yohekhwoi.*

7. *ikhra*: S, D, BS (man sp.), BD (man sp.), MBS (man sp.),
     MBD (man sp.), ZS (wom. sp.), ZD (wom. sp.) . . .

This term designates the child of any person with whom ego may have sexual relations, the child of any person whom a male ego calls by term 5, and the child of any person whom a female ego calls by term 6. Distant relatives who fall into this category may also be called *ituahum* if they are male or *ituamẽtxi* if they are female. These are descriptive terms meaning "father of my *itua*" and "mother of my *itua,*" respectively. See below under term 8 for a discussion of *itua.* Other forms used are *akamtére* ("your son") and *akatxwoi* ("your daughter").

8. *itamtxua*: SS, SD, DS, DD; ZS (man sp.), ZD (man sp.);
BS (wom. sp.), BD (wom. sp.), MBS (wom. sp.), MBD (wom. sp.) . . .

This term designates all children of people whom ego refers to by terms 7 and 8, all children of people whom a male ego refers to by term 6, and all children of people whom a female ego refers to by term 5. This term refers to the same range of relationships as the pair of terms *ia'para* (which designates only males) and *iapartxwoi* (which designates females). When ego bestows his own personal name on somebody else, he calls that person by the term *ipantu.* Since ego can only transfer personal names to people who would normally be designated as *itamtxua,* it follows that the category *ipantu* is a subclass of *itamtxua.* Finally, relatives in the category of *itamtxua* who are genealogically distant from ego may also be referred to by the term *itua.*

9. *impien*: H, HB, HZS, ZH (wom. sp.) . . .

This term designates all those with whom a female ego may have sexual relations.

10. *iprõ*: W, WZ, BW (man sp.), MBW (man sp.),
      ZSW (man sp.) . . .

This term designates all those with whom a masculine ego may have sexual relations.

11. *ipré*: WB, HZ, HZD . . .

There are two synonyms for this term: *impöye*, which is used only by male speakers, and *itïktïye*, which is used only by female speakers. This pair of terms is actually in more frequent use than the general term *ipré*, which I list as number 11 since it includes them both.

12. *ipréket*: HF, HFB, HFZS, WF, WFB, WFZS . . .

A synonym for this term is *ikrãtumye*.

13. *iprékei*: HM, HMZ . . .

The synonym for this term (*propéikei*) is more frequently used. I list the less frequent term for the sake of simplicity and to show the structure of the system since it shares a radical with terms number 11 and 12.

14. *hotxwïye*: WM, WMZ, SW (man sp.), . . .

A synonym for this term is *ipan*.

15. *itxwïye*: BW (wom. sp.), SW (wom. sp.) . . .

16. *ipiayõye*: ZH (man sp.), DH . . .

A female speaker uses this term in a more simple form: *ipiayõ*.

The terms which I have so far discussed are those used to refer to live relatives. The Krahó, however, have special terms to refer to dead relatives. In Table 1, I list the most important of these in the right-hand column and the corresponding terms, which would be used for those same relatives when alive, in the left-hand column.

An examination of these two columns shows that the terminology for dead relatives can help us considerably in the analysis of the Krahó system. We find repeatedly that relationships which are designated by separate terms for live people are subsumed under a single term when those relatives are dead, which clearly indicates that those separate relationships have something in common, since they may be classed together at a later stage. The terminology for dead relatives thus confirms my simplification of the terminology for the living as set forth in my presentation. But when we come to the terms for brothers and sisters, real or classificatory, then the opposite is the case. According to Krahó informants, there is no general term for a dead brother or for a

TABLE 1. Terms for living and dead relatives

Living	Dead
itxū	*txūtxua*
ītxe	*itïrïtxua*
keti	*ketxua*
tïi	*ipuptxua*
ikhra	*ikhraye*
ituahum	*ikhraye*
ituamētxi	*ikhraye*
itamtxua	*itamtxua*
itua	*itamtxua*
ipantu	*itamtxua*
ia'para	*itamtxua*
iapartxwöi	*itamtxua*
impien	*ipiye*
ipro	*iprõye*
ipre	*ipréwï*
impöye	*ipréwï*
itïktïye	*ipréwï*
ipréket	*ipréwamket*
ikrātumye	*ipréwamket*
iprékei	*ipréwamkei*
propéihei	*ipréwamkei*
hotxwïye	*ipantxua*
ipan	*ipantxua*
ipiayõye	*iwawï*
ipiayõ	*iwawï*
itxwïye	*itxwïitxua*

dead sister. There are only terms which indicate the relative age of dead brothers and sisters, real or classificatory. Thus,

dead older brother	*ihëye* or *ihërëtxua*
dead younger brother	*yõ?he*
dead older sister	*ipiatxua*
dead younger sister	*iapukhwoi*

Here I must make two points concerning the terminology. First, as was noted above, I have only listed against each relationship term a small number of kin types, normally those closest to ego. It would be an endless task to try to enumerate all the kin types covered by a given term. Second, although such an enumeration is possible in theory, it is impossible in practice, for the application of the terminology gets more and more snarled as one gets farther away from ego's genealogically closest kin. These apparent inconsistencies are a result of marriages which supersede kinship ties and also of other factors such as the transfer of personal names. I shall return to this problem below.

THE SYSTEM OF ATTITUDES

The body of a child is formed by the accumulation of semen in his or her mother's womb through the action of repeated sexual intercourse. This is the theory of procreation held by the Krahó, and it permits them to admit the possibility that a given individual may have a number of biological fathers. The mother's contribution to her child consists of blood and nourishment which is transferred from her body to the body of the fetus. Later on, she also contributes her milk during lactation. Directly after the birth of a child, both the father and the mother must abstain from certain foods, from sexual relations and other physical exertions. These restrictions are lifted little by little until finally the parents are released from all of them. However, the father and mother should submit to similar restrictions when their child, even in adult life, is gravely ill or is stung by some poisonous animal. Similarly, the child should observe the restrictions on behalf of his or her father or mother or on behalf of siblings where there is at least one parent in common.

The father and mother have the rseponsibility of seeing that the child wears amulets so that he or she need not suffer the consequences of any infringement of these restrictions on the part of the parents. They are also responsible for seeing that the child develops normally in a physical sense. Although the feeding of the child is equally the responsibility of the mother and the father, certain Krahó customs stress the father's importance. For example, fatherless boys take part in the ritual distributions of meat or other foods as if they were adult men. Similarly, women without husbands avoid having children and will even resort to abortion since they have no spouse to help them feed the child.

These restrictions do not apply to classificatory fathers, mothers, brothers, or sisters. Similarly, a man has no obligation to feed his classificatory sons and daughters unless they have been conceived by his actual wife. As a result, an individual does not treat all those people classified as *ĩtxũ, ĩtxe, ikhra, itõ,* or *itoĩ* in the same way. He distinguishes those who actually procreated him or whom he actually procreated and those with whom he shares a common procreator from the rest of the people in the categories named, in the same way as he distinguishes the members of his elementary family from the rest of the people in the categories named.

Similarly, a person does not behave in the same way toward all the people designated by the categories *keti, tïi,* or *itamtxua.* The unique characteristic of a *keti* or *tïi* and the only common denominator in their behavior is that they may transmit their personal names to their *itamtxua.* Among the Krahó, a personal name is made up of a set of words, but for the most part, there is no significant relation between these words. They are isolates. Each set of words, that is, each name, belongs to one of the moieties in the pair Wakmẽye/Katamye. Masculine names also belong to the eight groups which go to make up the moieties of the pair Khöirumpe-këtxë and Hararumpekëtxë. Furthermore, various personal names are linked to certain ceremonial roles which only their incumbents can perform. Each personal name is tied to certain others through the special relationship of *hõpin,* which will be discussed below. In fact, a given Krahó normally calls all other Krahó, with the exception of his closest relatives, by the relationship terms which are applied to those people by the individuals who bestowed names on the speaker.

Of all the kin types covered by the term *keti,* it is the mother's brother who is most preferred as the bestower of masculine names. This can be shown both terminologically and statistically. Terminologically, as we have seen, a male ego can call his real and classificatory sisters (*itoĩ*) by the term *ipantumẽtxi,* which means "mother of my *ipantu*" or "mother of a person who has the same name as I." This indicates that the preferred bestower of names for a masculine ego is the real or classificatory brother of his mother. Statistical data point to the same conclusion, although the sample is small. Out of eighty cases of masculine name transmission, twenty were bestowed by a mother's brother (this number increases to thirty-five if we include half-brothers and classificatory brothers of the mother), which is more than the number of bestowals by any other kin type within the category.

Similarly, the preferential kin type among those covered by the term *tïi* for the bestowal of feminine names is the father's sister, and this can also be shown terminologically and statistically. A woman may call her real or classificatory brother (*itõ*) by the term *ipantuhum,* which means "father of my *ipantu*" or "father of a person who has the same name as I." Out of forty-nine instances of feminine name transmission, I found that thirteen were bestowed by the father's sister (and this number rises to twenty if we include half-sisters and classificatory sisters of the father), which once again is larger than the number of bestowals from any other kin type within the category.

The relationship between the *keti* and the *itamtxua* to whom he has given a name (that is, his *ipantu*) is, as we have seen, largely a ritual one. It is customary also for the *keti* to give him a bow and a bundle of arrows from time to time. Similarly, the relationship between a *tïi* and her *ipantu* is also a ritual one, and it is the former who gives the latter a girdle (*ipré*) made out of various strands of tucum fiber when she reaches puberty.

Although a man can call various women "wife" (*iprõ*), this does not imply that he behaves in the same way toward all of them. The Krahó practice monogamy, and a man is only obliged to feed and clothe his actual wife. Nevertheless, certain characteristics of his relationship with his actual wife are extended to his potential wives, that is, to those whom he addresses by the same term. Thus he is expected to give small presents to the women with whom he has extramarital sexual relations. Similarly, the obligations of a husband toward the relatives of his actual wife, such as the giving of presents and the performing of services, are also found in the relationship between a man and the relatives of his potential wives. For example, a woman can demand of a man who has had sexual relations with her that he help her brother when the latter needs it.

There is at least one contradiction in the behavior of affines which shows up in the terminology. We saw that the term *ipré* can include both the wife's brother (*impöye*) and the husband's sister (*itïktïye*). But the first should receive presents from his sister's husband, while the second should give presents to her brother's wife. Thus a single term, *ipré*, covers two kin types with opposite expectations of behavior. It is, however, customary for a woman to be helped whenever she is in difficulties by other women who have had sexual relations with her brother. Thus the custom inverts the rule at the level of attitudes.

In sum, the system of attitudes is reflected in the relationship terminology, but there is no strict correspondence between them. Each individual applies one relationship term to numbers of people, but this only implies a clearly defined expectation of behavior toward a small number of them.

THE LIVING AND THE DEAD

Most of the terms used to refer to dead relatives take the form of terms for live relatives with the addition of an extra syllable: *ye*, *txua*, or *wï*. The linguistic change in the term implies a change in behavior. Indeed, the whole notion of death for the Krahó consists of a change of behavior. An individual does not die when his soul, *karõ*, leaves his body, for the soul may wander outside of the body for some time and return to it either spontaneously or when forced to do so by a shaman and without any interruption of life. A person only dies when his soul accepts food from the souls of the dead or, according to one informant, when the soul has sexual relations with the souls of the dead. At this point, the soul no longer wishes to return to the body. After death, an individual no longer maintains the same relationship with his live relatives. He is only seen by them in dreams and hallucinations, when, as the Krahó say, their own souls leave their bodies. Another way for the dead to communicate with the living is through the mediation of shamans, who can see the dead and talk to them. A few days after death the soul of the dead person appears to a shaman and asks him to tell the consanguineal kin of the deceased that the dead person wishes to eat some special food. The kinsmen then prepare the meal and put it on a platform outside the house. At nightfall, the shaman goes out to seek the soul. It comes and eats only the soul, *karõ,* of the food, leaving its material part intact. A dead soul never requests another meal after this first one, so that the meal is virtually a ritual of separation. The behavior of dead relatives is unpredictable. Sometimes they yearn to have the souls of their live relatives close to them and for that reason they desire their death. However, stories are also told of dead souls who refuse food to live relatives or in other ways prevent them from dying so as not to leave other consanguineal kinsmen unprotected on earth.

A Krahó, it seems, only remembers those dead whom he has known during his life. This seems to correlate with the belief that the souls of the dead also die and become animals, which, in their turn, also die and become stumps of woods or anthills, until finally they are annihilated completely by fire.

The dead, then, behave differently from their live relatives. They do not eat with the living; they do not have sexual relations with them; they do not live with them nor do they communicate directly with them.

There are at least two terms for the dead which are also used to designate live relatives: *itamtxua* and *iwawï.* I am unable to explain this overlap. It seems that the terms were originally used only for the dead.[5]

KIN AND AFFINES

The Krahó use the word *meikhïa* to refer to the set of people recognized as being consanguineal kinsmen. The term also has other connotations, as, for example, where it designates all those who inhabit the same village as ego. Those whom a speaker does not consider as being his consanguineal kin are called *mei-*

khïï'nare (that is, "not *meikhïa*") or *meka?krit*. The latter term
also has other connotations. It can be used to designate the members of another village or of another tribe.

It is characteristic of the behavior of consanguineal kinsmen
toward each other that a person gives food to his consanguines
without expecting to get anything in exchange for it. He knows
very well that the moment he needs food or help he can always
rely on his consanguineal kinsmen to provide it. Not all goods
are transferred between consanguineal kinsmen without repayment, but repayment for a specific gift takes place only when very
valuable objects, such as cattle, are being transferred. Consanguineal kinsmen may not have sexual relations with each other.
Furthermore, they are expected to support each other in conflicts,
to revenge each other's deaths, and so on.

Between affines, sexual relations are of course permitted, but it
is characteristic of the affinal relationship that explicit compensation is expected for services rendered or goods transferred. A
husband owes his wife's kinsmen presents and services in return
for the sexual and domestic services of his wife. The smallest
services, such as a hair cut or weeping for a dead relative, must be
paid for if they are performed for people who are not consanguineal kinsmen. There is an important difference between the
exchanges between consanguineal kinsmen and exchanges between affines. When a person does something for or gives something to a consanguineal kinsman, he does not think of which
particular favor or gift he is repaying. Gifts and favors between
kinsmen are a constant flow which lasts throughout their life-
times. An affine, on the contrary, performs services and offers gifts
in exchange for specifically determined repayments.

In spite of the fact that the expectations of behavior between
kinsmen can be clearly distinguished from the expected behavior
between affines, there is no clear dividing line between those relationship categories which are necessarily regarded as consanguineal and those which are regarded as affinal. In other words, it
is difficult to delimit the group of consanguineal kinsmen for
any given individual. The Krahó all agree that consanguineal kin
should not have sexual relations with each other. Thus a full
knowledge of sexual relationships in Krahó villages should enable
us to delimit the consanguineal kinsmen of every individual. Yet
there are examples of marriage or perhaps merely of sexual relations which take place between close kin, for example, with the
father's sister's daughter, the mother's brother's daughter, the
mother's half-brother's daughter, the mother's half-sister's daughter, and so on, even though these relationships are usually con-

sidered consanguineal ones. I know two cases in which a young man had sexual relations with his half-sister. In one case, the young man had more than one biological father, and one of these was the father of the girl. In the other case, the father of the young man was one of the biological fathers of the girl. I do not know whether these couples discovered their relationship to each other only after they had had sexual relations. In one of the cases at least, the young man subsequently called the girl by the term for "wife" (*iprõ*). I know of at least one case in which a father and son both had sexual relations with the same woman, but she was not the actual wife of either of them. I know of at least two cases of marriage with the brother's daughter. One of them has attracted no attention among the Krahó, but the other is always pointed out by them as being the prime example of incest. In this latter case, the girl was not only the brother's daughter of her husband but also the daughter of his effective wife. The Krahó say that the incestuous couple were punished since both of them died a short time after the marriage. In general, however, the Krahó do not invoke supernatural sanctions in cases of incest. I know of no case of sexual relations between a biological father and his daughter or biological mother and her son. Nor do I have any evidence of sexual relations between full siblings. There are no marriages between members of the same residential segment.

A marriage between consanguineal kinsmen is usually considered rather matter of factly in terms of its effects, and there are various ways of justifying such unions. In such a marriage, a man does not feel himself a complete stranger in the house he goes to live; a husband will receive the support of his wife's kinsmen should a conflict arise. The Krahó also justify such marriages by saying that Brazilians marry their consanguineal kin. However, when a man marries or has sexual relations with a consanguineal kinswoman, he has to give much more valuable presents to her kin than he would have had to do should the girl not have been his consanguine. As the Krahó say, "A good payment ends the shame." Besides, a man must take care not to have sexual relations with too many consanguineal kinswomen, because this transforms them into affines and he no longer receives food when he visits them. The more affines he has, the less food he will receive in the various houses that he visits.

When a man becomes the sexual partner of a woman who is his consanguine, he starts calling her "wife" (*iprõ*). The Krahó thus tend to adapt their relationship terminology to their behavior. However, when a male speaker transforms a consanguineal kinswoman into an affine, he does not usually transmute all of her kin into affines at the same time, but merely so considers some of them. It seems that there is no general rule for how this should be done, and much of it is a matter of individual preference. A concrete example will illustrate the procedure. Zacarias married his mother's father's daughter's daughter, in other words, he married his classificatory sister and started to call her "wife." He had always called the mother of the girl who was now his wife *ĩtxe* (mother), but he now started called her *hotxwïye*. However, he continued to call his wife's brother *itõ* (brother), yet at the same time he made him a present of a gun. In other words, he continued to refer to him as a consanguineal kinsman but started treating him as though he were an affine. The deceased sister of his wife left two daughters. Zacarias continued to call them *itamtxua* (not *ikhra*), and he continued to treat them as consanguines, watching over the stability of their respective marriages and enjoying the right to receive presents from their husbands. In another case, a man by the name of Secundo had sexual relations with the sister's daughter of one of his biological fathers. He also promised to marry the sister's daughter's daughter of this same biological father and had, therefore, given presents to the father. Thus the young man was treating his own biological father as an affine.

Thus the essential members of the consanguineal kin group of any given individual appear to be his lineal ascendants and descendants, those born in the same residential segment and those born of his actual genitors in other residential segments. As far as other consanguineal kin are concerned, it is not absolutely certain whether they will be included within the consanguineal kin group, and these are the relationships which are most likely to be transformed into affinal ones.

The possibility of transforming a consanguineal relationship into an affinal one increases the interest of certain similarities between the terms used for affines and the terms used for dead relatives. Various affinal terms are made up of terms used for consanguines modified by the addition of the syllable *ye*. One of these is the term *itïktïye*, a subcategory used by a female speaker of the general term *ipré*. There is no doubt that this term has a great deal in common with the term for consanguines *atïktïi*, one of the forms of the general term *tïi*. Another example is the term *ikrãtumye*, one of the forms taken by the term *ipréket*, and which derives from the term *ikratum*, one of the forms of the term *keti*. These two affinal terms are thus modifications of consanguineal terms in the same way as various terms for the dead are modifications of various terms for the living. Affinal terms thus have something in common with terms for the dead. This fact may be interpreted as reflecting something which is common to the behavior toward affines and the behavior toward the dead. Just as death causes both the behavior and the term applied to a given relative to be modified, similarly a sharp change in behavior and in the term applied to a consanguineal relative occurs when he is transformed into an affine.

CONSANGUINEAL KINSHIP: PROCREATION AND NAMING

I have already pointed out that there are no common behavioral expectations toward the various kin types covered by the term for given relationship categories. It is therefore useless to try to break down the appropriate behavior indicated by each relationship term into its constituent elements. We have seen, however, that certain kin types belonging to given categories do share some specific characteristic. This characteristic may apply only partially, if at all, to the more peripheral kin types within the category.

The central characteristic of the terms *ĩtxu, ĩtxe, ikhra, itõ,* and *itoĩ* is the biological relationship that the people called by these terms have with ego. This is not a biological relationship as we understand it, but a biological relationship in the Krahó sense of the term. These are the relatives whose acts can affect the body, the organism of ego himself, above all when ego is going through some particularly vulnerable phase, for example, immaturity, sickness, or suffering from a wound inflicted by a poisonous animal. This biological link is not held to exist between ego and his classificatory fathers, mothers, sons, daughters, brothers, and sisters. Nevertheless, there is no exact correspondence between these biologically linked kinsmen and ego's elementary family. We know that ego's genitor can procreate children with women of other elementary families and in this way produce siblings who are joined to ego in the biological way I am discussing. Furthermore, ego is of course biologically linked to two elementary families, the family of orientation from which he came, and the family of procreation which he has set up.

The biological linkages between ego and his classificatory fathers, mothers, sons, daughters, brothers, and sisters remain merely unrealized potentialities. Classificatory fathers are simply men who could have procreated ego by copulating with his biological mother. They are in fact men who can actually procreate biological brothers for Ego. Similarly, classificatory mothers are women who could have been ego's actual mother and may yet produce biological siblings for ego by copulating with his biological father. A given individual can produce classificatory children either by having sexual relations with their mother in the case of a man or with their father in the case of a woman. Moreover, classificatory fathers may actually take the place of the biological father by marrying ego's biological mother, and in such cases they assume the responsibility of feeding and looking after ego. Similarly, classificatory mothers can take the place of the biological mother.

The basic characteristic of those people called *keti, tïi, itamtxua,* and even *itõ* and *itoĩ* is that they are related to each other through the transmission of personal names. A male ego receives his personal name from one or two (rarely more than two) *keti,* a female ego from one or two *tïi.* The other *keti* and *tïi* are those who are potential name-givers to male and female egos, respectively. A *keti* may actually take the place of another one as name-bestower. One informant, for example, told me that when a subgroup of Krahó called the Kré were attacked by an enemy tribe and annihilated, the children who had received their personal names from members of this group were renamed by members of other groups. It is for this reason that nowadays there is only one personal name left derived from this group of Krẽ.

The relationship terminology dealing with consanguines thus contains two sets of terms. One deals with those kin who have to do with the procreation of ego and the other with those kin who have to do with the bestowal of names on ego. Furthermore, those who contribute to the formation of ego's body may not transmit names to him and vice versa.

Within each one of these sets, the relationship terms vary according to the sex of the person to whom they are applied (although not invariably, as in the term *ikhra;* the term *itamtxua* also has a synonymous pair applied to males and females, respectively. Furthermore, the terms vary according to whether the individuals referred to are subjects or cosubjects, objects or co-objects of procreation or name transmission. Tables 2 and 3 sum up this analysis and are *almost* equivalent to a componential analysis of Krahó relationship terms for consanguines.

Subjects are those people who could either procreate or bestow names on ego; cosubjects are those who could procreate or bestow names on the same people as ego can; objects are those who could be procreated or could receive names from ego; co-objects are those procreated or named by the same people who could have procreated or bestowed names on ego. These tables do not exhaust all the terminological possibilities. For example, certain *keti* (such as the mother's brother) but not all could be considered cosubjects, of a male ego as far as procreation is concerned.

TABLE 2. Relationship terminology dealing with consanguines for the male ego

	Procreation		Nomination	
	Male	*Female*	*Male*	*Female*
Subjects	1-*ītxū*	2-*ītxe*	3-*keti*	
Cosubjects		5-*itõ*		
Objects	7-*ikhra*		8-*itamtxua*	
Co-objects	5-*itõ*	6-*itoī*	5-*itõ*	

TABLE 3. Relationship terminology dealing with consanguines for the female ego

	Procreation		Nomination	
	Male	*Female*	*Male*	*Female*
Subjects	1-*ītxū*	2-*ītxe*		4-*tïi*
Cosubject		6-*itoī*		
Objects	7-*ikhra*			8-*itamtxua*
Co-objects	5-*itõ*	6-*itoī*		6-*itoī*

An individual is biologically identified with his genitors since that which affects them also influences him physically, and in the same way that which affects his body produces physical effects in his genitors. In social relations, however, the individual is identified with his name-giver, but this identification is not total, since personal names are associated not with all pairs of moieties but only with two of them. Furthermore, the tendency of an *ipantu* to call others by exactly the same term as is used toward him by his name-bestower does not operate between close kin, at least between close lineal kin. An individual will therefore never call his own mother "sister," his own father "sister's husband," or his own maternal grandfather "father" merely because he has received his name from his mother's brother. Even so, the name-giver transfers to his *ipantu* the greater part of those social relationships which he himself maintains with other members of the society. It is as if the physical organism produced by the genitors is "clothed" by the name-giver. The term "clothed" in this context could even be taken quite literally since the *ipantu* (name-receiver) paints his body in the characteristic style of his moiety or according to the ritual role which he is carrying out. Every Krahó personal name thus corresponds to a social personality, that is, to a person who may be incarnated on different occasions by different actors but nevertheless always carries out the same actions and maintains the same relationships with other social persons. These Krahó social persons are not found only in rituals. Their presence is also felt in everyday life. An individual may not marry somebody because of his name set. In a dispute, a person may shrink from killing another because of the name he bears. On many occasions throughout the year, a person gets meat from the game animals which have been killed and divided up between the moieties, and this by virtue of his membership in one of them through his personal name. These social personalities thus permeate not only the rituals but also the economic and political life of the society and even its marriage possibilities.

We can see, then, that the Krahó stress two types of identity between consanguineal kin: a biological identity which links procreators and procreated; and a social identity which assimilates name-givers and those named. This does not, of course, mean that there are no social relationships between a person and his procreators and that there may not be biological relationships between a person and his name-giver, and the Krahó are well aware of this. It means only that the Krahó *stress* the fact that the procreators produce the physical body of a person and that the name-giver transmits to him his social personality.

Although consanguineal kin are thus divided into two sets, one connected with procreation and the other with the bestowal of names, there are cases where relatives of one sort do what is expected of relatives of the other sort and vice versa. We have already seen how a father or a husband can be a mediator between the elementary family and the public life, whether political or ritual, of the society. Then there is the matter of adoption. Krahó parents not infrequently give away a child to be brought up by kinsmen, either because they wish to diminish the number of children that they have to support or because the kinsmen in question have no children of their own. Out of fourteen cases of adoption, six children were adopted by their father's mother, two by the father's sister, two by the father's sister's daughter, one by the mother's mother, two by the mother's sister, and one by the sister. Consequently, in eleven of these cases the woman was *tïi* of the child adopted. Not all of the women doing the adopting had husbands at the moment when the data were collected, although where such husbands existed they were considered to be coadopters of the children concerned. When the women did have husbands, these men, with occasional exceptions, were called *keti* by the children adopted. Thus *keti* and *tïi* can carry out roles which are normally specific to *ïtxũ* and *ïtxe*.

AFFINAL KINSHIP: CREDITORS AND DEBTORS

Now that I have ordered the consanguineal terminology in terms of the transmission of physical and social elements, it may be possible to use similar criteria for the analysis of the affinal terms. Among affines, however, the element which is being transferred is neither the organism nor the name but rather matrimonial prestations. I shall therefore classify the affinal terms according to the direction of these prestations.

Among the Krahó, marriage does not usually involve a direct exchange of women, although there are one or two exceptional cases. Nor is there any form of prescriptive or preferential marriage. A man who is getting married must offer presents and perform services for the consanguineal kin of his wife. These matrimonial prestations are offered not all at once, but little by little, and neither their quantity nor their quality is determined beforehand. When a marriage is being arranged, the total of goods and services to be received by each consanguine of the bride is not calculated. Her relatives demand these presents over a period of time. Nor do they all receive the same amount. Her close relatives get more. These marriage prestations are considered a repayment for the sexual favors of the wife, for her virginity, and for her services, such as cooking, harvesting, and working in the fields. They usually consist of muzzle-loading rifles—which are considered the supreme present by the Krahó and which normally go to the brothers or the father of the bride—of cooking pots, bush knives, and hoes. The husband now accepts the obligation to help his father-in-law in his work and to assist at the burial of the kinsmen of his wife. The obligation to live with the parents-in-law might be regarded as one of the marriage prestations. A husband is thus caught by his wife's relatives and included in her domestic group even after her death, during the period of mourning, when he will make his final prestations resulting from the marriage.

No specific relative decides the marriages of a woman. The matter is discussed by various relatives together with the relatives of the future husband. In a majority of cases, it seems that the marriage invitation comes from the parents or from other relatives of the woman. I thus regard those relatives who arrange the marriage and receive presents on behalf of the woman as being the people who have the right to receive matrimonial prestations for her services. In the same way, those relatives who arrange the marriage and give presents on behalf of the man may be considered the people who have the obligation of repaying the services of that woman through the matrimonial prestations.

TABLE 4. Reciprocal pairs of affinal terms for givers and receivers of marriage prestations

Receive marriage prestations	*Make marriage prestations*
10. *iprõ*	9. *impien*
11. *ipré*	16. *ipiayõye*
12. *ipréket*	16. *ipiayõye*
14. *hotxwïye*	16. *ipiayõye*
14. *hotxwïye*	12. *ipréket*
15. *itxwïye*	11. *ipré*
15. *itxwïye*	13. *iprékei*

In Table 4, reciprocal pairs of affinal terms are arranged in two columns. When ego refers to a person by any term in the left-hand column, then that person will call ego by the corresponding term in the right-hand column. The left-hand column therefore contains terms which refer to people who receive matrimonial prestations, while the right-hand column contains terms referring to people who make matrimonial prestations. The woman herself, who is the focus of these prestations, is found in the left-hand column, since she too receives services and gifts in exchange for what she does for her husband.

Table 4 presents an immediate difficulty. Certain terms, such as *ipré* and *ipréket,* are found in both columns and thus appear to refer both to relatives who make prestations and relatives who receive them. We have already seen how the husband's sister is a debtor in that she has to make matrimonial prestations, yet on certain occasions she is treated as a creditor, according to the custom by which a woman must be helped by all those other women who have had sexual relations with her brother. The difficulty, then, of classifying these affinal terms lies in the fact that the terminology for affines not only reflects the transmission of goods and services resulting from what a wife does for her husband, but also reflects the institutionalized inversion of these matrimonial prestations as a whole. Thus the rule by which a man must live in the house of his parents-in-law is counterbalanced by an inverse rule which obliges a wife to live in the house of her parents-in-law in certain specific cases: (1) when the husband goes on a long journey, usually to the big cities, his wife moves into the house of her parents-in-law, who watch over her to see that she does not have sexual relations with other men during the absence of her husband; (2) when a husband is seriously ill, he goes to the house of his parents for the duration of the illness and his wife moves in with him; (3) when a husband dies, his wife passes the period of mourning for him in the house of his parents. There is thus an occasional virilocality defined by specific rules which is opposed to the general rule of uxorilocality. A similar inversion affects another obligation that is included among the matrimonial prestations, namely, the obligation of a husband or a lover to give presents in exchange for the virginity of his wife or mistress. Thus when a woman initiates a man into his first sexual experience, she is required to give his relatives (generally his mother or his sister) a small present, such as a pan or an enamel dish. The present to which the relatives of the boy are entitled is very small and does not come anywhere near the value of the present given by a man who deflowers a girl.

The Genealogical Distribution of Relationship Terms

I have so far ordered the relationship terminology on the basis of the connotations of the terms, but this does not tell us about the system which the Krahó use to order these terms genealogically. I shall now try, as far as possible, to show how the Krahó relate this system to the content of each category.

In the first place, when ego calls an individual by a certain term, he also tends to use the same term for all real or classificatory same-sex siblings of that individual. The group consisting of all real and classificatory same-sex siblings thus constitutes a unit. In fact, such individuals do have a great deal in common. They received or could have received body, name, and matrimonial prestations from the same individuals, and they give or could have given body, name, and matrimonial prestations to the same individuals.

Second, when ego calls a certain individual by a given term, he will not always apply the same term to real and classificatory opposite-sex siblings of that individual. Though a brother and sister are procreated or could have been procreated by the same individuals, the prohibition of incest which prevents them from marrying each other insures that they cannot possibly procreate the same individuals. Since they cannot do this, they cannot, as may be seen below, bestow names on the same individuals.

Third, consanguineal kin who could not have procreated ego, or been procreated by ego, or have joined with ego in procreating a child, or have been procreated by the same individuals who procreated ego, may bestow names on ego or receive names from ego. Such people are, therefore, referred to by terms associated with name-giving.

Fourth, based on the terminological equations father's sister's daughter = father's sister and mother's brother's daughter =

brother's daughter, the Krahó system of relationship terminology can be classified as being of the Crow type (Murdock 1949:224). Other equations of the same kind, both for kin and for affines, are consistent with a Crow terminology, namely, father = father's sister's son = father's mother's brother; father's mother = father's sister = father's sister's daughter = father's sister's daughter's daughter; husband's sister = husband's sister's daughter; husband's father = husband's father's sister's son; wife's father = wife's father's sister's son, and so on. The problem then is to discover why the Krahó have a Crow-type relationship terminology. This will be discussed below.

These four characteristics of the Krahó terminology may be used as rules to order it according to a genealogical scheme; but first it is necessary to say something about certain relationship categories for which there is no clearly defined term. Some of these problems are related to the transmission of personal names. We have seen that the preferential transmission of masculine names is from the mother's brother to the sister's son and that this is consistent with a Crow-type relationship terminology. This is not the case, however, with female names. To correspond with a Crow-type terminology, feminine names should be passed down preferentially from the mother or the mother's sister, but this does not happen. According to the Krahó system, these categories cannot under any circumstances transmit names. The name-giver par excellence is the father's sister. But if a woman receives her name from one of the sisters of her father, then she will call the children of that sister of her father by the same term that she uses for her own children. She will, however, continue to call the children of the other sisters of her father by the same terms as she uses for her father and her father's sister. Thus an Omaha characteristic appears in the terminology in cases where there is an actual transmission of name from father's sister to brother's daughter, while the system otherwise retains its Crow features intact.

Since the term *tïi* is applied both to the father's mother and to the father's sister, one would expect the term *keti,* which refers to the husband of the former, to be also applicable to the husband of the latter. This is in fact the case. There are cases, however, where a female speaker calls her father's sister's husband by the same term as she uses for her own husband (*impien*). Where the father's sister has actually bestowed her name on ego, it is easy to understand the identification of father's sister's husband and own husband. Occasionally, however, the term "husband" is used for the husbands of father's sisters who have not given their names to ego. This shows that the rules of name transmission influence terminology even when an actual transmission has not taken place. Thus just as a woman may make the equation husband = father's sister's husband even when there has been no name transmission, the sister of her father may make the equation husband = brother's daughter's husband under similar circumstances. Correspondingly, a man should normally call his wife's father's sister *hotxwïye*. Nevertheless, there are occasions when, even without any name transmission, he makes the terminological equation wife's father's sister = wife.

The Krahó use more than one term for kin types such as husband's father's sister, husband's father's sister's daughter, and wife's mother's brother. Accordingly, although the term for husband's sister (*ipré*) is different from the term for husband's mother (*iprékei*), a woman calls her husband's father's sister and her husband's father's sister's daughter either *ipré* or *iprékei* indiscriminately. Similarly, although the term for wife's brother (*ipré*) is different from the term for wife's father (*ipréket*), a man can call his wife's mother's brother *ipré* or *ipréket* indiscriminately. The following list shows these usages:

A wife's *itõ* is called *ipré* by her husband.
A wife's *ĩtxũ* is called *ipréket* by her husband.
A wife's *keti* is called *ipré* or *ipréket* by her husband.
A husband's *itoĩ* is called *ipré* by his wife.
A husband's *ĩtxe* is called *iprékei* by his wife.
A husband's *tïi* is called *ipré* or *iprékei* by his wife.

This list shows that there is no special term which a man can use for those people whom his wife calls *keti*, and so he can call them either by the term he uses for her *ĩtxũ* or the term he uses for her *itõ*. Similarily, there is no special term which a woman can use for the *tïi* of her husband, and she can, therefore, call them either by the term she uses for his *ĩtxe* or the term she uses for his *itoĩ*.

TERMS NOT SUSCEPTIBLE TO GENEALOGICAL DISTRIBUTION

I have left until the end of this discussion two terms which cannot be fitted into any genealogical scheme. They can, nevertheless, be regarded as relationship terms, and their nature can be partly explained by the distinction between consanguineal and affinal kin. I am referring to the relationship between *ikhïonõ* and between *hõpin*.[6]

According to the Krahó, the following individuals call each other *ikhïonõ:* those who are born on the same day; those males who are simultaneously either "directors" of the village, leaders of age-sets, or leaders of the boys in the initiation rituals; those women who were simultaneously associated with moieties or with the boy's groups at initiation. In addition to these instances, it seems that two individuals may become *ikhïonõ* to each other spontaneously simply by wanting to. *Ikhïonõ* are characteristically companions. They work together, play together, and go out with girls together. Some informants insisted that in the old days *ikhïonõ* used to exchange wives with each other. One informant told me that a man could not call a woman *ikhïonõ*. Another explained that the term *ikhïonõ* is always used between people of the same sex. However, a man calls a woman *inõ* and she calls him *ikhïoré*. It seems that there is a certain identity between *ikhïonõ* and *inõ* (real or classificatory sibling). There are other indications apart from those cited above which seem to support this suggestion. First, there are numerous cases of a man calling another person *ikhra* (biological or classificatory child) because that person is the child of his *ikhïonõ*. Second, one informant who gave me his genealogy and all the terms that he used for his relatives applied the term *ikhïonõ* to all those individuals who were husbands of his potential wives. Now the men who called ego's children by the same term as their own children and ego's wives by the same terms as their own wives are his *inõ* or some of his *keti*. There is further evidence yet. The term *ikhïonõ* appears to be made up of two elements, *ikhïa* (consanguineal relative) and *inõ* (real or classificatory sibling). If this breakdown is correct, there is an identification of *ikhïonõ* with consanguineal relatives and specifically with the brother or the sister. Furthermore, a dead *ikhïonõ* is referred to as *inõye,* in other words, by the term *inõ* followed by the suffix *ye,* which is commonly used to transmute the term for a live relative into the term for a dead relative. One informant said that one should give tobacco and food to *ikhïonõ;* another that an *ikhïonõ* is a person who, although not a consanguineal relative, nevertheless gives one food and sells to one on credit. In short, just as the Krahó allow for the transformation of consanguines into affines, the *ikhïonõ* relationship refers to the inverse transformation of affines into consanguines.

The term *hõpin* is more complex still. Every individual refers to one or more males as *hõpin* and females as *hõpintxwöi* (the latter term is usually abbreviated in the form *pintxwöi; txwöi* is a feminine suffix). There is a term for dead relatives, *ikritxua* (sometimes also applied to living relatives) which corresponds to these two terms. Each individual, on receiving his personal name, also acquires all the *hõpin* and *hõpintxwoi* of his name-giver.

People may not utter the personal names of their *hõpin* or *hõpintxwöi* and may not talk to them. If he meets one of them when out walking, he must go by with lowered head. All sexual relations between *hõpin* and *hõpintxwöi* are forbidden. Nevertheless there is extreme solidarity between people who refer to each other by these terms. Thus a man who is running with a racing log will slow down if he sees that the log of the rival moiety is being carried by his *hõpin*. During initiation rites, the *hõpin* or *hõpintxwöi* of a youth will protect and help him. A *hõpintxwöi* only needs to appear at the maternal household of her *hõpin* during a ritual period and she will be given meat from any game which the latter has killed. No aggressive act, not even a symbolic one, may be carried out toward a *hõpin* or *hõpintxwöi*. While the relationship is considered one of extreme solidarity, all the help and all the presents it implies must be repaid. Generally, this repayment is made by the consanguineal kin of the people concerned. When the moon is new, the first person who notices it at dusk calls the attention of the village to the phenomenon by a series of piercing cries. This is considered to be the moment when anybody who wishes to make any accusation against the consanguineal kin of a *hõpin* or a *hõpintxwöi* should do so, and he or she does it quickly in a loud voice.

It is very difficult to explain this relationship. It shares certain aspects of consanguinity: extreme solidarity, prohibition on sexual relations, and complete absence of aggression. It also has some of the aspects of affinity: the repayment of each present or favor received, and the hostility against the consanguineal kin of ones *hõpin* or *hõpintxwöi*. It is impossible to say for certain whether there is a common element between the terms *ikritxua,* which refers to dead *hõpin* and *hõpintxwöi,* and *meka?krit,* which means an affinal relative or a member of another village or another tribe. Nevertheless, during one variation of the ritual known as *pembkahëk,* a hut sheltering the young initiates is at a given moment protected by two lines of defenders. One of these is made up of people who come from other tribes and who are resident among the Krahó, and the other by the *hõpin* and *hõpintxwöi* of the initiates. This ritual appears to identify the latter with foreigners, or strangers to the tribe. Moreover, the Krahó themselves translate the terms *hõpin* and *hõpintxwöi* into Portuguese as *compadre* or *comadre,* respectively. I assume that they translate them this way because they themselves find some similarity between the relationships so designated among the Krahó and among the Brazilians. In fact, in the north of Goiás, the *compadre* relationship is among the local backwoodmen one of extreme solidarity, although we cannot go so far as to say that in this region sexual relations between people who stand in this relationship to each other are considered incestuous. This is, however, the case in other parts of Brazil (Câmara Cascudo 1962, see *comadre, compadre*). Yet at the same time as the terms *compadre* and *comadre* refer to a relationship of extreme solidarity resulting from the ritual of baptism or from a rite celebrated around the fires during the festival of São João, they can also be used when referring to strangers. Indians and Brazilians in this part of the country refer to each other as *compadre* and *comadre,* showing that these terms may be used with the connotation of "stranger" or "foreigner," but I am unable to push this analysis any further.

The terms *hõpin* and *hõpintxwöi* thus serve to distort the use of the relationship terminology, since they often supersede other relationship terms. I have, for example, seen an old woman refer to a very small boy, the son of her daughter, as *hõpin* instead of *itamtxua*. Similarly, a man used to call his own son *hõpin* instead of *ikhra*, but the son, instead of referring to the father as *hõpin*, referred to him as *ĩtxũ*. Finally, in spite of the stress on the avoidance which should characterize the relationship between *hõpin* and *hõpintxwöi*, more than one Krahó has transformed his *hõpintxwöi* into his *iprõ*.[7]

CONCLUSION

I have already stated that it is currently impossible to provide a satisfactory explanation for the Crow-type terminology of the Krahó. Nevertheless, I would like to put forward a tentative explanation for it.

Lounsbury believes that Crow- and Omaha-type terminologies express laws of succession (Lounsbury 1964:382–383). Let us accept this explanation as a point of departure, noting that it is a more general one than the explanation in terms of the unity of the lineage group offered by Radcliffe-Brown (1965:75–76). I must first establish which laws of succession are clearly defined among the Krahó. One of these is the law of biological succession according to which the organism is transmitted by both mother and father to the child. Since, however, this law is a bilateral one, it will not serve to explain a system which tends toward the unilineal. Another type of succession found among the Krahó is the tendency of the son-in-law to take the place of his father-in-law in the leadership of the domestic group, but this type of succession seems equally unrelated to a Crow-type terminology. A third type of succession is the one defined by the transmission of personal names, according to which an *ipantu* comes to incarnate the social personality of the individual who transmitted names to him or her. Men's names, being transmitted by preference from the mother's brother to the sister's son, follow a rule which is perfectly coherent with a Crow type of terminology. Women's names, however, are transmitted preferentially from the father's sister to the brother's daughter, a practice which would correspond to an Omaha-type terminology.

In spite of the fact that the rules for transmitting male and female names are contradictory, they appear to cast some light on the problem of the Crow terminology. We have seen that the Krahó stress the bestowal of personal names as a way of transmitting social relationships, although there are social relationships which are not passed on nominally. The fact that they give greater emphasis to the mother's brother → sister's son succession than to the father-in-law → son-in-law succession is an ideological factor which is reflected in the terminology. It indicates that ritual relations are accorded greater importance than economic ones. Meanwhile, it is established beyond doubt that name transmission does affect the terminology, so that female name transmission actually gives it an Omaha character as used by some individuals. But while the transfer of female names proves that name transmission affects relationship terminology, it also creates a problem. If the rules for the transfer of male and female names are the inverse of each other, why is the terminology so clearly of the Crow type?

One answer to this question would be to suggest that the transfer of male names was more important than that of female names and that female name transmission was simply the inverse reflection of male name transmission. This hypothesis receives support from the fact that name transmission is of great importance in filling ritual roles and determining the membership of ritual groups and that men are clearly predominant in ritual activities. Furthermore, we are not dealing here with the only case of such inversion. We have already noted the inversion in the rules of marriage prestations. So the Crow terminology would therefore reflect the rule of male name transference.

On the other hand, personal names are closely related to the rule of residence. When a man leaves his maternal household to take up residence with his wife, he leaves behind part of his social personality, incarnated in his sister's son, to whom he preferentially transmits his name. Moreover, he takes with him to his new place of residence part of the social personality of his sister, whose name is given to his own daughter. In this way, the transfer of names acts like a compensation for the transfer of residence. Given the preferential rules for name transmission, certain male names

tend to accumulate in certain domestic groups or residential segments, while female names, which follow men as they move from
one residence to another, tend to be spread throughout Krahó
society. Perhaps the concentration of these male names tends to reinforce the individuality of these segments and to emphasize their
continuity via mother's brother → sister's son succession, which in
turn contributes to the greater importance of men's names in the
domestic sphere.

To sum up the argument: the residential segment is not only
important in the regulation of marriage, since it tends to be exogamous, but it is also the stable nucleus of an individual's group
of relatives. The rules for the transmission of men's names result
in their tending to accumulate in given residential segments.
Since personal names are crucial in Krahó ritual and their transmission also influences the use of the relationship terminology, it
is only to be expected that men's names, the rules for whose transfer correspond more closely with the other rules of Krahó society,
should be the ones which most strongly influence the ordering of
the terminology itself.

This analysis of the Krahó relationship system seems to have
shown that it is not only related to their marriage rules, their residence rules, and their domestic organization. To understand the
system, one must also take into account the dualism which imbues
all Krahó institutions.

Thus the transmission of personal names appears to be a negation of uxorilocality. The man's name stays in his sister's household, while his sister's names goes with him to the household of
his wife. This is due to the fact that every Krahó has two aspects:
body and name.

Body and name form yet another opposition which is reflected
in the terminology and in the behavior associated with it, distinguishing relatives connected with procreation from relatives
connected with nomination. Here nomination appears almost as
the mirror image of procreation. While husband and wife procreate the bodies of their children, brother and sister transmit the
social personalities which the children incarnate. It is as if name
transmission became a negation of the incest prohibition.

The relationship system also shows the Krahó penchant for opposing oppositions. The occasions for virilocality, the indemnity
paid for the sexual initiation of a boy, the fact that *ipré* is the reciprocal of both *itxwïye* and *ipiayõye,* the limited Omaha characteristics of their relationship terminology resulting from female

name transmission, all contradict the distinction between male and female and insist on the equality of the two sexes.

Perhaps the relationship designated by the terms *hõpin* and *hõpintxwöi* should also be considered a case of opposing oppositions. It is, as we have seen, associated with consanguinity (prohibition of incest, extreme solidarity) and also with affinity (obligation to repay goods and services and aggression, albeit indirect). Perhaps this relationship has the effect of opposing the affirmation that consanguines are different from affines by another which insists that they are the same.

But what is the rationale for these oppositions among oppositions which mark the entire Krahó social system and their relationship system too? Every opposition between two elements is also in some way a comparison of them. Naturally, if we are dealing with distinct elements, there is some difference between them. But it is only elements which have something in common which are compared. For the Krahó, then, the opposition of oppositions is a way of stating that when two distinct elements are compared, they must have something in common. The oppositions of oppositions also seem to have some effect on Krahó behavior. Since they counteract the absolute nature of social rules, they are in all probability the reason for the fact that Krahó behavior is not at all rigidly determined by those same rules.

THE APINAYÉ

I N 1971 there were about 350 Apinayé living in two villages near
Tocantinópolis in the far north of the state of Goiás, and there are
now over four hundred.

The first contacts between the Apinayé and Portuguese settlers date
from the eighteenth century, but it was not until the late nineteenth
century that there was much pressure on the Indians. At that time, a
wave of immigrants who lived by cattle rearing and the gathering of
wild products reached the Tocantins River. Since these immigrants did
not produce anything of great value to the outside world, their pene-
tration into the area was relatively weak and the Apinayé managed to
come to terms with it. Thus modern Apinayé have godparents among
the local settlers and vice versa, even though there may be tension between them, usually as a result of the disappearance of cattle, which is
systematically blamed on the Indians.

Apart from their contacts with the backwoodsmen of the region and
with the citizens of Tocantinópolis (who do their best to ignore their
inconvenient presence in the area), the Apinayé have regular contact
with the Krĩkatí and with the Krahó.

Since 1970, their traditional territories have been occupied by cattle
ranchers and settlers who earn their living by gathering babassu nuts.
Meanwhile, the work on the Trans-Amazon Highway has led the Apinayé to await the legal demarcation of their lands with understandable
anxiety.

The Indian Protection Service maintains a post for the Apinayé and
has recently been encouraging them to manufacture handicrafts for
sale to tourists. The FUNAI arranges to distribute these to the cities in
the south of Brazil.

Current conflicts between the Apinayé and the settlers in the region
revolve around the issue of land. The Indians have been severely pres-
sured of late by the massive occupation of their territories and the almost total disappearance of game. They now live by engaging in
subsistence agriculture and gathering wild products of the region, especially babassu nuts, which bring them a cash income. They are handi-
capped by having no Brazilian representative to speak for them at the
level of the municipio and the state. The Indian Protection Service is
a federal institution and thus represents them at the less immediate
national level.

A casual visitor to modern Apinayé villages might think that these
people had totally adopted the life-style of the local Brazilians. This is

81

not so, however. In spite of the forces which have been pushing the Apinayé in the direction of Brazilian society for over a century, they still maintain their traditional way of life, especially as regards religion and their system of social interrelationships.

3 | The Apinayé Relationship System: Terminology and Ideology[1]

Roberto da Matta

Translated from the Portuguese by J. Christopher Crocker and David Maybury-Lewis

Introduction

THE APINAYÉ MADE their appearance in anthropological theory in 1937 when Curt Nimuendajú and Robert H. Lowie, in an article entitled "The Dual Organizations of the Ramkokamekra of Northern Brazil," mentioned this Western Timbira tribe.[2] The Apinayé were referred to as a group which did not practice the sororate, in the context of a discussion where Lowie compared various forms of marriage with his usual precision (1937:579). The inclusion of the Apinayé in a work devoted to the Ramkokamekra appears accidental, but it is important to note that, as early as the thirties, Lowie was using the available ethnographic data on the Central Brazilian Indians to compare certain aspects of their social organization. He paid special attention to two problems which, from then on, would be fundamental issues in all discussions of the Gê. I refer to the dualism expressed in the symbolic and ritual order of all these tribes and, paradoxically, the lack of any prescription or even preference for marriage between cross-cousins.

Lowie, furthermore, was the first to note the structural similarity between Ramkokamekra kinship terminology and the terminologies of certain North American tribes (Crow, Choctaw, and Hopi), and to seek forms of preferential marriage which might indicate how the dualism expressed in Ramkokamekra ritual was implemented in their social organization.

Two years after this work, Curt Nimuendajú published his book *The Apinayé* (1939), and in 1940 Lowie explicitly took up a crucial aspect of the ethnography by stating: "The four marriage-regulating *kiyé* of the Apinayé do not conform to any type

83

of organization hitherto described. Descent differs according to sex, sons following the father, daughters the mother. The *kiyé* are thus neither clans nor Australoid sections, though there is the pseudo-Australoid rule that an individual may marry into only one of the three other *kiyé*." He concludes, somewhat perversely, "Incidentally, once more to confound the diffusionists, whence does this curious institution come? So long as it is known from just one tribe, shall we not simply treat it as a creature of Apinayé culture?" (1940:428). This was the origin of "the Apinayé anomaly."

After 1940, various anthropologists tried to interpret this system of four matrimonial "groups." Jules Henry called attention to inter-*kiyé* endogamy. This resulted from the descent rule which separated the sexes and a marriage rule specifying that a man of *Kiyé* A had to choose a spouse from *kiyé* B, a man of B, from *kiyé* C, and so on, until the circle was closed with a man of D taking a wife from *kiyé* A. The result, as Henry perceived, was four other "groups," now formed by the men of *kiyé* A and the women of *kiyé* B, men of B and women of C, men of C and women of D, and, finally, men of D and women of A (Henry 1940; after Maybury-Lewis 1960). In 1942, Kroeber used the same material, calling attention to the fact that the two-by-two grouping of the four *kiyé* produced a system of latent moieties (cf. Kroeber 1942; after Maybury-Lewis 1960).

In 1949, two classic works in the study of kinship systems appeared, and both dealt with the Apinayé and their curious marriage system. George Peter Murdock characterized the Apinayé as a society possessing a cyclical marriage system with matrilineal descent, but, in a most confusing note, suggested an evolutionary sequence for this tribe (Murdock 1949:242–243, 332). Claude Lévi-Strauss in his *Les structures elémentaires de la parenté* used the *"kiyé* marriage system" to illustrate the relativity of concepts of exogamy and endogamy (1949:61, 287). Lévi-Strauss made another attempt in 1952 (reprinted in 1963), when, in a pioneering article, he once again used the Apinayé to demonstrate that actually the dualism of the Gê and Bororo was much more apparent than real. The ethnologists who had studied these societies, argued Lévi-Strauss, took the dualistic model because it was the natives' own model. It was only among the Apinayé that this apparent dualism could be seen in its proper perspective without the importance that the natives themselves lent it. He therefore used the Apinayé marriage system to confirm his analysis of Bororo social organization, which, he argued, was really based on the endogamy of a system of three superimposed and hierarchically arranged groups. Since the *kiyé* system led equally to a latent endogamy, Lévi-Strauss commented, "To regard the Bororo as an endogamous society is so startling that we should hesitate even to consider this possibility had not an analogous conclusion already been drawn for the Apinayé by three different authors working independently with documents collected by Nimuendajú" (1963: 125).

The Apinayé anomaly seemed to have been resolved by Lévi-Strauss, but in 1960 David Maybury-Lewis raised the problem anew and attempted a total, detailed analysis of the Apinayé system. In his article, Maybury-Lewis took a direction opposite to that of Lévi-Strauss and sought to demonstrate, through statistical reasoning and a study of the relationship terminology, that the *kiyé* were a secondary institution in the Apinayé social order, that they did not regulate marriage, and, furthermore, that the best hypothesis to be applied to the Apinayé material was that this society operated within a two-section system.

After Maybury-Lewis's work, three other attempts were made to resolve the Apinayé anomaly: one by Robin Fox (1967), another by R. T. Zuidema (1969), and a third by Floyd Lounsbury and Harold Scheffler (1971).

An analysis of all these interpretations reveals some constants. First, there is a successive abandonment of the primary sources as the interpretations of the Apinayé system follow one another (this is the case with Fox, 1967). It is as if the analyst were suffering from a "passion for models," so that, seeing his diagrams operate on paper, he instituted them as the true Apinayé reality. Second, the interpretations are based on paradigms derived from other ethnographic sources and are applied to the Apinayé so as to accommodate Nimuendajú's data (as the analyses of Maybury-Lewis [1960] and Zuidema [1969] show). That which cannot be included in the paradigm is interpreted either as an error on the ethnographer's part or as a consequence of social change. The third is common to all sociological analysis where the native ideology is scorned and the analyst's perspective is correspondingly ethnocentric: having many variables to choose from, the analyst arbitrarily selects those which best fit his model. Fourth, as a result of all these factors, the system is reduced to a more or less arbitrary and disjointed conjunction of components (rules of residence, descent, cousin terms, and so on) and is so classified. That is why it is essential to examine the explicit beliefs of a group, for it is these beliefs which demonstrate the significance (or lack of it) of each of these components. In this context, it is appropriate to recall the words of Dumont. Writing on India and dealing with a situation analogous to the one I am discussing here, he said, "Another way of remaining shut in upon ourselves consists in assuming from the outset that ideas, beliefs and values—in a word, ideology—have a secondary place in social life, and can be explained by, or reduced to, other aspects of society" (1970:3).

It was through consideration of this Indian lesson that I resolved, in this analysis, to contrapose terminology and ideology. These expressions refer not only to the verbal conventions employed by the Apinayé to classify persons and social relations, but also to the anchoring of this set of terms or categories in a system of ideas capable of being explicated and/or discussed by the natives themselves. Terminological systems are generally studied in the opposite manner. It is felt that the terminology reveals the ideology, or at the least aids in its examination, and this examination, in so-called formal analyses, is usually most limited. Here, the reverse direction is taken: ideology is taken as the basis for the analysis of the terminology.

Put this way, it is clear that the purpose of this paper is to describe and interpret the ideology which informs the ensemble of terms employed by the Apinayé to classify persons and social relations. I will seek to avoid, as much as possible, treating this ensemble as "kinship terms," again for an "ideological" reason, since the terms, as I shall try to show, form a continuum in which it is not easy to segregate terms which can be given genealogical and biological referents from those which cannot. Since social anthropology has never been able to define precisely what is meant by "kinship" or "kinship system," I prefer to transfer my analytical attention to a "relationship system" rather than arbitrarily to treat certain categories as "kinship terms" and others as "fictive kinship terms," "ritual kinship terms," and so on, as is common in the current literature.

In this essay, my point of departure is a set of terms and its ideological foundation. To each set of terms (or terminological subsystem) corresponds an ideology relevant to some domain of reality, as it is defined and carved out by the Apinayé. To move, then, from an underlying ideology to a terminological system is to attempt the construction of an Apinayé ontology, that is, a system of categorization which sustains this dimension of their culture.

Terminology

The terminological systems used by the Apinayé to classify social relations can be divided into two parts. The first is made up of relationship terms for general or more inclusive categories, with no explicit genealogical referents; these I call comprehensive terms. The second part involves those terms conventionally called "kinship terms," for the majority have an explicit genealogical and/or biological referent. These are the terms most commonly used by the Apinayé, and they are as much a justification of behavior toward given persons as a mode of address. These I call specific terms, and they are divided below into four groups. In the following discussion, the five terminological subsystems are designated by Roman numerals, terms themselves by Arabic numbers, except the four terms constituting the comprehensive terms.

I. COMPREHENSIVE TERMS

a. *kwoya;* b. *kwoya kumrendy;* c. *kwoya kaag* (or *kwoya puro*),
and d. *kwoya ket*

All but the first of these expressions are formed from the word *kwoya* and an additional suffix. Thus the word *kumrendy* signifies "true," "real," in contrast to *kaag* or *puro,* which means "false," "imitation," and to *ket,* a negative particle. The expression *kwoya,* furthermore, may be combined with other terms, as in, for example, *iprom kwoya,* which designates relatives by marriage (*iprom* = wife). None of these terms, including *kwoya* itself, is ever used in address. They are fundamentally reference categories, employed to specify a person or, more frequently, categories of persons and of social relations.

Contemporary Apinayé gloss the word *kwoya* into Portuguese as *parente* ("relative") or *meu povo* ("my people"). Just as the word *parente* applies to all kindred or just the nuclear family in Brazilian usage, the term *kwoya* has a semantic field which expands and contracts according to the vicissitudes of daily life and as a function of what is being emphasized or specified in a particular context. The term *kwoya* can thus apply to the inhabitants of a given village, in contradistinction to the inhabitants of another village or tribe (the *kwoya ket*). More rarely, it can also be used to refer to the members of a residential group (the *kwoya kumrendy*), in opposition to other residential groups of the same village, the *kwoya kaag.* Since the category *kwoya* has no specific reference to social groups on the ground, it lends itself to this classificatory flexibility, as do our own terms "relative" or "family."

It is possible, then, to make a preliminary ordering of such categories in the following manner: (A) *kwoya* in opposition to *kwoya ket;* (B) *kwoya kumrendy* in opposition to *kwoya kaag.* These expressions allow a greater or lesser precision in defining any social field to which the terms are applied. In its more general sense (A), the category *kwoya* denotes all the social relations characterized by a sentiment or duty of solidarity, actual or potential. The expression thus establishes a contrast with an area where this sentiment or duty does not exist. In its more specific sense (B), the expression amounts to a gradation within a more limited social field. Thus *kwoya kumrendy* specifies persons whose residence is nearby and with whom genealogical relations can be traced easily; persons who support one in disputes and with whom one freely exchanges gossip, food, and labor. In short, *kwoya kumrendy* denotes primarily, but not exclusively, persons who recognize categorical obligations toward each other. These are people who, according to one informant, "one does not need to ask, for they always offer hospitality." But the category *kwoya kaag* (or *puro*) applies to such areas as adoptive relations and persons who are not included within the preceding terms. While it is possible to exchange meat and work with them, this occurs unsystematically and discontinuously.

As can be seen, the specifications of these categories are vague. They are applied to fields of relationships and do not generate any absolute dichotomy between *kumrendy* and *kaag* which might correspond with discrete and well-defined social groups, capable of corporate action. Consequently, in each Apinayé village there is a continual flow of individuals from one category to another, since there are always *kwoya ket* in the process of being transformed into *kwoya* (through marriage or common residence) and *kwoya kaag* metamorphosing into *kumrendy* through name-giving, friendship, food, and service exchange. The categories, then, overlap in a way which might be approximately represented by a Venn diagram. Let us now proceed to examine the nature of the overlapping and how the Apinayé are able to manipulate this general system of relational terms.

Every Apinayé invariably claims that he has a great number of *kwoya*. But when the subcategories of *kwoya* to which the members of a village belong are specified, it becomes clear that the number of *kwoya kumrendy* and *kwoya ket* is quite small, while the number of *kwoya kaag* is large, composing the majority of a given ego's *kwoya*. In fact, a detailed inquiry into this topic utilizing sixteen Apinayé individuals of both sexes and different ages clearly substantiated their normative statements.[3] In a universe of 152 persons, only 20 percent were classified as *kwoya kumrendy,* while 75 percent were included in the *kwoya kaag* category; the remainder were composed of *kwoya ket.* These figures obtained from sixteen informants are very consistent with verbalizations obtained less systematically.

However, a detailed investigation of the *kwoya kumrendy* recognized by various informants shows that it is possible to establish another distinction within this subclass itself. This is because the Apinayé distinguish between *kwoya kumrendy* with whom restrictions on food exchanges and behavior (*piangri*) are obligatory, and those other *kwoya kumrendy* toward whom such obligations do not exist. The Apinayé sometimes call the former group "birth relatives" or "relatives whose blood is near," using the expression *kabro atpen burog*. These persons are invariably members of the nuclear family of origin and/or of marriage of the informants (depending on their marital status) and are thus segregated from the other *kwoya kumrendy,* who constitute an "unmarked" class, with no special term. The class *kwoya` kumrendy* is thus subdivided into two classes: one which includes the members of a given ego's family of origin or of marriage (or both) and another which includes other "true relatives." Affines, especially those who reside with ego or who are connected to his wife or her husband through primary ties, are considered *kwoya kumrendy* of the type toward whom no restrictions obtain.

The ideological basis for this distinction is discussed below. For the moment, it is sufficient to point out that, in its most general use, the category *kwoya* refers essentially to a nucleus made up of people whose interrelationship is seen by the Apinayé in terms of physiological or biological ties or bonds of common substance. This does not mean that any given ego's family of origin or of marriage is inevitably defined in this rigid fashion. In fact, relations of respect or common substance frequently include persons connected to a certain ego by more distant ties. But one quickly discovers that their inclusion in this category is due to the fact that they have had an intense intimacy with ego. In all cases of this type, the Apinayé justification is the statement that such persons have come to smell alike (*me-kutxe*) through having slept together for a long time. And this demonstrates that some social relationships can be initiated from outside the *kwoya kumrendy* class and subsequently become an integral part of it, since such social relations can be justified through an idiom of common substance. In fact, among the Apinayé, this idiom of substance is the best translation for what we term "kinship" or, rather, "consanguinity."

In the Apinayé system, therefore, there is a set of obligations and/or restrictions which obtain among a restricted group of people (an average of 6.5 for each of 7 informants). This group consists of the nuclear family of origin or of marriage of a given ego or, rather, of those persons with whom a given ego maintains

systematic and constant but not exclusive physiological relationships.

These general categories can thus be seen in terms of two dimensions of contrast. One of them separates classes diametrically,
establishing a division which might be equivalent to the classic
dichotomy between "us" and "them." The other, however, establishes a series of gradations outward from a restricted circle of persons. Thus the *kwoya* are subdivided again into "persons toward
whom ego observes restrictions in cases of sickness or birth" and
"persons toward whom such precautions are not taken." Gradations can be distinguished among *kwoya,* in a series of discriminations departing from a central nucleus or primary group around
ego, but the dimension which makes these distinctions is one involving natural, physiological, or other components of common
substance. These terms can therefore be ranged in a series as
follows: *kwoya ket* —— *kwoya* —— *kwoya kaag* —— *kwoya kumrendy* —— *kwoya* "of restrictions" —— ego.

There is no difficulty in distinguishing the poles of the continuum, but there are problems in an *a priori* specification of the
classes in the middle of the series. This goes to show the difference
between these categories and actual social groups, but also demonstrates that these categories are always used from an egocentric
perspective.

The categories presented above cover areas which intersect, but
within certain limits. An Apinayé is thus able to manipulate his
classificatory system up to a certain point. For example: although
in cases of conflict he can change the classification of certain relatives considered *kumrendy,* this is not possible if these *kumrendy*
relatives are members of his family of origin (his father, his
mother, and his uterine siblings) . The same holds true for his children. Thus restrictions can be relaxed, but the relationship is life-
long. In reverse fashion, an Apinayé can transform some of his
kwoya ket into *kumrendy,* but there are limits to such transformations, for they can only take place after regular and intense social
bonds have been formed between ego and the persons previously
classed as *kwoya ket,* which very rarely happens and then usually
in cases of adoption.

In sum, I think it important to stress the following aspects of
this general terminology:

1. The terms cover social fields and relations; they do not refer
to social groups.

2. The only *kwoya* who can be unambiguously specified are the
members of the nuclear family of origin or marriage directly tied

to ego, that is, his genitors, uterine siblings, wife, and children; and interaction with these people is justified through an ideology founded on notions of common substance.

3. It is precisely because this indivisible and life-long nucleus of persons with whom a given ego has categorical relations exists that the manipulation of the system occurs within certain limits.

4. Besides this group which shares a common substance, there are also intense social relations which can be spoken of as belonging to the class *kwoya kumrendy,* but which lack a biological foundation; these are relations created and maintained by common residence, marriage, nomination, and exchanges of food, presents, and services.

II. Specific Terms: Common Substance

In addition to the comprehensive terms, the Apinayé use a system of terms to classify specific relationships, such as those of common substance or initiation ritual friends. These terms are used to classify relations and persons situated within the field defined as *kwoya.* There are no terms for relations within the contrasting field, the *kwoya ket.* Such people are called by personal names or by terms referring to special relationships. For example, if a person is classified as a "formal friend," the circle of relatives around him can be designated by terms appropriate to this type or relation, as will be seen below. If the person is a spouse, there is a system of terms used to define such relations, or rather, a system for relations established by marriage, also presented below.

1. *pam:* F, FB, MH, MZH . . .

This term is applied only referentially, without further specifications. The term *txun,* in its variations *txun-re* or *txun-ti* (where *re* = diminutive particle, *ti* = augmentive particle, both referring to the physical size of a person) , is used as the vocative term. Some informants used the Brazilian *papai,* limiting its application to the genitor or *pam kumrendy.* The most frequent use of *papai* occurs in those under twenty. Both *pam* and *txun* may be used within the categories *kumrendy* and *kaag,* when it is wished to signify the distance or specific position of a *pam* in relation to a given ego. The *txun* form may also be used with a proper name, as well as with other suffixes (such as *prek* = old or *prin* = young) , as the vocative or the necessity for individuation may require. It is also possible to employ the descriptive term *nipeitxo* ("he who made me") to designate the genitor and/or the "adoptive father" (who arranged names), with the following distinction: *nipeitxo* is used here as a reference term for the genitor but as a term of address for the name-arranger. The use of this descriptive form will become clear in a moment. For the genitor, the vocative form is always a nickname, that is, an individualizing term whose use does not extend beyond the boundaries of a very much reduced group of persons. It is also possible to use the term *to-re* to address the genitor, thus indicating intimacy and affection. When a *pam* dies, the particle *pinrog* is used immediately after the term. This particle is interpreted by the Apinayé as a death marker. Besides these forms, the Apinayé use the term *me-papam* (where *me* = collective) to refer to the sun or, nowadays, to God, and sometimes to the Chief of the Goiânia Inspectorate or to the President of Brazil.

2. *na:* M, MZ, FW, FBW

This term is used in reference. The term *dyil* in its various forms is used as the vocative which results from the addition of particles (*ti, re, prek, kumrendy,* or *kaag*). A proper name may also be used to distinguish an individual in this category. As with the previous term, the expression *kator-txo* ("she from whom I came") may be used to indicate the genetrix or to refer to the "adopted mother" (who arranged names for ego) or to the wife of the name-arranger. Again, as with the preceding term, the genetrix is never addressed by a term, but addressed by a nickname used only by the members of her nuclear family or by those persons resident in her primary group. When a *na* dies, the term *pabo-txoi-ti* is used to refer to her.

3a. *to:* B, MS, FS, MZS, FBS
3b. *tody:* Z, MD, FD, MZD, FBD

To and *tody* are the vocative forms. Referentially, they are used with *ti* (augmentative) and *re* (diminutive) to indicate physical size. With *kumrendy* or *kaag* they indicate social distance. The form *kambu* is used in address by a female ego and the form *pigkwa* by a male ego. Like the genitors, uterine siblings are always addressed by a proper name or nickname, the preceding forms being used much more for adoptive or ceremonial siblings, in contexts where social distance is emphasized. The term *pinrog* is added after these forms to indicate that the "sister" or "brother" in question is dead. The expressions *kro-ti* and *kro-re* are used, respectively, for the older brother and younger brother, but they are never employed as vocatives for uterine brothers, who are always addressed by name.

4. *kra:* S, D, BD, BS (man sp.) ; ZS, ZD, S, D (wom. sp.)

The term is used as a vocative and as reference. The forms *akatxoi* and *akante-re* are used, but very rarely, to distinguish, respectively, a male from a female *kra*. However, ego's own children are always addressed by names or nicknames, never by relationship terms. As with the preceeding terms, it is possible to use this category to specify social distance, through the addition of *kumrendy* and *kaag*.

5. *geti* (*ngeti*): FF, MF, MB, FZH

This term is used both vocatively and referentially. When a person in this category passes his personal names to a male ego, the expression *krã-tum* may be used referentially or vocatively for him. Now, the reciprocal term is commonly *krã-duw*. The form *tum* can often be used, but it is always accompanied by the suffixes *re, ti,* or *prek,* or by the proper name of the *krã-tum*. The Apinayé have a verbal and behavioral tendency to treat as *krã-tum* the name-giver or other persons of the same generation as the parents. Meanwhile, the term *geti* implies old age, as in the term *pinget* (age-class of "grandfathers" or "old people"), or *imbre-geti,* a term used as reference for the father-in-law (see term 8). When a *geti* dies, the term *pinrog* is appended after *geti* to indicate death. Some informants of various ages use the Brazilian form *vôvô* or *vóvó* (without making the vowel contrast which differentiates male from female in Portuguese) to translate this term, and often use it in address. The term can also be accompanied by the specification *kumrendy* or *kaag*.

6. *tui* (*tukatui*): MM, FM, FZ, MBW

The term is used for both address and reference. As with the other terms, the particles *prek, prin, ti,* and *re,* or *kumrendy* or *kaag* can be used to indicate differences or specify a particular *tui*. The same end can be achieved by using the proper name after the term. When, however, a *tui* gives her names to a child in the category *tamtxua* (specified below), there is no change of terms, as in the previous male case. When a *tui* dies, the term *pinrog* is added as a suffix to indicate death.

7. *tamtxua:* SD, SS, DD, ZS, ZD, WBS, WBD (man sp.) ;
    SS, SD, DD, DS, BS, BD, HZS, HZD (wom. sp.)

The term is used for both address and reference. It is possible to distinguish the sexes by using the expression *parxiote* for a female *tamtxua* and *apare* for a male *tamtxua*. Yet the term is rarely used in address for *tamtxua* closely related to Ego (his grandsons, for example). For persons thus related, the proper name or nickname is used. This term also is used with *pinrog* to refer to a deceased person.

III. Specific Terms: Affinal

8. *imbre-geti:* WF (man sp.); HF (wom. sp.)

Imbre-geti is a reference term. The vocative form is *tukoya*. The Apinayé never use personal names as terms of address for affines, always calling them by the appropriate relationship term. Similarly, such terms are rarely used with the suffixes *re* or *ti*, and are never employed with the categories *kumrendy* or *kaag*. They are therefore situated outside of the general system of classification. This holds true for all the following terms.

9. *papam-geti* (address and reference): WM (man sp.); HM (wom. sp.)

10. *improm:* W

The term is only referential. The husband never calls his wife *iprom*, always using her name and/or nickname, especially after the marriage has been stabilized through the advent of children.

11. *idpien:* H

The term is only referential. As with term 10, a wife always addresses her husband by name or nickname, especially after they have children.

12. *papany* (address): WZ, BW

The referential form is *ipany*.

13. *imbre:* WB

Imbre is a reference term. The vocative form is *imboi*.

14. *idpienhon:* ZH

The term is used for both address and reference and is always accompanied with the suffixes *re* or *ti*. The term *tuko* can be equally used for address.

15. *txoiti:* SW, BSW, ZSW, BW (wom. sp.)

The term is used for both address and reference.

16. *tukoti:* DH

The term is used for both address and reference.

17. *ponmre-geti:* HM

The term is used for both address and reference.

18. *ponmre:* ZH

The term is used for both address and reference.

IV. SPECIFIC TERMS: "FORMAL FRIENDS"

19. *krã-geti* (masc.) ; *krã-gedy* (fem.)

These terms are used in reference and address for a person who establishes highly ceremonial ties with ego, giving him a set of ornaments for the chest, arms, and legs, in addition to the insignia of one of the Ipgnotxóine or Krenotxóine moieties. These terms do not permit any modification or specification in terms of physical size or relative age. Formal friends are never addressed by their personal names or nicknames.

19a. *pa-krã*

This is the reciprocal of the terms given above, used in address and reference toward a formal friend younger than ego. This relationship also affects the children of the "formal friends." The children of persons thus related treat each other reciprocally as *ikamde-re* or *ikamde-ti* (the suffixes indicating relative age), if they are both male. If they are of opposite sexes, they treat each other as *improm-ti* (man speaking with the daughter of his *krã-geti* or *pa-krã*) and as *ikande-ti* (woman speaking with the son of her *krã-geti* or *pa-krã*). These are both terms of reference and address.

V. SPECIFIC TERMS: INITIATION RITUAL FRIENDS

20. *krã-txua*

The term is used to classify persons of the same age who participate together in the rituals of male initiation, in their first or second phases (respectively, *pēb kaag* or *pēb kumrendy*) (cf. Nimuendajú 1939:37 ff., 56 ff., and 1956:chap. 9). The selection of these friends is made through personal preference, but the terms are employed for life, replacing personal names or the relationship terms discussed previously. As with terms 19 and 19a, this class does not allow any gradations. Friends thus related are of the same age (or, to be more precise, of the same age-class), and their relations are symmetrical, as witnessed by the modern Apinayé term for them: *companheiros* (companions). Occasionally, the relatives of *krã-txua* are affected by the relationship, so that two people who are *krã-txua* to each other call each other's children *kra*.

All these terms are invariably preceded by the possessive *id* (= my).

This is the complete list of the Apinayé relationship terms. As their primary and partial definitions reveal, these terms refer to various subsystems of social relations. In fact, the presentation of the system itself implied a decision on my part to segregate them into subsystems. A cursory analysis of such terminological subsystems reveals certain features which indicate that these subdivisions do not violate Apinayé classificatory thought. For example, subsystems II and III, unlike the others, are genealogically determined. Besides this subsystem I is somewhat relative, being—as I define it—an all-inclusive system of classificatory relations. But subsystems II and III are automatic in their application, being for that very reason determined biologically and genealogically. Subsystem IV (that of "formal friends") is difficult to translate genealogically, and V (that of *krã-txua*) is frankly dependent on individual choice. Similarly, subsystem II can be used with particles or categories which differentiate persons and social relations (the particles *re, ti, prek, prin,* and the categories *kumrendy* and *kaag*), but subsystems III, IV, and V do not permit such nuances. The same thing holds true with reference to the address terms which accompany such terminological fields. While subsystem II permits the use of personal names in address, this does not happen with subsystems III, IV, and V, which are thus much more formalized. These subsystems, consquently, always supersede other relationships and in so doing indicate new social relations.

I argue here that, in an orthodox analysis, the terms and their morphological distinctions would guide the analyst. Undoubtedly, then, the Apinayé relationship terminology would be promptly subdivided under the classic headings "consanguineal terms" and "affinal terms," leaving aside the two last subsystems, which refer to "formal friends" and "companions." But such a focus would certainly raise various problems. For example, how would one explain the extensive use of the term *geti* for "consanguines" and certain affines, as in terms 8 and 9? Or, again, how could one elucidate the use of the word *krã* (= head) in so many terms? Are these relations to be regarded as extensions of primary ones, that is, those which possess an indisputable genealogical determination? But, then, would the sole common denominator of such terms be a linguistic one?

It was in seeking to avoid such problems that I resolved to let my analysis be guided by a study of ideology. If, in fact, the Apinayé terminological system is subdivided into specfic fields, then there ought to exist corresponding ideologies for each one of these subsystems. Such ideologies would be explicated by informants in terms of rules of etiquette, prescriptions for behavior, distinctions between address and reference forms, beliefs relative to the human body and procreation, and so on—in a word, through a system of signs which in turn would indicate the fixed and irreducible points of Apinayé social order. It is these sets of signs that I have been calling ideologies. And it is these ideologies which refer not just to Apinayé relationship terms, but to their entire cosmos. Let us, then, examine the terms as a function of these systems of ideas.

Ideologies

In the Apinayé terminological system, there are various terms which specify members of the nuclear family. This holds as much for the comprehensive terms as for the terms applied to the genitors of a given ego. I shall, therefore, start this section by taking as my departure point the nuclear family and its ideology.

Among the Apinayé, each nuclear family has its own plot of ground to cultivate, and is the only socially recognized unit for the production of children. Marriage is strictly monogamous and spouses have mutually exclusive rights to each other's domestic and sexual services. To each nuclear family corresponds a specific area: either a house or a special area within a house. Like all the Gê, the Apinayé practice uxorilocal residence, so that a large number of households in their two villages contain more than one nuclear family. When this happens, the ideal is that the residential group operates as a unit, at least for the execution of specified duties. But, even so, the nuclear families remain independent in eating and sleeping, two activities by which the Apinayé define domestic life. Young unmarrieds of both sexes do not have the right to build a house, and the men do not possess a permanent residential structure in the middle of the village, such as occurs among the Bororo and the Kayapó.

Apinayé houses are arranged in a circle around a public plaza so that the opposition between these two areas, houses and plaza, and the groups which have rights to them is clearly expressed. In fact, the sphere of the family, economics, and socialization of the young is a domestic and daily order; while the ceremonial order, along with the groups formed to conduct it, is a public order essentially situated outside daily routine. While the first is regulated by persons who maintain intense and lifelong social relations, the second is formed by groups which come together sporadically and whose membership can vary from occasion to occasion.

The Apinayé domestic order is marked by two clearly expressed ideologies. The first, discussed immediately below, is expressed in so-called avoidance rules or rules of etiquette. The second, discussed next, has been treated in the anthropological literature, especially in South American ethnology, under the title of "couvade," which I here call precautions, abstinence, or restrictions. Last to be discussed in this section is the etiquette of ceremonial relationships.

ETIQUETTE

Every time an Apinayé speaks of marriage, he is always careful to enumerate the rules of etiquette which characterize conjugal life in his society. It is evident that these rules grow out of the asymmetry produced by uxorilocal residence, which compels men to leave their natal houses to their brothers-in-law and move to the houses of their wives. But this, obviously, is not all. In fact, the problem is not only that of having to live physically close to persons who are socially distant (affines). It is also that of creating within an originally unified nuclear family a social field for a new nuclear family, since most Apinayé households contain more than one, and of accommodating the relative political and economic independence of the latter. The problem therefore has equal repercussions for the affines.

Actually, the rules of Apinayé etiquette are of two types: toward the parents and the brothers of his wife, a husband must behave in a ceremonial and restrained manner. He never calls them by their proper names or by their nicknames, but always uses the appropriate relationship terms. He never speaks to them, unless prompted by a question. And even when he has succeeded in the hunt, he remains silent until his parents-in-law and wife have cleaned the animal and cut up the meat to distribute it. Apinayé etiquette stipulates that the father-in-law receive, butcher, and distribute the meat, always separating a portion for his son-in-law's parents; but the son-in-law says nothing and merely waits for his older affines to handle the matter. Similarly, a husband never enters the rooms of his parents-in-law or brothers-in-law, nor does he have the right to use their weapons or possessions. These are avoidance rules *par excellence*.

There are, however, other rules, more circumscribed than (and in a certain sense opposed to) these. A husband ought to and can converse freely with his wife's sister and treat her children affectionately, in the same way as he would his own wife and her children, because the relationship between them should, at the outset, be characterized by cordiality and restraint, virtues much admired by the Apinayé. In fact, when relations between a man and his *papany* (see term 12) are discussed, the Apinayé always say that such a woman is almost the same thing as a true wife.

The reverse of these rules also holds true. A father-in-law or brother-in-law never enters his affine's room, nor takes his personal possessions without permission. This reciprocal avoidance behavior shows that the tension of residence change is felt by both sides, that the husband as much as the original residents of the household group suffer with the former's change of residence. In the Apinayé case, this is clearly seen because there is no rigid definition of domestic authority. Since unilineal descent groups do not exist, either the father-in-law, mother-in-law, the husband, or the brother-in-law can occupy an important position within the domestic group and be the key point of articulation of its members' social activities. In some domestic groups the extended family is coordinated by an old man, in others by a woman, and in still others by a middle-aged husband. Since this coordination generally extends to neighboring houses, residential clusters tend to form, with important political consequences. Therefore, the presence of a strange man in a house generates tensions not just for him, but for all his affines.

These paradoxes are expressed by the Apinayé through an ideology which underlies such avoidance relations: the ideology of *piam*. All these relations are marked by *piam*, and this category defines qualities of shame, respect, and/or social distance implicit in certain social relationships. In fact, the ensemble of prescriptions expressed by this category is impressive. Persons who have *piam* cannot joke, they cannot speak lightly of each other, nor fight, ask each other favors, call each other by name, look each other in the eye, walk or bathe together, have sexual relations, urinate together, talk to each other, or observe ceremonial restrictions for each other. Persons thus united can, however, carry on formal transactions, an activity always marked by *piam* for the Apinayé.

The prescriptions determined by *piam* apply, with greater or lesser intensity, to all Apinayé social relationships. They do not exist in relations between persons of the same age, same sex, and same nuclear family (two uterine brothers or sisters), but begin to exist between a genitor and his children and even more between a genetrix and her son, the reverse being true for a woman in relation with her uterine brothers, her father, and her mother. *Piam* is, then, correlated with biological differences of sex and age, gradually increasing as other discriminations are added to these two fundamental dimensions of contrast in the Apinayé social system. Consequently, every time that persons of different sex, age, and social groups enter into formal transactions, their relations are marked by *piam*. Consistent with this custom, the passage from one of these categories to another is marked by some type of precaution. Young initiates ready to change their class follow alimentary regulations of the same kind as those obeyed by a man who has become sick through contact with an animal and by a husband and wife who are in direct contact with a newborn child (I will return to this topic below). The greater the difference between the fields and the categories in contact, the greater the *piam;* the less the difference, the less the *piam.* The corollary of this ideology is the expression *piam ket,* used to castigate those persons who egotistically cease to follow the more important prescriptions of Apinayé culture. Actually, a person "without *piam*" is equated with dogs, animals who understand all that is said, but nonetheless continue to act antisocially. A person being *piam ket* is therefore an individual who does not obey the natural order of things, since a world without *piam* is a world in disorder—a universe where the fundamental categories of Apinayé society would be confused and its social fields scrambled.

But in the ideology of Apinayé etiquette, it is not only the husband and his affines who have relationships marked by *piam.* A woman also has *piam,* not only with regard to her parents and brothers (but not her sisters), but also toward her husband. Her *piam* is centered in the fact of her public admission that she has permanent sexual relations with a man. While the Apinaye say that the *piam* of a woman is equal to that of her husband, vis-à-vis their respective affines, I suspect that the woman has much more *piam* with her own genitors and close relatives. This is due to the physical (and social) distance between her and her affines, who generally live on the opposite side of the village. Perhaps it is because of this that the Apinayé always discuss these rules of etiquette from the point of view of the husband, even when the informant is a woman.

The ideology of Apinayé etiquette rules marks a social field which was opened by marriage. This field is initially segregated by avoidance rules which rigidly separate the husband from his affines of the opposite sex and separate him from his wife and her mother in a more attenuated way. But as the marriage stabilizes through time, especially with the arrival of children, *piam* diminishes with opposite-sex affines and disappears with the wife. This diminution signifies not only that the husband and wife have adjusted to the marriage, but also that they are capable of creating a potentially independent zone inside an original nuclear family. An uxorilocal extended family is thus formed, and the group, when the *piam* is equilibrated, can operate as a unit in various social affairs. In other words, intensive *piam* expresses social relations in which persons who represent discrete and/or segregated social fields enter into contact. The relations marked by *piam* at its greatest intensity are relations in which the agents have clearly defined matters to transact; they are therefore exchange relations. In the case of relationships between a man and his affines, these matters are made clear at the beginning of marriage: he hunts and works for his parents-in-law and brothers-in-law, receiving in exchange the exclusive domestic and sexual services of his wife. But to the degree that his nuclear family is established and integrated into an extended family, the cycle of these relations becomes a long one (Sahlins 1965), with consequent diminution of *piam* between the man and his affines. Avoidance rules are strong and intense at the moment of marriage, when he and his wife create their own, potentially independent area.

"COUVADE"

Another ideological component of the nuclear family is the fact that this group is conceived by the Apinayé as being a natural group. That is, the nuclear family is taken straight from nature and the links between its members are expressed as part and parcel of the physical world. This means that the nuclear family has as its distinctive mark an ideology founded in Apinayé conceptions of the functioning of the human body.

For the Apinayé, the human body can function correctly only when it is maintained by a combination of substances. Meat, water, and tubers are fundamental for such functioning, although the first two are seen as having special qualities. Meat, it is believed, brings physical vigor (which is not obtained by the exclusive ingestion of tubers), while water aids in the production of blood. All food and water are always seen as descending from the head (*krã*) to the intestines (*inkrú*) and in this descent undergoing substantial transformations. Food is changed into feces "because it becomes very hot" and water into blood and urine. But blood itself (*kambro*) also is transformed. Falling into the genital organs, it can become sperm. This change occurs in the scrotum (*greniko*), with the assistance of the penis (*txeto*). Heat is responsible for this transformation, since during coitus (*baguni*) the man becomes very hot and part of his blood descends and changes into sperm. Heat causes the blood to change its color and appearance, but not its nature. Besides this, the blood is considered a vital substance, the volume of which in the body determines a series of specific behaviors. An aging man loses blood, a growing child gains blood, a man who has much blood is heavy and sluggish, and should bleed (*me-kupe*) himself; a woman who loses blood during menstruation becomes a recluse and is considered sick (*me-o*).[4] If a person loses all his blood, he also loses his image (*mekaron*), which goes to the world of the dead.[5]

The formation of a child is explained as the encounter of male sperm with female blood. For this reason women cease to menstruate during pregnancy and prepubesent girls do not menstruate (*kambro*). A physical union between the sexes is needed before a woman can menstruate. Once a woman ceases to have a menstrual flow, it is known that she is pregnant (*kambro ket* or *tuiaro*). The couple then ought to copulate frequently, since the Apinayé say that the woman has more blood than the man and it is necessary to balance her contribution to the new body with more sperm. The mixture of the two elements in the woman's belly produces the child, who is gradually formed throughout pregnancy. As a result, all the men who have sexual relations with a pregnant woman are obliged to observe restrictions. But the logical implication of this belief is not always taken into account by all Apinayé, some of whom are ambivalent concerning this problem. Therefore, at least nowadays, there is a visible tendency among the younger members of the tribe to identify the husband as the genitor, and thus as the only one who is obliged to observe the restrictions.

Once there is a mixture of the two elements in the uterus, the child begins to be gradually formed. It is then that precautions or restrictions on diet and behavior begin which are to last throughout life.

There are various kinds of precautions among the Apinayé. Abstinence from food is the crucial element of curing and rituals in which changes of status (and of physical nature) occur. There are precautions when a man kills an enemy, when a person is

sick, when a woman is menstruating, and when novices are se-
questered awaiting their change of social status. As I indicated
earlier, every time two elements of differentiated domains enter
into contact, alimentary or behavioral precautions are taken. The
more diverse the domains (and consequently such elements), the
more intense the precautions.

Here I shall focus in detail only on the precautions relevant
to the nuclear family, which are called *piangri*. *Piangri* begins
during pregnancy or, in the case of marriage with a virgin girl,
during her first menstruation. Husband and wife avoid taking
baths, eating rhea meat (which would make them as old as the
rhea, whose feathers are gray) and the meat of other animals considered heavy or slow, which is considered to be difficult to digest.
When a woman is pregnant, however, alimentary restrictions are
greater. Thus the man does not eat rice which sticks to the pot
(which would make childbirth difficult) nor cake made from
manioc dough (manioc being soft and sticky, it also would cause
problems in childbirth). Man and wife do not eat armadillo of
either kind common in this area (*Cabassous unicinctus* and
Euphractus sexcinctus sexcinxtus) or certain fish which, like the
armadillo, live in fissures in the river gullies, since both kinds of
food would make childbirth difficult.

After the birth, these precautions increase and become equivalent for husband and wife. Both cease to eat coatimundi (because it is an animal which is constantly defecating and the child
would be like it); fish and the liver of animals (which would
cause diarrhea in the child, since the liver is very rich in liquids
and blood, and the fish has sticky flesh); cutia, which makes the
child cry constantly; monkey, which would cause the infant to
stay awake all night (as the animal does); seriema, which would
cause the semblance of madness (the seriema moves its head very
rapidly from side to side), and so on. During this period of
piangri, husband and wife eat principally dry flour and tapioca
cake, foods which according to the Apinayé contain very little
water. Both cease to bathe (water would chill their bodies abruptly
and this cooling would cause the loss of hair); the husband cannot do heavy labor or copulate with other women (the production
of heat during copulation produces sweat and this in turn causes
intense crying in the child); and husband and wife can only
scratch themselves with special instruments (no longer used
today) since scratching with the hands provokes wounds because
their skins are very weak. (Nimuendajú 1939:75, 1956:60). In
other words, the physical frontiers (skin) of the couple become
weakened, a process which reveals their identification with the

newborn (defined as having a weak skin) , as well as the suppression of the social frontiers between three individuals differentiated in terms of sex and age, but united in a special grouping.

These same precautions, in a more attenuated form, are followed for the rest of their lives whenever any member of the nuclear family becomes sick.

Asked why they take such precautions, the Apinayé say that they do so because the *kra-re* (infant) does not yet have much blood and it is necessary to assist the formation of his or her body. Infants are seen as incomplete beings, and until children are seven or eight years old, they are subject to soul loss. A fright or violent scolding can cause a child to leave his or her soul at the place where the shock occurred, and this loss is manifested by the loss of appetite or sleep, prolonged crying, and headaches.

Because a human being is gradually created, the precautions are thus gradually intensified or diminished, there being a clear correspondence between the process of the child's formation and the beginning and end of the precautions. The "couvade," however, focuses on the child and his or her process of initial development. Of all the relatives, the genitors are exclusively responsible for this growth. And although the Apinayé say that "blood is scattered throughout the village," the nucleus (or paradigm) of its concentration is the nuclear family. Parents, in fact, are responsible for the physical well-being of their children until death, and children are most careful in their relationships with each other and with their parents. Among the Apinayé, consequently, there is not the asymmetry encountered among the Kayapó and Shavante, where the genitor can affect his children but the latter cannot affect him (cf., respectively, Turner 1966:xviii and Maybury-Lewis 1967:66) . The precautions of childbirth, however, last until the child begins to crawl and walk, activities which indicate that he is "hard" and that "his blood is guaranteed." The genitors are responsible for this increase of the vital substance, not just because their offspring has received it from them, but because they are the only adults socially formed by Apinayé culture who have direct contact with him. It is for all these reasons that when the Apinayé are asked why they practice such restrictions, the reply is always, "The parents do not eat meat because the child has not yet done so."

It seems clear, therefore, that *piangri* reveals an identification of the genitors with the child and of the genitors with each other.[6] The so-called "couvade," at least in its Apinayé version, can be considered a rite of passage, in which the genitors as much as the child are in a marginal and dangerous position. It at once defines, puts in focus, and rationalizes the bonds between genitor, genetrix, and newborn child, and delimits an area or social field which will be occupied by the completely established nuclear family.

The alimentary precautions therefore create a continuity between persons physically and socially separated: genitor/genetrix and newborn child, a being partially submerged in nature. The restrictions create what might be called, to paraphrase Victor Turner, a *community of substance,* symmetrical to but also the inverse of the *community of affliction* brought about when an Apinayé becomes sick or when he is contaminated by the killing of an enemy (Victor Turner 1968 and 1969). In the "couvade" for childbirth, the precautions and abstinences abolish the frontiers between persons separated by age, sex, and social position. The precautions associated with sickness and murder, by contrast, are undertaken to reorder the frontiers between the ingested animal and the sick man (who ate it) or between the dead man and his assassin. The community of affliction in this way reconciles persons or elements situated in differing domains of the Apinayé cosmos: its therapy is to separate them. The community of substance is exactly opposite. It begins with the abstinences (which correspond to the therapeutic process of the first case) and from there attempts to establish and found social relations between persons initially distinct, but who should remain together. The mechanism of abstinence is, therefore, used to implement two inverse processes, and it cannot be stressed too often that its meaning is given exclusively by its context.

The interpretation of the etiquette rules and the alimentary precautions of childbirth and sickness as elements in the ideology of the Apinayé nuclear family facilitates our understanding of how it is perceived in this society. In turn, this allows a more reliable analysis of the reasons for certain terminological usages. In fact, once we adopt the perspective that rules of avoidance and childbirth restrictions are two sides of the same coin, some aspects of the terminology are immediately clarified.

1. Among the Apinayé, the terminology of marriage and terminology for relatives of substance are not dichotomized by the classic dimensions of "consanguinity/affinity" or "we/they," such as occur among the Shavante (Maybury-Lewis 1967). In fact, the wife is an affine who is transformed gradually into a *kwoya kumrendy* of common substance, since once the marriage is consummated and stabilized by children, husband and wife mix their blood and follow mutual restrictions in cases of sickness. This transformation also affects the immediate circle of affines (the parents and uterine siblings of the wife) who are part of her

substance group. This influence is expressed by the inclusion of such affines in ego's bilateral kindred, and also by the repetition of terms which are common to both systems. Such is case with the term *geti* (number 5), which is used to denote the positions of wife's father and wife's mother (man sp.) and husband's father and husband's mother (wom. sp.), otherwise *imbre-geti* and *papam-geti* (see numbers 8 and 9). The area of terminological overlapping is precisely the area covered by the genitors of the wife (or husband, in the case of a female ego), a fact which shows how the ties of marriage are superimposed on the relations of common substance, and vice versa.

2. The ideologies presented above also account for the terminological identification of genitors with their same-sex siblings and the separation of these from their cross-sex siblings and their genitors (classified as *geti/tui*). In Apinayé ideology, these distinctions are produced by the application of basic distinctions according to sex and generation. In this way, two siblings of the same sex do not have *piam* between them, while two siblings of the opposite sex do have *piam*. The same thing happens with two men or two women in the same descent line but of different generations. The rule of uxorilocal residence can be taken, in fact, as an expression of this principle. Cross-sex siblings are separated after marriage, an act which accentuates their sexual differences. The Apinayé express the formal principle of the equivalence of siblings, however, through their ideology of etiquette and of *piam*. As a result there is, for the Apinayé, complete social and biological identity between two uterine siblings of the same sex.

The terminological identification between cross-aunts, cross-uncles, and grandparents is thus nothing more than the expression of equivalence between the contrastive dimensions of sex and age. The genitors and their same-sex siblings are referred to as *pam* and *na,* but the cross-aunts and cross-uncles and the grandparents are called *geti* and *tui.*

3. We can now see why the members of the nuclear family are always addressed by nicknames and not by ordinary relationship terms or even descriptive terms. Being a community of substance, the nuclear family is based on an identity among its members. In it, responsibilities are biological, not jural or ceremonial. The Apinayé do refer to the genitors by descriptive terms (*nipeitxo* and *katortxo*), but also use such terms for their adoptive parents, who are ideally the parallel siblings of their genitors. This usage is a metaphorical form intended to express relations which are otherwise eminently jural and ceremonial in a biological idiom. Since the adoptive parents are jurally responsible for all disputes

in which their adoptive children are involved (especially divorces and rapes, where indemnities are demanded), these relations are transformed, through the descriptive terms *nipeitxe* or *katortxe*, into relations of substance. This metaphor shows that the nuclear family is outside the jural-political arena of Apinayé society but that its relationships are nevertheless fundamental: they imply permanency and consubstantiation, given the force of the metaphor and its significance.

But for the entire terminological system to be understood, it is necessary to move to the study of the ideology underlying the other terms, expecially those related to the transmission of ceremonial roles.

CEREMONIAL RELATIONSHIPS

I have sought to demonstrate above how the Apinayé nuclear family is set up as a group around the notion of common substance. Although the Apinayé ideology of substance is not focused exclusively on the nuclear family, since as the Indians themselves say, "blood is spread throughout the village," the nucleus (or the paradigm of such relations) is the group constituted by a man, a woman, and their children. This group, whose functions are defined in terms of the physical well-being of its members, is an authentic community of common substance.

The ideology which lies behind the terms yet to be examined does not refer to kinship groups, but to social relationships between members of a bilateral kindred. Such relationships imply social groups, but those groups only operate as units during well-defined ritual occasions: they are the ceremonial groups of Apinayé society. In contrast to relations of substance, such bonds are defined through their expression at an eminently public or ritual level. This means that when an Apinayé speaks of such relations and ceremonial units, he is speaking of events involving the collectivity, where the participation of all members is a prerequisite. Such relations and ceremonial groups, however, do not operate in daily life, either as reference groups for political support or as regulators of alliance in Apinayé society. Consistent with this mode of operation, these groups depend for their constitution and continuity on relations of adoption and the transmission of names, rather than on common substance between generations.

Names and the Kolti and Kolre Moieties

All Apinayé receive two sets of names (*itxi*). The first set, usually called "nicknames" or "household names," is received when the individual is born, and is not given ceremonially. A male is called Penguy and a female, Sit or Sire. Other words are generally added to such names in order to distinguish their bearers individually. When this happens, the added word specifies a part of the body, some accident which befell the child, or some other event capable of individualizing him or her. Very often, these names persist for some time, even after the child has grown older and received his second name-set. After marriage, however, such names are only used by the members of his family, and there is no adult Apinayé known in the community as Sit or Penguy. The second set of names is not regarded as composed of nicknames or "household names." On the contrary, such names are formally transmitted, giving their bearers certain rights, ceremonial roles, and/or membership in the Kolti and Kolre moieties.

Apinayé names are not, however, directly bestowed, as are names among the other Gê groups. There are adoptive parents (*pam kaag* and *na kaag*) who adopt the child to be named and then seek a nominator for him or her. Ideally, these adoptive parents are parallel siblings of the genitor and genetrix, but putative or classificatory siblings often establish such relations of adoption. The essential point is that the adopters must be considered same-sex siblings of one of the genitors. These *pam kaag* and *na kaag* then visit a woman who is about to give birth, take her some firewood or some food, and speak of their intention to adopt her child. After this, they become the name-arrangers and acquire the right to protect their *kra kaag* whenever the latter is involved in a conflict (particularly in cases of divorce or defloration). The parents, according to the Apinayé, could not take part in such disputes because they would be overwrought and unable to accept negotiated decisions calmly. Once a child has a *pam kaag* or a *na kaag,* all concerned await a public opportunity for the transmission of names. Such an opportunity generally comes in the summer, which is the ritual season. In 1970, for example, there was such a ceremony, and all the children in the village of São José who had been without formal names received them. The name-giving is carried out with some solemnity either in the house or in the village plaza. Names are bestowed in the village plaza only when they involve expensive rituals or social roles, and these have become obsolete nowadays. The Apinayé call these names *itxi maati* ("great names") (Nimuendajú 1939:24 ff., 1956:21 ff.). At a name transmission, the nominator (male or female) and the adoptive parents of the child walk in procession. The child is held by his adoptive parents, and the nominator, standing in front of him, says: "You who hear me are now going to hear our names.

When you ask something of the *na* or *pam* of this child, you must speak thus: I am going to ask something of the *pam* or *na* of . . ." (there follow the names of the child) . This formula, with minor variations, is used for all name transmissions among the Apinayé. The ceremony emphasizes that adoptive parents are responsible for the social life of the child and at the same time it publicly establishes the child's relationship with the name-giver.

In spite of the intervention of adoptive parents, Apinayé names have the same characteristics as names among the other Timbira: (1) they are given as a set; (2) they have no mystical connotation, as among the Kayapó, where the great names cannot be bestowed on very young children without causing their death (T. Turner 1966:171) ; (3) they are associated with ceremonial groups; (4) the relation between nominator and nominated is ceremonial, and has nothing to do with bonds of common substance; (5) they are related to the ceremonial moieties: they give rights of membership in the Kolti and Kolre moieties; (6) they are transmitted by persons classed as *geti* (see term 5) to persons classed as *tamtxua,* who, if they are men, come to call each other *krã-tum* and *krã-duw* ("old head" and "young head," respectively) ; (7) they establish strongly marked public relationships. All the holders of essential ceremonial offices are called *krã-tum,* as in the initiation of young men.

The Apinayé ideology of names and name-giving is clearly marked by the public aspect of social life in their society. Thus groups of names, which is to say the ceremonial moieties Kolti and Kolre, have nothing to do with political or matrimonial affairs. They effect the organization of Apinayé society via relations and groups which are distinguished and contraposed according to more general principles. While relations of substance incorporate marriage relations and influence the political system (factions are formed according to residential segments and around groups of substance) , relations of nomination and the groups constituted by them (the Kolti and Kolre moieties) refer to the Apinayé cosmic and symbolic order, stressing its integrative and complementary attributes. Thus the names themselves as well as the moieties can be associated with the oppositions sun/moon, winter/summer, men/women, wild/tame animals, and so on. This is an area where behavior is stereotyped and defined rationally through rules which are made by and pertain to the entire social group. The whole area, including the naming relations which determine it, is one where ceremonial ties are engendered, or to use once more Victor Turner's term (1969) , it is an area of *structure.*

"Formal Friends" and the Ipognotxóine and Krenotxóine Moieties

Formal friends (*krã-geti,* masc.; *krã-gedy,* fem.; reciprocal, *pa-krã*) transmit to their younger friends rights of membership in a second pair of ceremonial moieties, Ipognotxóine and Krenotxóine (henceforth referred to as Ipog and Kre). These names signify, respectively, "person of the center or plaza" and "person of the house or periphery." It can therefore be said that the dualism of the Kolti and Kolre moieties is of the diametric type, the emphasis being on the symmetry and complementarity of the two opposing groups; while that of the Ipog/Kre moieties is of the concentric type, with an emphasis on the asymmetry and hierarchy of the relations between the two opposing groups. In accord with this dualism, the Apinayé say that the Ipog are liars, deceivers, and people of little consequence, associating them with the moon, night, rain, woman, and other entities characterized by irregularity and unpredictability, while the Kre are associated with the opposing terms of each opposition: sun, day, dry season, man, and so on.[7]

The rule of recruitment to these ceremonial groups is tied to the bonds of formalized friendship in the following way. As soon as a child is about ten years old, his adoptive parents (*pam kaag* or *na kaag*) choose for him a "formal friend" from whom he receives the insignia of the moiety he will belong to. His *krã-geti* is, according to the rule, always a *pa-krã* of one of his *pam kaag* or *na-kaag,* so that the child ends up in the same ceremonial group as his adoptive parents. These, in turn, transmit their moieties to an adopted son or daughter of one of their *krã-geti,* perhaps the same individual who just transmitted his ceremonial insignia to ego. In an actual instance the procedure was as shown in Figure 1. All the cases I obtained among the Apinayé followed this complex rule. Just as with names, a man can have various formal friends, and there occur cases in which nominators and formal friends are of different sexes, although the ideal is that they be of the same sex.

There is, then, a formal continuity between the recruitment for this second pair of moieties and the connections between a man and his *pa-krã,* on the one hand, and his adoptive son, on the other. The result is that a minimum of two "lines" always exists. One consists of a man and his adopted son, the other of his *pa-krã* and his adopted son. The two lines, as can be seen in Figure 1, trade rights of incorporation into the second pair of moieties.

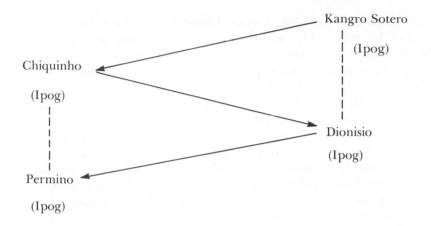

FIGURE 1. The rule by which Apinayé are recruited to ceremonial groups; the arrows indicate relations of *krã-geti/pa-krã,* the dotted lines, relations of adoption, that is, of *pam/kra-kaag*

However, just as with name-giving, so with formal friendship and the recruitment of new members to Ipog and Kre, there is an emphasis on the relationship between adoptive fathers and adoptive sons. The differences between these two relationships are as follows:

1. In formal friendship, "friends" are related by body paint, not proper names.

2. Formal friendship is marked by extreme *piam* and avoidance.

3. In formal friendship the relation between the two friends is from the very beginning one of direct exchange, as when the senior friend makes ornaments for his junior friend and receives a huge meat and manioc pie in return from the representatives *(pam kaag* and *na kaag)* of the latter. They are also responsible for each other at critical moments, such as when one of them wishes to leave the village or is threatened with violence or dies and requires burial.

4. Formal friendship has a mystical aspect. When a formal friend is angry with his partner, he suffers from extreme swelling of the eyes, or even blindness.

5. In formal friendship, relations are established outward in a circle of relatives who make up ego's kindred. With name-giving, the relation is established by reference to ego's own kindred from an internal perspective. Thus the relations of name-giving are categorically fixed (it is always a *geti* who transmits names to a male), while, with formal friendship, the terminology is established *a posteriori.*

Ideologically speaking, formal friendship is the relation most marked by *piam*. The emphasis is on separation, and a formal friend should, therefore, refer to the members of his partner's group of common substance by the terms already mentioned, as "things," or *iprom-ti* (which has sexual connotations). I have argued elsewhere (da Matta 1973) that it was perhaps these aspects of the relationship that caused Nimuendajú to equate these moieties with the names of their decorations and thus to suppose there were four matrimonial groups among the Apinayé. The arguments can be roughly summarized as follows. The names of the four *kiyé* which Nimuendajú took to be marriage classes referred in fact to the moieties I have already mentioned (Ipognotxóine and Krenotxóine) and to items of regalia characteristically associated with them—*krã-o-mbedy* with the Ipognotxóine and *kré'kara* with the Krenotxóine. Nimuendajú mistook the parallelism of the arrangement whereby a man's formal friend is the son of his father's adoptive father and a woman's the daughter of her mother's adoptive mother (see Figure 1) for parallel descent. Finally, he assumed that the strong relationship of *piam* existing between people and their formal friends indicated a tie of affinity, for here, just as in marriage, the relationship is marked by great restraint, and formal friends, just like affines, are always located on "the other side of the village." Although there can be marriage with the children of a *krã-geti*, I found no instances of it. In fact, such a relation would be difficult to maintain, and if it occurred, the formal friends would be transformed into affines and would cease to exchange the services indicated above.

This summary discussion of ceremonial relations is sufficient, I think, to demonstrate that such ties are public, formal, and complementary to the bonds of common substance. The expression of Apinayé dualism in their relationship system is thus not institutionalized in the way familiar to anthropologists. There is no system of exogamous moieties and/or marriage between bilateral cross-cousins. Instead, the dualism is expressed as an opposition between distinct social areas, mediated by persons connected to any given ego in substantially different ways. Thus we have persons related to ego physically and persons tied to ego ceremonially. The first create what I have termed a community of substance, and the second, relations of structure. The first are covered by the terms *na, pam,* and its reciprocal *kra;* the second, by the term *geti-tui* and its recriprocal *tamtxua*. The elucidation of the terminology depends on how such terms and relationships are stressed in each Northern Gê society. However, before passing

TABLE 1. Relations of substance and ceremonial relations among the Apinayé

Relations of substance	Ceremonial relations
Body	Social personality
Mixture, confusion of persons	Integration of persons into discrete groups
Physical union of the sexes	Separation of the sexes
Transmission of internal things: blood and sperm	Transmission of external things: names and ornaments
Groups difficult to separate	Well-defined groups
Groups unequal on the ground	Absolutely equal groups
Groups with political power	Ceremonial groups, with no power
Familiarity	Ceremonialism
Daily life	Ritual life
Continuity	Separation
House	Plaza
Intimacy	*Piam*
Long-cycle exchange	Short-cycle exchange
Restrictions	No restrictions
Community	Structure

on to a more detailed consideration of the terminological structure, let us clarify the relationships examined up to this point. These are shown in Table 1. The oppositions listed in Table 1 could be elaborated, but it should be stressed that such a schema is an abstraction and, although basically correct in terms of Apinayé categories, it is somewhat theoretical. This is so because these oppositions do not indicate the points of contact, of mediation between the spheres which they demarcate. A general interconnection of these two planes is made by the system of relationship terms. Another is accomplished by certain social relations which are structurally located on one side or the other. I can better explain this by means of the genealogical-type diagram shown in Figure 2.

Figure 2 is intended to show, as clearly as possible, the principal areas of Apinayé society, as well as its mediating dimensions and relationships. The areas marked I, II, and III, are as follows:

I. This is the area of the nuclear family, the domestic arena in which social relations are expressed through an ideology of common substance. In a way, this area mediates between all that lies outside the boundaries of Apinayé society (what I call nature) and all that is controlled by its rules (culture or society). This area corresponds topographically to the circle of houses which encloses the village, which is, significantly, a female area, and

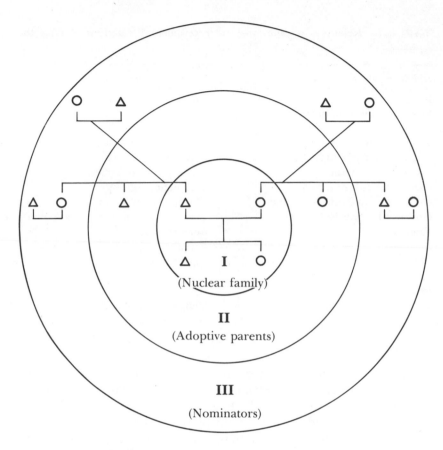

FIGURE 2. Spheres of relationship in Apinayé society

one to which sick persons should be confined. It is here that the body of a child is preliminarily formed and maintained through the alimentary and behavioral restraints practiced by its genitors.

II. This is the area of adoptive parents. In a way, it contrasts with area I, since it is here that the disputes in which ego is involved are mediated. It is here too that an Apinayé starts to extend his network of social ties outward. But this domain also contrasts with area III, since the relationships in II are neither formalized nor ritualized. The sphere of the "name-arrangers" is essentially "legal," but not completely public. From the terminological point of view, there are no differences in the system of reference for persons located here and ego's actual genitors. On the contrary, we have already seen that the former are precisely metamorphosed as "genitors" through the use of descriptive labels. In structural terms, the persons situated here are persons identical with ego's

genitors. In fact, such persons ought to be of the same sex, generation, and substance group as ego's genitors. The only difference
is they do not observe ceremonial restrictions for ego.

III. Ego enters this area through the sponsorship of his name-
givers. The third area is thus represented by his *geti/tui,* in the
same way as areas I and II contain his *pam* and *na.* The paradigmatic representatives of this area are the genitors' cross-sex siblings and ego's grandparents. Here it can be clearly seen that a
shift from one sex to another is equivalent to a shift between
generations. Thus, the cross-uncles and cross-aunts are identified
with the grandparents, and all are united by a common denominator: they are all real or potential name-givers to ego. For all
these relationships there exists some degree of *piam:* the cross-
aunts and cross-uncles have it because they are separated from
ego's genitors, the grandparents because they are two generations
removed. The third area, though, functions as the formal limit
of the Apinayé kindred. And the relationships established therein
are the mediating connections between the domestic sphere and
the rest of the village.

The area of formal friends and of "companions" (*krã-txua*)
cannot be included with these relations, for it is incapable of
genealogical translation. The same is true for the domain of
relatives by marriage.

Terminology and Ideology: A Synthesis

We now have sufficient information to enable us to reexamine
the Apinayé relationship system. An analysis of the ideology of
this system indicates that it contains two different types of expression. The first derives from native ideas concerning the
biology of sexual reproduction and concerns the nuclear family.
The second deals with the fundamental questions of social continuity in Apinayé society and is concerned with personal names,
which indicate membership in ceremonial groups, and with formal
friends, through whom membership in another pair of ceremonial
moieties is acquired. This expression is institutionalized through
exchange and could therefore be called a "sociological" postulate.

Although the Apinayé social system contains both relations
based on biological ties and those based on ceremonial ties, they
are differently weighted according to particular contexts and for
various ends. Any interpretation of the Apinayé relationship
system, then, must necessarily specify such contexts and such
ends, as well as the relationships which typify them. I hope it is
now clear that relations between an individual and his genitors
are characterized in terms of a common substance that serves as

a justification for the categorical obligations extant between members of the nuclear family. In terms of social position and the transmission of status, such an area is neutral, since the genitors contribute only indirectly to the rituals in which their children take part, through their contributions of meat to their own children and by acting as mediators in disputes in which their children are involved. The relations of common substance, in sum, do not operate in the public sphere.

An important relation from the public point of view is that established between an Apinayé and his ceremonial parents. But the relation between *pam kaag/na kaag* and their children has two dimensions. In one of them, *pam kaag* and *na kaag* function as mediators. They do this at the name-giving, where the adoptive parents serve as intermediaries between the nominator and the nominated. The other involves the relation between formal friends and membership in the second set of moieties (Ipognotxoine/Krenotxoine), when the adoptive parents are associated with their children through the indirect transmission of these ceremonial groups. In other words, the *pam kaag* and *na kaag* are eclipsed by the naming relationships and revealed through the bonds of "formal friendship."

These relations, as I have already specified, are those which create structure within Apinayé society. They not only establish highly formalized social bonds, but also transmit rights of incorporation into discrete, well-defined social groups: those of the moiety systems, responsible for all public events in Apinayé society. In sum, the relationships of nomination and of adoptive paternity are the basic modalities for the transmission of status in Apinayé society.

These points are fundamental because they explain some controversial problems in Apinayé ethnography, especially those related to the terminological system. I refer particularly to the position of cross-cousins, who—as the reader must have noted—are not mentioned in the section devoted to terminology.

In the Northern Gê societies, the variable definitions of cross-cousins can be seen relatively clearly, since these are the only terms which oscillate from society to society and even within the same society. All the terminological systems of the Northern Gê possess the same inventory of terms, with only dialectical variations. Thus the eight terms and their respective cognates presented in my list (*pam, na/kra; geti, tui/tamtxua; to/tody*) can be employed without any difficulty to define the same genealogical positions among the Krahó, Krĩkatí, Gaviões, Canela, and Kayapó. But it appears that the Kayapó define cross-cousins so as to produce equations with Omaha features, that is, the matrilateral cross-cousins are classified as *na* and *geti*, while patrilateral cross-cousins are classified as *tamtxua*. Among the Gaviões and Krahó, these positions are defined in such a way as to produce a terminology with Crow features, that is, the *matrilateral* cross-cousins are called *kra* and the *patrilateral* cross-cousins are classified as *pam* and *tui*. Among the Krĩkatí, there are terminological variations for these same positions, except when the cross-cousins are involved in the transmission of names (Lave 1967:197). And variations for these same positions are also encountered among the Krahó, as Melatti has already noted (1967:75).

Variations in cross-cousin terms is thus not unusual among the Northern Gê. Furthermore, it should be stressed that it is only the cross-cousin terms which vary and which are found in differing permutations from society to society. Thus the Kayapó have an Omaha-type terminology, while the Timbira possess a Crow-type terminology. But to adopt this perspective is to assume a completely typological position, especially when we know, as Lévi-Strauss noted over two decades ago (1952; see Lévi-Strauss 1963) that these social systems are based on a common set of institutions which only vary from group to group.

I believe that the resolution of such problems lies in the adoption of two perspectives. First, we should assume that these systems are not anomalies and that their relationship terms are not expressions of different types of institutions. Second, we should study these terminological systems as expressions of ideologies. Thus if the terms for cross-cousins are the oscillating parts of such systems, then it is necessary to study in detail the invariant terms, notably: *geti-tui/tamtxua; pam, na/kra,* which, as we have seen, are expressed in distinct ideologies.

At the risk of repetition, I should like to stress certain points here concerning these sets of terms:

1. In the Apinayé system, *pam* and *na/kra* are important terms because they influence the relations of formal friendship, determine membership in a second set of moieties, and also regulate name-giving.

2. The terms *geti-tui/tamtxua* are, however, the key to the Crow-Omaha features found among the Northern Gê. Such categories already blend consecutive generations, since *geti/tui* designate both grandparents and cross-aunts and cross-uncles. It is clear that such terms can be interpreted as a consequence of uxorilocal residence (which separates brothers from sisters), but it is not in such a way that the Apinayé interpret them. Indeed, they state that the opposition of sexes is axiomatic in their ideological

system, so that men and women have their specific places in the village, respectively, in the center of the community and at the periphery. Besides, women are naturally different from men: they are heavier, have more blood, are weaker, are less sociable, and are equated with the moon, summer, night, hypocritical behavior, and so forth. In Apinayé society, therefore, the sexes are rigidly separated. In accord with this pattern, each sex has its place in the village, and since the plaza is the men's domain, men can only retreat to reside in the houses either of their mothers or of their wives. Uxorilocal residence is, therefore, as Maybury-Lewis indicates,[8] a fitting solution, given this premise.

3. In the system of interpersonal relations, such a sexual distinction comes out clearly in the ideology of *piam* (respect, shame), which permeates the relations between elements representing differentiated aspects of Apinayé society. Thus there should be *piam* between a man and a woman even when they are uterine siblings; in the same way, there should be *piam* between persons situated in different age-classes. Passage through the age-classes among the Apinayé (as among all the Gê) is marked by elaborate rituals, seclusion, and stipulated diets. The motives for these rituals are clear: it is necessary to separate boys from women, from domestic life and their communities of substance. This being so, to change one's age-class (or to change one's generation) is equivalent to the separation of boys from their sisters and mothers. To put it another way, such changes are equivalent to the separation between the sexes, which should be completely effected after a boy's initiation and marriage.

Now, this equivalence is clearly expressed in the Apinayé terminological system by the equations of cross-aunts and cross-uncles with grandparents. In the same way, this equivalence is expressed in the vocative terms for brother/sister, in which the substitution for *tõ/tõdy* of *idpugkwa* and *idkambu* underlines the sexual difference and the respect that should obtain between them. Further, while the formal terms for elder brother and younger brother refer only to physical size (*tõ-ti* and *tõ-re*), the terms for opposite-sex siblings are morphologically much more differentiated. Thus siblings of the opposite sex from the genitors, as well as the parents of the genitors, are separated from the substance group by sex and age. It can even be said that the establishment of the nuclear family is correlated with this separation, which is completed through an exchange of relationships. This point needs to be amplified.

A nuclear family is only completed by the arrival of children.

Via children, bonds of adoption are established with same-sex siblings and ties of nomination are generated with opposite-sex siblings or with parents (the grandparents of the child). Now, each of these ties is marked by ceremonial transactions, which increase in quantity, formality, and volume as one moves from relatives of ego's same sex to those of a contrasting sex and generation. But as these ceremonial bonds are established, the ties of common substance between such persons and ego are broken. Indeed, relations of adoption, name-giving, and formal friendship are defined as different from those based on blood. As a result, when a brother gives his names to his sister's son, he acknowledges that his sister's substance group (her nuclear family) is a sociological fact. So at the same time as he severs the bonds of common substance that he has with her, he substitutes ceremonial ties, through his nephew, who receives his name. The same thing happens to women, when a father's sister transmits her names to her brother's daughter. When grandparents serve as name-givers, the situation is the same. They can bestow names because the generational distance equates them with opposite-sex siblings of their grandchildren's parents. Thus all persons situated in these genealogical positions are likely to exchange ties of common substance for ceremonial bonds, and all are the potential name-givers for any ego. Male Apinayé are taking such matters into account when they say that sisters' children (*itamtxua*) are farther away than brother's children.

As a corollary, the Apinayé consider what we call incest a transformation. They do not have a word for incest, and to express such a relation they must use circumlocutions. For example, if a man copulates with his mother, the expression is just this: *nã na ni* (where *ni* = to copulate). Actually, to copulate with relatives with whom one shares a common substance is to confuse two sets of relations and two entire social fields which are totally separate. It is not possible to maintain two such relationships at once because they imply different and opposed obligations, such as gift and trade, community and structure, body and social personality. To confound them invites the risk of becoming a being who transcends negatively the boundaries of human society: a monster, a "thing" or an animal (*mebo*). In a myth in which boys copulate with their sisters (Nimuendajú 1939:182 and 1956:136), they are transformed into birds, beings which in Apinayé taxonomy are very distant from humans. In cases I was told of, two men turned into monstrous animals, both with the characteristics of dogs. In the same way and according to the same logic, divorce involves an indemnification of the woman and her relatives of substance by the husband and his adopted parents, which amounts to a "reverse exchange."

It can be said, then, that all persons located outside the nuclear family are real or potential cross-relatives; they are marginal persons in terms of common substance and can be tied to ego by ceremonial bonds. Such relations have a component of identity (the bestowal of something shared, such as names) and a component of affinity (the short-cycle exchange of something different: services and food in the case of affines; blood and sperm in the case of spouses, who are transformed into relatives of substance after marriage has been established; moiety insignia and paint styles in the case of formal friends).

The continuum of Apinayé social relations is shown in Figure 3. Relationship terms are not used in area I, or rather, such terms are empty of any formal content. In area II, the terms *pam, na,* and *kra* imply relations of of "sociological paternity"; in area III, we find relations of name-giving (the terms *geti-tui/tamtxua*), paradigms of incorporation into ceremonial groups and of formal positions in the system. And finally, the fourth area is that in which distant relations are transformed into relations of substance, or are maintained at a distance. The former occurs with affines, the latter with formal friends.

To return to the terminology: the analysis of the invariant terms in the Apinayé system indicates a fusion of generations. The terms for grandparents and the terms for cross-aunts and cross-uncles are the same. What might, therefore, be the "generative" possibilities of such a system?

It is clear that if grandparents are equated with cross-aunts and

(−) (+) → Ceremonial exchange

Nuclear family	Genitors' same-sex siblings and ego's same-sex siblings	Cross-uncles, cross-aunts, and grandparents	Affines and formal friends
I	II	III	IV

Common substance
Gifts
(+) ← (−)

FIGURE 3. The continuum of Apinayé social relations

cross-uncles, then the cross-cousins can be classified in various ways:

$$geti = tui \qquad\qquad geti = tui$$

$$geti = tui \qquad pam = na \qquad geti = tui$$

$$tui \quad pam \qquad ego \qquad geti \quad na$$

or

na geti   pam tui

Whichever of these solutions, with its respective reciprocals (which, of course, eliminate the corresponding terms for the cousins on the opposite side), is adopted, it operates by ignoring the principle of generation. Thus the system has Crow-Omaha features, a fact which shows that the invariant equations of Northern Gê relationship systems are automatically capable of producing such features. There are, in other words, two fundamental principles which permeate these systems: the separation of the sexes and the formal equivalence between a sexual change and a generational remove. The cross-cousin terminology shows the ways in which these principles are put into effect, and it is this which accounts for its variations.

Among the Apinayé, however, we find *all* the terminological possibilities presented above. I made a special study of cross-cousin terms during my fieldwork and used photography in the investigation, but even so, I encountered the same variations. It made no difference whether the system of terms was presented abstractly or concretely (in genealogy) to the informants. It varied in the same way. In fact, in the Brazilian edition of Nimuendajú's book (1956), an edition "revised, annotated and corrected" by the author (Nimuendajú 1956:viii), there is an exact reproduction of one of the terminological solutions presented above:

FZD = *tamtxua*		MBD = *tui-re*
	and	
FZS = *tamtxua*		MBS = *krã-tum* (= *geti*)

This would be an "Omaha" equation, very close to the terminology found among the Kayapó by Turner and Bamberger. The equations for cross-cousins present some difficulties, since we have two siblings being designated by terms that, in the first and second ascending generations, are used for affinal relations (since WBW, MM, FM = *tui-re* and FF, FM, and FZH = *krã-tum* (*geti*). But although these equations are anomalous, they are not unique in South America, for a similar terminological system is found among the Siriono of Bolivia (Holmberg 1960:53). Such a use of the system among the Apinayé expresses an emphasis on the nuclear family as a unit of substance. Ego's nuclear family assumes preeminence and thus produces an Omaha terminology by virtue of the reciprocal terms.

The Apinayé, however, are also quite capable of producing the symmetrically inverse equations, such as:

$$FZD = tui \qquad MBD = kra$$
$$\text{and}$$
$$FZS = pam \qquad MBS = kra$$

These amount to a terminological solution with Crow features. Such equations would also be consistent with the Apinayé system, but would stress the relations between nominator and nominated. Thus, the MB = ego, and therefore, MBS and MBD would be *kra*.

The third possibility would be that in which the naming relations of women took precedence over the male ones. This happens occasionally among the Krahó, where specific naming relations are taken into account and acquire great importance (Melatti 1970). Such a solution would indeed be normal if the principle of sexual opposition were unresolved in the terminology, and naming relations between men were given precedence. In fact, if this practice did not occur, the terminological system would be split down the middle according to sex, with one usage for women and another for men. This solution would be correct in a formal account which assumed that the Northern Gê were characterized by some parallel transmission of social status. This is, incidentally, the solution proposed by Lounsbury and Scheffler, at least in the preliminary versions of their study of Northern Gê terminological systems (Scheffler 1969). It happens, however, that the terminology is used by the Northern Gê for the ideological resolution of natural paradoxes. Thus the male side always takes precedence, even among the Apinayé, where the terminological solution is as much female as male oriented, with no patterns of variation that correlate with sexual differences. This point is crucial because although, formally speaking, the opposition between the sexes is equivalent to a generational change or remove, it is only men who are subject to such changes. Women do not change age-classes and do not have rites of passage or initiation. In fact, the female sex is considered immutable in its essence, while male nature changes as a man ages. While there is a complementary opposition between the sexes, the male sex gains preeminence. As a result, female names do not acquire the power to influence the terminological system *qua* system. But the transmission of male names is the focal point of terminological usage among the Krahó and Gaviões. Among the Krĩkati, the naming terminology takes precedence over the terms for prior relationships.

Among the Apinayé, such variations are a function of the role of the *krã-tum* (name-givers) and of the *pam kaag* and *na kaag* as transmitters of status within the group. When an Apinayé stresses the relationship between himself and his name-giver, the system is used in Crow fashion. When, however, the *pam kaag* or *na kaag* is stressed, the system assumes Omaha characteristics. This was confirmed in the field in the course of various interviews. The Kayapó case could be explained by postulating the ceremonial preeminence of the *pam kaag*, who actually introduces a boy into the men's house. Thus while naming relationships are essentially public among the Timbira, among the Kayapó these relations are activated by the adopted father, who mediates between a boy and the men's house. It is this group among the Kayapó which replaces the ceremonial moieties of the Timbira. Among the Apinayé, however, both names and adoptive paternity are important, a fact which explains why the system permits a variety of usages.

Conclusion

The terminological system of the Apinayé appears eminently logical if we view it as the expression of a set of ideas concerning the nature of social relations and of human physiology. This paper has, in fact, shown that terminological equations which override generational contrast can be produced by a system which has nothing to do with unilineal descent groups, or with any strict sociological principle ordering all of Apinayé social structure, as would be the case if a rule of parallel descent were postulated. We have seen that such a system can be satisfactorily elucidated in terms of two fundamental principles: the opposition of the sexes and the passage from one generation to another.

The Apinayé express the opposition between the sexes in biological terms and do the same with generational differences. Every time that there is an encounter between sexes or some passage between generations, a mediator is recruited and a terminological change takes place. In the case of the sexes, such a mediation is accomplished through the rites of passage, which begin at marriage and reach their climax with the arrival of children, when rites of abstinence are carried out to maintain the well-weing of the entire social group involved. These relations create a biologically defined area and thus weight the ideology of the society in a specific fashion. In the case of generational passage, there are again mediators and again a clear definition of specific social relations, couched in terms of the exchange of names, ornaments, and services—or, in other words, ceremonially defined.

The terminological system itself is the instrument which unites these separate domains, which are expressed in differing but complementary ideologies. To use the terminological system is thus to resolve the contradiction between "given" relations and "constructed" relations: between relations of common substance and ceremonial relations. Each Northern Gê group takes a specific institutional direction for this resolution.

The Kayapó follow a pattern where men assume ritual and political preeminence, with the institutionalization of the men's house in the middle of the village. They introduce a boy into the men's house through an adoptive father, with the result that the men become internally divided into groups which are equivalent to symbolic patrilineages, since the fundamental relationship is not between a genitor and his son, but between a fictive father and his adopted son. It is a *pater* (and not a *genitor*) who mediates between the substance group and the political-ritual domain of Apinayé society, and this practice preserves the domestic field in symbolic isolation. But such an equilibrium, as Terence Turner's research shows, is tenuous. Among the Kayapó, there is a high level of aggression that reveals a contamination of the domestic sphere by the ritual sphere. It is equally possible that many beliefs concerning biological paternity and the conception of children might be a function of this paradox of having a pater and a genitor enacted by two separate persons, and a men's house which immediately channels all disputes into the terms of *pam-kra* relations.

The Shavante case contains the same Kayapó model in a more developed form. The Shavante have patrilineal descent groups, and the entire ritual system is influenced by the relations between a man and his father and, consequently, by the relations between brothers-in-law. The sexes are also separated among the Shavante, each having its symbolic place in the village, but the system is operated by stressing the bonds between father and son, not by separating the genitor from the father. Among the Shavante, therefore, the biological and domestic relationship is also the political-ritual relationship. For this reason, names among the Shavante are expressions of personal relations between MB and ZS, and the relationship is biologically determined. That is, the genealogical position of the MB is unique in the system, being covered by a single term.

In the Timbira case, it appears that the opposition between the sexes and the generations is used less drastically. Thus the most important mechanism for the creation of structural ties (names) is perfectly symmetrical: perferentially, women receive names from the paternal aunt (FZ) and men from the maternal uncle (MB). The same thing happens in the domestic area, in which pater and genitor are totally discrete figures, each one operating in a clearly defined area of the social system. In addition, the figure of the name-giver assumes prominence. In accord with the separation of the domains, he is determined categorically but not genealogically. In other words, while the mother's brother is preferred, the name-giver is not prescribed. Similarly, while there is a discrete and clearly defined group of common substance (the nuclear family), there is also a series of social relationships potentially capable of establishing structural relations among men: MB-ZS, MF-DS, FF-SS, and so on. Name-givers are lumped into a single category, in the same way that members of the nuclear family are lumped together. The domestic and ritual planes are balanced and rigidly separated. As a result, the opposition between sexes and generations is crucial in those groups, where rites of passage between generations (and sexes) are strongly elaborated symbolically. The equilibrium between the sexes among the Timbira is shown in the balance of political forces in their villages, where factionalism is less virulent than among the Shavante and Kayapó. It is also shown in the segregation of ritual from domestic life, as if they were two faces of the same coin.

The terminological subterfuge that produces Crow-Omaha equations can thus be a result of various ways of resolving such paradoxes. These appear all the more paradoxical since the relations between the sexes are well balanced and the separation between the domestic and ceremonial spheres is clearly established. Among the Krahó, the paradigm of conciliation between the sexes or between the domestic and ritual domains in the terminology is the *name-giver*. The system in use thus depends on the relations between nominator and nominated influencing the relations formed around the substance group. Hence, the Crow terms for cross-cousins. The Krĩkatí adopt the same solution, but stress naming even more, for without naming terms the cross-cousins are not precisely defined. Among the Kayapó, the domestic figure who emerges in the ceremonial area is the adoptive father. Thus the system takes on an Omaha cast and does not contain variations in the cross-cousin terms. Such variations are found only among the Krīkatí and the Krahó, where the name-giving relation is important but where it can be argued that the variations are exceptions to the rule. Finally, among the Apinayé, the two figures of *pam kaag* and name-giver are both sociologically crucial. From this fact derives, as we have seen, the oscillations in the system of terms.

These considerations are important because they do not appear to be uniquely characteristic of Timbira societies. Schneider and Roberts (1956:15) found them in their reanalysis of the Zuñi. Sol Tax (1937) observed Crow-Omaha variations among the Cochiti and even outside North America. Furthermore, Marvin Harris points out (1968:586) that such systems do oscillate. With the exception of the Bathonga, mentioned by Harris, what might be the common denominator of such societies? It is obvious that it is not just the form of transmission of jural-political status, since here we find groups with presumed matrilineages and patrilineages and bilateral societies (the Northern Gê). At first glance, what these societies have in common is an elaborate ceremonialism, a division between the domestic field and the ritual field,[9] and an accentuated tendency to proliferate ceremonial moieties. It is, then, a viable hypothesis to say that Crow-Omaha terminologies are ways of resolving paradoxes encountered by social systems in which social fields are rigidly divided. Such fields can express, as in the Gê case, an axiomatic division of the sexes (and generations), or just social groups with essentially different functions and relations. They would be integrated through internal divisions and by not allowing a relationship important in one domain to contaminate another domain. Thus if the genitor is basic to the domestic area, in the ceremonial sphere the sponsor of a child would be a ceremonial father (or some other personage) coming from another group and related to the initiate by another sociological principle. The paradigm of these societies would be the one already outlined by Kroeber in *Zuñi Kin and Clan* (1917: 185). It is worth noting that in this work Kroeber constructed a model for the Zuñi in which the society is interpreted as possessing a multilayered system, integrated by its relationship system. To this model, I would add that the relationship terms express, in their marginal areas (the area of cross-cousins), the different ways of integrating the system's internal divisions. In these systems, however, the genealogical distortion of the Crow or Omaha type is a result of some mediating relation between the domestic and ceremonial fields, which implies an identification of two persons situated in diverse and rigidly defined domains. Such a model is apparently similar to a unilineal system of integration. However, it is necessary to differentiate between a type of social continuity realized through an identification of pater and genitor (or between mater and genetrix), as in unilineal systems, and the type of continuity achieved by the Northern Gê, where the relation between the domestic and ritual fields is mediated by a person clearly distinct from the genitor. Although the formal result might be the same, since a single principle could be seen to operate in both types of systems, the ideologies of each type are sufficiently different to establish a crucial ethnographic distinction between them. I would say, therefore, that the continuity in unilineal systems is obtained through a continuum (Scheffler 1966) ordered in temporal terms (closer to or more distant from a common ancestor), while continuity among the Northern Gê is obtained through substitution. In these societies, a person assumes a social mask from another and substitutes for him jurally and and ritually. There is no obvious idea of continuum, but there is a clear notion of duality, even when substitutions over a long period are involved. For this reason, the Timbira do not exhibit any ideology related to ancestors or demonstrate any preoccupation with remote forefathers. And in the same way, the bonds which relate nominator and nominated, or as in the Kayapó and Apinayé cases, a *pam kaag* and a *kra kaag*, are typically dyadic relationships, where one substitutes for the other. This is an expression of the exchange between bonds of substance and ritual bonds that permeates these societies.

To confirm my hypothesis, it would be necessary to reanalyze the North American Crow-Omaha systems, viewing their terms not as expressions of rules without sociological content, but as expressions of ideology. This is what I have tried to do for the Apinayé system. To do the same for the Pueblos, however, is another story.

THE KAYAPÓ

THE KAYAPÓ (also occasionally known as the Northern Kayapó to distinguish them from an unrelated and now extinct people to the south who were called Kayapó in colonial times) now number about fifteen hundred people in seven or eight communities. They once inhabited a huge territory of about 130,000 square kilometers in what is now southern Pará and northern Mato Grosso. They certainly had intermittent contacts with settlers and travelers by the beginning of the nineteenth century, but there is little reliable information about their numbers and precise whereabouts at that time. Coudreau, whose estimate is probably the most accurate, calculated that there were about five thousand Kayapó in the late nineteenth century (1897:206). Their modern descendants derive from the Xikrin and the Gorotire groups. There are two villages of Xikrin, located respectively on tributaries of the Xingú and the Tocantins. The remaining communities all derive from the Gorotire group and are to be found between the Iriri and the Araguaia rivers in southern Pará or within the Parque Indígena do Xingú (the Xingú Indian Reservation) in Mato Grosso.

The Kayapó had a warlike reputation historically and probably expelled or exterminated other Indian groups in the area they controlled. They certainly clashed with the Mundurucú to the west of them and were feared by the tribes on the upper Xingú and the Tapirapé to the south and southeast. Until twenty years ago, their villages were still largely inaccessible to Brazilians, though air-strips had been built in this region and the Indian Protection Service maintained two posts with the tribe. Now the construction of the Trans-Amazon Highway system and the attendant immigration into their area has hemmed in the Kayapó and sharply curtailed their transhumant way of life.

Traditionally, Kayapó villages dispersed in small groups for hunting and gathering during the dry season, which lasts from about late April to early October. People would come together again for the first rains and remain in the village throughout the wet season, which was the time for agriculture and ceremonies. Nowadays, the Kayapó are cut off from the territories over which they used to travel and so they have expanded their horticultural activities, with the result that gardening has become less seasonal. Furthermore, the Kayapó are now accustomed to the manufactured goods and medical services which they can only obtain from the Brazilians, and so they tend increasingly to remain close to the sources of supply for these items and to engage in activities which will bring them some cash income, however modest.

129

4 | Exit and Voice in Central Brazil: The Politics of Flight in Kayapó Society[1]

Joan Bamberger

Introduction

THE FACILITY WITH WHICH Kayapó villages dispatch exiles, expel dissident groups, and divide into annual trekking parties indicates a flexibility in their community organization. This tendency may well have deceived earlier scholars, most of whom characterized central Brazil's Gê-speaking Indians as nomadic hunters and gatherers. Whatever wanderlust may once have motivated movements among the Kayapó (and perhaps other Gê groups), it is important to note that today the seasonal dislocations of the Kayapó would rarely place much distance between village and trekking camps, since it is proximity to the gardens for extra supplies of manioc and other staple crops that is usually the consideration in choosing a campsite. It is quite probable that distances even in prehistoric times rarely if ever exceeded the few days it might take to effect a hasty return from dry season camp to rainy season village. Only occasionally, and under specific circumstances, were rainy season villages totally abandoned, and new settlements initiated elsewhere. In no real sense, therefore, could the Kayapó be designated as true nomadic hunter-gatherers. For a more comprehensive argument against the depiction of the Gê as nomadic hunter-gatherers, see Bamberger 1971.

No doubt the lack of any recognized territorial limits and the absence of strictures on individual residential choices may have contributed to the prevalent view that the Kayapó were once nomadic. A review of the historical sources on the Kayapó of Para and Mato Grosso gives an indication, albeit sketchy, of village size, together with some of the reasons for their dispersals over the past hundred years. Reports from nineteenth-century explorers and missionaries depict internal dissensions and conflicts which ultimately led to the breakup of Kayapó villages.

Similar factional disputes persist today, although village fission is controlled in principle by the presence of the National Indian Foundation (FUNAI), formerly the Indian Protection Service.

At present, there are eight Kayapó villages located on approximately 130,000 square kilometers of land most accurately characterized as an ecological zone which is transitional between the *hiléia*, or cloud forest of the Amazon, and the central Brazilian *planalto*. Exact data for several bands which do not maintain regular contact with Brazilian settlements is not available, although approximate locations and to some extent numbers can be known from information supplied by immigrants and refugees residing in established villages. A head count of the three villages I visited and a rough estimate of the remaining five villages plus that of the unsettled bands gives a total rounded figure for the Kayapó of about fourteen hundred (see Table 1). This figure would represent a substantial reduction from the three to four thousand Pau d'Arco Kayapó reportedly encountered by Frei Gil Vilanova in 1896 (Audrin 1947:130). It is, however, improbable that Vilanova met anywhere near that number, because in the following year his countryman Henri Coudreau (1897:206) reported fifteen hundred for the same group. This latter estimate, based on an actual count of one village and derived from information given to Coudreau by Kayapó informants, may be more accurate than the earlier figures.

In general, the size of aboriginal settlements in central Brazil is small, with village populations ranging between 25 and 300 individuals. The relatively tiny size of these communities has led anthropologists to speculate about the kinds of limitations placed

TABLE 1. Estimates of Kayapó populations in 1966

Population	Number
Xikrin	
Itacayunas	80
Bacajá (Bemontire)	150
Gorotire	
Gorotire, Rio Fresco (including 34 Xikrin)	268
Kubenkranken, Riozinho	280
Kôkraymôrô, Xingu	80
Baú (Kararaô, Mẽkranoti)	90
Txukahamae	
Mẽtuktire (Bebgogoti), Iriri	250
Porori (dispersed 1970)	169
Total	1,367

on population growth which could account for the diminutive size of these groupings, especially when one considers the extensive tracts of land available to them. It was proposed by Meggers, first in 1954 and more recently in 1971, that an inhospitable tropical forest environment and a Stone Age technology were probably the major factors limiting the size of Amazonian populations. Carneiro (1961:27), disagreeing with Meggers, pointed to the existence of untapped natural resources, which if properly utilized could support populations far more numerous that those which exist now or have existed in the past, and suggested that instead a permissive environment, the absence of territorial restrictions, and the lack of strong political leadership were responsible for the pattern of village dispersals he reported for the Kuikuru Indians of central Brazil. The difference in the hypotheses of Meggers and Carneiro centered on the importance which each ascribed to the natural environment in the determination of village size. Carneiro, in fact, suggested that more consideration be given to certain social and political factors, unrelated to subsistence, which have led villages to fission. This paper takes up that suggestion, and in attempting to account for the small size of settlements, uses the theoretical concepts developed in Albert O. Hirschman's recent book *Exit, Voice, and Loyalty: Responses to Decline in Firms, Organizations, and States* (1970).

Histories of Village Fission

According to Coudreau's (1897:206) informants, four groups of Kayapó—the Pau d'Arco, Gorotire, Xikrin, and Purukaru—had split from a single ancestral village as a result of a disagreement among themselves. Today the Pau d'Arco are extinct, and there is some disagreement about whether there are any surviving Purukaru. There are now two villages of Xikrin, and Gorotire has thus far spawned eight settlements, not all of which still exist or merit the claim to village status. Records of Kayapó dispersals suggest that villages did not break up all at once, but that the process of village fission was a continual one occurring sporadically throughout their history. This tendency to fractionate continues among groups which have only recently been contacted by Brazilians, with the result being a reduction in village populations.

Division occurs usually over a question of the group's future alliances. Dissension about matters of policy, whether to remain independent of Brazilian national society for example, or whether to abandon their forest outpost in favor of some kind of regularized association with Brazilians, frequently makes for a divided community, with some members choosing to move to the "attraction post" set up by agents of the FUNAI, while others, preferring to remain in their "wild" aboriginal state, withdraw further into the forests of central Brazil. One motivation for joining forces with Brazilians is the anticipation that the contact will be beneficial. The flow of manufactured goods and medical services which the Kayapó have come to expect from friendly associations with non-Indians serves first to attract and then to bind them to government posts. The expectation of good relations with Brazilians also places a premium on a peaceful coexistence with them, and in general has been a deterrent to the renewal of any hostile activities.

Native accounts of village schisms document a long-standing pattern of factionalism and feuding among Kayapó males. Informants have claimed that the collective duels which preceded most village splits were usually fought over a woman. As far as the facts can be established, the separation of the Mẽkranoti group from the ancestral village of Gorotire (circa 1900), and later that of the Gorotire from the Kubenkranken (1936), the Kôkrâymorô from the Kubenkranken (1940), and the Mẽtuktire from the Mẽkranoti (1950) are said to have been precipitated by quarrels between men over the adulterous liaisons of their women.[2] The fact that these disputes were almost always settled collectively raises a suspicion that adultery, a not uncommon occurrence in Kayapó communities, was only made the excuse for a battle, while the underlying cause for it is to be sought in the existing conflicts between male associative groups. The Helen of Troy theory of war, so readily proffered by the Kayapó, while providing them with an apparently reasonable account of village subdivision, appears to deflect them from the true causes of division. A study of Kayapó political organization reveals the fundamental source of their divisiveness to be a function of their diffuse system of political authority.

Initiation into Political Life

Kayapó informants describe the locus of village politics in the old village as divided between two men's houses (*ngà*), the one eastern and the other western, which, tradition has it, faced each other across a central ceremonial plaza. Given the frequency of village fission, I assume that the village with two men's houses, although the stated ideal, presented a potentially explosive political situation, which may account for the fact that there have been no reports of villages containing two men's houses since 1936.

The *ngà*, or men's house,[3] serves the Kayapó as both meeting house and council chamber for all adult men of the village, and as the sleeping place for unmarried men and boys. *Ngà* membership is divided into societies (*tchêt*), of which there are usually two, and sometimes more. It is only at the birth of his first child that a man accedes automatically to full adult status in the *tchêt*, to which he first gained entrance at the close of his initiation ceremony. Until that time, his membership in the men's house is as a *mēnōrōnure*, or initiated young adult male. This stage is one of preliminary training for a later active membership in one of the mature men's associations (*tchêt*). As junior members of the men's house, *mēnōrōnure* from time to time may challenge the senior authority of the *mēkrare* in such sporting events as wrestling and field hockey. This structural opposition is also displayed in village rituals, through singing and dancing, and in periodic spouse exchanges.[4] Otherwise, the *mēnōrōnure* remain subordinate to the men of the *mēkrare* age-grade.

The political affiliations of the Kayapó are organized on a system of non-kin-based corporate groups founded on a hierarchically structured system of age-grades. All males and females are classified from birth to death in a series of age groups, which, with the exception of the oldest and youngest grades, are segregated by sex and arranged by chronological age (see Table 2). Kayapó age divisions, however, do not constitute uniform classifications based

TABLE 2. Kayapó age categories

Male	Approximate age span	Female
mēprire	1–4	*mēprire*
mēbokti ngàydure	4–8	*mēprīnti*
mēokre mēgōrōmānōrō	8–12	*mēkurêrêre*
mēintùkre	initiates 12–16	*mēkraytùk*
mēnōrōnure	12–18	*mēkraytùk*
mēkrare	18–45	*mēkrare*
mēkrapuyn	people with one child	*mēkrapuyn*
mēkrakramti	people with many children	*mēkrakramtī*
mēbêngête	over 45	*mēbêngête*
	people with grandchildren	

on age homogeneity, such as those of their Gê neighbors, the Shavante or Ramkókamekra. They are, instead, composed of individuals whose physical growth cycles may be only temporarily in phase, and who pass through a series of named age-grades as a result of the occurrence of an individual biological event (such as first menstruation, the birth of a first child, or the birth of a first grandchild). Progression, or promotion from a junior to a senior age-grade, is thus not automatic, but contingent on biological status, which is measured in terms of either physical development or number of offspring produced.

Promotion from one age category to the next is accompanied by rituals of transition which stress kinship as the major criterion for the allocation of ritual roles. In the case of the children's name-transmission rites and the initiation ceremonies for boys, the ties between noncoresident kin are revitalized in village-wide celebrations which bring together members of a cognatic kin group (*ombikwa*) who otherwise would appear to share no common set of functions. Indeed, the principal function of the *ombikwa* is ceremonial, although interactions of individual *ombikwa* in behavioral settings other than those formalized for ritual occasions can and do occur.

No Kayapó word exists for family or kin group other than *ombikwa*, which refers to a nonlocalized group of bilaterally extended relations. *Ombikwa* is the term used to refer to "my own people," or all those individuals whom ego recognizes and calls by a relationship term (see Table 3). Relationship terms are applied to many persons who are neither kin nor affines, strictly speaking, but who may be adoptive or fictive relations. For an outside observer, it is quite impossible to distinguish between relatives by blood and those by marriage, on the one hand, and relatives by adoption, on the other. When pressed to do so, however, the Kayapó will distinguish "those born from the same womb," half-siblings born of different mothers or fathers, and putative kin. All of these relatives who are considered some kind of *ombikwa* are terminologically differentiated from nonkin, who are called *mẽbaitebm*, "people to one side (or outside) of my own people."[5]

The Kayapó *ombikwa* is an "occasional kin group" in the sense specified by Murdock (1960:5). No formal obligations exist between kindred members aside from the rights and duties manifest during the celebrations of the rites of passage of one of the group's members. And since the transmission of social statuses from senior generation to junior generation is accomplished through the joint activity of one's cross-sex collaterals, the major

136 • *Joan Bamberger*

TABLE 3. Kaypó relationship terminology

	Kin Terms of Reference
Male ego	
1. *ngêt*	men of second ascending generation, uterine male descendant of *ngêt* and *kwatuy*, FZH
2. *kwatuy*	women of second ascending generation, FZ, wife of *ngêt*
3. *bam*	agnatic male descendant of *ngêt* and *kwatuy*, husband of *nã*
4. *nã*	uterine female descendant of *ngêt* and *kwatuy*, wife of *bam*
5. *kamu*	male descendant of *bam* and *nã*, male sibling
6. *kanikwoy*	female descendant of *bam* and *nã*, female sibling
7. *kra*	own descendant, descendant of *kamu*
8. *tabdjuò*	descendant of *kra*, descendant of *kanikwoy*, FZS, FZD
Female ego	
1–6.	same as male ego
7. *kra*	own descendant, descendant of *kanikwoy*, FZS, FZD
8. *tabdjuò*	descendant of *kra*, descendant of *kamu*
	Affinal Terms
Male ego	
9. *prõn*	wife (W)
10. *'ùpayn*	wife of *kra* and *tabdjuò*, BW, WZ
11. *'ùdjuò*	husband of *kra* and *tabdjuò*, ZH
12. *'umrê*	WB
13. *'ùpayndjuò*	WM
14. *'umrêngêt*	WF
Female ego	
11. *'ùdjuò*	husband of *kra and tabdjuò*, HB
12. *'ùmrê*	HZ
13. *'ùpayndjuò*	HM
14. *'umrêngêt*	HF
15. *miedn*	husband (H)
16. *wóy*	wife of *kra* and *tabdjuò*, BW

Source: Data are after Terence S. Turner, Social structure and political organization among the Northern Cayapo, Ph.D. diss., Harvard University 1966:xxiv–xxvi.

responsibility of the life-cycle rituals is seen to be deflected from the parental pair to their cross-sex siblings. Thus *ngêt* ("mother's brother") and *kwatuy* ("father's sister"), instead of *bam* ("father") and *nã* ("mother"), play the leading ritual roles in the drama of young Kayapó lives (cf. da Matta on the Apinayé, Melatti on the Krahó, and Lave on the Kríkatí in this volume; see also Bamberger 1974).

In the initiation ceremonies which occur at the threshold between the age categories of *mẽôkre* and *mẽnõrõnure* for boys, and
between the female categories of *mẽkurêrêre* and *mẽkraytuk,* the
initiates are assigned ceremonial guardians or companions known
as *krabdjuò.* These individuals are nonkin whose formal connection to their wards' fathers and mothers is "patrilineally" inherited (the only such relationship which exists among the
Kayapó). Parental concerns are thus the delegated responsibility
of substitutes who, in taking charge publicly of the initiation
rites, seem to annul the crucial early familial ties of the initiates.
Although the termination of dependency on the natal family is a
long drawn-out affair, beginning with the ceremonial transmission
of names to children between the ages of two to four, and cul-
minating in initiation rites some eight to ten years later, it is the
period of initiation which serves as the watershed between childhood and adulthood, between the private and public domains.

The attainment of adulthood for males is signaled by the twin
possibilities of procreation and politics, whereas female initiation,
a much more abbreviated rite than that performed for males,
heralds only incipient motherhood and marriage to the child's
father. Women, excluded from the obligations, pressures, and
responsibilities of any corporate group membership as these are
seen to apply to men, have a nonexistent role in formal village
politics. Newly initiated *mẽnõrõnure,* however, are first introduced
into one of the men's associations (*tchêt*) at the close of their
initiation period by a *bam kà'àk,* a substitute or "false father,"
who leading his young charge by the hand takes him to his own
tchêt's sitting place within the men's house. As a new member of
the *mẽnõrõnure* age-grade, however, the young man does not become an active member of his *bam kà'àk*'s *tchêt* at this time. In
fact, his commitment to a *tchêt* is only settled after he marries and
his wife bears him a child. He has then become a *mẽkrare.*

The assignation of a stranger, or nonkinsman, as "false" or substitute "father" for the introduction of the novice into the life
of the men's house has certain social and political consequences.
First, it reduces or weakens the intensity of the family by placing
the crucial outcomes of the process of initiation outside the domain of kin relationships. Although both the *krabdjuò* and *bam
kà'àk* are patri-appointments, the first hereditary, the second not,
they technically belong to the *mẽbaitebm,* or nonkin class of relationships. Having been thrust temporarily into the influential
roles of political "fathers," or initiators, *krabdjuò* and *bam kà'àk*
stand in for senior generation kin, who are forbidden to assert
themselves in these roles. The sphere of influence of kin stops

short of the men's house and its political associations. Entrance into village politics, thus devoid of any inputs from the private domain, becomes the responsibility of *mēbaitebm*, who represent the public domain. Political alliances between *mēbaitebm* are formed at the center of the village in the *ngà*, whereas private alliances through marriage to *mēbaitebm* are primarily the concern of the residents of the uxorilocal households on the village periphery. The *ombikwa-mēbaitebm* dichotomy, conjoined through marriage, is kept distinct and separate in the *ngà*. Thus it is unlikely that a man's political liaisons will be formed on the basis of a family interest, because kinship and politics are entered into as if they were two mutually exclusive domains.

Village Leadership

Robert Lowie (1948), when referring to the limited authority of South American headmen, spoke of them as "titular chiefs" who served the people primarily as "peacemakers" and "go-betweens." These phrases are apt descriptions of Kayapó *ben-iadjuòrò*, or village leaders, whose lack of coercive powers renders any chiefly authority ephemeral. Even the honorific title *ben-iadjuòrò*, which can be glossed as "those who give the ceremonial chant," specifies two seemingly apolitical roles of a leader, namely, his privilege to intone the *ben* (a traditional ritual chant or blessing given in falsetto voice) and his right to deliver public orations on the subject of village morality. This latter prerogative is sometimes shared with a small group of respected village elders. Besides these two communitywide functions, a *ben-iadjuòrò* is also expected to lead one of the village's men's societies (*tchêt*), which he at least nominally directs, in its collective enterprises, whether these be economic, ceremonial, or military. The *tchêt* constitute the politically active group in the men's house, and jointly serve as village council under the aegis of the village leaders. A *tchêt* is identified as following, or "working for," a specific *ben-iadjuòrò*, who mobilizes its forces and guides its activities largely by example and exhortation.

The position of *ben-iadjuòrò* is recognized by the village at large, although each headman has his own following of adult men who belong to the same *tchêt*. It appears that a single village may have any number of active *ben-iadjuòrò*. Krause (1911:401) reported that one of the Pau d'Arco villages had five or six leaders. The Txukahamae of Porori had four; the larger villages of Gorotire and Kubenkranken had two each. The specific powers of Kayapó leaders are not easily defined. The amount of influence each leader has is directly contingent on personal qualities. To achieve a reputation for being a "good" *ben-iadjuòrò,* it is said that a man should be even-tempered and, above all, generous. The leader who knows how to distribute largess is a popular one, commanding respect and augmenting his following (cf. Lévi-Strauss on the duties of Nambikuara chiefs, 1955; chap. 29). Krause (1911:401) suggested that Kayapó "chiefs" had little power or function other than that of dealing with Brazilians and other visitors, and he concluded from his observations that leaders must have been chosen primarily for their ability, however rudimentary, to speak Portuguese. But Krause had chanced to consider only that aspect of leadership immediately obvious to all visitors; he did not record other responsibilities of headmen, such as their powers of mediation in internal as well as in external affairs.

A *ben-iadjuòrò,* in addition to dealing with the outside world, should be able to appease disputants in arguments which threaten to involve more than a few persons in their solution. He should also be prepared to deal effectively with any threats to his own position as the recognized leader of one of the men's societies. If a *ben-iadjuòrò* is unable to hold his own *tchêt* in line, or to maintain peace in the village, he is at once in danger of losing his status as leader, and of destroying the tranquility and unity of the village. The establishment and maintenance of harmonious relations is therefore one of the major functions of Kayapó headmen.

Should traditional leadership fail to reestablish harmony after a dispute has broken out, the contestants and sometimes their supporters, who in the most dramatic instance include the entire community, may engage in physical combat. Fighting of this kind is institutionalized among the Kayapó in the formal duel, known as *aben tak* ("hitting together"). According to the rules, whoever loses an *aben tak,* whether it is a two-person fight or a community brawl, must leave the village. The Kayapó say that the vanquished depart because they have too much "shame" (*piaàm*) to remain in the same village with those people with whom they have fought, and to whom they have lost.

The Consequences of Fission

A decisive victory in intravillage conflict is won usually by the headman with the more numerous following, while the less popular leader and his group may be forced out of the village. It is said that the entire *tchêt* must follow its leader into exile, although this rule is by no means enforceable. For instance, it is always possible to choose to exercise an option to remain in the village if one has numerous kin relations on the winning side.

The ties of kinship and marriage, which cross-cut the men's political associations, which are recruited on the basis of friendship rather than kinship, can be activated at times of village fission to circumvent a full exodus of the losing *tchêt*.

Once the village has divided after a collective duel, the two factions continue to remain hostile. Reprisals are a source of fear in the old village, where the possibility of surprise attacks from vengeful former associates is a recurrent theme in daily conversations. Fear does not preclude curiosity, however, and hostile bands may welcome news of kinsmen who now reside permanently elsewhere. Although there are few opportunities for groups once they are severed by feud to recombine as a single unit, kinsmen separated by village schism enjoy visiting each other on an individual basis, and can do so without endangering their lives. Today, visiting back and forth between Kayapó villages is greatly facilitated by the Brazilian air force planes that supply government Indian posts during the dry season, and on which a small number of Kayapó are occasionally permitted to fly. The distances between villages are deemed too great for foot travel, and only refugees fleeing hostile communities will venture to make the long and hazardous journey through difficult terrain to reach another village.

The group exodus which takes place after an *aben tak,* or duel, has an effect on the size of the community quite apart from that of the sporadic movements of individual visitors. The latter displacements reflect essentially voluntary and, for the most part, temporary moves influenced by economic and psychological needs, while the former constitutes a more or less permanent migration of a dissident faction. The *aben tak,* viewed thus as a convention for relieving the village of its dissidents, becomes a force for the preservation of peaceful coexistence within the home village.

Both of these types of movements or migrations would seem to be the result of an ethnocentric view of territorial prerogative, based on traditional access and right of way to an apparently limitless quantity of land in central Brazil. Until quite recently, the absence of political boundaries and geographical barriers has meant that the Kayapó could continue uninterruptedly their unstated policy of group dispersal as a means of dissolving village factions. How frequently these disruptions took place in the distant past is not known, although there is good evidence that villages were splitting before the moment of contact in the nineteenth century. It is only in recent times that the Kayapó have been forced to share their habitat with other non-Indian groups, so that the old system of fission at times of crisis may have been especially well adapted to the former lack of limitations on land use. Today the story is different, since the factional disputes, once so characteristic of traditional political relations, are to a large extent now controlled by outside forces.

A view of Kayapó history as far as the scanty records and informants' memories permit reveals a population in the throes of an endless mitosis. Villages which split in the nineteenth century seemed to have spawned even more splinter groups in the twentieth. At the very time that their overall population seems to have declined, Kayapó settlements have become more numerous. At the present time, there are six spin-off groups from the village of Gorotire, which divided as late as 1936, accounting by my calculations for some eleven hundred persons of the total modern Kayapó population, estimated at fourteen hundred. The recurrent pattern of subdivision would seem thus to represent both an aboriginal mode of action and a current reaction to acculturative distress.

It is possible that a stronger commitment to communal organization would have curtailed the amount of freedom available to individual Kayapó. Today, for instance, many Kayapó have chosen to join Brazilian road gangs, to tap rubber trees, and to cut Brazil nuts for wages, further contributing to the weakening of traditional village management. Since migrant work groups may represent substantial spin-offs from settled communities, they, like the losing factions in village feuds, are effective in reducing village populations. In terms of absolute numbers, the departure of a group, regardless of its rationale for migration, may represent a crucial decrease in population size in such small village communities as those discovered in central Brazil.

Since any substantial reduction can result in the immediate curtailment, or even the stoppage, of traditional social and ritual activities, it may be assumed that the breakup of villages, past and present, has had some deleterious effect on aboriginal social organization. Here it is worth noting also that ritual performances have served frequently as catalysts for village disturbances, generating tensions and ill-feeling between the participants of these lengthy village festivities, such that the halting of communal rituals, however temporary, may be regarded as finally advantageous to any small enclaves of Kayapó trying to reestablish themselves in new villages. Although informants seem to consider that one of the disadvantages of breaking away from an established village is the inability of the new group to perform most of the Kayapó "great" ceremonials for lack of enough personnel, the absence of ceremonialism has its benefits, especially the minimization of certain kinds of conflicts which inevitably arise during performances.

Judgments rendered by Kayapó informants when queried about preferred village size expose their own negative view of the effects of village fission on communal life. For them, the ideal village, or "beautiful village *(krĩn mêtch)*," is much like the ancestral village of Gorotire as described by Coudreau in 1897. Its population was reputedly large (Coudreau estimated fifteen hundred), and it apparently provided the Kayapó with a population numerous enough for the support of two men's houses and an extensive ceremonial life. Yet in spite of their preference for larger over smaller villages, the process of fission continued unchecked until recently.

Small bands of Kayapó living apart from larger parent communities, and faced with the task of rebuilding their society, initially would have little of the leisure time necessary for participation in the traditional rituals. Since village subdivision is as much a means of social preservation as it is a method of self-determination, and of regional expansion, the absence of ceremonialism is viewed as only a temporary state by the Kayapó. Ritualism is resumed either when the new village has become firmly established, or when an exiled group joins another larger community. Its resumption signifies both a stable population and one sufficiently large for the proper staging of group performances.

Small splinter bands of Kayapó numbering less than one hundred persons (a figure cited for three groups of Kayapó living on the Iriri, Itacayunas, and Baú rivers, Table 1) must be considered only provisional social groupings by Kayapó standards, since they seem to expect that such groups may eventually want to increase in size, or to become reintegrated into larger communities. This was the case with a much smaller band, the Kruòtikangu faction which split off from the village of Kubenkranken after the outbreak of a measles epidemic in 1958. At that time, twenty-four men, women, and children went to live near a small creek, the Kruòtikangu, from which they took their name. A few days' walk from the parent village, which after the split ignored their existence, they continued separately for five years until one day the dissidents suddenly returned, and were ceremoniously welcomed by their estranged kin.

The "Exit Option"

In the resolution of serious conflicts, village fission ultimately serves as a conservative mechanism for the preservation of the old social order, which is later replicated in the new village. It also gives the Kayapó, now faced with adjusting to the presence of Brazilians in the Amazon, an option other than the traditional native response, which had been to withdraw further into the forests. Withdrawal, or flight, no longer represents the only choice open to the Kayapó. Today, the community may split its decision, with part of the village opting for long-term arrangements with Brazilians, while the rest may decide to leave the village and settle in seclusion elsewhere. Those who have responded favorably to the new association with modern Brazil have had to realize a definitive loss of autonomy in the conduct of their village affairs. This loss has affected the nature of factional disputes because the major catalysts influencing Kayapó choices are now located outside the aboriginal villages. While in the past, the typical reaction to internal pressures had been to divide the village, the response to new external constraints is frequently, but not definitively, to consolidate community forces.

The pattern of subdivision which represents the old social process still persists among some recently contacted Kayapó, however. The persistence of this particular mode of response to external stress can be analyzed most productively in terms of a theoretical construct borrowed from Hirschman's book *Exit, Voice, and Loyalty: Responses to Decline in Firms, Organizations, and States* (1970).[6] According to Hirschman's theory, both exit and voice (as well as a mixture of the two) can play crucial roles in the maintenance of social systems, but it makes a great deal of difference which mode of reaction to discontent on the part of individuals or groups predominates. Voice, for example, represents the mode of self-development as well as that of progressive change. When voice is activated, it can demonstrate the internal strengths and the stability of the group by permitting members to express dissenting opinions about the group's leadership. Rigidity and stagnation, by contrast, are the possible outcomes for the organization which chooses to suppress voice.

Exit, when it is the dominant mode, indicates either the absence of strong leadership, and hence a loosely organized group, or conversely a situation so tightly controlled that any discontented members are encouraged to leave the group rather than to stay and express their opposition to it. Hirschman (1974) cites Cuba as a contemporary example of the suppression of voice and the concomitant encouragement of exit for political dissidents.

Among the Kayapó, however, the relationship between exit and voice is rather different. Exit has not been resorted to because voice was impossible or dangerous; rather, it was the availability of exit which prevented any substantial development of voice. As a result, voice has remained an underdeveloped and negligible political mode. Certainly, exit has been the mode *par excellence* for the handling of conflict situations, with village fission as the end result of the favoring of exit over voice. The almost total absence of a Kayapó voice, with the sole exception of the *ben-iadjuòrò,* whose voice is that of tradition, and as such is nonprogressive, reflects their lack of political development in general.

Among the Kayapó, there is no recognized outlet for the expression of dissatisfaction either with customary behavior or with infringements on individual freedoms. As a result there is no way of changing the status quo. Disagreements may be dramatized periodically through the collective duel, or *aben tak,* with the emigration of the weaker faction as the expected outcome. But as Hirschman (1978:95) has pointed out "the practice of exit is self-reinforcing. Once this avoidance mechanism for dealing with disputes or venting dissatisfaction is readily available, the contribution of voice, that is of the political process, to such matters is likely to be and to remain limited." The absence of a Kayapó voice is not surprising given the diffuseness of the leadership roles, and the absence of any binding loyalties either to particular leaders or to particular political groups (the *tchêt*). The absence of loyalty to figures of authority seems to be symptomatic of a general Kayapó problem, one that is also manifest in the ease with which marital ties are dissolved and new marriages established. This flexibility and fluidity in the matter of changing both spouses and political affiliations must be viewed in conjunction with the lack of any real opportunity to effect a structural change in the nature of institutions, which are so firmly fixed by custom that personnel changes scarcely would affect them.

Hirschman (1970:83) has predicted that where the possibility of exit is either "too easy or too attractive," the concept of voice will be undeveloped. Since exit is a less effective political mode than voice, the result of a preference for exit over voice is the deterioration of the organization. In the Kayapó case, the exit of a faction represents a substantial reduction in the village population, yet this reduction is not without certain advantages for the village, since the immediate effect of fission and exit is to mitigate conflict and to preserve the social order from destruction.

An alternative solution to this continuing process of fission would be the development of a voice for the Kayapó. Hirschman's suggestion that voice could be strengthened at the expense of exit "directly, by reducing the cost and increasing the rewards of voice, as well as indirectly, by raising the cost of exit and even reducing the opportunities for it" (1970:123), is pertinent to the issues considered here, for he seems to have predicted precisely what is now occurring in central Brazil. The National Indian Foundation (FUNAI) has severely reduced opportunities for the Indians to continue their practice of exiting, while at the same time raising opportunities for voice, not from any grand concern for the preservation of indigenous communities as such, but from a more practical interest in promoting peaceful relations between Indians and Brazilian settlers in the Amazon region. FUNAI's rationale is that the Indian confined to government posts is less likely to cause trouble than the Indian still free to leave a natal village in quest of another territory. As a result of FUNAI's explicit policy, exit is no longer a possible option in villages over which the government of Brazil has some control.

A New Voice for Brazil

With the suppression of exit, the level of Kayapó voice has been raised. The emergence of a Kayapó voice seems to be as much the result of the appointment of native leaders from the outside as it is the outcome of a direct curtailment of their physical movements. Voice in the possession of the *ben-iadjuòrò* was the traditional voice of customary behavior. As such, it was far from becoming a powerful political tool. The necessity for communication with Brazilians, however, has created a new role for village leaders, and another kind of leadership seems to have become necessary. The man who, with the support of his village, can negotiate forcefully with Brazilian officials is more important today than the old style of *ben-iadjuòrò* whose mannered harangues and exhortations served to safeguard village traditions.

A young leader of this new variety emerged recently from the now-defunct Txukahamae village of Porori in the Upper Xingu, a settlement which had felt particularly threatened by the confiscation of its land for the Trans-Amazon Highway. His name is Robni (Rauni); and he has been featured prominently in newspaper articles and books concerned with the plight of central Brazil's Indian populations. When I met him more than ten years ago, Robni had just been appointed a *ben-iadjuòrò* by Claudio Villas Boas, who had successfully persuaded his people, the Txukahamae, to settle within the confines of the Xingu National Park. Robni has since become the accepted spokesman for his group, although there are still several traditional *ben-iadjuòrò* who are active in village politics. He can be said to exemplify a new voice which has been activated from the outside. It appears that the Kayapó voice mechanism, once so rudimentary, needed only to receive the right impetus to discover itself.[7]

The presence of Brazilians and other foreigners in central Brazil has induced changes in certain aspects of aboriginal life which must now be considered irreversible. In many ways, the most obvious effect of this intrusion has been the decimation of native populations through epidemic disease and warfare. Less obvious a change to the outside world, perhaps, has been the gradual development of a voice, or national consciousness, among Brazil's Indians, many of whom, like Robni, have become concerned about the future of their own groups. Some of them have already understood that with the building of the Trans-Amazon Highway they no longer have the option of withdrawal into forests which once belonged exclusively to them. Robbed of their ancestral lands and hemmed in by new roadways, many of these Indians currently see the best opportunity for their survival in active membership in government-supported villages.

Once they have capitulated to living at an Indian post, how much of their traditional culture will they be able to maintain, and for how long? These questions, already posed by a vast literature on culture contact, have been answered to some extent as if decline and disintegration must be the certain fate of non-Western societies brought into contact with the Western world. Were we to take into consideration, however, certain historical facts which indicate that decline was as often as not a part of the prior history of a particular group's dynamics, rather than stimulated solely by external events, then the situation of contact could be viewed from yet another perspective—one in which social and political decline has been stemmed and a reversal put into effect. In central Brazil, it may be shown, for example, that contact with the West abruptly ended the twin processes of fission and exit, operating as native forms of conflict control. In their place, a recently discovered political process, strengthened from the outside, seems inadvertently to have helped the Kayapó to reassert some control over their declining social environment, even to the extent that certain Kayapó villages might be said to be flourishing today.

5 | The Gê and Bororo Societies as Dialectical Systems: A General Model

Terence S. Turner

Introduction: Ethnographic Questions and Theoretical Dilemmas

THIS PAPER IS OFFERED as an experiment both in ethnographic and in theoretical synthesis. It is also an attempt to formulate a general model which can be tested by application to specific cases, as I attempt to do in the following paper on Kayapó social structure.

As the title implies, the paper represents an attempt to identify and in some sense explain the common features of the structure of the Gê and Bororo societies. At this level, the paper raises and attempts to answer such questions as: Why should the uxorilocal extended family be the common form of residence of all of the societies of this group (as well as a number of other similar lowland South American societies)? Why should societies with this form of residence possess communal corporate institutions, forming a distinct level of social relations set apart from the domestic and personal kin relations centered in the uxorilocal households? Why should these corporate communal institutions so regularly take the form of moieties? Why should all of the societies of the group share the same peculiar bimodal form of economy, based on a cyclical alternation between slash-and-burn agriculture, practiced in large base villages, and the dispersion of these villages into seminomadic hunting-and-gathering bands? Why are the villages of this group, and other uxorilocal societies of the region, so much larger than those of most other societies of the same general habitat?

Infrastructure: Material Subsistence, Socialization, and the General Features of the Social Division of Labor

To begin with, let me define the term "infrastructure," which I shall be using in a special sense somewhat different from the usual

147

Marxist meaning of the term. I shall employ the term to denote the forces and relations of production (understood to include both material and social production) as generalized, potential factors, as yet lacking the specific forms they take on through integration in the social structure of a particular society. "Infrastructure" in this sense represents the general constraints that the forces and relational forms in question impose upon any social system into which they are incorporated, as well as the positive potential of those forces and relations for the construction and maintenance of the social order. The term "base" will be employed to denote the specific structure of productive relations and forces formed by the integration of infrastructural factors into a specific society according to the dictates of its "superstructure," or set of collective institutions, norms, and values which serve to regulate the relations of production and the reproduction of those relations and the society as a whole. In the spirit of this definition, then, I shall begin by giving a general account of environmental conditions, productive techniques, and economic organization broadly corresponding to those of the Gê and Bororo, but not yet cast in the specific forms they assume in Gê and Bororo society.

MATERIAL SUBSISTENCE

There is space here for only the most cursory overview of Gê-Bororo subsistence patterns and environment (these have been described in detail elsewhere: Bamberger 1967, 1971; Crocker 1967, n.d.; Lave 1967; Nimuendajú 1939, 1942, 1946; Maybury-Lewis 1967, n.d.; Melatti 1970; Seeger 1974). The country is a mixture of forest and savannah, which reaches a balance of almost equal parts of each in Kayapó country in the northwest of the Gê area and thins out to a predominantly savannah environment with "gallery forest" along the banks of rivers and creeks to the south and east. Population density seems always to have been very low, with villages separated by great distances of open country from one another (100–150 kilometers being the average distance between Kayapó villages). Villages are typically situated on the margin between forest and savannah land, enabling convenient exploitation of all three of the ecozones involved: the forest (primarily used for garden land, hunting and gathering); the savannah (hunting and gathering); and the marginal zone of transition from forest to savannah, the richest of the three in wild plant and animal species and thus especially productive for hunting-and-gathering purposes.

Five gross aspects of Gê-Bororo subsistence activities must be taken into account in attempting to understand the specific social forms they assume in the social division of labor in the various Gê societies. I emphasize at the outset that I am arguing not that these features, in and of themselves, "determine" the social form of the division of labor, but only that the latter is formulated with reference to them and cannot be understood without them. They are: (1) the relative proportion of the contribution of the productive activity in question to the overall productivity of the economy; (2) the limitations and demands imposed by the techniques and material forces of production upon the social control and organization of the relations of production; (3) the susceptibility of the productivity of the activity in question to human control (that is, the uniformity, continuity, and predictability of the production involved) ; (4) the social character of the productive activity in question, that is, whether it is more easily and efficiently performed individually or collectively; and (5) the ability of the activity in question to be combined with the early phases of the socialization process, that is, the care of young children.

With respect to the first criterion, the most important Gê-Bororo subsistence activity is swidden agriculture, which generally accounts for more than one-half of total food production. Hunting, fishing, and gathering are also highly developed and account for the remaining one-half to one-fourth of food consumed. Gê horticulture has an unusually varied repertoire of crops: bitter manioc and maize are the most important staples, but maize, yams, squash, sweet manioc, and fava beans are also important. Other tribes of the same general area relying upon the usual tropical forest subsistence pattern (swidden horticulture based more exclusively upon manioc) survive quite comfortably without anything like the development of hunting and fishing or long-range gathering expeditions characteristic of the Gê in general. Carneiro has calculated the population that could be indefinitely sustained in the same place on the basis of the tropical forest type of manioc-based swidden agriculture, without any input from other sources such as hunting and gathering, at around 2,000. These calculations were made for the Kuikuru of the Xingú headwaters, and thus pertain to the same general ecological area (Carneiro 1960). The more complex Gê economic pattern should thus be capable of supporting village communities of populations approaching 3,000, especially taking account of the standard Gê practice of moving the village site every ten years or so and the virtually unlimited supply of fresh garden land. Kayapó villages of between 1,500 and 2,000 are vouched for by early explorers like Coudreau (1897) and Kayapó accounts of times as recent as 1936. The sizes of the existing Kayapó communities, however, vary from around

400 to less than 100. These figures seem typical for the Gê and Bororo as a whole.

With respect to the second criterion, the point to emphasize is that communities of more than 100 could not survive as cohesive villages on a hunting-and-gathering basis alone, even in the comparatively rich Gê environment. Nor could groups larger than this come together for the extended periods (two to four months) necessary to celebrate the communal rituals which serve as the major foci of Gê and Bororo social life. Gê society, with its characteristically large villages and collective ceremonial institutions, must therefore be regarded, in its present form, as based on the productivity and reliability of swidden agriculture. I emphasize that I am not saying that Gê societies necessarily rely for the preponderant share of their food supply on agriculture. My point is that the large communities which are the distinctive expression of Gê sociality could not have developed and cannot stay together, during such periods as they are not divided into trekking bands, without a substantial contribution from agriculture. At a more fundamental level, all Gê societies could support themselves entirely by agriculture, given their large supplies of land and their varied crop repertoire. They could not, on the other hand, support themselves entirely by hunting and gathering. More to the point, the hunting, fishing, and gathering that can be done by individuals and small groups in the neighborhood of the base village would be sufficient to supply the minimal protein requirements not fulfilled by the agricultural diet. The collective trekking pattern of the Gê and Bororo societies, and the fact that some, like the Shavante, obtain the majority of their food in this way, must therefore be regarded as a cultural choice rather than as a result of ecological necessity. Since the alternation between dispersed trekking groups and large base villages is a prominent feature of the social organization of all of these peoples, its explanation must be accepted as one of the primary tasks of any adequate theoretical account of Gê and Bororo society.

It must also be taken into account that the ability of fairly large groups to support themselves by hunting, fishing and gathering alone (the ceiling in this respect is perhaps between 50 and 100), and the virtually unlimited supply of open land for both hunting and gathering and agricultural uses, effectively forestall the development of any institution of property in agricultural land, or more generally of any form of domination or control of economic resources capable of serving as a basis for organizing social relations at the communal level, or of restraining the mobility of individuals or factions who might wish to leave the community at any time, either to join another village or to found a new one themselves.

In regard to the third criterion, it is of prime importance that bitter manioc in particular, and the gardens in general, provide a dependable source of food the year around, which can be harvested at will on a day-to-day basis in the amounts desired. In these respects agriculture differs fundamentally from gathering of the more important wild foods, such as piki fruit, Brazil nuts, or açaí and bacaba berries, which are seasonal and often at distances from the village that make harvesting them a question of cooperative endeavors which produce large amounts at sporadic intervals, thus requiring collectively organized distribution and consumption. Hunting and fishing are also fundamentally different from agriculture in this respect. They are less uniform and predictable in their results, of course. They have a seasonal aspect, becoming more difficult in the rainy season when the fish are less concentrated in low rivers and shallow pools, and animals leave the rivers and disperse themselves over the land because of the abundance of water sources. It is also important that fish and animal meat are highly perishable and that the Gê have developed no techniques for preserving them. The result of these factors is that a fisherman's catch or a hunter's game inevitably has something of the character of a windfall, both in the sense of its essential unpredictability and in the sense that while one hunter is lucky others are unlucky, and the product is thus unevenly distributed. Fishing and hunting, like the heavier, long-range gathering activities, thus place a premium upon the distribution of the product over a wide range of consuming units. In this they contrast with agriculture, whose productivity can be controlled to conform to the needs of individual consuming units without risking inequalities of distribution of the sort represented by unlucky fishermen or empty-handed hunters.

The social character of Gê-Bororo subsistence activities, the fourth of the five criteria, is relatively straightforward. There is no technique or productive process, from the manufacture of tools to fishing with timbó (a vine whose sap, when beaten in the water, has a suffocating effect upon fish and causes them to float to the surface), that cannot be performed by a single individual acting alone. In a few cases, efficiency is improved, or the work significantly lightened, by cooperative effort: fish "poisoning" with timbó, long-range gathering expeditions for babassu or Brazil nut, the slashing and clearing of fields. Now that the Brazilian style of house building has been adopted, the construction of at least the frame of the structure is necessarily a job for two or three men at least. All other hunting, fishing, gathering, agricultural, food-preparation, and tool-making tasks can be done as or more efficiently by individuals as by cooperative groups.

The fifth criterion, the compatibility of subsistence activities with socialization activities, sharply differentiates the former into two categories. By far the most important socialization activity in this respect is the care of young children. All activities involving extended periods of silence, total concentration, abrupt and violent physical effort, danger, or relatively rapid movement over long distances associated with the carrying of heavy burdens (that is, hunting, fishing with bow and arrow or by hook and line, and long-range gathering expeditions) cannot be carried out by persons simultaneously charged with the responsibility for caring for young children. All gardening activities, the gathering of wild products growing close to the village, the cutting of firewood, the preparation of food, and the construction of the aboriginal lean-to style of house, are, by contrast, quite compatible with child care.

SOCIALIZATION

The relationship between socialization roles and activities on the one hand and subsistence activities on the other does not end with the question of child care. The human life cycle from birth to death, including sexual reproduction and the necessity of nurturing young children, comprises a set of psychobiological, therefore infrasocial, and therefore "infrastructural" factors in the sense in which the last term is employed here. This entire set of infrastructural factors must be accommodated by society and assimilated into its organization. "Socialization" properly refers to this process as a whole, not merely to that phase of it that deals with early child care and training.

Let us consider in a general way what is implied by "socialization" thus defined. Five major phases of the process may be distinguished, each with its own mechanisms of social integration. The first phase is that of birth and early childhood, with its tasks of nurturance and primary socialization, accomplished primarily through the family and domestic group. Second is the phase of transition to adulthood, involving the process of loosening the dependent relationship with the natal family and orienting the individual toward adult forms of participation in the wider society, tasks usually accomplished through ritual mechanisms of a communal or at least extended-family character. Third comes the phase of reproduction, typically reached in young adulthood. This phase involves two distinct sets of tasks, associated with distinct levels of social structure: the nurturance and primary socialization of offspring, typically carried out within the family of procreation; and the social integration of the unit of primary socialization itself (the "socialization" of the family of procreation as a whole), accomplished through maintaining it in a pattern of prescribed relationships with more stable and inclusive groupings or networks of relations. Fourth is the stage of full, or senior, adulthood, which begins with the dispersion of the family of reproduction, or procreation, and extends for the remainder of active adult life. It usually corresponds to the zenith of the individual man's or woman's social authority and prestige. Finally comes the fifth stage of old age and death, typically managed through dependency in the context of extended-family relationships.

Gê-Bororo age-grading and patterning of socialization conform to this general pattern. Women are charged with the responsibility for early child care and the primary socialization of both sexes. In the second phase, a sexual distinction is made, with boys being more sharply separated from the natal family and associated with extrafamilial groups of a communal nature, while girls remain primarily attached to the intrafamily level of maternal concerns. As young women, girls make the transition from their natal families to their families of procreation without ever detaching themselves from their primary association with this intrafamily level of structure: as wives and mothers they continue to be preoccupied with primary socialization functions carried out at this level. Young men, by contrast, approach their adult family roles as fathers and husbands from the vantage point of a primary association with extrafamilial (or suprafamilial) levels of social organization. Consistent with this, they assume the complementary set of adult socialization functions, that is, the mediation of the relationships between their immediate families and other families and the community at large. The dispersion of the family of procreation at the onset of the fourth stage of full adulthood leads to a redefinition of status for both sexes at the suprafamily level of affinal and grandparental relations. This "move" becomes the basis of the structure of the extended family, which provides the framework for the accommodation of the fifth stage of dependent old age.

Two points of fundamental importance for Gê and Bororo social structure follow from this general outline of the structure of socialization relations. The first is that through their dominance of the higher level of interfamily and, *a fortiori,* communal relations, men are in a position to dominate and control women and the lower structural level of intrafamily relations with which they are identified. The second is that the level of complexity of social organization required by socialization far transcends that *required* by any subsistence activity, or set of such activities, in which the Gê engage. I stress the word *required* to emphasize that I speak here of the technical requirements and material exigencies of these processes as they have been set forth above: in short, their infrastructural features. The Gê and Bororo do, in fact, organize certain subsistence activities at a level considerably beyond that dictated by the infrastructural requirements of socialization. For such cases, however, reasons other than material exigencies or economic requirements must be sought. The result of the greater infrastructural complexity of socialization relations is that the domain of social relations within which they are articulated, namely, the system of family, kinship, and domestic group relations, tends to become the dominant framework for the organization of subsistence activities.

Structure: The Social Division of Labor

THE DIVISION OF LABOR IN SUBSISTENCE ACTIVITIES

The last point may now be developed in relation to the account above of basic subsistence techniques and activities. The fundamental division of labor in the sector of subsistence activities conforms to that laid down in the socialization sector. The economic "division of labor by sex," which is the basic form of the organization of productive activities and relations, is thus, strictly speaking, a division of labor according to socialization functions. Women perform such tasks as can be carried out while discharging their functions as socializers of young children. Men perform the tasks incompatible with these functions. Many of the men's tasks are, moreover, directly consistent with *their* adult socialization functions, which, as we have seen, focus on the level of interfamily relations. The subsistence activities of both men and women, moreover, are not simply distributed in accord with their socialization functions, but are socially defined so as to emphasize the structural distinctions following from these functions, that is, the association of women with the intrafamily and men with the interfamily levels of kinship and family structure.

Women do virtually all of the work in the gardens with the exception of the slashing and clearing, which are typically done by men. The daily routine of harvesting food, carrying it home, and preparing it is completely a female province. The technical quality of agricultural production noted above (its reliability and controllability as to frequency and volume of production) is drawn upon in the culturally prescribed form taken by this productive activity, which is tailored to the limited sphere of social relations with which a woman is identified by her socialization functions. A woman harvests only enough to feed her immediate family. She only begins to have her own gardens when she is ready to marry and have children, and the gardens are considered to belong to her for the duration of their productivity in her capacity as an actual or potential materfamilias. Women also gather wild produce within easy range of the village and gardens. The products of a woman's gathering, as of her gardening, are destined for consumption within her immediate family unit.

Men, as I have mentioned, do the heavy work of slashing and burning the gardens, and also assist with planting and weeding. Their basic economic occupations, however, are fishing, hunting, and gathering commodities obtainable only at great distances from the village, which require journeys longer than one day. A man brings his hunting, fishing, or gathering produce to his wife, that is, to his own individual family of procreation, but its subsequent distribution and consumption follow a different pattern from those of a woman's produce. Men's fish and game, or, as the case may be, babassu or Brazil nuts, are typically shared out (usually by the wife) among a network of relations comprising the kindreds of both husband and wife. The kindred, for such purposes, is operationally defined as including affinal and fictive relations.

Men's produce thus tends to be distributed in an interfamily pattern, whereas women's produce tends to be consumed totally at the intrafamily level. It is also true that even though the basic techniques of hunting and fishing can be, and usually are, performed by individual men working alone, there are collective forms of hunting and fishing which receive considerable cultural emphasis, and men's gathering expeditions are similarly collective in form, usually organized on an age-set or other corporate-group basis. Women occasionally mount ritualistic collective gathering expeditions that last for only part of a day, and they do cooperate to produce and cook the food for ceremonial feasts (for which the men hunt collectively). Aside from such minor exceptions, however, men's productive activities have a less family-centered, more collective aspect than women's, while the distribution and consumption of male produce is sharply contrasted with those of women in terms of their focus at the interfamily, rather than the intrafamily, level of relations.

DOMINANCE AS STRUCTURAL RELATION AND AS VALUE

The Generation of Dominance and Value through the Social Division of Labor

I have sought to show how the Gê and Bororo societies formulate the division of labor according to sex in both of the two basic types of production (socialization and the production of the material means of subsistence) in such a way as to concentrate female activities within the lowest level of social structure (the internal structure of the individual family) and male activities, by contrast, at higher (interfamily) levels of structure. This distribution of productive tasks has, as I mentioned, implications for the patterning of control. In any internally stratified group, those who control the group's relations with other such groups or with society at large must be in a position to control, to some extent at least, those whose activities and responsibilities are focused wholly within the group. This is so if only because the latter lack any point of external leverage upon the former such as is possessed by the former, through their identification with the structure of the group as a whole, over the latter. This relationship of hierarchical control between the higher (intergroup-oriented) and lower (intragroup) levels of group structure, of course, presupposes some effective ground of integration of the levels and thus of the group as a whole. Such a ground is provided by the interdependence of the complementary sexual roles as defined in the social division of labor in socialization and economic activities. This same complementarity, by giving to men control over the interfamily level of family structure, guarantees their general social position of dominance over women and over the lower, intrafamily level of relations with which women's productive activities link them. I use the term "dominance" to denote a generalized, structurally grounded relationship of hierarchical control.

The dominance of men over women in Gê society cannot, of course, be understood as an accidental by-product of the social division of labor or, still less, of the biological and material factors which provide its most general set of constraints. It should, rather, be seen as a social value which informs the pattern of the distribution of tasks within the division of labor. The tendency for women to be charged with the responsibility for early child care, and thus to be allotted such tasks as are compatible with this socialization role, may doubtless be considered a basic infrastructural input into the shaping of this pattern, but this does not by itself dictate the social exclusion of women without young children from male hunting, fishing, and gathering tasks, nor the concentration of women's production and its consumption at the intrafamily level. These aspects of the division of labor are "arbitrary" from the point of view of the material and technological exigencies of the processes in question, and must be accounted for as the results of the imposition of a superordinate set of social values. The central value of this set is what I have called male dominance.

The plasticity and divisibility of most garden production, above all that of bitter manioc as the staple crop, is thus socially exploited in such a way as to define agricultural productivity as well as women, in their capacity as agricultural and human producers, in terms of a level of family structure capable of being controlled and exchanged by those in control of the higher levels of that structure: to wit, men. In dialectical fashion, however, the same procedure maximizes men's dependence on women, as the exclusive channels of what is by far the most important subsistence activity in the Kayapó economy, in terms of both quantity and reliability. The division of labor can be seen, in this respect, as simultaneously maximizing the value of women in exchange within the system of family relations and the dependence of men upon that structure of relations, through which alone they can gain access to women and their productivity. The dependence of men upon the structure of family relations and the value of women in exchange may be regarded as constants for the whole social system (that is, all its members, male and female), whereas the distribution of control over women among men within the system is variable. This discrepancy between the constant and variable features of the relations between men and women forms the point of departure for the whole of the following analysis.

From Dominance in the Relations of Production to Dominance in the Relations of Reproduction; or, How to Transform Control over Women into Control over Men

The problem of dominance has been considered up to this point solely in relation to the simplest unit of coordination of the relations of production, to wit, the individual family. This unit has been considered only as a static set of normatively defined roles, rather than in terms of its total developmental cycle from formation to dispersion. Let us, then, consider the problems arising from the dispersion of such a unit, that is, the crisis precipitated by the coming of its sons and daughters to maturity and their formation of their own families of procreation.

This event constitutes a decisive diminution of the original family unit, terminating the early socialization functions that constitute the primary basis of the intrafamily level of structure, with respect to which both the mother's socialization functions and the father's dominant role had been defined. The parental couple are now potentially left as a rump unit with no social function beyond that of sustaining themselves. The process by which the male family head had first freed himself from the subordinate position he had held within his father's family and then founded his own family and attained within it a position of dominance in his own right has now potentially gone into reverse.

This is no small matter where a man's general status and prestige in the community are concerned. A man's position of dominance as paterfamilias is defined with direct reference to both of the major categories of productive activity in Gê society. There is no alternative basis, at the level of primary productive relations, for reasserting or recouping the effective dominance and prestige that are the corollaries of the real functional importance that has been lost. The loss of a mother's functional role as socializer of her daughters (and much earlier of her sons) at this point carries an analogous if less acute threat of loss of the public status that accompanies functional authority. The loss of the daughters' contribution to the family economy (daughters assist their mothers with all gardening, cooking, and other household tasks) is a loss to both parents, and raises the further potential problem of support and security in old age.

If there is no redress for these losses nor solution for these problems to be found at the level of the organization of primary productive relations—that is, at the level of the individual family—an opportunity not only for solution and redress but for a further aggrandizement of status and reinforcement of both functional dominance and economic security presents itself at the higher level of the relations of *reproduction* of the family. The latter consist of the relations of spouse exchange by which a new family is formed by the male and female offspring of two families in the process of dispersion. The problem of reasserting dominance presents itself at this level as one of defining and manipulating an effective medium of control of family units as wholes (including both their adult male and their adult female members).

There exists, as I have already noted, no form of fixed or movable property, control over which might provide a man with leverage for exercising control over his sons (or sons-in-law). The control a man exercises over his daughters, in their capacity as female members of the intrafamilial level of structure of his own family of procreation, does, however, represent a valuable resource capable of being manipulated in exchange with other men (specifically, the prospective husbands of the daughters). This resource might be used in one of two ways. In one, the daughters could simply be given to men of other local groups, in direct or indirect exchange for wives for a man's sons. This solution is relatively ineffective in terms of the control a man can exercise thereafter over his sons, for example, in such matters as retaining them and their wives as contributing members of his household. This remains true to some degree even in the case where marriage exchange is transformed into affinal alliance between groups of men constituted as exogamous, patri-virilocal patrilineages.

The second solution, and the more effective one in terms of the father's (and mother's) ability to exercise continuing control over the resulting situation, is to allow the sons to move out and marry into other households, while retaining the daughters as resident members of the household, thus compelling their husbands to move in with the parents-in-law. The continued coresidence of the daughters would make it possible for their parents to surrender their family control over them only by slow degrees, exacting in return the maximum amount of deference and assistance from their husbands, and above all preventing them from removing the daughters from the household to join other residential groups. This solution consists, then, of the establishment of matri-uxorilocal households linked to one another through the exchange of men as husbands.

It should be clear that this "uxorilocal solution" consists essentially of parlaying the control men are able to exercise over women within the family at the level of the primary relations of material production and early socialization into control over other men (sisters' and daughters' husbands) exercised at the higher level of the *reproduction* of the family unit as a whole. The "control" thus generated takes the relatively diffuse and generalized form that I have called "dominance." It consists above all in the negative power of a woman's parents to prevent her removal from the household by her husband, and to exact from the latter recognition of and respect for their continuing and overlapping claims on her family allegiances. This recognition on the part of a husband of the claims of his wife's parents upon his wife, and thus upon himself, takes the form of deference and "respect" behavior, and is concretely manifested in his obligations to contribute to his in-laws a portion of his production of fish, game, labor on heavy projects, such as slashing new gardens and building Brazilian-style houses, as well as such masculine artifacts as mats and storage pouches woven of buriti palm fiber.

Such concrete contributions have their material importance, which grows as the wife's parents advance in years. They are, however, more important as the symbolic indices of the dominant position of the parents-in-law, and particularly of the wife's father. It is, in effect, only as a "wife's father," that is, as the head of an extended-family household, that a man (or, in the analogous role of mother-in-law, a woman) attains the status of full adulthood and the social prestige that accompanies it. The structural basis of this status and prestige should be clear: the level of dominance represented by control over the relations of reproduction of the family, and thus over individual family units as wholes, is to the lower level of dominance represented by a man's control as husband-father over the women and children of his own family as the position of the husband-father is to that of the wife-mother and children within the family. The dominance of the extended-family household head constitutes, in short, a higher step on the same scale of structural contrast on which the dominance of the male head of the individual family is defined.

The difference in prestige and authority between male heads of extended-family households and young husbands who have not yet established their spheres of dominance beyond the level of their own families of procreation is a striking feature of public political life in all Gê societies. It is generally only the former who engage in political oratory and debates in the communal men's councils, and they who take the lead in ceremonial organization and other forms of public activity, while fathers and husbands of the younger age-grade generally play the role of silent followers. The character of the "dominance" of the fathers-in-law, or household heads, as a generalized social value is attested by the fact that it is not mechanically tied to the actual structure of a man's household: a man with three sons-in-law is not thereby counted more prestigious or higher in status or authority than one with two sons-in-law, or for that matter than one who has no sons-in-law (for example, a man who had only sons, and therefore has only daughters-in-law as junior affines). Any man of the age-grade at which he would, other things being equal, be expected to attain the status of "wife's father" and household head can, as it were, capitalize upon the generalized status and prestige accruing to his age-grade. What I am suggesting is that the latter is to be understood in its turn as an expression of a generalized structure of dominance relations grounded in a collectively stereotyped norm of family and extended-family organization.

The Uxorilocal Extended-Family Household (and the Interhousehold Relations It Entails) as the Structure of the Social Relations of Human Production (Socialization)

The individual family is the primary unit of the sexual division of labor as it applies to the relations of production of material subsistence. There exist, as I have outlined in the last section, certain relations of cooperation in the production and distribution of material goods above the individual family level, primarily involving the obligations of sons-in-law to aid their fathers-in-law and to supply their mothers-in-law with certain male food products and artifacts. These extrafamily or interfamilial relations of material production, whose strategic symbolic importance far outweighs their relative quantitative significance, are thus concentrated within the extended-family household, although, as I emphasized earlier, men's production of fish and game is distributed among a man's and his wife's bilateral kindreds, extending over many such households.

The relationship of the organization of the other major category of productive activity, socialization, to the structure of the household is obviously quite different from that of material production. The individual family unit, constituting the basic structural framework of material production, is the focus of only the earlier phases of socialization: birth and childhood, for women adolescence, for both men and women reproduction as young adults. The phase of reproduction closes with the dispersion of the family of procreation. Potentially one-half, or at least one-third of the life cycle remains to be lived, beginning with the stage defined in all Gê societies as that of full maturity or adult man- and woman-hood, and continuing through the distinct stage of old age to death. The social appropriation of these latter stages of the life cycle is, I have argued, as much a question of the production of social forms and meanings from psychobiological (infrastructural) forces, not to mention lower levels of social integration, that is, as much a question of "socialization," as the initial socializing of young children.

The individual family is obviously *not* the social framework for the socialization of the latter phases of the life cycle of either sex, since these phases can be said to begin only with the dissolution of the second and last minimal family unit to which individuals of either sex normatively belong (the family of procreation). The minimal family unit, the setting of the earlier phases of socialization, is reproduced and dispersed on the average of three times during the course of a normal life cycle, that is, a normatively complete socialization process. The third of these cycles of reproduction of the family, that constituted by the families of procreation formed by the offspring of an adult couple, is exploited through the device of uxorilocality by the parental couple to produce or socialize themselves as members of the age-grade of full adults: in this way, the reproduction of the earlier phases of the socialization process, or (which comes to the same thing) the lower levels of the structure of socialization relations, is made the medium of the reproduction of the final phases (or upper structural levels) of the process as well.

Socialization, in other words, is never a simple organization of productive relations, but is a hierarchically stratified system of relations of production and reproduction. At a higher level, the system as a whole (that is, the total system of personal kinship relations generated from the reproduction of the family) is in Gê societies reproduced according to a certain externally imposed pattern through the agency of institutions such as descent, exogamy, moiety structures, and so forth. I shall reserve the term "superstructure" for institutions of this type, that is, institutions that can be shown to affect or mold the process of reproducing the system of socialization relations (the "kinship system") as a whole.

In my initial discussion of the concept of socialization, I suggested that just as the specialized socialization functions of the female are allocated in the social division of labor to the earlier phases of the process, so those of the male are concentrated in its later phases and at its higher levels of organization, specifically those dealing with relations between and among minimal family units. The present discussion has translated this general thesis into concrete terms. The move by which the parents of a dispersing family of procreation exchange their role as parents for the more prestigious status of parents-in-law within the structure of the extended-family household constitutes the decisive step in the socialization of the later, mature phases of the life cycle. It establishes the structural terms in which maturity and old age are integrated, together with the earlier phases of childhood, youth, and reproduction, within a total structure of kinship and domestic relations. This decisive step, I have suggested, is negotiated primarily in terms of the transformation of status and dominance relations that accompanies it, which is primarily, although not exclusively, a male concern.

The transition from the stage of reproduction to that of full adulthood, or from the status of parents to that of parents-in-law, is not the last of the major transitions of the socialization process. There remains, of course, the transformation of the dominant parent-in-law into the dependent elder. This transition occurs, in the extended-family household, in coordination with the trans-formation of the daughter and son-in-law into dominant parents-in-law in relation to their own daughters' husbands.

The structure of the uxorilocal extended-family household can thus be regarded as a coordinated series of exchanges of domi-nance and subordination (dependence). A male begins by ex-changing his status as a dependent child within his natal family for the status of youth-initiand, which is socially defined as rela-tively free of family-level dependence but still subordinate, at the communal level, to the collectivity of adult men. The latter, in their symbolic capacity as embodiments of a youth's future, stand to him most immediately in the role of father-in-law. A youth's next transformation, is, then, into a young husband-father, with a dominant position in relation to his wife and children within his own family of procreation (the reverse, in this respect, of his sub-ordination as a child to his own father), but still a position sub-ordinate to his father- (and in a lesser and more oblique sense, mother-) in-law.

As the parents-in-law age and the man's own children grow toward reproductive age, the father next transforms himself into a father-in-law. His own father-in-law, now dependent upon him, occupies an honored but no longer actively dominant place in the structure of the household. The man now stands at the pinnacle of his dominance and prestige in both household and community. Finally, he in his turn yields his place of dominance to his son-in-law, in exchange for the role of honored but dependent elder. The character of the honor accorded to the elderly of both sexes, but especially to old men, is determined by the nature of this final exchange: they are honored as having yielded up and thus tran-scended their particular interests (that is, their dominance) in both household and communal affairs, and thus are considered qualified to serve as spokesmen for communal values at their most impersonal, altruistic, or transcendental level.

A woman's life cycle follows a similar but somewhat simpler tra-jectory, since it is not complicated by the shifts in household affili-ation required of men by the uxorilocal rule of residence. A girl's childhood and youth are spent as a dependent member of her natal family, under the authority of her father and mother. She continues in this status until she is ready for childbearing and thus for marriage in the full sense of the relationship, as it is defined in Gê society. With marriage and motherhood, she passes under the dominance of her husband as a member of his family of procreation, a dominance, however, severely restrained in its exercise during the early years of marriage by her husband's subordination to her parents within the household.

With the marriage of her daughters and the removal of her sons to other households, the woman exchanges her functional authority as mother over her children and adolescent daughters for the prestigious role of mother-in-law, with sons-in-law to pay her deference, do her bidding, and submit, if she pleases, to her scolding, beyond anything her own sons would be expected to tolerate from her. Her relations with her daughters, however, remain open, relaxed, and free: there is a direct continuity to them lacking in a man's relationship to his sons-in-law or to his sons, now residents of other households. This continuity makes the final transition to old womanhood a more gentle and continuous affair than the parallel male transition, since there is less overt dominance and discontinuity in the central relationship (in this case, mother-daughter) to give up or "exchange," and the deference of the son-in-law continues to be paid in recognition of the contrast in sex roles and the structural continuity of mother-daughter relationships within the household, regardless of the content and directionality of real authority or dominance relations.

In the foregoing cursory account of the typical pattern of the male and female life cycles in Gê and Bororo society I have attempted to show how the structure of the uxorilocal extended-family household, together with the pattern of affinal relations between households, can be considered to constitute the organizing framework of the relations of socialization, considered in its turn as the most structurally complex and demanding, and therefore the dominant, form of production in Gê society. The essential point I have made is the central importance of the patterning of dominance, and specifically the translation of the intrafamily dominance of husbands and fathers over their wives and daughters into the interfamily dominance of fathers-in-law over sons-in-law, as the basis of the structure of the extended-family household and thus of the relations of production and socialization.

Superstructure

COMMUNAL CORPORATE GROUPS IN RELATION TO THE STRUCTURE OF THE UXORILOCAL EXTENDED-FAMILY HOUSEHOLD

Under the general social and economic conditions of lowland Amazonian society, matri-uxorilocality, as I have suggested, can be more potent and effective than patri-virilocality as a medium for binding the members of successive, overlapping minimal family units within a pattern of dominance relations, consisting, in the uxorilocal case, of the control of the wife's parents over the daughter's husband. It can be maintained, conversely, that the effectiveness of matri-uxorilocality in this respect, while more intense at short genealogical range, falls off more rapidly in terms of genealogical distance than virilocality, and becomes less effective as a binding principle for groupings organized at greater genealogical depth.

The reason for this is that the effectiveness of uxorilocality rests upon the control exercised by parents over their daughters (or, to a lesser extent, of brothers over their sisters) in the latters' capacity as members of the same minimal family unit. This intrafamily basis of the effectiveness of uxorilocality is difficult to generalize or extend beyond the range of direct overlap between minimal families: that is, beyond the range of parent-in-law—son-in-law (or sister's husband–wife's brother) relations. It does not, for instance, provide an effective basis for controlling the relations between the otherwise unrelated husbands of a pair of sisters, after the death of the latter's parents and brothers, or still less the relations between the husbands of matrilateral parallel cousins. Fission of the uxorilocal household therefore tends to occur beyond this point.

Virilocality, by contrast, whether or not it is reinforced by patrilineality and exogamy, provides a more flexible and extensible basis for the integration of local groups under the same economic conditions. The reason for this is the same as for its relative weakness, compared with uxorilocality, at short genealogical range: to wit, that it is not based to the same extent upon subordination within the minimal family unit. Sons are less effectively subordinated to their fathers, or older to younger brothers (especially after the younger men have become husbands and fathers in their own right), than are daughters to fathers, or sisters to brothers, even after the former's marriages under uxorilocal circumstances.

The matri-uxorilocal residence pattern of the Gê and Bororo thus tends to generate units that are relatively smaller, genealogically shallower, but more stably and effectively integrated within that shallow depth, than the patri-virilocal pattern of many Carib, Arawak, Tupi, and Tukano-speaking lowland Amazonian groups. The relatively small size and low threshold of segmentation of the uxorilocal extended-family household lead to the constitution of communities as agglomerations of multiple households. This segmentary character of Gê and Bororo communities may again be contrasted with the single long-house form of community typical of the patri-virilocal societies, in which the long house is on the average larger than a single extended-family household of the Gê-Bororo type.

The relatively tight integration and strong pattern of dominance at the core of the uxorilocal household, considered together with the formation of the community as a segmentary plurality of such households, call for a correspondingly effective mechanism for coordinating the relations of spouse exchange between households. The structure of interhousehold relations in this respect and the internal structure of the individual household, such as it has been described in the preceding section, are of course simply two sides of the same coin. The pattern of interhousehold spouse exchange can be regarded as the relations of reproduction of the dominance hierarchy, based on affinal relations, that form the core of the internal structure of each individual household. The need, then, is for a regulatory institution, or set of such institutions, capable of operating at a level above that of household structure, capable of coordinating the system of exchanges between all of the segmentary household units of the community according to a uniform pattern.

The structural requirements for the fulfillment of this function are simple enough, as far as the general features of affinal relations and household structure as described up to this point are concerned. The degree to which males as sons, brothers, and maternal uncles are separated from their natal households, and the rate or phasing of this process, must be matched with the degree and rate of the integration of males as husbands and fathers into their wives' households. This might be put in different terms as the problem of correlating the degree to which (and the rate at which) parents surrender their filial attachments to their sons to the latters' affines with the degree (and rate) to which they surrender their filial control over their daughters to the latters' husbands.

In all of the Gê and Bororo societies there exists a set of communal institutions, recruitment to which has the effect of coordinating precisely this set of relations. These institutions (which typically take the form of moieties) can therefore be said to have the function of defining and reproducing the structure of the extended-family household, and specifically the dominance of the parents-in-law that lies at its core. From the sociocentric point of view, however, the primary function of these collective institutions might equally well be defined as the reproduction of themselves as collective, corporate institutions (in a word, as the super-structure of the community as a whole) through the repetitive, standardized reproduction of the households constituting the productive base of the society. These two views represent the two moments or phases of the functional relation between communal groups and extended-family households, which in analytical terms are aspects of the same dialectical process of social reproduction. From the perspective of this process, the gross contrast between the level of collective institutions and the level of domestic and personal kin relations focused in the uxorilocal household, which is probably the most salient single feature of Gê social structure, stands in an internal relation to the contrast within the structure of the uxorilocal household between the level represented by the structure of the household as a whole (associated with the parents-in-law) and that represented by the individual families within it (associated with the daughter and daughter's husband). These two interfaces between contrasting structural levels, apparently so disparate and overtly unrelated, must, in other words, be regarded as complementary manifestations of the same underlying structure.

The identity of this common structure has already been revealed: it is the pattern of dominance and subordination that forms the organizational core of the extended-family household and, at the communal level, the principle of the relationship of the age-grade constituted by senior men of the father-in-law/grandfather category to younger men and women as expressed in the structure of collective groupings and political life. Now although the effective basis for this pattern is the principle of uxorilocal residence and the relationship between the wife's parents on the one hand and the daughter and daughter's husband on the other, the extended-family household is not the primary setting for the realization and expression of the hierarchy of dominance and subordination generated from it, just as it is not the primary locus for the social specification of the structure of extended-family relations *per se*. Both the overt relation of dominance and the structure of relations through which it is generated are more directly and fully expressed at the communal level of relations. The displacement of the form and substance of dominance relationships from the extended-family household to the relations between collective groups and categories defined according to social age, moiety, and other criteria may be seen as the return accruing to the latter from their function of reproducing the basic structure of extended-family household relations according to a standardized pattern, which is the effective basis of their integration within a unified communal society. The process of reproduction according to such a standardized pattern, mediated by collective ritual and recruitment to collective institutions, serves to concentrate the effective control inhering in the separate intra-household relations into a single set of relations between collective groups, and thus to amplify them from an effective basis of household integration under the control of the wife's parents to an effective basis of communal solidarity under the dominance of the age-grade of senior men (fathers-in-law).

Gê and Bororo social structure appears in this perspective as a form of political economy based on social rather than material production and reproduction (although subsuming material production in the ways I have indicated earlier as a subordinate sector of productive activity). It is a political economy based upon the exploitation of young women and men actively engaged in producing the basic social units of human production (that is, nuclear families of procreation) by older men (and to a lesser extent older women), who form a dominant "class" by virtue of their control of the crucial means of production (in this case, the obligatory setting of the productive activity in question), the residential household. Uxorilocality is the formal principle through which this control is exercised.

MOIETY STRUCTURE

The general proposition upon which this analysis is based is that form and function, or structure and dynamics, are directly related, so that a correct account of the general dynamic properties of the collective institutions of Gê and Bororo society should also be capable of generating a satisfactory explanation of the general structural properties of the same institutions. The most pervasive general structural characteristic of Gê and Bororo collective institutions is that they take the form of moieties. The question, then, is: can a dynamic analysis along the lines of that presented above serve as the basis of a satisfactory explanation of moiety structure—an explanation general enough to fit all the varied forms of Gê and Bororo moiety organization, but also capable of accommodating the specific details of each case?

Gê and Bororo society presents a wide variety of forms of moiety structure: exogamous and agamous, matrilineal and patrilineal, some based on nondescent criteria such as personal names or ritual fosterage, others on age-set criteria. It is clear, therefore, that any explanation capable of accounting for the gamut of Gê and Bororo moieties must approximate to a general theory of moiety structure.

Let me begin by defining moiety structure. A moiety structure is a normative construct according to which all the members of a specified category (for example, all men, all adults, and so forth) in the society as a whole are assigned to one or the other of two groupings, according to the same recruitment principle in both cases. The two groupings are therefore structurally symmetrical. As Lévi-Strauss has pointed out, however, the relationship between the two moieties tends to be expressed symbolically in an asymmetrical way (Lévi-Strauss 1952, 1956).

The uniform principle of recruitment of the two moieties is socially embodied in a recruitment relationship. This recruitment relationship (for example, patrilineal descent, adoption by an unrelated "substitute father" as among the Kayapó, and so on) is itself contrastively defined in relation to a complementary relationship (for example, matrilateral and, more generally, affinal relations in the case of patrilineal exogamous moieties, or the relationship of the son to his true father, in the case of moieties recruited through an unrelated foster father). Recruitment to membership has the effect of aligning the individual recruited with the recruitment relationship in opposition to the complementary relationship for purposes related to the substantive nature of moiety membership and the relationship between the moieties. These purposes include, in all Gê and Bororo societies, the pivotal alignments and transformations constituting the weighted pattern of extended-family and household relations.

I suggest that moiety structure embodies or "models" such a socially uniform pattern of asymmetrical or "weighted" alignment with one of a pair of complementary status-role relations (the complementarity of the pair of relations involved being defined with reference to the situation and purposes of recruitment). The pair of moieties models the pair of statuses; the symmetrical structure of both moieties (their recruitment on the basis of the identical relationship) represents the socially symmetrical (that is, uniform) pattern of alignment with one of the two in contrast to the other. The relationship between the two moieties models the relationship between the recruitment relationship and the complementary relationship. The asymmetrical symbolic attributes of the moieties (for instance, "people of the above" and "people of below"; "people of the center" and "people of the periphery," and so on), meanwhile, model the asymmetry of the differentially weighted relationship between the same pair of statuses. All in all, then, a moiety structure constitutes a sociocentric model of a uniform social pattern of differential weighting (expressed in terms of the alignment of all members of the relevant social category with one rather than the other of the two for the social purposes in question) of a pair of complementary relationships. Through the recruitment process by which the moiety system renews itself, through the concrete character of the activities and relations which constitute moiety membership, including the relationship between the two moieties, the moiety structure affects the paired relationships that constitute its reference as a "model" in such a way as to reproduce the asymmetrically weighted relationship between them which it "models." Form and function thus coincide: moiety structure can be understood as a collective mechanism for reproducing a uniformly asymmetrical or biased pattern of relative alignment between a pair of complementary statuses, where the reproductive process to which it relates is structurally defined in terms of the complementarity of the two statuses in question.

Moiety structure serves not only as a collective device for reproducing a uniform pattern of differential alignment between a pair of status-role categories and the relational principles they embody, but also to stabilize this pattern over time by counteracting tendencies toward cumulative drift in the contrastive weighting of the two relations: that is, the long-run tendency for the unevenly weighted contrast between the pair of relations to alter, either in the direction of intensifying or of equalizing the discrepancy in weighting between them. Moiety structure serves as a "governor" for counteracting tendencies of this nature by the simple device of confronting each of the two groups embodying the dominant relationship not with a group representing the complementary, subdominant relationship, but with a mirror image of itself, while at the same time formulating the relationship between the two groups in terms of the relationship between the dominant and subdominant relationships. The effect of this is to cancel changes in this relationship by pitting them, as it were, against themselves. Variations in the asymmetrical relationship between the original pair of complementary statuses, in other words, are transformed at the moiety level into symmetrical and reciprocal modifications in the relation of each moiety toward the other, which each has the same structural resources both to enforce and to resist.

The Structure of Superstructure: The Plurality Communal Structures as an Expression of Conservation in the Reproductive Process

One of the most important notions of system theory is that a self-regulating system of transformations (such as any system capable of institutionalizing cyclical or repetitive reproductive processes) must be based upon a principle of conservation or invariant coordination of the transformations of which it consists. This invariant aspect may be thought of as the common ground of the various phases or permutations of the system and its component processes.

In any system focused on the reproduction of the same structure of relations, that structure becomes the basis of definition of the principle of conservation governing the relations among the transformational operations which make up the reproductive process. This is so because this relational structure is the constant object and standard of coordination of the reproductive process through all its successive phases. To put this in more formal terms, the principle determining the coordination of the relations constituting the structure of an entity is also the principle determining the coordination of the set of transformations that connect the various forms that entity assumes at the different stages of its production (and dissolution). This set of coordinated transformations leading from stage to stage of the reproduction of the entity *is* the structure of its process of reproduction. The invariant principle of coordination regulating all of the stages of the reproductive or developmental cycle of an entity must obviously be of a higher order of abstraction and generality than the structure of the particular phases considered separately. It can only be defined analytically by analyzing structures as developmental (that is, productive or reproductive) processes rather than as static finished products. The implications of this point for the present analysis can be simply stated in Marxist dialectical terms. The invariant structural properties of the set of relations that constitutes the product of the reproductive process will be reproduced reflexively as the invariant structure of the relations of reproduction, or in other words of the relations between the structural components of the reproductive process: in sum, of the institutions and ideological forms of superstructure.

The Gê and Bororo societies, considered as self-reproducing systems, are focused upon the reproduction of the pattern of dominance/subordination relations that forms the core of the structure of the extended-family household. It follows that the invariant formula or principle of conservation regulating the relations between the various moiety sets, age-set systems, and ceremonial organizations that make up the superstructure of Gê society must reflect the invariant conditions of this pattern of dominance relations. This pattern has been shown to consist in a form of manipulation of the reproductive cycle of the minimal family, in such a way as to produce a certain pattern of relations between families with overlapping members. The invariant conditions of its structure are therefore the principles of invariance governing the reproduction of the family (that is, the system of interfamily exchanges immediately involved in this process), and in addition the distinctive feature of the uxorilocal pattern, that is, the retention of residual control over a daughter by at least the parental members of her natal family after her marriage and formation of a family of procreation.

The invariance relations governing the process of the reproduction of the family may be simply stated. The solidarity or positive integration of relations within a minimal family unit, whatever form it takes, must be balanced by the negation or dispersion of the complementary relations of the spouse-parent members to their previous, natal families. Second, these negated relationships must themselves be transformed into positive relations of equal value linking the various natal family relatives of the parents to the other members of the latters' new family of procreation (that is, their spouses and children). The second of these requirements is the corollary of the first, since, without it, the first would simply issue in a direct conflict between natal and conjugal family ties, in which each would tend to cancel the other, thus leading to the paralysis of the system. The expression of the second constraint is the existence of the array of "secondary" relations (grandparents, uncles, aunts, and so on) which must, in the stress placed upon them, balance the stress upon intrafamily relations, albeit in a mode or modes that emphasize their distinctness and complementarity.[1]

Within the broad constraints imposed by conservation in the reproduction of the family and the uxorilocal pattern of dominance, there is still considerable latitude for variation in the patterning of interfamily relations, and thus in the precise form both of the pattern of dominance relations within the household and of the communal institutions of superstructure. This latitude defines the limits of variation of the Gê and Bororo systems, each of which may be analyzed as an expression of a different pattern of formulating and weighting the interfamily relations of reproduction of minimal family units within the confines of the uxorilocal structure.

The "weighting" of interfamily relations can be analytically defined as a product of several factors: the relative degree of discontinuity in natal family relations, balanced against the relative degree of integration into the affinal family and household; the rate at which the process of separation and incorporation that engenders this balance is made to occur (that is, its relatively abrupt or gradual character); and the way in which these two sets of considerations are combined and balanced against each other for male- and female-linked sets of relations (various combinations being possible within the broad constraints of conservation) .

The particular form and internal structure of the minimal family does not affect the relevance of these broad conditions. Whatever form the minimal family assumes in a particular society, in response to that society's pattern of weighting of the interfamily relations through which it is reproduced, its reproduction will necessarily involve the transformations of all the dimensions of family structure affected by the process, for example, generation, consanguinity/affinity, and the various forms of contrast between "primary," or intrafamily, and "secondary," or interfamily, relations recognized in the societies of the Gê-Bororo group.

The constraints of conservation applying to the system of family relations as a whole mean that these transformations are not free to vary in relation to one another: that is why their coordination is the essential action through which the system defines itself (that is, maintains its own conservation) . There are, however, a limited number of "degrees of freedom" in the system: the specification of one transformation does not mechanically determine all the others. There are, nevertheless, fewer degrees of freedom than the total number of transformations, reckoned for both males and females. The number and form of these "degrees of freedom" varies somewhat for each system, but for all of them it suffices to specify the forms of a subset of the total set of transformations making up the reproductive process of the family and the dominant pattern of interfamily relations in order to determine the rest.

The "specification" of the form of the transformation of a dimension of family structure is achieved by designating that form of that transformation as the context and criterion for recruitment to a communal institution. Recruitment has the effect of realigning the individual in the appropriately weighted relationships with the other categories of status/role actors to whom he is related upon the dimension in question. The coordination among the transformations is specified through the institutionalized pattern of relations among the total set of institutions which embody them. Sometimes more than one dimension and its transformation can be embodied and coordinated in the same institution (for example, a pair of exogamous moieties based on unilineal descent, exogamy and descent being transformations of different dimensions of family and interfamily structure) . Often, however, each dimension and transformation will be embodied in a distinct institution.

The superstructures of the Gê and Bororo societies consist of small sets of such institutions, each embodying the transformation of some dimension of interfamily relations, with the weighting attached to it in the process of reproducing the pattern of family and interfamily relations. Taken together, these sets of institutions correspond to the subsets of relations which suffice to determine the form of the other transformations that go to make up their respective systems.

The analysis presented in this section is essentially a development of the point made at the end of the last section, that the contrast between the domestic, or household, level and the communal institutional level of village structure must be seen as a dialectical refraction of the contrast between the two levels of the structure of the extended-family household, respectively represented by the minimal family unit and the extended family as a whole. The latter contrast is epitomized by the relationship of parents-in-law to son-in-law: it is, in other words, identical with the structure of dominance relations that has been identified on other grounds as the focus of articulation between the base and superstructural levels of Gê society. What I have attempted to do in this section is to specify the formal basis of this relationship in system-theoretical terms. While this discussion has of necessity been confined to an abstract and general level, the following article on Kayapó social structure is intended as a concrete illustration of the general approach developed here.

LARGE VILLAGES AND LACK OF FORMAL INTERVILLAGE STRUCTURE

The differentiation of a set of communal institutions, constituting a level of social structure distinct from that of the extended-family households that constitute the segmentary units of the society, provides Gê and Bororo society with a mechanism capable of integrating large numbers of such segmentary units. Since the communal level as a whole arises out of the regulation of relations among segments within the community, and since these relations are focused on the marriage exchange of spouses among households, the community takes on the character of a self-contained, endogamous society. It has no need for formal exogamous relations with other communities. Its communal superstructure is therefore not defined in terms that require or imply links with other villages. The individual village community, as a self-regulating, self-reproducing, autonomous social entity, thus effectively defines the highest level of Gê-Bororo social structure.

This may again be contrasted with certain Amazonian groups of the virilocal, patrilineal, exogamous, single long-house community type (for example, the Tukano of the Vaupés region: Goldman

1963; Hugh-Jones n.d.). The villages of these groups lack the differentiation of household and communal levels of structure, since the minimal patrilineage, as the minimal segment of social structure, forms the structural core of the extended family with its long house, and thus defines the structure of the local community as a whole. They accordingly seem to lack the structural capacity to form large, polysegmentary villages on the Gê-Bororo pattern. However, these societies achieve a far broader structure of intercommunal relations than the Gê or Bororo. This is created through the extension of the principles defining the structure of the individual segment (the exogamous patrilineage) to form a system of internally ranked, exogamous patriclans standing in relations of marriage alliance with other such clans. This system is capable of integrating local communities over wide areas, albeit at a lower level of effective solidarity than that achieved among the extended-family household segments of a Gê village. The contrast between these two forms of Amazonian intracommunal and intercommunal organization clearly repeats, at a higher structural level, the contrast noted earlier between the structural potential of uxorilocality and virilocality as forms of domestic grouping.

The Relationship of the Gê-Bororo Bimodal Economy to Social Structure: The Hypertrophy of Hunting and Gathering and the Institution of the Trek as Superstructure

Among the general questions put at the beginning of this paper was that of why Gê and Bororo social structure should be so closely correlated with the bimodal economic pattern peculiar to these groups (and others of similar structure). This pattern is characterized by an alternation between the practice of swidden agriculture, supplemented by hunting and gathering done on a predominantly individual basis, in a large base village, and the dispersion of this village into hunting-and-gathering trekking bands for part of every year. The traditional explanations of this pattern have been either that the Gê are essentially hunting-and-gathering people still in the stage of transition to agriculture, or that they are the remnants of former tropical forest agriculturists displaced by more aggressive groups from the richer agricultural land along the larger rivers of the Amazonian basin, and forced to turn to hunting and gathering to supplement the more meager food-producing (and especially protein-producing) capacity of their new habitat on the forest periphery. Proponents of both views have tended to share the assumptions that the Gê-Bororo ecological niche on the margins of the forest that covers the lowland Amazon basin is poorer than that of at least the more favored agricultural areas of the forest (specifically, the silted floodplains along the banks of the major rivers; Lathrap 1968) ; that hunting and gathering, at least when conducted on a seminomadic basis for part of the year by the society as a whole, is a more primitive economic adaptation than agriculture, *and therefore* an indication of social and cultural backwardness in contrast to more fully agricultural peoples; and that the complex and therefore culturally "advanced" social organizations of the Gê constitute an anomaly in relation to their relatively "primitive" economies and "impoverished" ecological niche (Cooper 1942; Haeckel 1952; Lévi-Strauss 1944, 1952; Steward and Faron 1959; Lathrap 1968; cf. Lowie 1952) .

All three of these assumptions are in my opinion unfounded and erroneous. The first has been exploded by Bamberger, who pointed out not only that the margin between the forest and the savannah, the preferred site of Gê villages, is a distinct ecozone richer in floral and faunal resources than either the savannah or the tropical forest in themselves, but that the Gê mixed economy, in making use of all three zones, is actually far more complex and sophisticated in the range of resources it exploits, and thus richer in terms of productive potential, than the more narrowly based economies of either the forest or the savannah tribes (Bamberger 1971) . As I have already argued, following Bamberger and Carneiro, the Gê and Bororo, with an overabundance of good agricultural land, a relatively rich and diversified agriculture, and ample supplies of fish and game in the immediate vicinity of their base villages, have no pressing economic need to go on their collective trekking expeditions.

I should now like to challenge the remaining two assumptions of the set, on the basis of the analysis of the social relations of Gê production and reproduction presented in this paper. To begin with the last (that the complex social organization of the Gê and Bororo stands in an anomalous relationship to their emphasis upon hunting and gathering) : it is odd that the proponents of this view have insisted upon the primitive or culturally regressive character of Gê and Bororo hunting and gathering without taking account of either the true richness of the Gê ecological niche, the more complex and productive resource base that the development of hunting and gathering within that niche gives the Gê in contrast to the more narrowly agricultural societies of the same area, or the fact that the hunting-and-gathering trekking groups are invariably organized on the basis of communal corporate institutions, such as moieties or age-sets, that form the highest level of structural complexity of the social systems in question. Far from

standing in a contradictory or anomalous relationship to the complexity of Gê-Bororo social organization, in other words, hunting
and gathering (or better, the organizational requirements of integrating the trekking adaptation with the agricultural base village adaptation) appears to be directly constitutive of the organizational complexity it is held to contravene.

The second of the two assumptions (that the economic atavism
of hunting and gathering can be directly interpreted as a sign of
the cultural and social regressiveness of the society practicing it)
rests upon the more fundamental assumption that the sector of
material production is invariably the dominant sector of production and thus *ipso facto* the primary criterion of classification of
the social and cultural systems of which it forms the "base." As
the model developed in this paper has shown, this assumption is
unfounded for most primitive societies, and certainly those with
which we are directly concerned here. It leads to the equally unfounded and misleading assumption that forms of economic activity are always primarily to be accounted for by reference to
their ostensible economic motives. As I have argued, this assumption leads directly to bad economic analysis in the case of the Gê
and Bororo (for example, the attempts to explain their trekking
adaptation in terms of the need to offset the nonexistent scarcity
of resources in their chosen ecological niche) .

This whole set of assumptions fails to take account of the need
to analyze the relations of relative dominance of different categories of production, and where material production turns out to
be subordinate to another mode (viz., socialization) , to consider
that the primary *raison d'être* of the forms of material production
should be sought, not in terms of economic needs, but of the requirements of supporting the structure of the relations of production in the dominant sector. I have earlier shown that the structure of productive relations in the sector of swidden agriculture
is to be accounted for in just such terms. I shall now make the
same case for the sector of hunting and gathering, and specifically
for the institution of the collective trek.

The dominance of the father-in-law over the son-in-law, which,
I have argued, forms the basis of Gê and Bororo social structure
in general, depends upon the ability of the father-in-law to exercise meaningful control over his daughters. This means, mini-
mally, to prevent them from leaving his household, since residential contiguity is the essential medium of control. Under normal
circumstances, however, this control is rarely put to the test in the
households of the base village. The establishment of the uxorilocal
residence rule in effect constantly threatens to undermine the prin-

ciple of male control over the household, because the group of
women that form its core remain together by simple inertia, while
men come and go around them. There is no context in which the
male head of the household can assert his control over its female
members and thus give social meaning to his "dominance." On
his ability to do so, however, hangs not only his private position
in his own household, but the consistency and integration of society at large.

The context for the assertion of male control over household
structure is provided by the annual hunting and gathering treks.
The treks are always organized on the basis of collective male
groups (for instance, moieties and age-sets) from among the superstructure of communal institutions. In normal communities
there is always more than one trekking group, and often there are
several. A father-in-law takes his wife, his daughters, and their
husbands with him (that is, with his collective men's group) on
trek, regardless of the collective group affiliation of the sons-in-
law. In normal households where there is more than one father-
in-law, for example, where two or more sisters or matrilateral
cousins have married daughters, these men divide the household,
if they happen to belong to separate groups, each taking his own
wife and daughters (and sons-in-law) with his own group. Thus
do senior men assert their dominance over the female core of the
extended-family household, and their ability to extend this control
over their sons-in-law, through the collective assertion of the
dominance of the male productive mode of hunting and long-
range gathering over the female mode of agriculture, associated
with static households in the base village.

The Gê use of hunting and gathering to reinforce the structure
of dominance in the relations of production in the dominant
sector of production, socialization, well exemplifies the way in
which subdominant productive modes are restructured to conform
to the requirements of the dominant mode. The seminomadic
hunting-and-gathering adaptation of the Gê and Bororo plays a
vital role in the maintenance and reproduction of the structure of
dominance in the relations of production in the dominant sector
of socialization, and thus the structure of society as a whole. It does
not do this, however, in the capacity of infrastructure, or of productive base, but in the capacity of superstructure.

6 | Kinship, Household, and Community Structure among the Kayapó[1]

Terence S. Turner

Introduction: Purposes of the Analysis

IN THIS PAPER I present a systematic analysis of Kayapó kinship and domestic group relations as a case study in the application of the general model developed in the preceding essay. The focus of the analysis is on the shifting pattern of relations of attachment to and separation from families and domestic households, as manifested in formal and informal patterns of behavior, dominance and subordination among their members. These relations are conceived as an organized system undergoing a regular and continuous process of development over time. This system and its temporal process are in turn conceived as a self-regulating and self-reproducing structure, with both formal and dynamic properties. One object of the analysis is to give a comprehensive account of both the structural and dynamic properties of the system, and particularly of the relationship between the two.

A second goal of the analysis is to compare the resulting model of kinship and domestic relations with a descriptive model of the structure of Kayapó communal corporate groups and their activities. The object of this comparison is to test the hypothesis put forward in the preceding paper that Gê and Bororo communal institutions, through their recruitment criteria and other aspects of their collective structure and activities, serve to define and generate a specific, communally standardized structure of household, extended-family, and kinship relations, and that they reciprocally embody the weighted pattern of relations they inculcate on the domestic level in their own structure. The basic principle of this pattern is the dominance of the wife's parents over the wife and, through her, her husband, within the uxorilocal household; but as I suggested, the reproduction of this pattern of rela-

179

tions at the segmental (household) level or organization is exploited to project its analogue, in a concentrated and amplified form, as the basis of the dominance of the age-grades of senior men (and to a lesser extent senior women) over the younger age strata of the society at the level of communal institutions.

The analysis, then, is formulated in the terms of the preceding general paper as a hierarchically organized feedback system, in which the upper level of communal institutions determines the specific structure of the lower, or segmentary, level of extended-family and household structure within the limits of certain general constraints and positive resources for social integration and control implicit in the latter (that is, the infrastructure of the system, in the terms of the preceding paper). The model is thus based on the principle of circular causality: it is explicitly antireductionistic, while at the same time insisting that the formal (ideal-normative) structure of categories and institutions at all levels must be understood as an aspect of their dynamic (causal-functional) coordination and interaction.

Extended-Family, Household, and Kinship Organization

A SUMMARY DESCRIPTION OF KAYAPÓ KINSHIP AND DOMESTIC GROUP STRUCTURE

The Kayapó share the basic Gê pattern of uxorilocal extended-family household structure, with its characteristic internal articulation into discrete family units. In the Kayapó case these units take the form of monogamous nuclear families. The husbands of women in the active reproductive phase (that is, the expansion stage of the family of procreation) stand in a subordinate or subdominant relation to their wives' parents. The Kayapó family is "nuclear" in the exact sense that it serves as the focus or center of reference for a radially organized bilateral kindred. Like all of the Northern Gê societies, the Kayapó lack descent or any form of kin-based corporate groups or categories standing in relations of perscriptive exogamy to one another.

The Kayapó nuclear family, considered at the completion of its reproductive cycle (that is, at the point at which it is ready to disperse) is bilaterally symmetrical. By this I mean that in the long run its male and female members strike much the same balance of separation and integration between it and the families from which they came to it or to which they go from it.

Before this ultimate point of equilibrium is reached, however, the structure of the family, and the radial network of kinship relations immediately linked to it, is weighted in a markedly

asymmetrical way. The uxorilocal residence pattern, as I suggested in the preceding paper, can be understood in dynamic
terms as a setting for the exchange of sons for daughter's husbands,
in a way that exploits men's control over women (and to some
extent mothers' control over their daughters) to gain control over
men. The Kayapó have developed the principle of the exchange
of sons for sons-in-law about as far as it can go in the direction of
severing sons' ties with their natal families and households and
integrating them into their families of procreation as (initially)
subordinate daughters' husbands. The result is a marked patrilateral skewing in the weighting of intra- and interfamily relations
during the expansion phase of the family. This is, however,
counterbalanced by matrilateral emphasis at the higher (suprafamilial) level of extended-family structure, in the form of the
domination of the young husband-father by his wife's parents.
As the family passes into its dispersion phase, this patrilateral
emphasis progressively diminishes, as does the matrilateral dominance of the wife's parents at the suprafamilial level, until the
point at which the husband and wife are ready to assume the
role of dominant parents-in-law toward their own daughters'
husbands and the cycle begins anew. The point is that the pattern
of weighting, for all its asymmetry considered at a given level
within a given stage, conserves overall (that is, over both stages
of the devolopmental process and over both levels of structure
within any given stage) a balanced relation of bilateral symmetry among all of its component parts considered as a set. The
structure of the Kayapó system of kinship and domestic group
relations can be understood as a continuously evolving dialectic
between the asymmetrical and symmetrical tendencies of the
system, focused on the shifting position of dominance within the
uxorilocal extended family.

INTRAFAMILY RELATIONS, I: THE MALE LIFE CYCLE AS AN ASPECT OF THE DEVELOPMENTAL CYCLE OF THE DOMESTIC GROUP

The intrafamily class of relations, in contrast to the marginal
class, is the focus of the sexually asymmetrical pattern of weighted
relations to which I have alluded. It will be convenient for purposes of exposition to present the male and female aspects of this
pattern separately before attempting to show how they actually
form complementary aspects of a symmetrical whole.

A boy spends his infancy and early childhood under his mother's
care as a member of his natal family. At the beginning of the
period of later childhood, at around eight years of age, he is taken
from his maternal household to be domiciled in a men's house

in the center of the circular village plaza, round the circumference of which the extended-family households of the village, among them his mother's house, are ranged. Induction into the men's house is under the auspices of a pair of ceremonial parents called the "false" mother and father. We shall hear more of these figures later: suffice it to say here that their function is to sever the boy's relationships, for public social purposes, with his own parents in particular and his natal family and household in general. After a half dozen years or so of residence in the men's house, the boys, now youths, undergo initiation. This rite is again under the sponsorship of the "false" parents, and stresses marriage and the youth's subordination to his future parents-in-law, with the active collaboration and support of his own parents and sisters.

Following initiation with its ritual marriage, a youth is licensed to court any girl he pleases as a future wife. If she and her parents approve of the match, a liaison develops and pregnancy follows in due course. Upon the birth of the baby, the new father is considered a married man, and moves out of the men's house to take up residence with his wife and parents-in-law. For the next years, during the active reproductive (expansion) phase of his family of procreation, he remains bound by conventions of strict formal deference in his relations with his parents-in-law and of respectful restraint toward his wife's sisters and their husbands.

These restrictions have the effect of retarding his full integration into the household, and thus both accentuate and prolong the dominance of his affines over him in the household context. A young husband-father's position in his affinal household is further isolated by a normative proscription prohibiting his brothers (or male parallel cousins, who are classificatory brothers) from marrying into the same household. This rule completes and emphasizes the separation and mutual incompatibility between affinal and natal family relations, and underscores a man's dependence and subordination in relation to his uxoral affines during the expansion of his family of procreation.

A man's relations with his own household in the same period, as in his earlier period of men's house residence, are even more constricted. The focus of formal restraint in this direction is his relationship with his sister's husband. A wife's brother should preferably not even come to the house, or remain in it, when his sister's husband is there. If he must be there, he should remain silent and make himself as inconspicuous as possible. There is also some feeling that a man should not enter the house if his sister is there alone. Otherwise he may come to the house and even keep possessions there, but not sleep there. His relations with his sister's children, in their early years, involve rough joking with a high aggressive content. At the same time, a man's "marginal" relationship to his sister's children and hers to his children are given positive ritual emphasis as the preferred channels for the bestowing of personal names on the children (see Chapter 4 of this book). The main thrust of this relationship is to counterbalance (and thus to reinforce) the separation of the brother and sister from their common natal family, and in particular (in the skewed pattern of emphasis on the sister's relationship to her brother's children) the separation of the brother from the sister's household.

It can be seen that the emphatic severance of the relations between a son and his parents at the close of the expansion phase of his natal family is the complement, in terms of the structure of the uxorilocal extended-family household, of the equally emphatic integration of a man as a father-husband into his affinal household at the beginning of the expansion of his own family of procreation. The negation of the intrafamily relationship of son to parent, as a means of separation from the natal household, in other words, is counterbalanced by the positive stress upon the relationship of the spouse-father to his children as the basis of his integration into his affinal household. Conservation is, then, preserved in male intrafamilial relationships, in a way that leads to a stress upon the role of the father-husband over that of the maternal uncle-brother at the level of nuclear family relations.

At the higher level of extended-family structure, however, this "patrilateral" emphasis at the level of nuclear family structure becomes the condition for the equally stressed domination of the young father-husband and his family by the wife's parents (who are, of course, "matrilateral" relatives from the standpoint of the dominated family). This is so because, as I have briefly indicated, the conditions of the young father-husband's "integration" into the household also involve his isolation (and, in a more general sense, the isolation of his family unit) within the household and his entanglement in a framework of behavioral restrictions that impede his and his family's full integration into the household on equal terms. This degree of separation from "full integration on equal terms" in the structure of the household measures the degree of subordination of the young father-husband, in his capacity as daughter's husband, to his parents-in-law (themselves the embodiments and arbiters of "full integration" in the household).

It should be emphasized that the separation of the son from his parents at the close of the expansion phase of his natal family removes him from the household before his parents rise to a position of dominance within it. He is thus never a part of a dominant family or faction within the household of his birth. This in turn greatly facilitates his total transference from his natal to his affinal household in the subordinate role of the new father-husband. He does not move from a position of strength in his natal household, gradually submitting to the constraints of subordination to his affines in his wife's household while applying what leverage he is able to prize out of his remaining position of strength at home to mitigate or hold aloof from their domination. The institution of the men's house as boys' dormitory and the separation of boys from their natal households at such an early age have the primary effect of delivering young men to their affines in as unmitigatedly weak, isolated, and subordinate a position as possible. This at once maximizes the ease and completeness of their integration into their affinal households and makes possible a relatively complete yielding at marriage of direct control over their brides on the part of their parents-in-law (that is, a strong marriage exchange), which of course maximizes the strength of men's attachment to their new household in their roles as fathers and husbands.

INTRAFAMILY RELATIONS, II: THE FEMALE CYCLE AND THE COMPLETION OF THE DEVELOPMENTAL CYCLE OF THE DOMESTIC GROUP

Intrahousehold Relations

Just as a man relies for his initial attachment to his affinal household upon his wife's womb (since it is only the actual birth of a child that is considered to "consummate" a marriage, and thus provide the proper basis for the male genitor to move in with the mother as her recognized husband), so it is his wife's function as primary socializing agent that provides his means of escaping his initial subordinate position in the household and eventually moving into the dominant position in his own right. As the father of growing children, a man becomes regarded less as an affinal member of the household and more as a consanguineal member of it. By the time the expansion phase of the family is over (by which time his sons are moving to the men's house and his daughters are beginning the process of sexual initiation and relations that ultimately lead to marriage) a man is primarily identified as a parental (consanguineal) rather than as merely a conjugal (affinal) member of the extended family. In this capacity, he may be thought of as a prospective father-in-law, standing together with his wife toward a new generation of incoming affines (daughters' husbands) in the position of a consanguineal core member of the household.

It should be noted that concomitant with a man's movement toward full integration in his affinal household, his relations with his sister's household and family become greatly relaxed. His joking relationship with his sister's children lapses, and one day his sister invites him back to the house for a formal dinner with her husband. This occasion marks the relaxation of the avoidance and respect relationship between the two men.

The main point for present purposes is that the transformation of a man's household status from that of subordinate daughter's husband to that of dominant wife's father, that is, male head of an extended family, is defined primarily in relation to the growth of his children, that is, to the development of the intrafamilial level of his family of procreation, for which his wife has specific functional responsibility and with which she is, for structural purposes, primarily identified. It is a man's daughters who bring sons-in-law into the house, and his sons who, by leaving it, indirectly make possible the sons-in-laws' arrival in it on terms favorable to his own dominant role. The development of a man's position in Kayapó domestic group structure is thus closely tied to the development of the female sector of family and domestic relations, and therefore, in general terms, to the female life cycle.

A girl is not separated from her parents and natal household at the close of the expansion of her natal family, in contrast to her brother. For the whole period of her brother's separation in the men's house, she remains integrated in her natal family. Then, at the dispersion of that family, when she has reached the age at which she is ready to bear children (that is, when she is ready for marriage in the full Kayapó sense of the word), she goes through a ceremony of adoption by "false" parents very similar to that which boys go through upon induction into the men's house. This rite involves, among other things, divesting her of the bodily ornaments associated with childhood status, which women wear up to this point in their lives. Marriage and childbearing follow soon after this ceremony.

The emphasis upon the severance of a woman's intrafamilial relations with her parents in the rite of adoption by the "false" parents, and the association of this separation with her imminent marriage and motherhood, manifest the Kayapó emphasis upon the separation of the bride in marriage from her direct ties with her natal family. The force of the marriage exchange from the woman's side is the basis of the strength of the husband's subordinate attachment to the wife's parents. The separation of the woman from her natal family in marriage is in its way as emphatic, and as significant for the development of the structure of household relations, as the man's earlier separation from his natal family at the time of his induction into the men's house.

A woman's parents, at the point at which she is separated from them in the premarital rite just described, have attained a position of dominance or full integration into the household. Dominance and full integration are synonymous: as I have described, the subordination of the father of the family, in his capacity as daughter's husband, to his wife's parents is maintained by various relational and behavioral mechanisms which emphasize his social distance (that is, *partial* integration) from other members of the household, especially those more centrally and fully integrated into it than he (above all, his wife's parents). Marriage for a woman involves her in the same structure of differential levels of integration into the structure of the household. It means, on the one hand, the attenuation of her family relationship as daughter to her mother and father and, on the other, her exchange of this subordinate intrafamily role for the role of link between her parents and her husband. She is, of course, still fully integrated into her household, but within it she is prevented from becoming fully integrated into her own family of procreation by the continuing force of her tie to her parents.

In this new role the woman, as a young wife and mother, functions as the medium of subordination of her husband to her parents. Her effectiveness as a medium of control depends, on the one hand, upon her remaining under the ultimate control of her parents (expressed in their control of her residential attachment to the household) and, on the other hand, upon a significant degree of control over her being yielded to the husband (since it is this measure of control that becomes the basis of the husband's attachment to her family and household, and thus to the structure of relations controlled by her parents). The husband's control over the wife within the new family is expressed in the subordination of the intrafamily domain of relations (focused upon the children and primarily presided over by the wife, with relatively minor participation by the husband) to the level of interfamily relations, including the relations between the new family and the other families within the household, and especially the wife's parents. This level of interfamily structure is, as we have seen, primarily the responsibility of the husband.

The relationship of dominance between the inter- and intrafamily levels of family structure is thus dialectically related to the dominance of the wife's parents over her husband and family of procreation as a whole. Neither relationship is static, and each changes in relation to the other. The turning point in the development of both comes at the close of the first (expansion) phase of the family cycle. This is the point at which sexual reproduction ceases, the family has attained its maximum growth, and the children have already begun to grow up, acquiring social identities in their own right. At about this point, as we have seen, a husband exchanges the primary household identity of "affine" for that of resident consanguine. By this time, also, the parents-in-law have begun to age and withdraw from active domination of the household.

For both reasons, the asymmetrical relationship of dominance-subordination between the wife's parents and the daughter's husband tends to move toward one of symmetrical reciprocity. The wife's parents' ultimate sanction of forcible divorce and expulsion from the household is much harder to use against a father with strong consanguineal ties to the household through his children than against a new husband with only a single infant, with still uncertain prospects for survival, to his credit, so their power over the former is in any case considerably undermined. The pressure for the subordination of the wife-mother to her parents as a medium of domination over her husband is thus removed. At the same time, the substantial completion of her functions of early socialization and the consequent atrophy of the intrafamily domain of relations undermine the structural basis for her subordination to her husband within the family.

The beginning of the second (dispersion) phase of the family cycle, immediately following the phase of expansion, thus marks the point at which a woman emerges from her relative subordination, both to her husband within the family and as an instrument of her husband's subordination to her parents at the interfamily level. This is, as I have already described, the point at which her husband moves toward assuming a dominant role in the household, but this dominance is for a change not exercised through her as a medium but rather through her daughters, over their husbands as they arrive upon the scene. The woman participates in her own right in this exercise of dominance through the medium of her daughters, from her secure base as a fully integrated member of her own household. Only in the matter of following her husband's men's society on hunting-and-gathering treks does she remain, in any pragmatically significant sense, "subordinate" to her husband. From this point on, her relations with him rather assume the character of an easy alliance based upon a complementarity of subsistence activities and spheres of social interest, with a common basis of interest in the affairs of their household.

The final stage of the life cycle for both sexes, that of old age, may be said in general to approach the sexually symmetrical pattern of the first (infantile) stage: the contrast between patrilateral and matrilateral relations is submerged and transcended, and that between consanguineal and affinal relations is likewise superseded. The life cycle, with its bilaterally symmetrical terminal phases bracketing the asymmetrically weighted central stages, thus parallels the structure of the kinship system as a whole, with its framework of bilaterally symmetrically marginal relations bracketing the asymmetrically weighted sector of intrafamily and affinal relations.

A woman's achievement of full integration into her own family of procreation, and her consequent attainment of a dominant household position in her own right, occur at the beginning of the dispersion phase of her family of procreation. They thus complement her separation from her natal family at the close of its dispersion phase. This separation takes place when her parents have already attained a position of integration and dominance within the household (it is this which allows them to "negotiate" from strength in the marriage exchange with her husband, in contrast to the weakness of her husband's position). The woman's own subsequent full reintegration into her family of procreation occurs as she and her husband are attaining a similar dominant position. A woman's points of separation and integration in the structure of the family and household thus balance each other: the terms of integration exactly reverse those of separation. The development of a woman's family and domestic group relations, considered as an aspect of the family cycle, thus conforms to the same formal pattern of conservation as does that of a man.

Affinal Relations

The strength of the transference of the woman in marriage from her natal family to her husband and family of procreation is overtly expressed, not in her direct relations with her husband, but rather in her relations with his mother and (especially) his sister. A young woman pregnant for the first time (thus a bride-to-be in Kayapó terms) often goes to the house of the mother and sister of her prospective husband to have her baby. She returns to her own house soon afterward, but the gesture is emblematic of the close relationship that develops between sisters-in-law and, to a somewhat lesser extent, between mother-in-law and daughter-in-law. The relationship emphasizes mutual visiting, sharing of possessions, and complete openness and self-expression in speaking. If a husband has a grievance against his wife in the first years of marriage, he often feels too constrained by the standards of formal respect governing his relationship to his wife as an affine to take it up directly with her, and instead applies to his sister to remonstrate with her on his behalf. The husband's sister does often take her brother's part in marital disputes with his wife. This is the other side of the open and unrestrained relationship between husband's sister and brother's wife. It is important to note that the brother/husband must avoid the two women whenever they are together. If his sister comes to his wife's house for a visit, he must leave for the men's house.

The relationship between sisters-in-law is thus the diametrical opposite of the relationship between brothers-in-law, in which the wife's brother must avoid his sister's husband when in the presence of his sister (whereas, before the marriage is consummated, the sister's would-be husband must avoid her brother in her presence). The opposition between the affinal relationships of male and female siblings-in-law is a particularly clear-cut case of the operation of the principle of conservation defined above. The original cross-sex sibling relationship between brother and sister, as a direct, intrafamily relationship, is severed for public social purposes by the brother's removal to the men's house and his concomitant severance of ties with his natal family as a whole. The principle of conservation of family relations would require under these circumstances that to the degree that intrafamily relationships are severed, they must be transformed into positively stressed interfamily relations. One way of achieving this would be to institute solidary relations linking each (male and female) sibling with the structurally complementary members of the other's family of procreation (that is, the same-sex sibling-in-law). The extreme bias of the Kayapó system toward the separation of a man from his natal family and household, however, is incompatible with the development of a relationship of positive solidarity with his sister's husband, counterbalancing the severed relationship with his sister. The same asymmetrical pattern of weighting, however, means that a man's sisters are in the opposite position in relation to his wife. There is no conflict between a husband's sister and her brother's wife or his household such as exists between her brother and her husband: on the contrary, the sister-in-law relationship is open to become the channel for all of the positive force of the original cross-sex sibling relation-

ship, unable as it is to be expressed between brothers-in-law. The
sole condition of this is simply that the linking member of the
relationship be absent, since the radical incompatibility, for him,
of his natal family and affinal relationships is an intrinsic feature
of the situation defined by the severance of his relationship with
his sister and his subsequent displacement to his wife's household.

The exiguousness of a woman's relationship with her husband's
father is in direct contrast to a man's relations with his wife's
father (and mother). The emphatic attenuation of a woman's
husband's link as son to his father is the precondition of his
equally emphatic bond as husband to her and her household. Son's
wife and husband's father thus have a purely negative basis of
relationship, and in fact tend to have virtually nothing to do
with each other. This contrast in a man's and a woman's father-in-
law relations in a sense reverses that between the relations between
a woman and her husband's sister and a man and his sister's
husband.

The Male and Female Life Cycles as Complementary Aspects of a Single Developmental Process

The outline of the development of male and female intrafamilial and affinal relations just presented has brought out four
important points. One is the emphasis for both sexes upon a
relatively extreme degree of separation from the natal family in
favor of attachment to the family of procreation. Another is that
the stages of separation or integration in the developmental process of each sex are, in relation to the level of relations at which
they are formulated, of a radical or total character. The Kayapó
system works not in terms of gently graded, continuous processes
of transition, but rather by a series of relatively abrupt and dis-
continuous steps. Third, the phases of separation and integration
for the two sexes occur at opposite times. Finally, in spite of the
asymmetry of the sequences of the male and female developmental
phases, both sequences conform to the same structural pattern
(stressed attenuation of connection with the natal family, followed by stressed integration into the family of procreation), and
thus "balance out" in the same way. As a completed pattern, in
other words, the coordinated developmental cycles of a man and
woman linked in marriage form a bilaterally symmetrical structure. The ultimate expression of this bilateral symmetry is the
relative symmetry in the roles of the man and woman as dominant
parents-in-law at the completion of the cycle of their family of
procreation.

These relationships between the male and female sequences of

TABLE 1. Relationships between male and female sequences of developmental phases

Phase of family cycle	Separation/integration in family structure	
	Male	Female
End expansion of natal family/begin dispersion	—	(+)
End dispersion of natal family/begin expansion of family of procreation	+	—
End expansion of family of procreation/begin its dispersion	(+)	+
End dispersion of family of procreation/move to level of extended family as head of household	++	++

Note: Minus signs signify separation from the family indicated, plus signs integration into it. Parentheses surrounding a sign signify no change in status. The double plus signs indicate integration into the higher level of structure represented by the extended-family household.

developmental phases are summed up in Table 1. It should be borne in mind that the end of the expansion phase of a family coincides with the beginning of its dispersion phase, while the end of its dispersion phase coincides with the formation by the offspring of the family of a new family of procreation (and thus, the beginning of a new phase of expansion). The table clearly indicates how an asymmetrically weighted pattern of relationships is generated within the limitations of the invariant constraints imposed by the principle of overall bilateral symmetry. Weighting, one of the main components of the general model developed in the preceding chapter, was there defined as a conjunction of three factors: (1) the specification of the degree of transference of actors between the natal family and household and the family and household of procreation; (2) the manner of phasing this process as a sequence of distinct stages or transitions; and (3) the mode of coordination of these two factors for actors of opposite sexes. The table and the aspects of Kayapó family and age-grade transitions it summarizes exemplify the way these three factors interact to determine the pattern of social relations and institutions in a particular Gê instance.

Conformity to the principle of conservation of bilateral symmetry is manifested at each stage by the way the radical separation of one sex from a given level of structure (for example, that of the family) is counterbalanced by an equally radical emphasis upon the integration or continuity of incorporation of the op-

posite sex, and the way that this pattern is reversed in each successive stage. The coordination of the separation and integration
of the spouse of each sex in relation to each's respective natal
family and mutual family of procreation constitutes, at the same
time, a higher level of structure than that represented by the
pattern of either sex alone. This level of coordinated interfamily
relations corresponds to the level of structure of the household
as a whole, considered as a system of coordinated interfamily relations. The dispersion of the family of procreation that coincides
with the female spouse's final attainment of reintegration at the
family level thus also coincides with the accession of the pair of
spouse-parents to the higher level of interfamily structure, where
they become the point of reference for the attachment of their
daughters' and daughters' husbands' families of procreation to
the household. The completed pattern of interfamily relations
embodied by the older married couple thus becomes the framework for the reproduction of the same pattern in the next generation. The "dominance" of the older couple over this next phase
of the reproductive cycle is from this point of view simply the
expression of the higher level of household structure, which consists of the completed pattern of coordinated interfamily relations
they have attained. All of this illustrates one of the key points
of the preceding paper. The reproductive cycle of the family is
weighted in such a way as to reproduce a specific hierarchical
pattern of dominance relations as the axis of the extended-family
household.

MARGINAL RELATIONS AND THE PRINCIPLE OF BILATERAL SYMMETRY

Basic Structural Properties of Marginal Relations

The categories of marginal relations are structurally symmetrical in a sexual sense. For both men and women, they consist, in ascending generations, of the cross-sexed parental siblings
and grandparents, and in descending generations of the offspring
of cross-sexed siblings and grandchildren.[2] The main expression
of marginal relations, the passage of names and other ritual
paraphernalia from senior to junior marginal kin, also follows
sexually symmetrical lines: women pass names to their fraternal
nieces and granddaughters, men to their sororal nephews and
grandsons. The details of these relations are given by Bamberger
(1974).

Marginal relations consist of transformed intrafamily relations
of the linking relative: there is thus a dialectical relationship between the two categories, in which marginal relations take the

form of positive transformations of the direct intrafamily relations of filiation and cross-sexed siblingship severed in the process of forming the new, complementary set of intrafamily relations (that is, relations within the family of procreation). The severed relations of a linking spouse-parent to his or her parents and siblings are thus positively transformed in two parallel ways. While the linking parent exchanges them for a complementary set of intrafamily relations (to spouse and children), they become the marginal relations of his or her children.

These two sets of transformations, according to the principle of conservation defined above, are interdependent and equal in force (weight). The requirement that names be transferred between marginal relatives in the first years after the formation of the family of procreation of the linking relative (that is, before the children have reached late childhood) reflects the dynamic interdependence of the two classes of relations. They are, in effect, internally linked as the complementary expressions of a dialectical unity, on both the structural and dynamic levels, the one representing both the final transformation and the condition of the other. Marginal relations, in other words, act both as the indispensable corollary of the formation of a new set of intrafamily relations and as the final transformation of relations of this class (that is, the form assumed by the intrafamily relations among a set of linking relatives at the dispersion of their common family). In both capacities, marginal relations frame intrafamily relations as a class with an overt expression of the structural principle basic to them both: the conservation of bilateral sexual symmetry, manifested as the concomitant of the conservation of the solidarity of the basic unit of the system, the bilateral nuclear family.

The Place of Marginal Relations in the Structure of Weighting

The overriding feature of the structure of intrafamily relations for both men and women can be identified, on the basis of the preceding account, as the weighting of the intrafamily roles associated with the family of procreation (spouse, parent) over those associated with the natal family (sibling, child). This pattern of weighting is, however, transformed from its initial asymmetrical form into a symmetrical configuration at the point at which the category of intrafamily relations as a whole is transformed into marginal relations. This point, as I have described it in the preceding section, is the dispersion of the family, the point at which parents become grandparents. This is also the point at which the basis of the initially asymmetrical marginal relationship between the parents' cross-sexed siblings and their offspring is undermined by the relaxation of the restrictions attaching to the relationship between sister's husband and wife's brother, and by the resulting equalization of the relationship between brothers-in-law and sisters-in-law. The point of juncture and transformation between the two categories, in short, is the point at which the invariant principle of bilateral sexual symmetry manifests itself as the basic principle regulating the structure of both.

The initially asymmetrical marginal relationship alluded to above between the father's sister and the brother's children, on the one hand, and the mother's brother and the sister's son, on the other, consists in the attachment of more weight to the tie of the father's sister to her brother's family of procreation than to the relationship of the mother's brother to his sister's son. It is the essence of this asymmetrical weighting that it pertains as an ideal norm, not to all female or all male marginal relations alike, but to the actual sister of the father (that is, his actual ex-conatal family member): it is she, and not a grandmother, who ideally gives her female names to her brother's son, so that he may in turn bestow them upon her daughter's daughter (thus departing from the otherwise uniformly followed rule of parallel sexual name-transmission). The significance of this is that the mother's brother and father's sister, in contrast to the maternal and paternal grandparents, pass through the developmental cycles of their families of procreation contemporaneously with the linking parental siblings. The asymmetrical aspects of the father's sister relationship, as contrasted with the mother's brother role, are concentrated in the expansion phase of the family of procreation of the linking parental siblings (for example, the naming of sororal nephews and nieces), and are thus contemporaneous with the asymmetrical aspects of intrafamily and affinal relations (which likewise stress patrilateral and fraternal over matrilateral and sororal ties) reviewed above.

In these asymmetrical features, marginal relations are simply conforming, in their fashion, to the asymmetrical constraints affecting the total structure of relations of which they form a part. This conformity is dictated, in other words, by the internal relationship that binds them to the ostensibly distinct and opposing category of intrafamily relations, and that impels them to reassert the solidarity of any set of severed intrafamily relationships in proportion to the degree and weighted direction of the severance. These asymmetrical features of marginal relations are concentrated, as I have pointed out, in the roles of the actual parental siblings. The marginal category as a whole is, however, focused on the relations of grandparents to grandchildren (the father's sister and mother's brother are terminologically assimilated to the grandparental roles of the appropriate sex). These basic marginal relationships are, relatively speaking, sexually symmetrical, because they embody intrafamily relations severed and transformed at the point at which *they* become sexually symmetrical. Marginal relations therefore constitute the category in which the principle of bilateral symmetry is expressed as the overtly dominant pattern, in contrast to intrafamily relations, where sexually asymmetrical (patrilateral) bias is the overtly dominant pattern.

The marginal category consists, as we have seen, of transformed severed intrafamily relations, which link an individual's conatal family members with the offspring of her or his family of procreation with a force or weight equivalent to the severance of the complementary category of intrafamily roles. In the Kayapó case, where the natal intrafamily roles are the ones severed in favor of the formation of the complementary set of procreational intrafamily roles, the marginal category of relations is accordingly defined in terms of the compensatory reassertion of the solidarity of severed natal family relations in relation to the offspring of the family of procreation of the linking relative. The family of procreation, as the locus of positively weighted intrafamily relations, thus becomes the focus, and therefore the prior condition, of marginal relations. Marginal relations in the Kayapó system, in other words, are directly correlated with, and depend for their consummation upon, the severance of natal family relations and the formation of the new family of procreation as a positively integrated unit.

This is not the only possible arrangement within the general limitations of the bilateral, sexually symmetrical, nuclear family–based kindred structure that the Kayapó share with the other Northern Gê societies. The Eastern Timbira, for example, display virtually the opposite pattern of weighting within and between the categories of intrafamilial and marginal relations (see Chapters 1 and 2 of this book). Among them, natal family relations are not abruptly or sharply severed, and there is no emphatic shift of weighting to spouse-parent roles in the family of procreation. The weighting of relations of the intrafamily category, in other words, favors the continuity of natal family relations over procreational family roles.

This opposite pattern of weighting within the intrafamily category of relations is correlated with an opposite pattern of weighting between the complementary categories of intrafamilial and marginal relations. With minor exceptions, the kin types assigned to the two categories in the Timbira societies are the same as among the Kayapó. The mode of correlation of the two categories, however, follows a pattern opposite to that of the Kayapó. Timbira marginal relations oppose their positive solidarity, not to severed natal family relations (in direct correlation with consolidated procreational family roles), but to as yet unconsolidated procreational family relations (in direct correlation with as yet relatively unsevered natal family roles). Note that this opposite mode of coordination of the two categories of relations aligns Timbira marginal relations with a matrilateral pattern of weighting, as opposed to the Kayapó patrilateral pattern (that is, the weight of the role of the maternal uncle over that of the husband-father). A corollary of this matrilateral emphasis is the alignment of marginal relations with the continuity of the status quo before the formation of the families of procreation of a pair of cross-sexed siblings. The transformations through which the latter is affected are therefore treated as *following upon* and complementing the prior assertion of marginal relations, rather than vice versa, as among the Kayapó.

Support for this formulation of the Timbira pattern of weighting comes from many details of kinship and domestic group structure, ritual, and the sharply differing patterns of institutionalization of the two categories of relations at the level of communal group structure. The point for present purposes, however, is not the structure of the Eastern Timbira systems in themselves, but rather simply that different patterns of weighting are possible within the structural and dynamic constraints governing the Kayapó system, and that the relationship between the categories of marginal and intrafamily relations is a crucial factor in determining the specific pattern adopted in a particular case.

The emphasis of the Timbira system upon continuity of alignment with the natal family is associated with the heavier weighting of the role of the mother's brother (whose tie with the sister's son is a tie to his natal household) than of the role of the father's sister (whose tie to her brother's children links her to his family and household of procreation). This bias toward the mother's brother is reflected in the far greater array of moiety and society memberships and ritual prerogatives passed down from mother's brother to sister's son than the array of those passed from father's sister to brother's daughter. The Timbira internal pattern of asymmetrical weighting of marginal relations thus differs, in a consistent way, from the patrilateral Kaypó pattern of emphasis upon the father's sister over the mother's brother.

The asymmetrical pattern of weighting of intrafamily relations must therefore be understood as part of a larger structure consisting of the relationship between the intrafamilial and marginal categories as wholes and the internal patterns of weighting within each category. The Kaypó stress upon procreational as opposed to natal family ties, with its initial patrilateral bias and ultimate sexual symmetry, is reflected in the internal structure of both categories. At the higher level of the relation between the categories as wholes, it is manifested in the priority, in structural and dynamic terms, of the intrafamily relations of procreation over marginal relations, even while the latter remain equally stressed and indispensable in relation to the former. This relationship of "priority" is, as we shall see, the focal point in the organization of the Kayapó system of communal groups and ceremonial activities.

AFFINAL RELATIONS

Structure, Weighting, and Conservation in Affinal Relations

In the structure of the Kayapó kindred, affinity is a transitional category, a phase through which relationships pass on their way from original unrelatedness to full kinship (marriage is prescriptively with nonrelatives). Affines are said to be "kin by marriage" and "to become kin." A man's wife's family, for whom he will employ affinal terms, will be classified as consanguines by his children; similarly, he will recognize no affines in the generation of his parents, since the spouses of parental siblings are all classed in the corresponding consanguineal categories. The structure of affinal relations is therefore focused in the relation of spouses to each other and each other's consanguines. It is this focal group of affinal relations that I shall discuss here, omitting the relatively trifling cases of the spouses of nephews, nieces, and grandchildren.

For individuals of both sexes, the universe of affinal relations may be divided, for purposes of the content of social relations rather than terminological classification, into three classes: the spouse, a second class of affines to whom ego is positively related in terms of either alliance or integration, and a third class toward whom ego stands in the opposite relationship of separation or negative integration. The structure of these categories and the mode of the positive and negative relations among them differ for each sex in a way that reflects, on the one hand, the structure of the relationship of an individual of a given sex to her or his spouse, and on the other, the manner of separation of the linking spouse from his or her natal family as a preliminary to marriage.

The pattern of weighting that regulates the structure of kinship and domestic relations has been shown to rest, on the one hand, upon the opposite significance of marriage for the two sexes and, on the other, upon the opposing patterns of separation of males and females from their natal families.

A man is separated from his natal family toward the end of its expansion, before his parents consolidate their marriage into a symmetrically integrated, relatively egalitarian relationship. The dominant structural opposition in the family is still that of sex: his mother and sister make up the subordinate core of intra-family relations; his father presides over the interfamily level of relations from his dominant position within the family; and his brothers, through their separation from the family and induction into the men's house (the first step in the process leading to marriage and fatherhood) are launched upon the complementary, negative (separative) phase of male involvement in the level of interfamily relations. Although the adoption of a boy by his substitute father emphasizes the opposition between the boy and his father at this point, in a larger sense this opposition (which is later resolved, in the sense defined above, by the boy's marriage and accession to fatherhood in his own right) is merely between two complementary phases of a male pattern of participation in interfamily relations of affinal exchange, in terms of which both father and son stand together in opposition to the female "core" of the family.

A woman, by contrast, is separated from her family when it reaches the end of its dispersion phase. Her mother and father now constitute an integrated subgroup of the family, in opposition to the complementary subcategory comprising the separated offspring. The dominant plane of structural opposition in the family has thus shifted from that of sex to that of generation. The consolidated parental group now jointly presides over the interfamily relations of the family (its affinal ties to the spouses of its offspring), while the dispersed offspring are beginning their own families of procreation.

Both the male and female patterns of natal family separation and marriage are subject to the same invariant principle of the bilaterally symmetrical conservation of the solidarity of the family unit that regulates the rest of the system. The implication of this rule for affinal relations, as for consanguineal relations of the intrafamily and marginal categories, is that one-half of the total weighting of relations constituting a family unit is rechanneled into the families of procreation of family offspring of each sex. We should therefore expect that affinal relations would follow a pattern of stressing the positive integration or alliance of a spouse with half of the relationship categories constituting the natal family of the linking spouse, and separation from the complementary set of relations. We should further expect that this pattern of differential weighting in each case should conform to the asymmetrically skewed pattern of weighting appropriate to each sex and the stages of the family cycle that serve as the points of separation (from the natal family) and integration (into the family of procreation) of each.

These expectations are confirmed by data already given. A husband, on the one hand, stands in a relationship of alliance with his wife's parents, the dominant family collectively from which his wife is separated in order to marry, and in a relationship of separation and inhibition (negative integration) toward his wife's siblings (the complementary subcategory of family relations at that point in its dispersion). A wife, on the other hand, stands in a relationship of positively stressed alliance with the women of her husband's natal family (his mother and, especially, his sister), and a relationship of negative integration (inhibition and avoidance) toward his male natal family relatives (primarily his brother).

The husband's father, I suggest, is largely neutralized for purposes of this opposition by the husband's attainment of fatherhood in his own right, thus "negating the negation" of his original relationship to his father represented by his adoptive "false" father, or antifather, and embodying in his capacity as husband/father the aspect of the male interfamily role embodied by his father in his natal family at the time of his separation. In terms of the logical structure of Kayapó family relations, in short, a man's father becomes redundant, for purposes of both consanguineal and affinal relationships, when the man and his brothers become husbands and fathers. A wife's avoidance behavior is thus directed almost wholly toward the brother; the husband's father is virtually ignored.

Note that the subcollectivity of the family which becomes the object of a positive affinal relationship is the one from which the linking spouse is separated as a concomitant of marriage. The structure of affinal relations thus follows the same principle as the structure of marginal and severed intrafamily relations of the consanguineal category: an intrafamily relationship attenuated in the process of affinal exchange is transformed into a positively stressed relationship of equivalent weight at the interfamily level.

The same principle holds in reverse: the subcollectivity (that is, the complementary half) of the natal family of the linking spouse with which the latter is not forced to sever relations as a concomitant of his or her marriage, and which thus remains the focus of positive relations on his or her part (a husband's brothers, a wife's sisters and, indirectly, brothers), becomes the focus of negative affinal relations on the part of the spouse. This conforms to the principle of conservation: if the alloted share of positive weighting is exhausted in the main, positively stressed relations of affinal alliance, the complementary category must be as emphatically negatively weighted. This pattern of sharply contrastive positive and negative weighting is, as we have seen, equally characteristic of the corresponding contrasts in consanguineal relations, and for the same reason.

The sharpness of the contrast between the positively and negatively weighted categories of interfamily affinal relations is, of course, a function of the Kayapó emphasis on marriage as a relationship of abruptly complete and total attachment at the intrafamily level. The positive stress on marriage for each spouse thus balances the negative emphasis on the abrupt separation of that spouse from the relevant subgroup of his or her natal family. That separation is in turn balanced by the positive inter-family-level affinal relationship between the members of that sub-collectivity and the linked spouse. The relationship of positive interfamily alliance is in turn counterbalanced by the negative relationship between the linked spouse and the complementary subgroup of the linking spouse's family, which also offsets the continuing positive relationship between that subgroup and the linking spouse. The whole system of affinal relations, thus defined, follows the same asymmetrical pattern of weighting as the system of consanguineal relations, and is in fact the same pattern seen from the complementary (interfamily rather than intrafamily) point of origin of the relationships involved.

The Place of Affinal Relations in the Structure of the Kinship System

The Kayapó are a bilateral society, lacking descent-based categories or corporate groups standing in relations of exogamy or prescriptive affinity, such as the exogamous moieties of other Gê societies. Marriage and affinity in such a system serve, not to articulate the relations between standing groups or fixed categories, but as the mechanisms of transition and transformation between groups and categories that are themselves impermanent and in constant process of development. Marriage, of course, serves to mediate the transition between the natal family and the family of procreation, and thus to articulate the two complementary sets of intrafamily consanguineal relations (natal and procreational) for both sexes. Interfamily affinal relations (that is, those between siblings-in-law and between parents-in-law and children-in-law) constitute an intervening step between natal intrafamily relations (of the linking parent) and marginal relations (of the offspring of the linking parent), since, in accord with the general Kayapó principle that affines "become kin," all such affines are transformed into marginal consanguineal relatives by the next generation of the family of procreation of the linking parent, with the exception of parental same-sexed siblings, who are classified with the parent. Interfamily affinal relations are thus bracketed, in terms of the developmental process of family and kindred relations, between the two polar categories of consanguineal relatives: intrafamily relations, on the one hand, and marginal relations, on the other. Their structure, at the same time, is merely a complementary refraction of that of the consanguineal categories. They might therefore be regarded as relatively secondary and redundant in terms of the system as a whole. Marriage, on the contrary, emerges as the central coordinating principle and focus of the weighted structure of intrafamily relations of the two sexes.

REDUNDANCY AND REPRODUCTION

The analysis of Kayapó family, domestic group, and kinship relations given up to this point has focused upon the structure and dynamic equilibrium of the system, and avoided the question of how the system is reproduced, or, more precisely, how it is constrained to reproduce itself according to the relatively tightly coordinated and finely balanced pattern that has been described. What I claim to have shown so far is that the structure of kinship and domestic group relations does in fact constitute a dynamic system, characterized by a consistent pattern of weighting and governed by an invariant principle of conservation, focused on the maintenance and reproduction of a specific pattern of dominance of wife's parents over daughter's husbands as the axis of the structure of the uxorilocal extended-family household: in short, that it conforms in these respects to the specifications of the general model set out in the last paper and the first part of this paper.

It remains to show that the reproduction of the system fulfills the specifications of the central hypothesis of the model: that the superstructure of communal groups and their ceremonial and economic activities constitute a collective mechanism for re-producing a certain pattern of household and extended-family structure or, more precisely, for constraining the reproductive processes of the family and domestic group level to replicate such a fixed pattern.

In connection with this hypothesis, it was suggested that the set of communal institutions of a given Gê society would tend to embody and inculcate a "restricted set" of the total system of family and household relations, specification of which would suffice to determine the set as a whole.

Redundancy and its opposite, unique specificity of implication, as aspects of the relationship between a subset and the total set of relations from which it is drawn, are defined in terms of the rules governing the relations among the elements of the set as a whole. In order to generate the structure of the total set it is necessary to specify (1) the total subset of nonredundant elements and (2) the rules or operations governing the relations among the elements of the set as a whole. Parenthetically, it is worth em-phasizing the importance of nonredundancy in the sort of model I am developing, since many commentators on primitive social and conceptual systems have emphasized precisely the opposite point, viz., the importance of redundancy in such systems. I argue that where exact coordination is required, "redundant" elements (most of which are not *perfectly* redundant, and thus render less precise the structure and content of the common information or meaning they encode) are apt to present more difficulties of ambiguity and imprecision than advantages in re-inforcing the communication of a structure of meaning or action. A precise, unambiguous, and nonredundant structure is therefore far less problematic and more useful for purposes such as the reproduction of a collectively standardized pattern of social re-lations than a structure rich in redundancy but therefore low in precision and specificity of message.

A nonredundant subset of relations, together with the set of operations (rules of transformation, weighting or coordination of transformations, and conservation or invariant constraints govern-ing the pattern of weighting) necessary to generate the structure of the total set of Kayapó kinship and extended-family relations, can be defined on the basis of the foregoing analysis. In the simplest possible terms, a nonredundant description of the system is provided by the asymmetrically weighted male and female patterns of separation and integration at the level of consan-guineal intrafamily relations, coordinated with each other in relation to marriage, balanced against the symmetrically weighted male and female pattern of marginal relations. Interfamilial affinal relations form the redundant class, which conforms to the structure specified by the relations among the other elements. A key point in the description is obviously the relationship between the marginal and intrafamily classes. In complementary opposition to marriage, the other key point of articulation of the structure, this relationship determines the pattern of weighting within each class and the principle of invariance governing both. The essence of this relationship is the alignment of marginal relations in reinforcement of the shift from the natal to the procreational family at the intrafamily level of relations of both sexes, and the consequent emphasis upon the priority (in dynamic or causal terms) of this development in the structure of intrafamily relations over the consummation of marginal relations.

This description of the content of a nonredundant model of Kayapó extended-family and kinship structure can be reduced to a simplified list of relational elements. To begin with the class of intrafamily relations, including marriage: since the asymmetically weighted structure of the class is defined in terms of the staggered pattern of relatively abrupt and total separations of men and women from their integrations into families at different stages in their development, and since the staggering of the male and female patterns is coordinated with reference to marriage (which represents both the completion of the male intrafamily-level pattern and the beginning of the female pattern), it is necessary to specify the following set of conditions:

1. Male totally separated from natal family and household at end of expansion phase of natal family (female remains totally integrated in same)
2. Male totally attached to family and household of procreation upon marriage (i.e., beginning of expansion of family of procreation)
   a. Male remains subordinate to his wife's parents throughout expansion phase of family of procreation
   b. Male becomes dominant at dispersion of his family of procreation (note that phases 2a and 2b are defined with reference to marriage and the development of the family of procreation in terms corresponding to the female phases 3 and 4)

3. Female totally separated from natal family at close of its dispersion phase (N.B.: immediately prior to marriage, which is thus the key point of reference for coordination of this phase with male phase 2)
4. Female totally integrated into her family (and household) of procreation at beginning of dispersion phase of family (N.B.: married status of woman remains key point of reference for this transformation)

For the class of marginal relationships, it is clearly necessary to specify:

5. Sexually distinct but formally symmetrical classes of marginal relations

The relationship between the two classes must then be specified in terms of asymmetrical interdependence, in which

6. Marginal relations depend for their fulfillment upon the prior formation of the subset of intrafamily relations identified with the family of procreation (specifically, marriage and the transference of the male from his natal to his procreational family household)
7. Intrafamilial relations reciprocally depend upon the consummation of marginal relations (symbolically expressed in the bestowal of names and ritual paraphernalia) for the compensatory positive reassertion of severed intrafamily ties, essential to the fulfillment of the dynamic requirements of conservation.

This set of seven elements specifies the structure of relationship within and between the intrafamilial, marginal, and affinal categories of relationship in a nonredundant manner, but with sufficient precision to imply or contain: (1) the basic structural unit of the system, the bilateral nuclear family; (2) the weighted pattern of coordination of the transformations of the structure of this unit that generate the structure of the total set of kinship relations; and (3) the invariant principle of the bilaterally symmetrical conservation of the solidarity of the nuclear family. The structure of the redundant subclass of interfamily affinal relations has been shown to constitute a simple transformation of the structure of the consanguineal categories, generated by taking the interfamily relationship of marriage rather than the intrafamily relations of filiation and siblingship as the point of origin. It is therefore adequately specified by the restricted set of elements that has been presented, since it includes the relationship of marriage (the point of origin for the transformation in question) and specifies the structure of consanguineal relations.

Kayapó Social Organization at the Community Level

Two basic kinds of data must be taken into account in describing the communal structure of a Gê society: the corporate groupings into which the community as a whole is organized and the formally prescribed activities, chiefly of a ceremonial nature, in which they engage. These data may be summarized for the Kayapó in the following form.

CORPORATE GROUPS

1. *Junior set of men's moieties.* These are recruited by the "false" father (and "false" mother, his wife) when a boy is about eight years old (thus at about the end of the expansion of the boy's natal family). Recruitment takes the form of symbolic social separation from the natal family and household, and induction of the boy into the men's house to which the "false" father belongs. The "false" father and his wife, the "false" mother, are recruited for their roles on the basis of being totally unrelated to the boy.

2. *Senior set of men's moieties.* These are recruited on the basis of a man's actually becoming a father and, thus, a husband. Upon recruitment, a man moves out of the men's house to take up residence in his wife's household, but joins one of the men's societies that constitute the corporate components of the senior men's moiety set, which meet regularly in one of the two men's houses. Members of the senior men's moieties are subdivided into junior and senior subage-grades:

   a. *"Fathers of a few children" or "new fathers."* These are men whose families of procreation are still in their expansion phase. These men generally play only a passive and subordinate role in the collective debates and politics of their men's society.

   b. *"Fathers of many children."* These are men whose families of procreation have entered the dispersion phase. Men of this subgrade dominate the affairs of the men's societies, and thus the political life of the community. The chiefs of the village (leaders of the men's societies) are drawn from their ranks.

3. *Junior set of women's moieties.* Girls are recruited to these moieties by a "false" mother (and "father," her husband), who are selected on the basis of being totally unrelated to the girl. The age of recruitment is the late teens, just before marriage, and corresponds to the final stage of dispersion of the girl's natal

family. The girl joins the society of young women (called "mothers of few children") belonging to the moiety of the "false" mother. If she marries a man of the opposite moiety, she shifts her membership to the young women's society of his moiety. Moiety membership for women is thus made dependent upon marriage.

4. *Senior set of women's moieties.* These moieties consist of women of the age-grade of "mothers of many children," to which women matriculate at the onset of the dispersion of their families of procreation. A woman of this age-grade remains in the women's society belonging to her husband's moiety, and in case of re-marriage shifts her moiety affiliation if necessary.

CEREMONIAL ACTIVITIES OF CORPORATE GROUPS

5. Most ceremonial activity is devoted to name-giving and other forms of celebration of marginal relations. Typical name-giving ceremonies last around two months and are celebrated either by men or by women, although at least one naming ceremony of each sex should be celebrated every year. The ceremonial system embodying marginal relations thus embodies a principle of sexual symmetry.

6. The celebration of naming ceremonies is initiated and carried out by either the men's or women's moiety sets. For ceremonial purposes, both moieties of each (junior and senior) set combine into an undifferentiated body, and the two age-ranked bodies cooperate in performing ritual, while remaining distinct. It is not automatic or assumed that ritual names will be bestowed in this way upon everyone. The performance of a naming ceremony for a particular child depends upon the moiety sets of the appropriate sex agreeing with the child's parents to perform the ritual, in exchange for gifts of food from the latter. The consummation of marginal relations through naming ritual and other ceremonial activity is thus made contingent upon the action of the moiety groups, that is, the collective embodiment of intra-family relations.

7. The performance of ceremonies by the fused moiety sets is primarily directed toward bestowing ritually distinguished names, belonging to the category of "precious (ritual) belongings" (*nêkrêtch*), upon the name-receiver(s), and also provides the context for many special ritual performances and displays by individuals or small groups which are passed down between marginal relatives in the same way as names. All those having the right to such special ritual distinctions, as well as all those receiving names, in a given ceremony are referred to, in that

ritual context, as "the owners of the *nêkrêtch* (precious possession) ." All others (that is, the ordinary celebrants, organized in
their fused moiety sets) are referred to as "those who own nothing." Ceremonies thus take the form of a continual series of
performances by "the owners of nothing," grouped on the basis
of symbolic intrafamily relations, directed toward bestowing, or
providing the necessary context for the display of, *nêkrêtch,* that
is, the symbols of consummated marginal relationships. Ceremonial activity thus dramatizes the reciprocal dependence of
intrafamily relations upon the consummation of marginal relations.

ECONOMIC ACTIVITIES OF CORPORATE GROUPS

Trekking groups (see the concluding section of the preceding
paper) are organized on the basis of the men's societies of the
senior men's moiety set, under the leadership of men of the age-
grade subgroup of "fathers of many children."

CONCLUSIONS OF THE ANALYSIS THUS FAR

The seven points relating to the structure and activities of
Kayapó communal corporate groups listed above should be compared with the seven-point model of the structure and reproduction of Kayapó kinship and domestic group relations given at the
end of the last section. Note that the recruitment criteria of the
various corporate groups, and their ritual, political, and economic
activities, are defined so that their pragmatic and/or symbolic
effects tend to inculcate the relationship of transformations or
reciprocal interdependence indicated under the corresponding
number in the restricted set of kinship and domestic group relations listed above.

Comparison of the organization of the communal superstructure of Kayapó society with a model of the minimal (nonredundant) requirements for generating the system of kinship and
domestic group relations, I submit, supports the working hypothesis advanced at the beginning of this analysis and developed at
a more general theoretical level in the preceding paper: to wit,
that the superstructure of collective institutions of the Gê societies
functions as a reproductive mechanism for the structure of kinship and domestic group relations, and stands in an internal
structural and dynamic relationship to that system. Its structure
and dynamic organization, in sum, must be understood as an
embodiment of the structure and organization of the pattern of
kinship and extended-family relations that it serves to reproduce.

As a final point in support of this conclusion, I call attention to the role of the senior men's societies, the collective focus for the expression of the authority of "fathers of many children" over "fathers of few children" (that is, fathers-in-law over sons-in-law), as the structural basis of the trekking groups organized for the annual hunting-and-gathering expeditions. In the preceding paper I argued that the function of the hypertrophic development of hunting and gathering in the form of such collective seminomadic treks among the Gê and Bororo was precisely to reinforce the ultimate authority of the senior male (s) of the household over his (their) wife (wives) and daughter (s), that is, over the female "core" of the household, and thus over the junior males of the household, the daughters' husbands. The utilization of the senior men's societies as the organizational basis of the hunting-and-gathering treks is consistent with this interpretation.

It should be pointed out that the pattern of relations formulated in the seven-point analytical model of kinship and household structure and found to be embodied by the communal super-structure of Kayapó society has been shown in the main body of the analysis to be coordinated in such a way as to reproduce a specific pattern of dominance of fathers-in-law over their daughters' husbands. This point is in line with the general contention of the analysis of both this and the previous paper, that the focus of the structure of the uxorilocal extended-family household and its reproductive process is the maintenance of a pattern of dominance by wife's fathers over daughter's husbands.

Kayapó Moiety Structure: Redundancy, Instability, and Contradiction

The recruitment criteria of the junior and senior sets of men's and women's moieties have been shown in the foregoing analysis to be the decisive pivotal points in the alignment of both sexes within the developing structure of the extended family and household. In each recruitment situation, moreover, it has been shown that the recruitment relation is opposed to one other complementary relationship, and that moiety recruitment is the means by which the alignment of individuals with the recruitment relationship, in contrast to the complementary relation, is effected as a socially uniform pattern. The Kayapó case is thus fully consistent with the general hypothesis as to the nature and dynamic functions of moiety structure put forward in the preceding paper.

CONTRADICTION AND INSTABILITY IN KAYAPÓ MOIETY STRUCTURE

The integration of the specific analysis of the Kayapó moiety system presented in this paper with the general theoretical model presented in the last one in one sense rounds out and completes the theoretical argument I have tried to develop in the two papers. The value of this argument, however, remains to be proved in concrete terms by its ability to account for the most puzzling aspect of Kayapó moiety organization, to wit, its great instability. In spite of the fact that all Kayapó remain committed to the principle of moiety organization as a normative ideal, and in spite of the important regulatory and stabilizing functions which (according to the hypothesis developed in this and the preceding paper) moiety structures perform, all nine existing Kayapó villages lack a moiety organization in being.

How is it, then, that all Kayapó villages are now, and have been for several decades, one-moiety villages, when the larger ones could, if they wished, easily regenerate the other moiety from within the village? If moiety structure plays a stabilizing role, how does it happen that moiety structure itself appears to be the most unstable element of Kayapó society? And why do we find that the one-moiety villages, all of which have been formed as the products of breakdowns of two-moiety villages, have proved to be relatively stable?

The basic reason for the instability of the Kayapó moiety system is implicit in the negative nature of the relationships modeled by the moieties. These relationships (the negation of the relation to the "true" parent by the interposition of the "substitute" parent, followed by the negation of the tutelary relation to the "substitute" parent on the basis of matriculation to the status of "true" parent/spouse) take the form of negative separation and inhibition. This means not only that they lack the character of positive reciprocity associated with exogamous and most other varieties of moiety structure, but that they lack the structural interdependence of other forms of moiety structure in which the members of the overlapping relationships of the original pair must belong to opposite moieties. The sole criterion of the Kayapó "substitute" parent relationship, that it should be filled by a complete nonrelative, supersedes and renders irrelevant any regular affiliation of the "substitute" parent with the moiety opposite to that of the "true" parent. There are therefore no strong bonds between the moieties of any moiety pair or set, in the sense of either prescriptive structural interdependence or positive reciprocity.

In contrast to the relatively exiguous bonds between moieties of the same set, the internal bonds of solidarity that link the members of a single moiety group are very strong. The mature men's, or "fathers'," moiety societies, in particular, are strongly solidary and become potent military, political, and, on occasion, factional units. The relations between these units, by contrast, are extremely tenuous, based upon mutual *pia'àm,* or restraint and "respect" behavior. There is, then, a contradiction implicit in Kayapó moiety structure between the political solidarity and potency of individual moiety groupings and the weakness of the available mechanisms for regulating relations between these groupings. The two parts of this contradiction are, as I have shown, functionally related to each other as reflections of complementary aspects of the underlying status and role relations modeled by the moiety system. The results of this situation have been a high rate of fission along moiety lines in two-moiety villages, leading to the current situation in which all the extant villages consist of single-moiety remnants of factional splits in earlier two-moiety villages.

The Kayapó themselves are skeptical and pragmatic about the advantages and disadvantages of their moiety organization in this regard. I was present during an interesting debate in the village of Porori early in 1966, when a proposal for reuniting the community with another, larger group representing the opposite moiety was being considered. There had been considerable antagonism between Porori and this group in the past, and several of the political leaders of Porori were uneasy about the prospect of being thrown into such close proximity with a large number of men who had good reason to nourish grudges against them. The possibility of reestablishing the other men's house in the village upon the other group's arrival was discussed in this context. One side took the orthodox view that this would be a good thing, as the normative *pia'àm,* or restraint, enjoined upon the behavior of members of opposite moieties to one another would tend to prevent outbreaks of violence. The other side (about equal in number) maintained to the contrary that it would be a grave mistake to allow the other group to perpetuate its own corporate identity and cohesiveness as a separate moiety group. Far better, these men argued, to expand the existing men's house and absorb the newcomers into the same "moiety" group as themselves: with everyone mixed together under one (men's house) roof, it would be more difficult for the other group to retain a separate capacity for unified factional action. The debate became moot when the merger failed to go through.

The contradiction of which I have spoken does not arise or exist solely at the level of communal organization (that is, of moiety structure). It is implicit in the extreme contrast between the stress on fatherhood as the basis of attachment to the wife's household and the stress on the total displacement of sons from their fathers' households to the men's house, which is of course created by the recruitment of the junior and senior men's moiety sets through the "substitute" father and the attainment of true fatherhood, respectively. The point is that the moiety structure projects and amplifies at the communal level not only the relational basis of dominance, control, and integration which it generates at the level of segmentary household and extended-family organization, but the tensions and latent contradictions as well, and that it generates the latter as intrinsic corollaries of the former, through the same process.

REDUNDANCY AND (RELATIVE) STABILITY IN THE ONE-MOIETY VILLAGE

Granted that the model that has been presented does help to account for the instability of the Kayapó moiety structure, can it also account for the opposite phenomenon of the relative stability of the single-moiety village?

The most unusual and distinctive characteristic of the Kayapó moiety structure is unquestionably that Kayapó moieties embody not a permanent pattern of relative alignment between a pair of complementary relations, but instead an inversion of that pattern of alignment between the same two relational categories. This inversion is embodied in the consecutive junior and senior moiety sets, which inculcate an alignment with the "substitute" parent as against the true parent (junior moiety set) and then with the status of true parent (or grandparent, depending on sex) as against the "substitute" parent. These opposite values of the same relational opposition are, however, associated with relationships to opposite families (and, for a male, households as well), namely, the natal and the procreational, and these relationships are themselves opposites (separation and attachment, respectively). Given the Kayapó pattern of weighting of affinal over consanguineal relations described in the earlier part of this paper, a negative relation (that is, of separation) to the natal family (and household, for a male) and a positive relation (that is, of attachment as an autonomous adult) to the family of procreation (and household of procreation, for a male) are structurally compatible expressions of the same relationship. It is like saying "half empty and half full." In this sense, the consecutive junior and senior moiety sets are related in a symmetrical way analogous to the relationship between the two moieties of a normal moiety structure.

There are, at the same time, two obvious respects in which the relationship between the junior and senior moiety sets is asymmetrical, and thus unlike the relation between moieties proper. In the first place, the two sets embody alignment with opposite members of the basic pair of recruitment relationships; and in the second, the two sets are related as consecutive stages or phases of the development of the basic recruitment relationship, rather than as simultaneous (temporally symmetrical) expressions of it. The interesting point is that these two differences to some extent offset or neutralize each other from the standpoint of the analysis above. The contrast between the junior and senior moiety sets (or, more to the point, between individual moieties of the two sets) bears a consistent "modeling" relationship to the same pattern of weighting of the same basic pair of recruitment relationships and is to this extent structurally and functionally analogous to an orthodox moiety structure. To this extent, the relationship between the junior and senior moiety sets renders the internal moiety division of each set structurally redundant. It is, at the same time, the more indispensable of the two partially redundant aspects of the moiety structure as a whole, because it models the temporal inversion of the relative weighting of the two relationships which is the heart of the Kayapó system, as well as the overall balanced opposition between the negation and affirmation of the two recruitment relations, which I have argued is analogous, under Kayapó conditions and up to a point, with the relationship between two moieties of the same set.

According to this interpretation, we should expect to find the opposition between junior and senior moiety sets, or single moieties of the respective sets, taking on the sorts of functions performed in other Gê societies by the relation between two moieties of the same set (for example, serving as opposing teams in athletic contests or assuming complementary ceremonial functions), and this is precisely what we do find. There are, in short, good theoretical and empirical reasons to accept the proposition that the opposition between the junior and senior moieties of a single side of the plaza (that is, a single-moiety structure) can take over most of the functions fulfilled by orthodox moiety structures in other Gê societies.

INSTABILITY AND CUMULATIVE DRIFT IN SINGLE-MOIETY VILLAGES

It will have been noted that I have consistently qualified my statements about the ability of the single-moiety form of Kayapó society to perform all of the functions of the full moiety structure. The general model of moiety structure put forward above would predict that in certain respects the social structure of Kayapó single-moiety villages should be less stable than it would be if both moieties were present and functioning. These respects constitute the ability of moiety structure to contribute to preventing "drift" (that is, a tendency toward long-term change in the relative balance between the dominant or recruitment relationship and its complementary paired relationship) . This is the one class of functions detailed in the model that the single-moiety form of organization is unable to fulfill, since it depends upon the symmetrical opposition of two structurally equivalent groups based upon the same recruitment relationship.

Kayapó moiety structure, of course, has the special problem not only of stabilizing a given pattern of asymmetrical weighting between a pair of status and role relations, but of coordinating two consecutive transformations or inverse forms of this asymmetrical pattern. The two problems are inseparable, since altering the relative weighting of the pair of relations within one form or transformation of the pattern should have the effect of unstabilizing the pattern of weighting in the complementary form in the opposite direction. The issue of the stability of the weighting of the two moiety recruitment relations is thus inseparable from the issue of the stability of the relationship of relative dominance and subordination between the senior and junior moiety sets. The general model of moiety structure and functions put forward earlier would indicate that, deprived of the stabilizing effect of the full complement of moieties, this relationship should become a focus of cumulative drift and instability. This prediction can be checked against the observable variations and conflicts surrounding the relationship in the existing single-moiety Kayapó villages.

The available data are far from conclusive on this point, but they do point to a high degree both of latent conflict and of structural variability in the relationship between the junior and senior men's moiety groups in contemporary Kayapó single-moiety villages. Overt conflict and village fission between the two groups is enacted in ritual and recounted in myth.[3] Although the youths of the junior men's moiety group are not supposed to play any direct role in politics, and do not, for example, in the village of Gorotire, there had been an attempt by the youths (*mẽ nõrõ-nu-re*) to set themselves up as a "men's society" like the political groups of the mature men in the village of Kuben-kran-ken a few years before I arrived to do fieldwork there in 1963. In the village of Porori, the *mẽ nõrõ-nu-re* had been designated as a "society" with a chief, along the lines of a mature men's society. This was part of a political reorganization of the village in which four age-graded men's societies, including that of the youth's age-grade, were founded to serve as *pro forma* followings of the four rival chiefs in the village, in an effort to neutralize the latent conflicts among them. The data, in short, do suggest considerable variability and instability in the relationship between junior and senior moiety groups in single-moiety villages.

The analysis I have presented has been an experiment in the synthesis of structuralist, functionalist, and system-theoretic notions with a dialectical point of view. The model developed in the preceding general paper has been put to the test of accounting for the normative and dynamic features of a particular Gê society, including the contradictions implicit in its structure and the short-run and long-term forms of instability and structural change resulting from them. I suggest, on the basis of the success of the model in meeting this test, that it might profitably be applied, *mutatis mutandis,* to other societies of the same type.

THE CENTRAL GÊ

THE CENTRAL GÊ are believed to have comprised two branches, the Akroá and the Akwẽ. The Akroá speakers died out toward the end of the eighteenth century (see Nimuendajú 1942:1). The Akwẽ speakers included the Sherente, and Shavante, and the Shakriabá. The Shakriabá probably ceased to exist as an identifiable people in the early nineteenth century (Nimuendajú 1942:2), though there are still occasionally reports of people claiming to be Shakriabá in the interior of the state of Minas Gerais. This chapter deals with the known Central Gê peoples, the Sherente and the Shavante.

In the eighteenth century they came into conflict with the Portuguese settlers who were moving into what is now central and northern Goiás in search of gold. These hostilities are much discussed in the colonial records, as also are the unsuccessful attempts to resettle the Indians and the embarrassing visit of 2,000 Shavante to the minuscule capital of the province of Goyaz in 1788. At this time the Sherente and the Shavante were believed to be virtually indistinguishable. The ancestors of the modern Shavante probably moved southwestward away from the Tocantins River at the beginning of the nineteenth century (Maybury-Lewis 1965c:355). By the second half of the nineteenth century, the two peoples had lost touch with each other.

The Sherente (also known as Šerente, Cherente, or Xerente)

The Sherente have been in constant contact with the Portuguese (later the Brazilians) since the late nineteenth century. In the sixties they numbered approximately 330 individuals who inhabited four main villages near the small town of Tocantinia on the east bank of the Tocantins River. The population has now increased to approximately 800.

There have been missionaries, both Catholic and Protestant, working with them and the Indian Protection Service has intermittently maintained one post and at times two posts for them. By the 1960s virtually all Sherente men and most women spoke Portuguese, and some of them could read and write it. Many had traveled and knew the Brazilian cities of the interior and sometimes even of the coast. There was a steady stream of emigrants from the villages, yet the population stayed roughly constant.

In their material circumstances and manner of gaining a livelihood (from slash-and-burn agriculture with very simple tools), the Sherente were little different from the neighboring backwoodsmen.

215

They did, however, speak their own language among themselves and maintain their own customs in their villages, in spite of all the centrifugal tendencies to which they were subject. Above all, they had very few cattle. Their major conflicts with the Brazilians in the *municipio* of Tocantinia were over land and cattle, the Brazilians claiming that the Sherente killed their cattle, the Sherente arguing that the Brazilians' cattle ruined their crops. The Indian Protection Service has tried repeatedly to persuade the Sherente to gather in one portion of the *municipio* so that it can be demarcated as Indian land. But the Sherente refused to abandon their traditional lands in the various corners of the *municipio,* and this dispute over their right to be there simmers constantly.

The Belém-Brasília highway passes well to the west of the Tocantins at this point. The river is now less important as a means of communication, and its east bank is a region of economic stagnation. This has protected the Sherente from even more severe pressure.

The Shavante (also known as Šavante, Chavante, or Xavante)

By the late nineteenth century the Shavante had already established themselves to the west of the Araguaia River along the Rio das Mortes in the state of Mato Grosso. At this time their neighbors and enemies were the Bororo to the west and the Karajá, who lived along the Araguaia River itself. It was not until President Vargas created the Central Brazil Foundation to open up the interior in the nineteen-thirties that the Shavante were contacted again, though systematic peaceful contacts between them and the Brazilians were not established until the early fifties. There were in fact some Shavante still uncontacted in the sixties.

At that time the known Shavante numbered somewhere between fifteen hundred and two thousand, and were to be found scattered through about ten communities, two at the headwaters of the Xingu River, two on the Rio das Mortes upstream from Xavantina, and six in the general region of the Rio das Mortes between Xavantina and the Ilha do Bananal. Most of these communities were attached either to mission stations or to Indian Protection Service posts. Yet they continued to live in traditional fashion, using the mission or the post as a base and trekking for months at a time through the surrounding countryside, which provided them with the game and wild plants off which they lived. Their gardens were still quite rudimentary and they spent correspondingly little time in them.

In the past decade there has been rapid change among the Shavante. Their population has increased to over thirty-five hundred. The region in which they live is being invaded by ranchers and agribusinesses encouraged by the government's incentives to develop the interior. The

Shavante have found themselves surrounded and sometimes threatened. They have been gathered at mission stations and Indian posts, where they live by agriculture, assisted by outside agencies. Meanwhile a number of Shavante have learned to read and write and are capable of traveling to Brasília to take their complaints directly to the government. Now the Shavante are struggling to defend themselves and their land against settler invasion, and they are threatening to fight for it if necessary.

7 | Cultural Categories of the Central Gê

David Maybury-Lewis

IN THIS ESSAY I shall base my discussion of the Shavante on the materials I published in 1967. Since my data on the Sherente are still largely unpublished, however, I must begin with a discussion of Sherente society.

The Sherente

The Sherente have achieved a minor notoriety since Nimuendajú published his monograph on them in 1942. Kroeber was intrigued by them, as he was by the other Central Brazilian peoples Nimuendajú described, because they appeared so clearly to be engaged in social innovation and experimentation (Kroeber 1942, 1948:397). Homans and Schneider singled them out later as one of the rare patrilineal societies in the world which was reported to practice patrilateral cross-cousin marriage. They were therefore forced to consider the Sherente a possible counterinstance to their theory that marriage with the father's sister's daughter would be found in matrilineal societies. They concluded, however, that if potestality (that is, who had authority over a boy) was the predictor rather than lineality, the Sherente would not constitute an exception, for although they were patrilineal, they vested authority over a boy in his mother's brother or some individual other than his father (1955:49–51). Needham argued later that Homans and Schneider had misrendered the Sherente data in support of an untenable hypothesis (1962:65–66, 102–103). Meanwhile Lévi-Strauss, taking a different tack, suggested that there were so many inconsistencies in the data that we could not analyze Sherente society satisfactorily in terms of the institutional arrangements which Nimuendajú had stressed. Instead he proposed a thoroughgoing reanalysis along different lines (1952).

I studied the Sherente in 1955–56 and again in 1963. My results, which I can better interpret with the aid of my material from the Shavante (see Maybury-Lewis 1967 and 1971) suggest a view of Sherente society which is somewhat different from the one presented by Nimuendajú. But before I attempt to investigate this contrast it is important to emphasize certain features of Nimuendajú's own data. He was fascinated by "true Sherente culture" and saddened by what he considered latter-day deviations from it. His book does not, therefore, describe the Sherente as he found them in the 1930s, but rather mixes such description with his own reconstruction of Sherente culture as it was in some unspecified previous time. In that previous age the Sherente were divided into two patrilineal moieties, which derived from their dualistic view of the cosmos as a whole. Each moiety contained four patriclans. This moiety and clan system not only had cosmological and ceremonial significance but also determined marriage and residence patterns. Sherente villages were small and autonomous, but people could move freely from one to another. They fitted easily and automatically into new communities since each moiety and its constituent clans had its assigned place on the village semicircle (as in Figure 1). The rule of postmarital residence was necessarily virilocal.[1] The moieties were exogamous, and each clan had a special bond with the one located directly opposite it on the village arc. Many of the practical activities of the society, such as hunting, gathering, gardening, and even making war, were carried out by four men's associations, which also had considerable ceremonial functions. Nimuendajú suggested that these associations had originally been age-sets, and he considered them vital elements of traditional Sherente culture.

When Nimuendajú came to study this culture, however, he found it, to use his own words, "in a state of collapse" (1942:8). Villages no longer were laid out in the traditional semicircle but were mere agglomerations of huts. Moieties and clans could not, therefore, have any special locations. Membership in them was still mandatory, but the Sherente had begun to ignore the rule of exogamy and marry within their moieties. Initiations were no longer performed, and the *warã*, or bachelors' hut, was only a memory. Above all, the associations no longer functioned, and it was this more than anything else which Nimuendajú considered fatal to the Sherente way of life (1942:59).

I found the Sherente in very similar circumstances twenty years later. Their villages were aggregates of huts with no symbolic significance. Their moieties and clans were not spatially located and nobody gave a thought to moiety exogamy. Their traditional

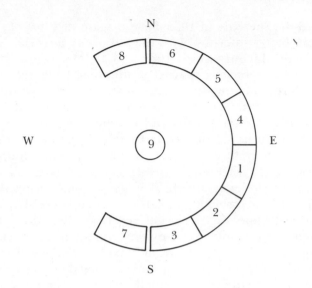

N

W   9   E

S

FIGURE 1. Traditional Sherente village plan (from Nimuendajú 1942:17)

Šiptató clans	Sdakrã clans	Incorporated tribes	
1. Kuzę́	4. Krẽprehí	7. Prasé	9. Warã (bachelors' lodge)
2. Ĩšibdú	5. Ĩsauré	8. Krozaké	
3. Kbazipré	6. Ĩsrurí'e		

ceremonies were performed amidst confusion and bickering over precisely what should be done and by whom, and this contrasted with the efficient organization of the alcoholic parties which they gave for neighboring Brazilians as well as for fellow Sherente. Yet I would not have said that their culture was in a state of collapse even then, although it had obviously changed since the ideal period represented in Nimuendajú's reconstruction. Consider that the Sherente have numbered no more than three to four hundred people for over half a century and that they still maintain themselves as a distinct cultural and linguistic entity, interspersed though they are with the surrounding Brazilian population, and you might conclude that their way of life has shown surprising resilience. They have even succeeded in maintaining their population in spite of their precarious social and economic situation and of the considerable emigration from their villages. Their associational system was indeed moribund, but from this I conclude that it was less vital to their society than Nimuendajú supposed.

In fact, the persistence of moiety and clan reckoning contrasted sharply with the disappearance of the associations. It was the moieties as a conceptual matrix and the clans as potential factions that constituted the essence of Sherente culture as I found it.

Even the moieties were on their way out, however. The most vital traditional institution still functioning was the clan system because it determined recruitment to Sherente factions. Sherente communities are not generally on good terms with each other. At the time of my fieldwork, the Sherente to the east in the community of Rio do Sono (see Map 1) were comparatively isolated from the rest, as were those in the community of Funil to the south. Hence there was most ill-feeling between Gurgulho and Porteiras, the two major communities that had frequent contact

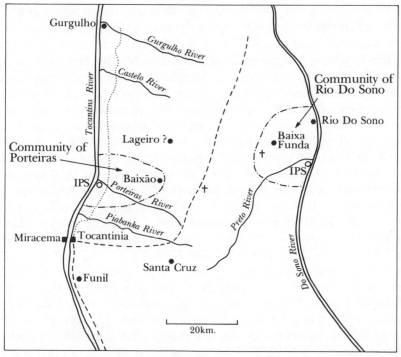

The map contains the area of the municipo of Tocantinia

- - - - -	Road
··············	Horse trail
†	Mission
o	Indian Protection Service post
●	Sherente village
■	Brazilian Town

MAP 1. Sherente country: the municipio of Tocantinia

TABLE 1. Factional structure of Sherente communities

Community	1956		1963	
Gurgulho	Wairí 1	: Wairí 2	Wairí 1	
Porteiras	Kuze 1	: Wairí 3	Wairí 3	: Kuze 1, Wairí 2
Rio do Sono	Krozaké	: Kuze 2	Kuze 2	: Krozaké
Funil	Klitó	: Wairí 4	Klitó	: Wairí 4

Note: Factions are indicated by clan name and a distinguishing numeral where there is more than one lineage in a given clan. The dominant faction is the one to which the chief of the community belongs. It is underlined and appears on the left-hand side of each column, while the opposition factions are shown on the right-hand side of each column.

with each other. But hostilities were by no means confined to them, and there was considerable intracommunity feuding as well. It is not necessary to go into the details of this factionalism, but the broad outlines can easily be stated. They are summarized in Table 1, where I have set out schematically the factional alignments in the four communities for which I have detailed information. The table does not show all the lineages represented in each community; it merely shows those which constituted factional groups. Thus in 1956 Gurgulho was split between two Wairí lineages, one of which (Wairí 2) moved to Porteiras before I returned to the field in 1963, leaving Gurgulho not only depleted but also essentially a one-party system. Porteiras was split in 1956 between a dominant Kuze lineage and another Wairí lineage which was in opposition. In 1963 the latter, Wairí 3, controlled the village, with Kuze 1 and Wairí 2, newly arrived from Gurgulho, in opposition. In Rio do Sono the conflict was always between a Krozaké lineage and Kuze 2. In 1956 the chief was Krozaké and he had not only weaned the community away from their previous Kuze 2 chief but persuaded them to move away from him physically to the hamlet of Baixa Funda, leaving one solitary household at Rio do Sono. But by 1963 this tendency had been reversed. The son of the deposed (and now deceased) Kuze 2 chief had reassumed the leadership of the community and persuaded most of it to move back to Rio do Sono and the nearby Indian Protection Service post. Only Funil remained stable from 1956 to 1963, owing to the powerful personality of the Klitó chief who ran things there.

It should be clear from the above that Wairí, Kuze, Krozaké, and Klitó are patriclans whose constituent patrilineages may be located in different villages and have little to do with one another, or may even be located in the same village and be hostile to one another (as with Wairí 2 and Wairí 3 in Porteiras). A fifth clan, the Kbazí, also exists but does not appear in Table 1 because there was no significant lineage group of Kbazí which appeared as a faction in any of the four communities for which I have data.

By the time I came to work among the Sherente their ideas about the moiety system had grown a little hazy. There was general agreement that in the old days every Sherente belonged to one of the two moieties called, respectively, Sdakrã (or Wairí) and Šiptató (or Doí). It was also generally agreed that members of one moiety had to marry only people selected from the other moiety. This rule was no longer applied when I knew the Sherente and indeed could not have been applicable, since many of them no longer knew which moiety they were supposed to belong to. In recent times men have only divided up by moiety affiliation for the ceremony marking the formal bestowal of boys' names. This ceremony is infrequently performed now, and on the one occasion when I saw it, I was impressed by the fact that it appeared to be in organizational shambles. Two criers, one from each moiety, should have stood facing each other and bestowed the names belonging to the opposite moiety on the children of the opposite moiety (see Nimuendajú 1942:45–46). In fact, the criers stood there to represent the moieties, but they named boys indiscriminately. Even though the moiety system appeared to be obsolescent, though, I found that people knew about clan affiliations and that any knowledgeable Sherente could work out moiety membership from that. Furthermore, there was general agreement as to the principles according to which this should be done, and they corresponded well to Nimuendajú's ideal model. I have set out these correspondences in Table 2, which shows that Nimuendajú's informants re-

TABLE 2.   Sherente moieties and clans

	Nimuendajú's model (using his orthography)	
Moieties	Sdakrã or Wairí	Šiptató or Doí
Clans	Krẽprehí	Kuze
	Isauré	Išibdu
	Isruríe	Kbazi (prẽ)
	Krozaké	Prasé (or Klitó)
	Maybury-Lewis' data	
Moieties	Wairí	Doí
Clans	Wairí	Kuze
	Krozaké	Kbazí
		Klitó

membered each moiety as having comprised four clans, of which one on each side (Krozaké and Klitó) was thought of as an alien tribe incorporated into the Sherente. By the time I reached the Sherente the various clans of the Wairí moiety were no longer distinguished. Instead there were a number of different patrilineages all known as belonging to the Wairí. These were regarded as being "on the same side," conceptually speaking, as the Krozaké. On the opposite side three of the four clans mentioned by Nimuendajú were still in existence.

There was a residual feeling among the Sherente when I was with them that fellow clansmen ought not to marry, but only older men felt such marriage was really shameful. In fact, such marriages did take place and most people remained unconcerned. They were more concerned to insure lineage exogamy, though some marriages did take place within lineages. Indeed, it was clear at the time of my fieldwork that there was considerable disagreement among the Sherente concerning their own values and whether or how they should insist on them. This was of course reflected in their views on marriage and the obligations of kinship. Under the circumstances, it was surprising to discover that they were still using a system of kinship categories perfectly adapted to their obsolescent moieties.

Sherente Relationship Terminology

The Sherente relationship terminology was first set out by Nimuendajú (1942:23–25). Lévi-Strauss published some analytical comments on it some years later (1952) in the course of his reinterpretation of Nimuendajú's material. In 1958 I published a list of Sherente kinship terms which was intended to supersede Nimuendajú's, which I had found to contain some inaccuracies, and at the same time made some critical comments on Lévi-Strauss's analysis. I would write a critique of Lévi-Strauss's interpretation very differently today and find similarly that the list of Sherente terms I published previously is unsatisfactory. I explain my errors of interpretation in a fuller treatment of Sherente kinship now in preparation. Briefly, they were due to my inexperienced seeking for an exhaustive list of genealogical referents for each Sherente kinship term. Since then I have had the opportunity to work over my material and return to the Sherente once again, and I now feel able to elucidate the structure of their relationship terminology. It so closely resembles that of the Shavante that I shall set it out in the same way as I set out the Shavante terminology in *Akwẽ-Shavante Society* (1967). The structure of the system can best be shown by the use of a binary matrix like that in Figure 2. This matrix expresses the distinction the Sherente make between *wanõrĩ* and *wasimpkoze,* a we/they distinction exactly analogous to the Shavante distinction between *waniwihã* and *wasi're'wa* (Maybury-Lewis 1967:167), people on my side and

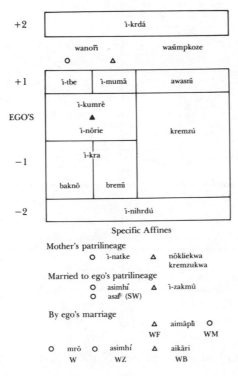

FIGURE 2. Sherente kinship terminology

people on the other side. In Figure 2 I place certain terms within the matrix and list others underneath. The terms in the matrix are those which are at least partially defined by it. For example, any female who is *wanõrĩ* to ego and in the first ascending generation can be addressed as *ĩ-tbe.* The terms which I have listed below the matrix are those which denote subcategories or genealogical positions. I have throughout listed terms of address as used by a male ego. A similar figure constructed for the Shavante termin- ology. (Maybury-Lewis 1967:342) is reproduced for comparative purposes as Figure 3, though I shall not repeat the discussion of the Shavante terminology which may be found in Maybury-Lewis 1967:214–239.

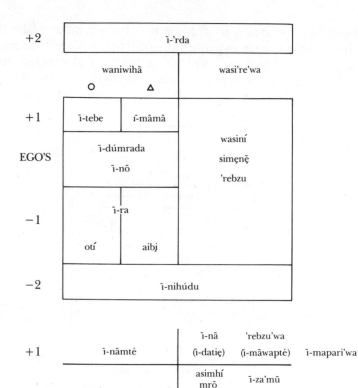

FIGURE 3. Shavante kinship terminology (from Maybury-Lewis 1967:214)

The connotations of the terms in Figure 2 are as follows:[2]

1. *ĩ-krdá:*   any person who is in ego's grandparents' generation or over
2. *ĩ-nihrdú:*   any person who is in ego's grandchildren's generation or below

wanõrĩ
3. *ĩ-tbe:*   any female in the first ascending generation who
is *wanõrĩ* to ego
4. *ĩ-mumã:*   any male in the first ascending generation who is
wanõrĩ to ego
5. *ĩ-kumrẽ:*   any person older than ego who is in the same
generation and *wanõrĩ* to ego

6. *ĩ-nõrie:*   any person younger than ego who is in the same generation and *wanõrĩ* to ego

7. *ĩ-kra:*   any person in the first descending generation who is *wanõrĩ* to ego

8. *bremĩ:*   any male in the first descending generation who is *wanõrĩ* to ego with the exception of ego's son

9. *baknõ:*   any female in the first descending generation who is *wanõrĩ* to ego with the exception of ego's daughter

wasimpkoze

13. *awasni:*   any person of an older generation than ego's who is *wasimpkoze* to ego

15. *kremzú:*   any person who is *wasimpkoze* to ego, and in ego's or a younger generation

17. *ĩ-natke:*   any female in ego's mother's lineage

18. *nõkliekwa:*   (or *kremzukwa,* less common): Any male in ego's lineage; also MBW

21. *asimhi:*   any woman who has married a man of ego's lineage, with the exception of anyone who is *ĩ-natke* to ego and of SW; also WZ

22. *ĩ-zakmũ:*   any man who has married a woman of ego's lineage

23. *ĩ-mrõ:*   wife

24. *aimãplí:*   wife's parent, wife's parents' siblings

26. *aikãri:*   WB

27. *asai:*   SW

The Sherente assured me that in the old days every person in their society could and did address any other person by a kinship term. If a given alter were much older than ego, he would be addressed as *ĩ-krdá;* if much younger, as *ĩ-nihrdú.* Beyond that a man only needed to know the moiety affiliation, sex, and approximate age of another person to be able to classify him at once. In fact, for those who were of the opposite moiety, there were generic terms correctly applicable even if one did not know the age and sex of the person to be addressed. Out of this broad category of people who were *wasimpkoze* (of the other side) and could be addressed as *awasni*[3] or *kremzu,* ego would then separate certain subcategories of specific relatives and address them by special terms. So all the members of his mother's clan, including his mother and those much discussed kinsmen, his mother's brothers, would be referred to as *ĩ-natkę* (female) and *nõkliekwa* (male). A man could not marry his *ĩ-natkę,* that is, any woman in his mother's clan. Since he had to marry a girl from the opposite moiety, he therefore had to marry his *kremzu*, that is, any woman in the opposite moiety of his generation or younger and not of his own mother's clan. After marriage he would refer to her as *ĩ-mrõ*. It was regarded as a good thing for a group of brothers to marry a group of sisters, or for a group of fellow clansmen to marry a group of fellow clanswomen. At the same time, brothers were prohibited from taking each other's sisters in marriage because a man could not be simultaneously *ĩ-zakmũ* (ZH) and *aikãri* (WB) to another.

It is clear that the use of this terminology by the Sherente has changed since the period which my informants referred to as the olden days; but in the absence of comprehensive information about those times, it is impossible to document the precise nature of those changes. What can be documented is a striking continuity. Knowledgeable informants all agreed that in the old days people applied *wañorĩ* terms to members of their own moiety and *wasimpkoze* terms to members of the other moiety. I therefore set out to discover how the Sherente could apparently go on using the same system at a time when they no longer knew people's moiety affiliations.

In 1963 the Sherente still accepted that all other Sherente should properly be addressed by kinship terms. They did not always so address them, but I do not find that necessarily significant. I had already seen how the Shavante, who certainly did apply kinship terms to all other members of their own society, were sometimes uncertain about how other people should be classified and would avoid using kinship terms until this problem had been solved (Maybury-Lewis 1967:230–231). In fact, the Sherente who did not use kinship terms for others, or who could not tell me which kinship terms they would use, were in one of three situations: (1) they were relative newcomers in their community (cf. the Shavante situation above); (2) I was asking them about Sherente in other communities with whom they had infrequent dealings; (3) they were denying kinship with the individual concerned. I consider the first two situations to be part of the normal functioning of the system. Only the third type of situation—which occurred exceedingly rarely—represents a modification of it. One of the two instances of it in my notes refers to a man who was by Sherente standards very prosperous and was therefore often accused of meanness in his community. "He forgets his kin," I was told. "In his house you are offered nothing. Everything is for sale." The man himself, discussing these sentiments with me one day, remarked "We [the Sherente] are all related, but I have no close relatives, the sort that have to be treated like kinsmen, in this community." Indeed, his closest kin lived quite far away and he rarely saw them. I believe that his prosperity was partly due to the fact that he had succeeded in establishing himself in a community where he could deny that he had kinship obligations. It was he who did not always use kinship terms for all the members of that community. This is an option which has only recently become acceptable among the Sherente, and it is invariably used in order to husband economic resources against the demands of kinsmen.

Apart from such exceptional cases, though, the Sherente did use the kin terms toward each other when they knew how to. The principle of their application was quite simple. In theory, people knew which lineage and therefore which clan other members of the community belonged to and from this their kinship status followed automatically. For example (see Table 1), in Rio do Sono a Krozaké person used own side (*wañorĩ*) terms for Krozaké people and other side (*wasimpkoze*) terms for Kuzę people. Furthermore, they were aware of the associations set out in Table 2, so that a Krozaké person would also use own side terms for all Wairĩ and other side terms for all Kbazí and Klitó. When I asked an informant how he would address a person in another community and the informant did not know that person (or did not recognize him from the name I gave him), he would ask me what his clan was. Once he had that information, he could suggest a classification. The Sherente were thus continuing to apply the terminology as if Wairí and Krozaké were one side (or moiety) and Kuzę, Kbazí, and Klitó were the other. Interestingly enough, it made no difference if lineages of a single clan were pitted against each other in a given community, as were two Wairí lineages in Porteiras in 1963. They continued to call each other by own-side terms.

The system works with a beautiful simplicity provided everybody knows everybody else's clan affiliation. But everybody did not. To return to our example, young people in Rio do Sono might not know that they were Krozaké people and that the "others" were Kuzę people. But they grew up applying own-side and other-side terms appropriately. Hence they also applied own-side and other-side terms to individuals in the community who were not known to be related to the Krozaké or the Kuzę, according to whom they sided with. It was thus possible for a man in that community to be treated as if he were, let us say, a Kuzę without actually being one, provided that he had no close or known (usually the same thing) genealogical links to the Krozaké and threw in his lot with the Kuzę. In such situations the we/they distinction was at once a terminological one and a distinction between factions in the community.

This was not always the case. In Porteiras, for example, two Wairí lineages were separate factions in 1963, but addressed each other as if they were on the same conceptual side of the kinship terminology. But this was a transitional moment in the affairs of that community. The first column of Table 1 shows that in 1956 the two competing factions in all the communities except Gurgulho were from opposite sides (moieties). Gurgulho was a one-party community when I arrived in the field and the split between lineages of the Wairí took place while I was there. Significantly, Wairí 2 established itself some way away from Gurgulho proper, at a distance of about four miles, though I still considered them to be part of Gurgulho when I left the field. When the breach did not heal, the members of Wairí 2 went to Porteiras in the expectation that they would there join up with Wairí 3. The quarrel between Wairí 2 and Wairí 3 took place while I was in the field in 1963, and it could only have had one of the following possible outcomes: it would be patched up, and the two Wairí lineages would no longer be on bad terms with each other; Wairí 2 would split off or move to another community; some members of Wairí 2 would make up with Wairí 3 and others would move away. In other words, the Wairí would either patch up their quarrel or some dissident Wairí would move away. In either case, the problem of what to call people would be solved and the community would conform once again to the Sherente model.

It seems then that, although the Sherente are individualistic and quarrelsome, their communities are generally divided between two principal factions which come from opposing sides or moieties. Their kinship terminology both expresses and serves as a matrix for this fundamental distinction.

Special terms are then used to single out classes and individuals on the opposite side. Thus ĩ-natke and nõkliekwa are used to denote the members of ego's mother's lineage. These are the people whom ego effectively separates from the "others," who are potential enemies and wives. From his mother's lineage he expects and receives affection and support. A man without maternal uncles (nõkliekwa)[4] is regarded as peculiarly unfortunate, for he lacks the security and protection which they provide. The Sherente sometimes compared this relationship to that between godfather (compadre) and godchild in Brazilian society, and this is a very apt analogy, as we shall see.

The other special terms which the Sherente use to distinguish relatives from the other side all refer to specific affines—men who have married into ego's lineage (*ĩ-zakmũ*), women who have married into ego's lineage (*asimhi*), ego's wife, her parents and her siblings. I cannot explain why there is a special term for son's wife, distinguishing the daughter-in-law from the other women who have married into ego's lineage. It is also noteworthy that the wife's sister is addressed by the same term as the women who marry into ego's lineage, but this custom corresponds to the traditional Sherente preference for marriage between a group of brothers and a group of sisters. The theory behind such marriages equates wife's sister and brother's wife. Similarly, among the Shavante who *do* have separate terms for wife's sister and brother's wife, the term for wife's sister would under certain circumstances be applied to the brother's wife (Maybury-Lewis 1967:221 and 322, Fig. 7).

Cultural Categories of the Central Gê

We are now in a position to consider the cultural categories of the Central Gê. It is clear that the relationship terminologies of the Sherente and the Shavante are very similar. Moreover, they were being similarly used in the mid-sixties even though the Shavante were at that time a recently contacted, seminomadic, hunting-and-gathering people, while the Sherente were a small, settled enclave which had been struggling for a century to avoid being swallowed up in Brazilian society. On the evidence, then, the structure of the relationship terminology demonstrates a fundamental property of these two cultures.

Both the Sherente and the Shavante terminologies emphasize a binary division of society. They indicate other things as well and make other discriminations, as I have been at pains to show both here and elsewhere (Maybury-Lewis 1967:237–239). But the primary discrimination expressed through the system of relationship categories is the distinction between own side and other side, between *wanõri* and *wasimpkoze*, between *waniwihã* and *wasi 're'wa*. This bipartition of society is part of a world view which insists on a bipartition of the total universe.

I have shown elsewhere that the distinction between *people of my side* and *people of the other side* (literally: people separated from us) is an important leitmotiv in Shavante culture (1967: passim and summary on p. 299). It is a cosmic distinction which also permeates Shavante institutional arrangements. Similarly, in traditional Sherente belief the two culture heroes Waptokwa (Sun) and Wairí (Moon) represent a series of oppositions which are the very warp of existence: life and death, heat and cold, day and night, even cleverness and stupidity. The symbolic content of these oppositions is ambiguous and subtle, and I shall have to postpone a discussion of it until another time. It is, however, significant that in spite of all the changes and vicissitudes which the Sherente have experienced in recent years, the contrast between Waptokwa and Wairí and the stories concerning this contrast are still a living part of their culture. The contrast between the moieties explicitly provides a social and concrete dimension to this cosmic schema, for Waptokwa is associated with the Šiptato (or Doi) moiety and Wairí with the Sdakrã (or Wairí).

According to Nimuendajú's reconstruction of traditional Sherente culture, this pervasive dualism also determined the layout of Sherente villages. Each one was arranged in a semicircle as in Figure 1, with the Šiptato moiety and its constituent clans occupying the northern arc while the Sdakrã moiety occupied the southern one. Such a layout fits so beautifully with Sherente ideas about the structure of the cosmos that it might seem unnecessarily scrupulous to question it, but Nimuendajú's diagram is rendered suspect by my discovery that the Sherente practice uxorilocal residence after marriage and insist that they have always done so. It is unlikely that this is a change from their traditional residence rule, since we now know that all the other Gê societies, including the Shavante, are uxorilocal. But if postmarital residence among the Sherente has always been uxorilocal, we are faced with a number of problems. Patriclans could not have been located in the village semicircle, for their male members would have had to move over to their wives' households at marriage. Moreover it was not only Nimuendajú who said that residence among the Sherente was patrilocal (1942:16). I myself stated in a preliminary report from the field (1958:131) that there was a distinct tendency to patrilocal residence. The explanation of this apparent contradiction tells us something important about Sherente ideology and also brings out the unfortunate imprecision of the term *patrilocal*. The term usually implies at least two things and possibly three: first, that a wife normally moves to her husband's household after marriage (virilocality); second, that the husband's household is also the father's household; third—it is often assumed—that husband and father are members of a patrilineal descent group. Among the Sherente a man and his father are to this day members of a patrilineage (patriclan). Men like to have their sons living in their own household or at least close by. Their ideology is therefore patrilocal. However, their rule of residence is uxorilocal, so we have a situation where the Sherente stress patriliny and talk of patrilocality but actually practice uxorilocality.

This is precisely what happens among the Shavante. In fact, the Shavante data can help us to make sense of the Sherente anomaly. Shavante society consists of three exogamous patriclans. The Eastern Shavante insisted that a man might marry a girl from either of the other two clans. The Western Shavante considered it improper for two of the clans to intermarry. Their members had to marry people from the third clan, so that in effect they had a system of unnamed patrilineal moieties. The clans were in turn subdivided into named lineages. Theoretically, the rule of uxori-local residence ought to have resulted in the dispersal of the lineages throughout the village. However, the men of Shavante lineages deliberately stick together after marriage, and they are encouraged to do so by the society's preference for having a number of brothers marry a number of sisters. In this way, whole lineages contrive to marry into adjoining houses in the village arc. Eventually, as the older men in that arc (the fathers-in-law) die, that segment of the circle comes to be known by the name of the lineage which has married into it. At the same time, segments of the circle are commonly referred to as the territory of this or that clan, although they must contain the male members of at least two different clans at any given moment. A Shavante will therefore, if asked, draw a diagram of his village arc and locate the three clans on it and their constituent lineages, yet we know that this is a momentary and schematic representation of a complex residential situation.

Nimuendajú's plan showing how Sherente patriclans were located on the village semicircle can now be seen in a new light. He never saw such a village and I have been unable to discover any eyewitness description of one. The diagram is therefore based on the information given by a Sherente informant. What did the informant have in mind? He could have been drawing a model of Sherente society, showing that the moieties and their constituent clans were essentially in opposition to one another. Alternatively, he could have been tracing a Shavante-style simplified diagram of the residential situation in a hypothetical village, for we know that the Sherente too encouraged marriage between groups of brothers and groups of sisters. In all probability, he was doing both, showing the bipartition of his society as expounded in its ideology and also the fact that residential segments of the village arc were thought of as belonging to specific clans.

But why should these societies practice uxorilocal residence in the face of their patrilineal ideology? Comparative study has shown that uxorilocality is common to all Gê societies and the Bororo. It only stands out as anomalous among the Central Gê, who organize their societies around patrilineal descent groups. One might therefore better inquire why the Gê insist on uxori-local residence and why the Central Gê then blur uxorilocality with patriliny.

Uxorilocality is certainly not dictated by the external circumstances to which these Central Brazilian societies have to adapt. Nor does it seem to have immediate practical advantages. The grudging collaboration on household-connected tasks between men and their daughters' husbands contrasts sharply with the solidarity evident in the relation between fathers and sons. Sons seek out their fathers' company. Sons-in-law stay away from their fathers-in-law, though they live under the same roof. Among the Shavante, fathers and sons regularly hunted together, though their game would go to different households; yet men would never hunt with their sons-in-law, even though they contributed meat to the same household. Uxorilocality thus creates strains for the Central Gê men, of which they are painfully aware, since every husband is obliged at marriage to leave the bosom of his descent group and transfer into a household where he is regarded as an inferior and outsider. This transfer was so traumatic for young Shavante that they would avoid spending more than the minimum amount of time in their wives' households. Some of them would even stoutly insist they were not married, even after their wives had borne them children (Maybury-Lewis 1967:84–86).

The rule of uxorilocal residence becomes immediately intelligible, however, if we consider the symbolic significance of the village in all of these societies. The Northern Gê and the Bororo build circular villages. The center, whether it contains (at least theoretically) two men's houses as among the Kayapó, or a single men's house as among the Bororo, or simply cleared spaces where men's groups meet, as among the Apinayé and the Eastern Timbira, is the locus of public life. It is also symbolically a male place. The periphery of huts is the domestic sphere and is symbolically female. Men may actually do most of the building of these peripheral houses, but they are said to do so for the women. The men's place, conceptually speaking, is in the forum at the center, where the political and ritual life of the society, from which women are more or less strictly excluded, is carried on. When men leave this public, male sphere to get on with the private, domestic side of their lives, they go to do so in their wives' houses. This is the rationale behind uxorilocality.

The Central Gê also distinguish between the male forum and the female houses at the periphery, but the opposition is somewhat differently maintained. They strongly emphasize the distinctions between the male and female principles, between men and women as distinct classes. Similarly, the forum of society is the *warã*,[5] or men's meeting place, which is located close to the fulcrum of the village arc in their semicircular communities. It is here that the political life of the society, based on its patrilineal groupings, takes place. Women are not only excluded from participation in politics but are regarded as merely passive or, in a sense, invisible members of these lineage-based groups. The proof of this is that they are, among the Shavante, never accused of sorcery, which is the very heart of politics. Although politics among the Central Gê are by no means confined to the forum, it is a sharp contrast with most of their Northern Gê neighbors to find the forum used for political purposes at all.

Among the Eastern Timbira and the Apinayé, each male has two aspects to his person. His social self is assigned to the moieties, which conduct the ceremonial life of the society at the center. His physical self is assigned to the periphery, where unrecognized extended families engage in politics without formal institutional expression.

The Kayapó appear to have tried to adopt a similar solution. Each man is invested with a public self, whose role is played in the system of age-grades and men's houses at the center, and a private self, whose role is domestic and peripheral. Again the dual organization of Kayapó society was a matter of complementary men's houses in the central, ceremonial domain. The Kayapó system did not work as well as that of the other Northern Gê peoples in suppressing schismatic politics. On the contrary, political feuding between men's houses became the norm, with the result that there are today no villages which have the two men's houses that the ideal village is supposed to have.

The Central Gê clearly opted for a different system. They did not put their moiety system on center stage to serve as a paradigm for complementarity and harmony, while trying to suppress factionalism by relegating it to the domestic and therefore structurally insignificant sphere. Instead, they tried to balance various all-pervasive moiety systems against each other.

Nimuendajú reported that the dualism of the Sherente social system, based on patrilineal moieties, had a cosmic character. But it was not the only dualism bisecting Sherente society. Log races, which had enormous ceremonial importance, were regularly run between two sporting moieties, to which children of both sexes were assigned by their fathers (Nimuendajú 1942:43). Adult men were assigned to yet a third pair of moieties, which existed to perform the longest and most important ceremony of all (Nimuendajú 1942:93–95). At the same time the men's associations also had many important functions. My data from the Shavante confirm Nimuendajú's suggestion that these associations were in fact originally age-sets. I have shown elsewhere that the Shavante were quite explicit about the contrast between their dominant dualism (the *waniwihã/wasi're'wa* opposition, sometimes expressed in exogamous moieties) and their age-sets and age-moieties. Both institutions were supposed to embody the complementarity of opposites; but the major opposition based on descent groups had come to stand for the antithesis between opposites, while the age-moieties represented true complementarity. So the *waniwihã/wasi-'re'wa* opposition represented conflict, while the age-set and age-moiety system stood for harmony (Maybury-Lewis 1967:164). In both societies the antithetical principle proved more powerful. The Shavante referred ruefully to the fact the enmity between "sides" invariably triumphs over the harmony supposedly inculcated by the age-set system. Among the Sherente, the age-sets/associations became obsolete, while the antithetical moiety system continued in spite of everything to serve as a cultural matrix.

The Bororo system represents yet another variation on this theme. The Bororo too distinguish between an individual's physical and social selves and they allocate different roles to each. They too make much of the distinction between the male center and the female periphery. Yet their ideology calls for the village to be made up of a certain number of constituent clans, each with its own assigned and immutable place in the village circle. Their unusual form of "matriliny" is the mechanism which serves to knit these elements together.

Similarly, the patriliny of the Sherente and the Shavante serves to link the public male sphere with the domestic, female one. But the Central Gê do not make such a clear distinction between the physical and social aspects of the person. The physical self is assigned to descent groups which have a recognized social role throughout the system. These descent groups are then contrasted with antidescent groups, such as age and ceremonial moieties. It is consistent with the pervasive nature of their dual organization that the relationship systems of the Bororo and the Central Gê, unlike those of the Northern Gê, embrace the whole of their societies. There are, for example, no Shavante whom any other Shavante does not regard, in principle, as relatives to be addressed by the appropriate terms.

It seems that all of these societies were preoccupied with the ambiguity inherent in dual organization. They conceived of opposition as immanent in the structure of the universe and therefore also in their own societies. But the nature of opposition is notoriously ambiguous. Depending on whether complementarity or antithesis is stressed, it may be expressed in reciprocity or competition and result in harmony or disharmony.

The Northern Gê attempted to resolve this paradox by separating their social systems into levels. The formal, public level was characterized by dual organization, complementary antithesis and harmony. Factionalism was relegated to the informal, domestic level, where it would be structurally insignificant, though among the Kayapó it could not be contained there.

The Central Gê and the Bororo had no such separation of levels. They opted for a total systemic alternative which permitted unilineal descent, which also operated throughout the system. They then strove to counteract the schismic tendencies of such a system by allocating people to countervailing moiety systems or establishing elaborate networks of cross-cutting ties. The Central Gê explicitly hoped that in this way they would maintain the balance and harmony which they sought. Ultimately, as we know, they failed, but only in the sense that all systems eventually fail, namely, that they change and cease to exist in their original terms.

Theoretical Implications

The relationship systems of the Shavante and the Sherente are clearly variations on a single model which we may call the Central Gê system. This is readily distinguishable from the Bororo system, described in the next paper, and the Northern Gê system, which is common to the societies which were discussed in the earlier papers in this volume. Let me first try and sum up my understanding of the common Northern Gê model as elaborated by my colleagues.

A simplified model of the Northern Gê type of system is shown in Figure 4. The basic principles of the classification are very simple. Ego distinguishes four classes of relatives in ascending generations, which I shall call for convenience (while stressing that these are *not* correct translations of the terms) "fathers" (*chũ*),[6] "mothers" (*che*), "uncles" (*ked*), and "aunts" (*tui*). Male and female siblings and parallel cousins are referred to as *tõ* and *tõi*, respectively. Finally, ego calls *kra* everybody who addresses him as *chũ*, and he calls *tamchwẹ*, everybody who addresses him as *ked*.

The Krahó and the Krĩkatí say that a person acquires his physical substance from people in the categories *father* and *mother* and

Generation

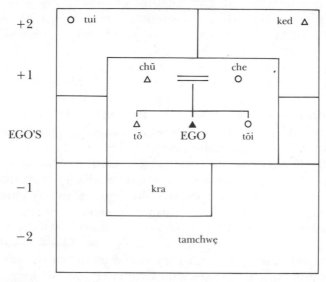

FIGURE 4. Northern Gê type of classification (using Eastern Timbira roots).

his social persona from people in the categories *uncle* and *aunt*. A boy's social personality comes to him in the form of names bestowed on him by people in the *uncle* category (normally mother's father or mother's brother) and through which he acquires membership in the ceremonially important name-based groups.

The Apinayé make the same distinction between physical substance and social persona and the means of acquiring them, but they introduce a new principle. A boy's father must find him an adoptive father, who may not be a man who is in the *father* category to the boy and may not even be a close kinsman of the boy. This adoptive father then arranges for someone in the *uncle* category to transfer names to the child.

The Kayapó give even greater emphasis to the adoptive father. A boy has to join the men's group of his adoptive father, and these men's groups are of critical political and ceremonial importance in Kayapó society.

We know that each of these societies makes a sharp distinction between the domestic, female sphere at the periphery of the village and the public, male forum in the center. At the periphery men, living uxorilocally, act together in coresident groups. Boys are brought into this realm of activity through their "fathers" (*chū*). The forum is, by contrast, dominated by groups formed respectively through name transference (Krahó, Krĩkatí), name transference via symbolic patrifiliation (Apinayé) and finally symbolic patrifiliation without name transference (Kayapó). Boys are introduced into this realm by their "uncles" (Krahó, Krĩkatí), by "uncles" through the intermediary of adoptive fathers (Apinayé), and by adoptive fathers without formal intermediary (Kayapó).

We are clearly dealing with a continuum, from the Krahó moving steadily westward through the Krĩkatí and Apinayé to the Kayapó. The basic system expresses a bilateral ideology focusing on the two aspects of a person, his physical substance and his social persona. At the Krahó end of the continuum, the social persona is bestowed unequivocally by the *uncle* category, with the *father* category confined to the domestic sphere. As we move westward, the *uncle* is assisted by a surrogate father and finally replaced altogether by a surrogate father. But there is no society which permits the actual *father* category to operate both domestically and in the forum. This would clearly lead to patriliny, which would effect radical alterations in the system, as we have seen in the case of the Central Gê.

These differences correspond exactly to the variations in the use of the terminology between the different societies, all of which occur in the cross-cousin category, that is, among people of ego's generation who are neither *tõ* nor *tõi*. The Krahó, who place most stress on matrilocal peripheral groups and the *uncle* category as a boy's bridge to the forum, use the terminology in a manner reminiscent of Crow-type systems. They call the patrilateral cross-cousins *keti* and *tïi*, and the matrilateral ones *tamtxua*.[7] The Krĩkatí emphasize name-based groups and accordingly use naming terms outside the immediate circle of kin, for cross-cousins among other people. The Apinayé are an intermediate case, where a father arranges for an adoptive father who procures someone in the *uncle* category. Their use of the terminology is accordingly balanced right in the middle. Some informants apply it more or less in Crow fashion like the Krahó; others apply it in something like Omaha fashion, calling their *matrilateral* cross-cousins *geti* and *na* and their patrilateral ones *tamtxua*.[8] Finally, the Kayapó tend to emphasize fatherhood and surrogate fatherhood as the bridge between the periphery and the forum, relegating the *uncle* category to the domestic sphere. They therefore use the terminology in consistently Omaha fashion (see Table 3).

The classic distinction between Crow-type systems and Omaha-type systems is thus neither discriminatory nor particularly informative for the Northern Gê. It is even less so when we consider

TABLE 3. Northern Gê cross-cousin terms

Society	Public-private link for males	Social emphasis	Cross-cousin terms
Krahó	*Keti/tïi*	Matrifiliation	Children of *tïi* called *tïi/txū*, children of *keti* called *tamtxua* (Crow)
Krĩkatí	*Ket/tui*	Naming relations	Called by naming terms
Apinayé	Surrogate father obtains *geti/ (tui)*	Neutral	Children of *tui* called *tui/pam*, children of *geti* called *tamtxua* (Crow) Also Children of *tui* called *tamtxua*, children of *geti* called *geti/na* (Omaha)
Kayapó	Surrogate father arranges men's groups	Patrifiliation	Children of *ngêt* called *ngêt/nã*, children of *kwatuy* called *tabdjuò* (Omaha)

the Central Gê systems together with those of the Northern Gê. According to the traditional classifications, the Sherente would be said to have an Omaha-type system, while the Shavante system would be considered of a Dakota type. Yet it is clear that they are identical in their essential features and in their internal logic. To distinguish them as Omaha and Dakota is to lay undue emphasis on peripheral variables and to miss the central point. If we attempt to classify all the Central Brazilian societies according to the same scheme, the anomalies become patently absurd. We would be obliged to distinguish the Kayapó system (Omaha) as radically different from the Krahó system (Crow) and to class Kayapó with Sherente (both Omaha) and Krahó with Bororo (both Crow), giving the following classification:

Omaha	*Dakota*	*Anomalous*	*Crow*
Kayapó	Shavante	Apinayé	Krahó
Sherente		Krĩkatí	Bororo

On the other hand, the essays in this volume amply demonstrate that we are dealing with variations on three different kinds of systems, which may be classified as follows:

Northern Gê	Central Gê	Bororo
Krahó	Sherente	Bororo
Krĩkatí	Shavante	
Apinayé		
Kayapó		

One may of course produce an infinite number of classifications merely by choosing different criteria for classifying. The question is why some criteria are preferable to others. In this case, I believe that the second classification is more useful than the first because it groups systems according to their central rationale, rather than according to the way they deal with something peripheral, like the cross-cousin category.[9]

The advantage of the approach used here is that it shows that the variations along the Crow-Omaha continuum in what I have called the Northern Gê system are oscillations in a basic system, differences of emphasis rather than of structure. In the same way, the Omaha-Dakota difference is a minor variation on the Central Gê theme. The kinship ideology of the Northern Gê is a theory about the relationship of the individual to society. The dialectics of society itself, which are so strikingly expressed in the Central Gê systems, are here removed from the sphere of kinship and played out in the forum. There the ceremonial moieties were free to perform the rituals of antithesis and synthesis which expressed the Northern Gê view of the world. This was not always a matter of serene complementarity, as the Kayapó evidence of severe feuding amply demonstrates. But the implications of symbolic opposition are notoriously ambiguous. It is, as we have seen, a short step from antithesis to antipathy.

It is similarly a central tenet of both Sherente and Shavante social theory that society is governed by the same principles of complementarity and antithesis which operate in the natural world. Yet, as we have seen, the Sherente and Shavante express this opposition through the kinship system itself, which is tied into the other major institutions of their society through patrilineal descent. At the same time, it is important to note that they, like the Northern Gê, show considerable ingenuity and flexibility in the use of their systems of classification. Kinship was for the Central Gê as much a matter of politics as of genealogy. It is therefore especially interesting to note that Christopher Crocker, writing of the ostensibly matrilineal Bororo, suggests that it may well be misleading to speak of unilineal descent at all for any of the Gê-Bororo peoples. What he appears to be saying is that a notion of unilineal descent which entails a simple, exclusive, and automatic allocation of children via genealogical ties to a given descent group is much too simplistic to encompass the societies with which we are dealing. I agree and would go even further and state that it is much too simplistic to deal with societies in general. As we get to know more about the societies we attempt to analyze from all over the world, it becomes increasingly clear that the concept of unilineal descent is not a neatly definable genealogical principle but a rather complex ideological statement. As such, it may operate in a variety of different ways, depending, as we have seen, on how a society defines a person, allocates his roles, uses its relationship system, and so on.

Furthermore, I would argue that the flexibility which we have noted in the Central and Northern Gê systems is not at all unusual. We have known at least since Robertson Smith's remarkably sophisticated analysis of Arabian kinship (1885) that even the most staunchly unilineal ideology with a strongly professed interest in bloodlines may be applied with this sort of flexibility. Yet kinship theory continues to be bedeviled by a sort of passion for neatness which leads anthropologists to make models of native models with insufficient regard for the use to which those models are put. It seems likely that the "neatest" unilineal systems may frequently, if not always, result in the sort of organizational fluidity which I have described for the Central Gê. The neatness, as other writers have recently been insisting,[10] is merely an artifact of the anthropologist's model.

The model used by the Central Gê and its expression in their system of kinship classification is, as I have argued, preeminently binary, but the system is not rigorously so. In fact, though the kinship systems of both the Sherente and the Shavante could be classed as two-section systems, they differ in some critical respects from the classical formulations of such systems (Dumont 1953; Needham 1958). The divergence which is of particular interest is in the classification of the maternal uncle.

According to Sherente theory, the mother's brother's clan (nowadays his lineage) is removed from the absolute opposition between the moieties. The mother's brother himself, as they say nowadays, is like a godfather (Portuguese *compadre*). Though he is by birth a member of the opposite moiety, *wasimpkoze* (of the opposite side), nevertheless, he and all the males of his descent group are like father, which is the paradigm for one's own side.

Their role is to be a person's "fathers" or protectors in the opposite moiety, which otherwise contains only remote and potentially hostile kinsmen. Similarly, women of the mother's brother's descent group are thought to be like women of one's own side, even though they belong by birth to the opposite moiety. They cannot therefore be taken in marriage.

The Shavante are just as explicit about the mother's brother being like a father. Their alternative term for the maternal uncle is *ĩ-mã-wapté,* a contraction of *ĩ-mãmã-wapté,* meaning "a sort of *ĩ-mãmã,*" or father. But the role of mother's brother as surrogate father is a temporary one. He plays it fully while his sister's children are small. At this time, he is usually still living in or spending a good deal of time in his sister's house. So her children call him a sort of father, and he addresses them as *ĩ-'ra-wapté,* sort of children. Later he moves away from the household, and he and his sister's children address each other as they would other members of the opposite side. The maternal uncle is not just like anybody else on the other side, and there may be enduring affection between him and his sister's children, but the relationship becomes a pale copy of the father-son tie (Maybury-Lewis 1967:226–229).

This Sherente-Shavante difference corresponds to another difference in their systems of classification. Among the Sherente, male names belong to specific moieties and clans. They ought not in theory to be bestowed on people outside the clans which own them, except as a mechanism for adopting such people into the naming clan. Male names, like the mother's brother's clan, were thus used as markers for categories at the level of the total system of classification, and their bestowal was an important public ceremony which demonstrated the dual paradigm of society. Among the Shavante, male names had no such classificatory functions at the level of the system. Receiving a name and changing a name had symbolic importance for individuals, but (except for certain names which went with offices) the name itself had little social significance. It was thus bestowed as we would expect, by the mother's brother of a young boy in a private ceremony involving only the households of the father's sister (father's natal household) and the mother's brother (child's natal household).

Sherente ideology thus allows for a category which mediates the opposition between the sides at the level of the system itself. In Shavante theory, there is no such mediation, although Shavante practice allows for it. The mother's brother category only operates at the private, domestic level, not at the public, systemic one. It is this difference in usage which accounts for the fact that the Sherente make a categorical distinction between matrilateral and patrilateral cross-cousins, giving their system the Omaha cast I have already referred to. The Shavante make no such distinction at the level of the system itself, which thus makes no corresponding distinctions between cross-cousins.

Now both Dumont and Needham stress that a crucial feature of the binary systems they discuss is the separation between father and mother's brother and the categorical identification of mother's brother with wife's father. Yet the Central Gê do something very different. They assimilate the mother's brother to the category of *father* and separate him from wife's father, with the result that marriage to the mother's brother's daughter is considered unacceptable—categorically prohibited among the Sherente, customarily so among the Shavante (Maybury-Lewis 1967:228). Thus the opposition which paradigmatically expressed the Central Gê relationship systems is not father/mother's brother (= wife's father), but father (= mother's brother)/wife's father. The opposition between father and mother's brother is therefore not a necessary structural concomitant of two-section systems, but a contingent feature of the ideology of certain societies which have such systems.

Furthermore, the Central Gê equation of the categories *father* and *mother's brother* directly contradicts much *a priori* theorizing about the nature of kinship systems and the atoms out of which they are built. There is, for example, no necessary psychological antinomy between these two categories, as many writers have believed. Thus Radcliffe-Brown argued (1952) that the mother's brother in patrilineal societies was a sort of mother, deriving his nurturant characteristics from association with the maternal side of the family, as opposed to the authoritarian associations of the paternal side. But the mother's brother is a nurturant and supportive figure among the Sherente and Shavante not because he derives these characteristics from the mother's role or the maternal side of the family (Homans and Schneider 1955:30–32), but because he derives them from the father's role and the paternal side of society.

The Central Gê systems also pose problems for Lévi-Strauss's argument (1958) concerning the "atom of kinship." He maintained that the minimal structure out of which all kinship systems are built up is not the elementary family, as in Radcliffe-Brown's theory,[11] but one containing four terms: brother, sister, sister's husband, sister's son. This was the atom of kinship because it contained (as economically as possible) all the positions necessary for the three basic kinds of relationship: that between siblings, that between spouses, and that between parent and child. The difference between this formulation and Radcliffe-Brown's elementary family is that Lévi-Strauss's elementary structure contains the relationship between brothers-in-law, which is entailed by the notion of affinity, for there must universally be wife-givers (wife's brother) and wife-takers (sister's husband).

Lévi-Strauss then went on to make some suggestions concerning the internal structure of this "atom of kinship." He argued that (1) the relationship between husband and wife would tend to be the inverse of the relationship between brother and sister; (2) the relationship between father and son would tend to be the inverse of the relationship between mother's brother and sister's son; and (3) that the brother/sister relationship would be to the mother's brother/sister's son relationship as the father/son relationship was to the husband/wife relationship.

If, following Lévi-Strauss, we indicate friendly and free relationships by a positive sign $(+)$ and antagonistic or reserved relationships by a negative sign $(-)$, we would get the following values for the Central Gê:

husband/wife	=	+
brother/sister	=	+
father/son	=	+
mother's brother/sister's son	=	+

Hence Lévi-Strauss' first two hypotheses are not confirmed and his third one is confirmed only in a manner which he had ruled out as impossible, namely, that all relations were positive.

Among the Central Gê, there is indeed a relationship of great reserve between brothers-in-law (sister's husband/wife's brother), but this does not prevent the husband/wife and brother/sister relationships from being positive. Similarly, we have seen that the mother's brother/sister's son tie, so far from being the antithesis of the father/son tie, is actually thought of as being modeled on it. The kinship systems of the Central Gê are not therefore built up out of the "atom of kinship" suggested by Lévi-Strauss. On the contrary, the particular concatenation of relationships contained in the atom is, among the Central Gê, isolated from the major opposition permeating their systems.

Lévi-Strauss's theory fares no better with the Central Gê than Radcliffe-Brown's or Homans and Schneider's because it is in one important respect the same kind of theory. All of these formulations insist that there is some sort of balance and opposition at the heart of kinship systems between the patrilateral and the matrilateral sides and that it is determined by the biological facts of procreation. From the logical entailments of the fact that in all societies man must copulate with woman to produce children (and with the additional rider that men everywhere give up their women to other men for this purpose), the theories attempt to deduce the social logic of kinship systems. But they do not succeed in bridging the gap between necessity and invention. Certainly all kinship systems have to conform to these requirements, but we cannot deduce their manner of doing so from the requirements themselves. The data from the Central Gê show once again how misleading such arguments can be. The moral is that the study of "kinship" will not emerge from the cul-de-sac where it is at present trapped until we develop theories which deal with social theories or socio-logics, which is what kinship systems are, instead of theories derived from the limiting factors which such systems have to take into account.

THE BORORO

W HEN THEY WERE first contacted by Brazilian explorers in the early eighteenth century, the Bororo occupied a great tract of land in north central Mato Grosso. The Western Bororo lived to the west of the Paraguay River. They were reduced to a single village by the time that Petrullo visited them in 1931 (see Petrullo 1932). At that time they were already in an advanced state of acculturation and no longer exist nowadays as a distinct group.

The Eastern Bororo have, by contrast, preserved their traditional culture to the present day even in the face of strong pressure. Traditionally, they occupied an area bounded by the Cuiabá River on the west, the Taquari on the south, the Araguaia on the east, and the Rio das Mortes on the north. Their modern remnants, or Orarimogu-doge, as they term themselves, live about 150 kilometers southeast from Cuiabá. Their villages are scattered along the São Lourenço River, its major affluent the Rio Vermelho, and the western headwaters of the Araguaia. The total population of slightly more than 500 (1967) is divided into three village clusters, differing in history and contemporary socioeconomic situation.

The first cluster now has a single village, located near the confluence of the São Lourenço with the Cuiabá, and near an Indian Protection Service post. Its inhabitants are the "pantanal Bororo," who differ slightly linguistically and culturally from the rest of the tribe, with whom they have but infrequent contact. They may originally have been a branch of the Western Bororo.

The second cluster is internally divided into villages above and below the boom town of Rondonópolis. The lower villages (two) are each associated with an Indian Protection Service post, but are indigenously regarded as the most traditional and least oppressed of all Bororo communities. Fieldwork was almost exclusively carried out in this area. The upper villages (three) include one near Rondonópolis, which in 1966 was little more than a disorganized camp, and two much further upstream on the Rio Vermelho, on its affluents the Poxoreu and Porube Aidjau, not far from the small Brazilian town of Jarudori. The historical association of the Bororo with this area is evident in all these Bororo-derived place names. Both of the last villages are in intensive contact with Brazilians, with precarious political and economic results. There is frequent contact and exchange of personnel between all villages of the second cluster, with a certain tendency toward permanent migration into the downriver set.

The last cluster is composed of two groups at the Salesian mission

247

stations of Meruri and Sangradouro, along the Rio das Garcas. They appear to be the most acculturated of all Bororo, and are settled with larger Shavante groups, their traditional enemies. There has been very little recent contact between them and the other Bororo.

With the possible exception of the last cluster, the Bororo seldom marry outside the tribe, nor do many live as individuals or small families among Brazilians except during brief periods of wage work. They now subsist mainly through agriculture, although fishing, hunting, and gathering constitute variably important activities, according to the season and the ecological resources of the regions in which the groups separately dwell. Fish in particular seem to have been an important feature of traditional diet, yet most species throughout the São Lourenço system have markedly declined in recent years, owing probably to intensive Brazilian commercial fishing. The continuing settlement of this rich valley has imposed great ecological, medical, political, and economic pressures on all existing Bororo communities, which yet persist in maintaining their traditional practices as far as possible.

8 | Selves and Alters among the Eastern Bororo[1]

J. Christopher Crocker

Introduction

AT FIRST GLANCE, the Bororo seem so unlike the Gê that one might wonder whether they should be considered in a Gê context at all. Yet there are a number of reasons for doing so. The linguists appear to agree that the Bororo language is related to Gê, but unfortunately they have not worked out the details of this relationship. Greenberg (1960:791–794) classes Bororo as "Macro-Gê," while Sarah Gudchinsky is more certain of a direct tie (personal communication). In terms of the social institutions and behaviors considered in this paper, the contrasts between the Gê and the Bororo initially appear formidable: the latter have matrilineal descent groups, exogamous moieties, one central men's house, a complete lack of age-sets, intervillage harmony, and so forth. But it will be one of my themes in the following pages that these traditional typological categories tend to distort the ethnographic facts and to conceal rather than reveal pan Gê-Bororo structure. As an initial demonstration of this, a personal remark is appropriate. As an ethnographer of the Bororo, thoroughly imbued with that curious acquired ethnocentrism of the ethnographer regarding "his" people, the various Gê groups constantly strike me as dreamlike anamorphoses of some basic principles of order, as if groups of Bororo had wandered off and somehow got things very badly wrong. But not so wrong as to be unrecognizable. Regardless of the true historical character of the relationship between the Gê and the Bororo, this haunting sense of strangely familiar patterns, a structural *déjà vu,* is enough to encourage one to attempt more systematic comparisons.

In this paper I shall focus on the ways in which the structural principles of Bororo society (Crocker 1967, 1969a, 1973a, 1973b) are reflected in the dynamics of the relationship system and domestic group. In so doing I try to present the reader with material comparable to that contained in the other papers in this volume. I shall be particularly concerned with topics traditionally identified as matrilineal descent, patrifiliation, and uxorilocal residence. The Bororo material has forced me to "rethink" these anthropological categories, however, and the ethnographic reasons for this as well as the analytical consequences must be set out in some detail. The major theme is how a series of interlocked indigenous dyadic principles serve to define the logical character of corporate units, domestic households, and agnatic/affinal bonds so as to provide the basis for social transactions. I try to show how these principles, which involve cosmological antitheses, the opposed nature of male and female, the categorical attributes of the moieties, and the symbolic transformations of ritual inversion, generate a uniquely Bororo processual dialectic, but one which is also related to those found among the other societies analyzed in this book.

The particular Gê themes relevant to the Bororo context (and vice versa) thus include (1) the relation between "public" and "private" spheres of existence; (2) the distinction between physical and social self; (3) the emphasis on age or generation as an organizational principle for certain social relationships as against the irrelevance of these factors in other relationships (that is, "Crow skewing features"); (4) the contrast between ritual and functional aspects of social collectivities; (5) the dyadic moral character of man; and (6), the connection between symmetrical relationships founded on shared identity ("common substance") and asymmetrical ones based on complementary oppositions ("mystical affinity") (Crocker 1969a). To order such diverse factors, and to avoid the dry formalism which sometimes seems inherent in a structural approach, I shall use as a constant point of reference the ways in which all these topics bear on the ways the Bororo define the self and the alter, in a variety of social and symbolic contexts. Since, in my view, these definitions provide the terms in which social transactions occur, the dyadic structural principles can thus be made relevant to the concrete details of social relationships, including those which are prone to conflict.

Before a discussion of these matters, a few of the more general attributes of Bororo society need to be examined. Even though these are noted extensively in the considerable literature on the Bororo,[2] they should be reviewed at this time because many involve the most notable "contrasts" between the Gê and the Bororo. The first of these apparently glaring "differences" involves the Bororo formally prescriptive exogamous moieties, between which the eight "matrilineal" clans are evenly divided. This classical feature of dual organization is accompanied by a cosmology predicated on dyadic principles (the *aroe-bope* categories) and by the almost total lack of any pan-social collectivities or institutions *not* associated with the matrilineal clan-moiety scheme. Thus, for example, the Bororo version of an age-set is now and apparently always was extremely weak, compared with that organization among, say, the Shavante. The Bororo completely lack the plaza groups, alternative moiety systems, and other sodalities found among the Northern Gê. In short, the Bororo elaborate a single organizational principle consistently or "harmoniously" to achieve a very considerable social and symbolic complexity, in contrast to the Gê pattern of mutually exclusive and perhaps opposed dyadic systems. It is for this reason that the Bororo are so very appropriate for structural analysis, particularly in terms of transformational codes through which analytical passage from one paradigmatic system to another can be effected; and this is why they have been so valuable an illustration for Lévi-Strauss.

Yet this apparently straightforward case of "an elementary model of direct exchange" has an elaborate, extensive system of ritual inversion which stands the whole society on its head, in an almost literal sense, and makes the Bororo ultimately much more Gê-like than they initially appear. I refer here to nearly the whole of Bororo ceremonial life, but most especially to the ritual representation of the dead, discussed in a later section of this paper. It would be helpful for the reader to bear in mind while perusing the intervening sections that little is as it seems among the Bororo, that for a substantial portion of their adult lives Bororo men act as if they were members of the opposite moiety.

The other major contrast between Gê and Bororo is quite directly related to the preceding point, at least in my view. It involves the very striking ways in which members of the Bororo communities still extant exhibit a strong sense of forming a single unique society, with quite definite social, symbolic, and geographic boundaries. These are manifested in many ways: by a fervent clinging to traditional Bororo practices, with the resulting identity of quite esoteric bits of culture (clan prerogatives, rituals, myths, and so on) throughout nearly all modern Bororo villages; by the near absence of schismatic conflict between or within these same communities; and by a strong awareness of the special values of the Bororo way, with its stress on balance between polar forces.

One sociological consequence of this sense of tribal identity is that there is seldom any ambiguity about whether someone is a Bororo, regardless of social context: a person either is, or is not.

To be sure, this identity can be lost, through adopting Brazilian residence and behavioral patterns. But at least nominal tribal membership, and attendant rights, can be regained by moving back to a Bororo village and assuming the responsibilities of one's natal roles. This equation of tribal membership with village residence is a critical point for understanding the Bororo, and it is a characteristic shared, although perhaps to a lesser extent, by all the Gê.[3] On the other hand, one must be born a Bororo to enjoy fully the privileges of village residence. Those few individuals, Brazilian and Indian, who have been assimilated to various degrees were thoroughly incorporated into the village scheme, but their natal origins were indicated by the ancillary and contingent nature of this inclusion. If females, they lived virilocally; if males, they were totally identified with the wives' clans; if families (anthropologists or missionaries), their houses were peripheral to the formal village plan. This plan, then, is basic to the Bororo system, as many anthropologists and others have noted for some time.[4]

Of all the aspects of Bororo communities, one of the most significant in Gê-Bororo comparisons is the lack of intervillage strife among the Bororo.[5] As I asserted above, this is associated with the "elementary" structure of Bororo society and more particularly with the way in which this structure is expressed through the details of the normative village plan. This model sets out the arrangement of the eight corporate groups in the village circle; stipulates, to a degree, their internal differentiation; and relates the whole to the natural and spiritual universe (the points of the compass, geographical features such as rivers, and the cosmological typography of the underworld).[6] The precision of the plan is far from a formal, empty norm. With the exception of those settlements in close proximity to Brazilian population centers,[7] every Bororo village attempts to recapitulate the model as nearly as local demographic circumstances will allow. It is this insistence on realizing a universally shared detailed plan for the community which, in my view, underlies much of the intervillage solidarity and tribal unity. In principle, and very often practice, a Bororo can enter a totally strange village, determine what clans are represented there, and proceed directly to his own (if present) or to that of his affines. Such experiences become, for the Bororo, a symbolic warrant of the "efficacy" of the model as a means of initiating and maintaining social relationships. The locations of corporate groups in the village express their relationships not only with one another, but also with extra-social forces reflecting the moral character of these relationships and with the natural-supernatural worlds (Crocker 1969a, 1971, and below). In terms of other dimensions, the paramountcy of the community's adherence to the plan is expressed in the corporate nature of all Bororo villages. In the traditional map of Bororoland, there were a limited number of communities, each of which was named and had proprietary rights over a defined tract of land (Albisetti and Venturelli 1962:0.26–0.27, passim). The village might often change its physical location, but it confined itself to the region with which it was associated. Even now, after the intrusion of Brazilians and the disappearance of most of these units, the Bororo regard their part of the world as segregated into distinct yet mutually replicating communal entities.

In the most dramatic instance of this known to me, the village of Pobojari consists of one man. He has cleared a village circle, and his hut is in the appropriate position of his ("matrilineal") clan. As long as he lives, that community has a sociological existence; but even after his death it will endure as a categorical entity, the Bororo village of Pobojari.

Admittedly, the drastic population decline over the last hundred years has made the demographic circumstances determining the actual sociological character of any given village most exigent. Real settlements are pale simulacra of the ideal. But, as at Pobojari, the residence groups construct their dwellings on the uxorilocal space categorically assigned to their female members, and gaping holes are left for the nonrepresented clans and lineages. Efforts are often made to entice representatives of a missing clan to move to the village, although it is true that such moral coercion is usually associated with self-serving political motives. The mingled character of adoption, discussed below, involves precisely this effort to reduplicate the village plan while serving more narrow interests. Because the tenets of Bororo transactions with nonempirical reality involve the participation of the complete village, with its component social units, major ceremonies must aggregate representatives of all the categorically requisite entities. Consequently, such rituals as funerals and initiations involve the participation of dozens of nonresident Bororo, and such mutual cooperation in fulfilling the demands of an abstract model becomes yet another existential confirmation of the medial success of "The Plan." There is no doubt that population loss and other consequences of the Brazilian presence have affected Bororo society thoroughly, and may have altered, as I shall argue below, certain aspects of the community model itself. But the Bororo continue to act on the belief that this plan provides the only way for them to live harmoniously with themselves, each other, and the forces in the natural and cosmological universe.

The Gê societies typically attach great importance to the ideal shape of the village, its nonsocial referents, and internal organization, but with the exception of the Sherente (who are anyway a doubtful case; see Maybury-Lewis in this volume), they do not specify the orientation of the domestic units to one another and to the cardinal points as do the Bororo. The reason for this among the Northern Gê is, of course, their lack of corporate unilinear descent groups. Yet these same societies specify quite exactly the relational positions of the various ritual societies within the central plaza, and the correspondence of this prescription with the siting of the Bororo clans at definite points on the village periphery has considerable significance. For the modern Central Gê, their practice of uxorilocal residence prevents the differentiation and articulation of their patrilineal corporate units through a fixed localization of domestic units. As Lévi-Strauss pointed out some time ago (1958:156–170), a principal feature of the Gê complex appears to be the association of male and female with, respectively, the village center and periphery, with its attendant symbolism. One institutional expression of this is the pan-Gê normative requirement of uxorilocal residence. The Bororo insist on the importance of a normative village model, which gives a geospatial referent for every social unit. The only way to achieve this in Gê terms would be through matriliny, which is the mechanism the Bororo use and which makes it possible to speak of a Bororo-Gê ideological complex.[8] Therefore, the next section involves a consideration of the Bororo version of matriliny in both its symbolic and its sociological guises.

Components of Corporate Identity: The Physical and the Social Self

The natal requirements for full membership in Bororo clan, village, and society are threefold: (1) birth to a Bororo woman; (2) acknowledgement of social paternity by a male member of the moiety opposite to that of the woman's; (3) the ritually correct imposition of a proper name, typically drawn from a stock of such names associated with the mother's corporate group. Much of the substance of this paper deals with the implications of these three conditions. The first of these to be considered is their "matrilineal" character. In such circumstances, anthropologists often try to demonstrate that the native theory of procreation is consistent with the jural aspects of descent. The Bororo material hardly lends itself to this strategy, for these people view the genesis of the physical self in terms of a "cognatic" ideology like that of the Northern Gê. The Bororo state that both parents contribute precisely the same sort of substance (*rakare,* "blood" or "strength") to the formation and development of the fetus, the male through his semen and the female through her menstrual fluids. Together with the Gê, the Bororo also assert that repeated copulation throughout pregnancy is necessary for the fetus's growth, and since different men may have intercourse with an expected mother, a child may have multiple genitors and even paters.[9] The only distinction made between sexual roles in reproduction is on the grounds of quantity rather than quality, in that younger persons are thought to have more "blood" (*rakare*) than older ones, unless they have dissipated it through laxity and self-indulgence. Since Bororo men tend to be substantially older than the women with whom they cohabit, most persons are perceived to have more of their mother's "blood" than their father's.

The Bororo have a very literal interpretation of the implications of different amounts of "blood" in individuals' physical appearances. Thus a man may be said to have his mother's brother's nose and mouth, his father's eyes, his father's brother's length of arm, and so forth. The physical resemblance of siblings and other consanguines is sometimes cited as an external reminder for them to act with solidarity and mutual respect; the fact that most Bororo take some pains to enhance their physical singularity both cosmetically and verbally indicates the ambiguity of this injunction, typical of the social interpretation of "consanguineal facts."

I could find no indication that the usual dominance of the maternal side in the physical transmission between generations had anything at all to do with the Bororo version of "matriliny." This dominance is, after all, circumstantial and presumptive, and cases in which the father is judged *post facto* to have contributed more "blood" to the child, on the grounds of its greater physical resemblance to him than to the mother, are not at all rare. Persons who share the same father but whose mothers are in different clans are said to be as closely related "by blood" as those individuals with common uterine but differing paternal ancestry. The presumed closeness of consanguineal ties is utilized by the Bororo as an idiom to organize and differentiate interpersonal transactions within the clan, within the moiety, and between moieties. Just as with the Gê, the Bororo appear to recognize some dichotomy between such physical, private ties and public, social group bonds. But it is essential to examine in detail the indigenous interpretation and categorization of this dichotomy, for differences between the societies concerning these matters are critical for pan-Gê comparisons.

At first, the Bororo concepts of physical reproduction appear to

contradict their practice of "unilineal descent," and such a paradox is in fact relevant to understanding certain aspects of the
society (Crocker 1969a). However, we must not be misled by the
anthropological assumption of a basic congruency between the
reproductive ideology and jural aspects of descent. One suspects
that such a premise is symptomatic of the literalistic biological
orientation that has so perturbed kinship studies since Morgan.
Somehow, our traditional wisdom has it, social rules must be
grounded in biological facts, even if we have now advanced to
the stage where it is "their" biology rather than ours. As mentioned earlier, Bororo society does rest on a categorical antithesis
between male and female, which has its expression in native con-
ceptualization of the radically differentiated nature of the relation
of a child with his father and that with his mother. But the
epistemological foundation of these relations is not a "physical,"
genealogical referent, but a symbolic, moral one. To anticipate
later arguments, the Bororo clan is indeed perceived as based on
common substances, but ones of logical identity, not physical
stuff. To be sure, its unity can be sometimes expressed in terms of
a unity of "blood" and shared uterine descent, but these are only
one set of idioms, and far from the most important set, that together express the nature of corporate membership. In one sense,
then, traditional anthropological premises are not so sharply con-
tradicted by the Bororo case, for since their mode of recruitment
to corporate groups is not a pure "unilineal descent" rule, their
notions about reproductive physiology are not inconsistent with
their jural norms concerning corporate membership. Or, to put it
another way, the Bororo are not the straightforward case of
matrilineality they first appeared to be.

Bororo cosmology is permeated by the antithesis between two
forms of spirit, the *aroe* and the *bope*. The latter is associated
with all processes of growth and decay, with such phemonena as
rain, the sun and moon, eclipses, and the seasons, as well as
specifically with birth, aging, and death. The *bope* might be seen
as representing some principle of vitality that destroys in order to
create. Not surprisingly, they are identified with human "strength"
or "blood," which is to say, with *rakare*. But every animate thing
has this *bope* component which animates it, and determines all its
existence. At the same time, every thing also has a name: the
Bororo might be considered to be thoroughgoing idealists, or
Platonic realists, in that they hold that nothing really exists
without a *nomens,* a categorical essence. The definitional ground
of universal order is the province of the *aroe,* and it is revealing
that the Bororo often gloss this term as *alma* in Portuguese, or

"soul." In some contexts, they speak of the spirit (*aroe*) that every natural species possesses, as a kind of transcendent idea of that entity (Crocker 1977). A man's own soul is closely identified with his proper name. Every clan has a fund of such names, derived from its *aroe*. The "spirit of categorization" is as intimately connected with social order as the "spirit of vitality" is manifest in nature. But, of course, this spiritual dyad cannot be directly equated with a contrast between society and nature, since man himself is a compound both of *bope* and *aroe*. It is true that males tend to be associated with the *aroe*, and females with the *bope*, but even these are partial and complex identifications, the exact character of which I try to clarify in later passages.

The point here is that just as the parents conjoin their *bope*-derived "blood" to engender physical life, so they must collaborate to endow a name, the social identity of an *aroe*. Not only does the proper bestowal of this name, which relates to the mother's clan *aroe* ("totems"), convey the perquisites of membership in clan, moiety, and village, but it also links the infant to one or more ceremonial roles critical to the enactment of Bororo rituals. Virtually no Bororo public ceremony (as distinct from private shamanistic rites) can occur without the participation of at least several such titled roles, and the funerals which are such a melancholy feature of contemporary Bororo life require the presence of these statuses ("great names") from all eight clans. In short, the Bororo clan is perceived as possessing sacred property, personnel, and other means essential to mediating between society as a totality and the power of spirits, *bope* as well as *aroe*. The point of emphasizing these aspects of nomination now is twofold: first, to point up the "spiritual" aspects of corporate membership, and second, to stress that, considered in this perspective, the Bororo clan bears a striking resemblance to the naming societies among the Northern Gê. These are not based, of course, on either a unilineal or a cognatic mode of recruitment, but they do add new members through much the same pattern of differentiated ritual participation by each parent as the Bororo employ.

The details of the Bororo naming ceremony are relevant both to the symbolic attributes of clanship and to the distinct contribution of each sex to social identity. When the infant is between two and six months old, the parents meet together with the senior members of both clans to initiate the naming ritual. Together they choose a name from the clan stock, which is also appropriate to the mother's lineage in a manner described below, and a name-giver, an *i-edaga*. Some consideration is given to the personal wishes of the parents in each selection, but with the following restrictions. No names may be selected that have been conferred on a Bororo within living memory. Nominally, the office of name-givers should be given to the mother's eldest uterine brother. He may be passed over for a variety of legitimate reasons, though: relative youth, or a reputation for irresponsibility, or simple personal dislike of either parent. Further, in these days of reduced population, a woman may not have a surviving uterine brother coresident in her village. In such circumstances, the normatively preferred name-giver is the consanguineally closest senior male relative of the mother, such as an eldest sister's eldest son, who fulfills the other qualifications. Whoever is chosen, the actual name-giver has a very particular and crucial relationship with the name-receiver as long as they both live. Some of the implications of this relation are contained in the practice of utilizing the same term, *i-edaga,* for the collectivity of the maternal clan totems (*aroe*). Further aspects of the relationship are discussed below.

The naming ceremony also involves the participation of the infant's agnatic relatives, most important of whom are the father (that is, pater) himself, his clan sisters and mother, and especially the father's *i-maruga* (prototypically a FFM or FFZ).[10] The agnatic women assist the father to construct a *kiogwara,* a pendant of macaw tail feathers that is worn hanging behind the neck (cf. Albisetti and Venturelli 1962:390–393 for description and illustrations). They also assist the mother's relatives to collect the materials for a feathered "skull cap," a *boe etao bu* (Albisetti and Venturelli 1962:392–394), made from the breast down of several macaw species. The construction of this cap, which is considered a very difficult art requiring great skill, is undertaken by the mother, assisted by her sisters and mother. Each clan owns a distinct pattern for each of these ornaments, and each parent must employ his or her clan's pattern. The symbolism of the two decorations is too complex to examine here; suffice it to say that the feather pendant represents the power of the *aroe* to transform states of categorical being, while the skullcap is associated with the *aroe* as principles of order. As later sections will demonstrate, this is indicative of the Bororo interpretation of paternity and maternity. The preparation and bestowal of the *kiogwara* is a proclamation of a man's willingness to assume the rights and obligations of paterhood, and as the Bororo say, no child can be named without a *kiogwara.*

In some recent cases, the putative genitor has refused to fulfill this role on the grounds that the child is not principally his, that he is only one among several genitors. In these cases, an agnatic relative of the mother, usually her own father, mother's husband, or father's brother, who is also an elder sister's husband, accepts the paternal role. But informants agreed that it was always preferable if the principal genitor was also the pater. The reasoning behind this has as much to do with the character of Bororo marriage (Crocker 1969b) as it does with any "consanguineal" ideology. In brief, the indigenous view is that fathering a child upon a woman, as distinct from merely having intercourse with her, creates strong obligations toward the child, its clansmen, and, very much less, the mother. The moieties are often spoken of as fathering children for each other, and a man's failure to comply with the continuing demands of this honorable duty marks him as an asocial and feckless creature who would deny one of the fundamental conditions of social life. Furthermore, the Bororo also suppose that the genitor is more apt to fulfill all the duties of the pater, "because he gave the child *rakare* (blood)."

For both the Northern Gê and the Bororo, then, the fundamental social self, as conveyed through the personal name and its associated rights of corporate membership, derives from the ritual activity of the mother's senior male relatives and the father's senior female relatives. These names are in both cases associated with name-sets intimately connected with the manifestations of spirit and with specific ceremonial roles. These societies consequently seem to manifest a dialectical origin of personal identity, in which opposition between male and female, physical self and social self, senior and junior, order and process, mutually interact to generate a social being. But the differences between the practices of the Northern Gê and the Bororo are equally important. Among the latter, it is a senior maternal male relative who bestows names on girls as well as boys; there is none of the "cross-sex sibling" transfer of one's own personal names, as among the Krĩkatí. A sexual distinction does pervade the Bororo naming ceremony, in that male infants must have a hole pierced in the lower lip just before the bestowal of the name. This is done by the *i-edaga,* the name-giver, who employs a *baragara* (the sharpened femur of a mammal), made by the pater according to his clan design. Adult males employ this hole for labrets made of pearl shell and macaw feathers following designs owned by the wearers' clans or by the clans of dead persons whom they ceremonially represent. There is no comparable physical marking of women to witness social identity. The operation symbolizes not only tribal membership, but also the very great differences in the implications of corporate membership for men and for women. Male social identity must be inscribed on the body, so that it can be at once obvious and yet mutable (for labrets other than the wearers' own clan's can be used), while no such care need be taken to mark women's social identity, which is "internal" in very sense of the term.

Finally, in the Bororo case the corporate units associated with personal names are localized in the village circle and isomorphic with domestic units, quite unlike the sharp bifurcation among the Northern Gê between public, ceremonial naming societies and the personal sphere of kindreds and households. It would appear, then, that it is the attributes of the Bororo clan which most sharply differentiate that society from the Gê. The next two sections consider those attributes in detail, surveying first the clan's formal characteristics and internal differentiation and next the dynamics of relations between clan members.

The Differentiation of Categorical Essence: Lineages and Corporate Property

The Bororo clan is not a wealth-holding and wealth-endowing unit in a strict utilitarian sense. But membership in it does provide an individual male Bororo with rights over the critical scarce resources of Bororo life: ceremonial ornaments, ritual privileges, esoteric knowledge, and, ultimately, titled status. These goods provide at once the material substances by which enduring social relationships are expressed through reciprocal transactions, and the very terms in which social personality is manifested and the uniqueness of the individual *persona* revealed. Each clan has rights over a very extensive set of particular decorations for bows, arrows, headdresses, woven items, arm- and leg-bands, belts, earrings, labrets, pots, somatic paintings, and many other items, including the "skullcap," *kiogwara* and *baragara* of the naming ceremony. All this amounts to a staggering variety of socially differentiated material culture; for example, the Bororo distinguish over sixty kinds of decorated ceremonial bows, more or less evenly divided among the eight clans. The clan also possesses control over various songs, dance steps, ritual ensembles, and even myths, in addition to the stock of names mentioned above. All of the clan property, immaterial and real, derives in Bororo theory from the categories of spirit associated with the group, its corporate *aroe,* or totems (Crocker 1972a). In principle, the categorical essence of all entities in the natural and cosmological world, including members of non-Bororo societies, can be subsumed under one of the eight clans as an *aroe*. In practice, most informants list only about forty to eighty principal *aroe* for each clan. The overt function of the clan property, especially the songs, somatic paintings, and ornaments, is to provide the material means of representing these spirits. The most valued wealth of the clan is thus five to ten *aroe etawuje* (literally, "spirit representation"), particular ceremonies in which the spirit entities which express the essence of clan identity can be personified by men. All details of corporate attributes are treated as secret, although they must be publicly exhibited.

The members of the clan seldom represent their own totemic *aroe*, but instead bestow the paintings, ornaments, and other items on members of the opposite moiety. This gift of representing an *aroe* is considered exceedingly valuable, so much so that, say the Bororo, a clan can sexually utilize "without shame" women of those clans which have represented its *aroe* spirits. These ritual transactions are usually reciprocal, so that if the Kie enable the Paiwoe to represent a Kie totem, the Kie are in turn allowed to personify a Paiwoe *aroe*. Consequently, the total set of spirit representations provides the symbolic matrix for all cross-moiety transactions, above all, the prestation of women. The identity of both owners and performers is traditionally specified in terms of the "great names," or ceremonial titles, referred to earlier. These are associated with the name-sets in a manner shortly to be described.

In strict jural principle, no name-set other than the one with traditional rights over the representation may sponsor it, and it must be enacted by members of the name-set, which are the historically stipulated performers of that representation. This principle is often waived, but in accordance with strict rules determining the legal rights of name-sets with regard to "borrowing" one another's property (see below). Informants often portray the village as a web of lines connecting those name-sets which represent one another's totemic spirits, and term such lines *utawara,* or "roads," to indicate the supposed extent of their dealings with one another. At one level of reference, then, the ceremonial representations provide the terms in which the clan is differentiated into component units. But in most contexts, these specific transactions are summarized under the single heading of the clan itself. Generally, the clan is defined as a corporate entity through its exchange of obligations and rights with regard to other such entities, and the representations are but one element in these exchanges. The moieties themselves, the Tugarege and the Exerae, emerge as collectivities through their mutual duties to provide each other with prestations of ceremonial food, ritual services at initiation and burial, wives, fathers, and the material means for representing spirits.

Within the framework of these categorical duties and privileges, members of the opposite moiety perform many *ad hoc* services for ego and his clansmen, services which are neither part of the daily routine nor elements within the prescribed sets of ceremonial prestations. The most important of these involve securing revenge when ego is wronged by nonsocial forces. If a person is harmed by some natural agency, such as a snake, fresh-water ray, jaguar, or venomous bee, any member of the opposite moiety should kill that agent and present its corpse to the victim. The avenger receives as compensation some of the clan property, such as a facial painting or necklace. In themselves, such transactions are rather trivial, but they do express one basic dimension of intermoiety relations, that of mediating between individual persons and both types of spirit forces (*aroe* and *bope,* the last being associated with hostile aspects of nature). This function achieves its social climax in the representation of deceased Bororo by persons in the other moiety.

This institution (that of the *aroe maiwu,* "new soul") is described in detail later, but briefly, the Bororo believe that all deaths are caused by a malicious act of nature (that is, the *bope*) comparable to the harms inflicted by animals. The deceased must be revenged by a member of the opposite moiety, who kills a jaguar, harpy eagle, or other large carnivore. The avenger also represents the deceased's soul in various ritual contexts. For these services he is allowed to utilize an extensive array of property belonging to the dead man's clan. Virtually the only element of clan property which is not thus involved in cross-moiety prestations is the proper names. These are the matrix of personal identity as well as the means whereby the clan's social components are segregated and related.

The internal organization of the Bororo clan is exceedingly complex, both in theory and in practice, but the details of its composition provide clues both to the nature of Bororo "matriliny" and to how the system works "on the ground." The "name-sets" into which the clan is divided are in theory fixed in number. They are combined into two units which, following prior usage (Albisetti and Venturelli 1962:434–445 and passim), I have termed subclans. Although a third, or "middle," subclan exists in Bororo tradition, it is very seldom mentioned these days even at the level of the model. Informants maintained that all the totemic spirits associated with the clan themselves had two subforms, such as sex and/or color ("red" and "black"), which are connected with the subclans, and that each name-set had further particularized versions of these subforms. Since all the ceremonial prerogatives, property, songs, and other elements of corporate wealth derive in some way from the clan's totems, there is, in principle, a formal scheme whereby specific items can be associated with given name-sets. Thus the Kie clan has the tapir (*ki*) as one of its totemic spirits; the Kiedu name-set "owns" a particular style of headdress, which is one of several connected with the male, red Tapir Spirit (Ki Aroe), since it is in the red Tapir subclan.

In indigenous theory, then, every element of clan property is properly owned by one name-set or another. Levels of specificity of these elements correspond to differentiated units within the clan, down to the final level of individual proper names. But in point of fact, only five or six of the clan's totems can thus be divided symmetrically even at the level of the subclans. The logical principles connecting specific names, or headdresses, or whatever else might be associated with those totems to the specific name-sets are obscure even for the Bororo. All that informants can say is that such-and-such an armband is owned by that name-set, and even then disagreements as to which name-set in the subclan actually has rights over the ornament are not uncommon.

There is agreement that the name-sets have very unequal amounts of ritual items and ceremonies associated with them. From this inequality derives the traditional hierarchical ranking of the name-sets in a single clan. Usually, the first-ranked name-set has jural title to the clan's most esteemed ceremony, the ritual representation of one of its major totemic entities. However, the second-ranked name-set is always in the other subclan, and has complementary rights over the representation of the other sub-form of that totem. Thus, for example, among the Bokodori Exerac clan (the "Giant Armadillos"), the lineage of Kaigu in the Xobugiwuge subclan has rights over the "small red armadillo spirit," while the Inokuri lineage in the Xebegiwuge subclan has rights over the "large black armadillo spirit." As the Bororo say, there is very little to choose from in terms of the relative prestige of these two great figures. But Kaigu generally disposes of more additional ritual roles (representing still other totemic spirits of the clan) than does Inokuri; so, "Kaigu goes first among the Bokodori Exerae."

Thus in Bororo theory, the traditional name-set hierarchy establishes the formal order of relative prestige, ceremonial precedence, and, in a loose sense, legitimate power among the units of a clan. Most important, in the view of informants, it sets forth what might be termed the fraternal order of substitution. When, as occurs inevitably in modern villages and apparently often occurred in the past, a given name-set is not represented in a community, members of the immediately subordinate name-set in the same subclan may utilize its prerogatives *pro tem,* until such time as its members are present. Consequently, it is possible for a very low-ranked name-set to occupy the most important ceremonial roles associated with its subclan. It should be remembered that these include both the honors involved in sponsoring the representation of clan *aroe* and those of performing as the totemic spirits of other clans, since the traditionally specified performing unit is nearly always the first-, second-, or third-ranked name-set in the clan receiving the prestation. There are very seldom more than two or three consanguineal units of the same clan represented in any modern Bororo village, and, as will be seen, these units are effectively identified as independent name-sets. Each of them, if not of a legitimate high rank, is or can be temporarily associated with a name-set of great prestige and traditional wealth-rights.

The distinction between such legitimate substitutions and "true" birth- and name-right membership in a prestigious name-set is sharply emphasized by all Bororo. Clansmen, of course, know the genealogies and personal histories of each other, and have a vested interest in keeping the record straight. However, there is much confusion about which proper names are actually associated with a given name-set, which is understandable given the enormous plethora of totems and derived proper names. Additionally, these days there are barely enough residents in any community to fulfill all the major ceremonial roles associated with the highest-ranked name-sets. The situation is, therefore, one in which truly there are all chiefs and no Indians. In other times, with villages of 500 and more, matters would have been quite different, and we might suspect that competition among the name-sets for a fixed amount of prestige was a chief feature of Bororo political life. The modern confusion over the details of name-set composition and property might be attributed to population loss and other aspects of Brazilian influence, for while the Bororo still jealously guard the allocation of ceremonial rights and property, they also envy the man who has a shotgun.

In brief, the traditional Bororo plan for the internal division of the clan is entirely comparable to the "genealogical charters" found outside of South America, in that there are a series of statuses allegedly fixed with relation to one another, but actually capable of great permutations. The formal scheme itself facilitates cross-village mobility and allows a smooth process of "lineage fissioning," otherwise frequently a great problem for "matrilineal" societies. If members of a name-set are dissatisfied with their position in the clan in a given village, all they have to do is move to a new community where their subclan is not represented. The scheme also permits the component units of any clan to differentiate maximally. If any clan has more than one such unit present, the chances are that these units are said to belong to different subclans. Even then, the ideology of "higher" and "lower" ranks serves to order their competition while giving each a maximum of traditional prestige and resources. This is a crucial point, for as the next section shows, relationships among individual clan members, including those of a single name-set, are also ordered on a "more-less" basis in which relative age and personal ability are as important as "blood" in determining the structure of interaction.

A few negative points need to be made concerning the formal properties of clan differentiation and corporate attributes. I have not been able to discover any common properties among the totemic *aroe* of any clan, let alone any overriding conceptual system (Lévi-Strauss 1963a:16–17, 83–91). It is true, though, that generally the Exerae clans are associated with mammals and fish, while the Tugarege groups are connected with birds, reptiles, and plants. In myths and other representations, the clans and name-sets are portrayed as collectivities of discrete entities, as separate lists of things rather than as single fixed identities. For example, the vital rights to represent an *aroe* spirit were originally acquired because an ancestor of the clan was the first Bororo to see *and name* that entity. Subsequently, many rights acquired in this way were transferred in totality to a clan in the opposite moiety; always the prestation went from a father to a son, a point of great significance for the remainder of this paper.[11] In the topography of the underworld, the land of the *aroe,* all the totemic entities and dead members of a single clan live together in the geographical wedge allocated to that clan in the village, except that there the wedge extends to the limits of the cosmos. This conception of a spatially bounded collection of discrete species, men as well as animals, seems to me the most accurate representation of the Bororo corporate group.

Now, as we have seen, the Bororo sometimes speak of the clan as if it were a single logical essence, differentiated through its various levels according to part-whole or other derivative relationships. In a few contexts, this essence is expressed in terms of common descent from a single ancestress. But I cannot stress too forcefully that this idiom of unified physical, uterine substance is only one of many such metaphors which describe corporate membership. Much the most important of these is the one couched in terms of the totemic *aroe,* and even here, while there are "greater" and "lesser" clan totems, no single one is regarded as basic or foremost. The clan does not express a single *persona,* one specifiable common element of any kind. It is defined as a unit primarily through its jural unity in transactions with like units, through its corporate responsibility for the actions of its members, and through its character as one of the eight categories into which the universe is subsumed. These attributes are expressed in daily life, in the transactions between clan members and in the residential system. These topics are the subject of the next section. One final comment, however, concerning the formal character of clanship needs to be made. The matters discussed in this section are all the concern of males; they have very little to do with women, who nearly always are ignorant of the details of name-sets and corporate property. But the domestic group is eminently their domain.

The Domestic Group: Sex, Seniority, and Affinity

A Bororo refers to his own corporate group both as a conceptual entity and as a collection of persons as *i-wobe* (plural, *pa-obe,* "our clan") , and generally contrasts this unit with those designated *i-medage,* the term he applies to all other Bororo, including affinal and cognatic relatives in other clans. But these designations are used with considerable flexibility, a practice which is typical of relational categories among the Bororo. In rhetorical public address, a man might term members of clans in his own moiety *i-wobe* to emphasize the closeness of his relations with them. In appropriate contexts, however, a distinction can be made between own clan and same moiety clans by the addition of the suffixes *remawu* ("true," "real") and *reno* ("similar") . But these terms are never used to differentiate between clan members. Ego refers to his name-set as *i-e,* which means literally "my name," and proper names (or nicknames) are commonly used in conjunction with relationship terms or alone to distinguish persons within the clan. Further, although the Bororo suppose that the clan itself is localized within the village circle, at no point in their assumptions or practices is the clan isomorphic with residential groups "on the ground."

Such a unit for an individual ego is always termed *i-bai,* literally "my house," which as a referential category includes the coresident male affines as well as any nonclansmen who may happen to have public allegiance to the unit as expressed through at least part-time residence in it. Generally, the assumption is that members of this group are consanguineally or affinally related. Further, informants said, each name-set should ideally have its own dwelling place, or at least its members' separate huts should be closely grouped. In other words, the Bororo assume that the *i-e* ("my name-set") should be physically congruent with the *i-bai* ("my house"), even though the latter category contains persons not of ego's clan. This implies, then, that the name-set is a shallow matrilineage whose identity as a domestic group is expressed through a distinct residence. None of these assumptions nor deductions are entirely true for the modern Bororo. The domestic unit appears eminently unstable and subject to rapid and dramatic fluctuations in composition and internal dynamics; it is the scene of apparently endemic conflict and strife. As I remarked in another context (Crocker 1969b), it might be said that the Bororo have sacrificed domestic peace for public tranquillity. This section will examine the factors behind this surface turbulence and the structural constants beneath it in terms of various Gê parameters, certain contradictions in the very premises of the Bororo system, and the disruptions deriving from population loss and participation in a money economy.

The most critical factor in residence is the clan/name-set/ matrilineage affiliation of the wife/mother. In principle, all the uterine female descendants of a woman should dwell together under one roof during her life. This means that by the third generation the domestic group will include collateral lines of "sisters' daughters," an arrangement which is practically never found in contemporary practice. But the principle is the ground for the supposition that each name-set/matrilineage is spatially distinct, if not actually coresident. Apparently, in traditional practice the growth of a lineage could be accommodated by having the more distant collateral members of the name-set establish their huts directly behind that of the senior woman. Thus the village was formed of concentric rings in which each slice of the corporate pie consisted of a single name-holding group. But for the modern Bororo, this "spatialization" of group membership conflicts with the fact that Bororo genealogies are very shallow even in the matrilineal line, never extending more than two generations beyond the oldest living "mother." Further, owing to population loss, it is rare to find uterine sibling groups of more than three or four adults.

In contemporary Bororo villages a fact of critical organizational importance is that clanswomen with no remembered uterine consanguineal ties are *de facto* considered to be of different name-sets. Even their membership in the same or different subclan is based on the formal system of name-set hierarchies rather than on presumptions of consanguinity. Perhaps in the past, with a much larger population and a fixed number of name-sets, the direct equation between narrow uterine lines and name-set/matrilineage was not so marked, or genealogies may have been better remembered. This would account for the presence of concentric residential rings in historical villages. But the crucial point is that for the modern Bororo the assumption that separate residences imply distinctive consanguineal lines and separate name-sets becomes "true by definition" and tautological. The distinctiveness and small size of the domestic unit facilitates the degree to which it can distinguish itself within the clan and village through association with the formal name-set system of ceremonial prerogatives discussed in the previous section.

The actual composition of any domestic group is considerably affected by the relative vigor and optimism of the attached males. By this I mean that a Bororo husband is expected to provide a house for his wife, her mother, and unmarried sisters if they lack their own residence. Some younger women even insist that they are entitled to their own house directly behind that of their mother and/or sister. However, Bororo men regard the construction of a house as a major undertaking. Actually, the labor and resources involved are not that great, but the act proclaims a commitment to the community and to the spouse. Given the fragility of most Bororo unions, a sensible man is quite prepared to live with any of his wife's clanwomen until his marriage is well established. Further, even long-standing domestic units of several generations are likely to leave one community and visit others for extended periods. Such groups nearly always stay with a uterine relative of the wife/mother if one is resident in the visited community. If none is available, any of the wife's clan mothers or sisters is normatively bound to accept the "visitors." In the village where I did most of my fieldwork, about one-third of all domestic units had such "temporary" families cohabiting with them at any given time. After two or three years and the birth of a child, in the case of new families, and after a year or so in the case of visiting groups, distinctive residences are finally built in a vacant section of the wife's name-set's portion of the village circle.

It is by no means true that all residential arrangements are based on the wife's group membership. Upon marriage a Bororo man tries, like his fellows in many other societies, to reside where he has rights to do so and where he perceives a clear advantage. Generally, this would be with the wife's own parents, but in their absence the husband's parents might support a couple for some time, especially if the wife has no uterine consanguines resident in the village. Indeed, the couple may even move in with a close female matrilineal relative of the husband's. On some occasions, when the mother was dead or absent, I have seen a visiting son and his family reside for a few months with his father and his current wife, or a visiting father stay with his son's family. These practices are significant in that they demonstrate how in domestic arrangements as in many other areas of Bororo life immediate short-term advantages are linked directly to consanguineal kinsmen, and above all to parents. But long-range strategy always dictates acceptance of the uxorilocal, "matrilineal" corporate group residential pattern. Aside from the normative stress on preservation of the village model that depends on this pattern, there are valid economic and political reasons for this preference.

Generally, the Bororo household group is much more integrated in terms of production and consumption than its counterparts among the Northern Gê. Individual couples, together with immature children and other dependents, do maintain separate garden plots, and in other respects as well the nuclear family constitutes the most constant irreducible economic unit in daily affairs. There is, however, a marked tendency for the couples of a single household to have adjacent garden plots, and nearly always the males of the group assist one another in clearing new land. Frequently, different proportions of crops, and even different crops entirely, may be planted on the plots belonging to the household's couples, to take advantage of topographical irregularities and perceived differences in the plots' fertility and suitability for particular cultigens. As this implies, garden produce is usually shared among the members of one household. When food is available, a single common meal is prepared twice a day by one or more of the women; the harvested food, especially corn, is combined with little concern for each couple's relative contribution. Further, the males resident in the household usually divide their days' labors for maximum efficiency, with one going hunting, another working in the gardens, and a third doing wage labor for Brazilians. Somewhat the same pattern prevails among the women, although they tend to work collectively at a single task if its technological character permits such collaboration. The Bororo clearly perceive and express the material advantages of such systematic division of labor within the domestic group. The joint pattern tends to prevail even after a daughter or sister's daughter establishes a home behind that of her senior kinswoman, even though such a move does tend to separate the families' joint enterprises to a considerable degree.

There are, of course, numerous exceptions to this economic integration of the domestic unit. It tends to prevail where there are direct, long-established ties of uterine descent and affinity among the household members, and to diminish to the point of vanishing altogether where the residents are related by classificatory membership in the same clan, or through ties of agnation/affinity, as when a son resides with his father. But the general Bororo rule that whoever works on the garden has a right to a share of its produce tends to prevail in all circumstances. Consequently, a newly married couple usually elects to assist another resident couple with a single garden, rather than establish one of their own. This often leads to difficulties, especially if the women are related as clan sisters. The least integration appears to occur in those households where one couple has a number of dependents, such as old collateral or lineal relatives who are virtually nonproductive, and another couple has moved in on a "temporary" or dog-in-the-manger basis. Yet even here the crucial point is that the Bororo clearly perceive it to be advantageous for a couple or even single persons to be members of a large, coproducing, and coconsuming unit.

So much is this the case that all unmarried individuals must be associated with such units in order to survive. The ties which integrate these "loose ends" into the domestic group are always matrilineality and agnation, in the particular sense in which these are manifested among the Bororo. The aged, the infirm, and young children are the obligation of their most direct uterine consanguineal kinswomen. If these "blood" ties are absent in the village, classificatory clanswomen must assume the responsibility, and the willingness with which women and their husbands carry out this duty testifies to the great power of clanship, however much it may be rent by the schisms described below. It is, however, also common for an old man to be supported by one of his children, whether this is a son or a daughter, but even in such cases his formal residence alternates between the men's house and his clanswomen's dwelling. Young bachelors must be given meals by their clanswomen, and if they lack mothers or uterine sisters, more distant female relatives assume the task. Within the traditional Bororo village, roughly half the households at any given time shelter such "classificatory" clan relatives. This gives the residence group a rather more corporate appearance than is actually the case, since these persons, whether visitors or incapacitated individuals, are constantly moving in and out of the household. I should stress again, though, that such mobility is phrased in terms of name-set, subclan, and clan membership, rather than in the idiom of "blood" relationship, even when such ties are present.

Nor is it always the case that consanguinity is the only precondition for stable, continuing integration of disparate family groups under a single residential roof. Uterine sisters often find it very difficult to reside together in the absence of the mother or a woman who has assumed that role for some time. In much the same way, uterine and clan brothers are seldom found living in the same household. Even though there is no specific injunction prohibiting male siblings from such an arrangement, as among the Northern Kayapó, it happens that couples or family groups tied only through uterine siblings simply do not persist as residential units through time. Yet when classificatory clanwomen have come to regard each other as virtual mother and daughter, and the men are related as *i-edaga* (name-giver/mother's brother) and *i-wagedu* (name-receiver/sister's son) within their own matrilineal group, the domestic unit may be exceedingly stable. In short, the most successful, enduring Bororo residential units are those based on cross-generation ties, whether these be of matrilineal, affinal, or agnatic character. It is quite rare to find more than one woman or man of the same clan generation in such a unit, other than as immature children. This means, of course, that the "extra" sisters (plus their husbands and children) occupy their own residences or, as is most frequently the case, have moved out of the village for an indefinite period.

I think this situation suggests two things. First, there seems to be some kind of endemic conflict between same-sex siblings which militates against their common residence, but which, at the same time, through their *de facto* exclusion and the emphasis on cross-generational bonds, allows stable domestic groups to emerge through the flux of constant change in the composition of the in-marrying males. Second, Bororo "matrilineages" do not fission; they simply move, to places where at least the wife's matrilineal/name-set kin are not present.[12] Again, the existence of multiple villages all attempting to replicate the same formal organizational models in terms of name-sets rather than matrilineal units is critical to the whole process, since it facilitates transcommunity mobility as a structural process. Any full account of the development of the Bororo domestic group, which the description above does not in any way pretend to be, would have to include such movements from one community to another, as well as the constant but changing presence of husbands/fathers and "visitors," agnatic and matrilineal, as basic features of the entire process.

Table 1 presents some figures on the actual composition of domestic groups. The senior woman in each household is not necessarily the oldest, but rather the one recognized as "owning the house." With two exceptions, each senior woman is resident on her proper name-set/subclan site. Two women occupy temporary shelters on their husband's clan land; in each case the husband is coresident with close matrilineal relatives, in one with his true

TABLE 1. Relation of adult coresidents to senior women householders

Relationship	Women	Men	Relationship
Uterine yZ	1	15	Husband
Classificatory yZ	2	1	Uterine yZH
Uterine D	10	8	Uterine DH
Classificatory D	2	1	Classificatory DH
Uterine DD	1	1	Uterine DDS
Classificatory MZ	1	1	Classificatory S (unmarried)
Uterine MZ	1	1	Classificatory MZH

mother and father. Table 1 reveals a marked congruence between behavior and norm in terms of a high proportion of uxorilocal, joint mother-daughter residences. What it does not reveal are the various maneuvers utilized to bring about such a pattern. For example, in one case a young woman named Kaigu is living in a household whose female head is of a different clan in the same moiety. She, however, calls this older woman *i-muga,* or "mother," on the grounds that her own mother died many years ago, and subsequently this woman "became a real mother to me." Her father is living in the adjacent residence, now married to a classificatory clan sister of his daughter's adoptive mother. Kaigu, who has two children but is currently unmarried, spends a great deal of time in her father's house and usually takes one daily meal there. She divides her productive activity between the two households, with the bulk of her effort going toward her adoptive mother's household. She also does not get along with her paternal half-sister, especially after the latter married a man who, it is alleged, has had an affair with Kaigu. Moreover, Kaigu is truly close to her adoptive mother and that woman's husband. Everyone agrees that when Kaigu marries again, her husband should build her a house on her own proper name-set site, which coincidentally will be adjacent to her father's household. While this example, which is diagrammed in Figure 1, shows the enduring character of consanguineal ties, it also demonstrates how the roles based on them can be filled by nonrelated persons. Perhaps owing to population loss, such "substitutions" are common among the modern Bororo.

The Bororo household, then, tends to be based on cross-generational consanguineal ties, with additional members recruited on the grounds of classificatory clan membership or adoptive relationships.[13] As we saw earlier, the household (or household group) is equated with the name-set, and consequently there are solid demographic reasons for the Bororo to assume that members of the

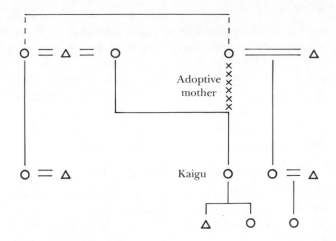

FIGURE 1. Kaigu's household affiliations

same name-set share a common ancestress. The normative rules for succession to ceremonial titles possessed by the name-set are consistent with this assumption, for in principle only true uterine consanguines can succeed to a title upon the death of an *i-edaga,* a senior matrilineal male name-giver. But even this putative genealogical relationship applies only within the name-set/matrilineage. Although, on occasion, the clan is spoken of as if it shared a single ancestress, never is the differentiation among the name-sets given a genealogical cast. In brief, although the Bororo do utilize an idiom of "blood" *(rakare)* to express certain aspects of personal relationship, and the attributes of intralineage transactions, they fail utterly to distinguish distinct social groups on the basis of contrasting *descent*. Further, the principle of uterine succession is as much honored in the breach as in the observance. An officeholder feels some moral obligation to impart the esoteric lore essential to his ritual duties to a direct uterine sister's son or sister's daughter's son, but such a relative may be lacking, incapable, or morally unworthy. The essential criterion of ritual-political legitimacy among the Bororo is accuracy and extent of esoteric knowledge, not the purity of genealogical position. To be sure, the sororal heirs of a notable leader have a certain presumptive prestige, but they are required to validate this in the public arena, in terms of their ability in ceremonial duties and general moral character. Basically, each political-ritual leader among the Bororo chooses his own successor through his training of an heir over time, and is inhibited in his selection only by a vague sense of obligation to his uterine line, offset by a much stronger commitment to preserving the details of Bororo tradition by the most able means possible. Finally, the Bororo have completely failed to elaborate any ideology of maternal descent. They do not dwell on a rhetorical image of breast milk or uterine continuity as do such matrilineal societies as the Ndembu (see Turner 1967:52–58). The principles of corporate continuity through time are expressed through figurative language relating to the proper names and name-sets discussed in the last section. The household is a matrilineage only presumptively and *de facto,* not *de jure.*

Siblings and Conjugal Units

As a result of these factors, personal relationships within the lineage and the clan are a dynamic amalgam of "biological" events and corporate attributes. I understand this to be a fundamental characteristic of all kinship systems, and believe that analysis must reveal how the unique cultural meanings attached to each element interact to produce a social structure.[14] I do not propose to present a full analysis of Bororo relationship terminology in this context, but will instead discuss aspects of dyadic relations within the clan that reveal the principles whereby clan members order their transactions with one another, including reasons why these principles engender conflict and strife.

The principles are those of relative age ("birth order"), sex, chronological generation, and "consanguinity," in rough order of importance. Jural authority (and its cognate, responsibility) within the sibling group, name-set, and clan derives from age seniority, in a strict parallel to the formal hierarchy of name-sets. It is this feature of Bororo corporations which most sharply distinguishes them from those of the Gê. In principle, the eldest brother has formal responsibility for the conduct of his younger siblings. Thus the father and mother's brother permit the obligations normally assigned to them in unilineal systems to devolve respectively on the eldest son/sister's son. An elder sister has somewhat the same formal relation to her younger sisters, but in her case authority is diluted by the presence of the elder brother and by the fact that the mother, while still alive, exercises a good deal of control over her daughters. But even here, in principle, the elder brother has the final word over whom his sisters should marry, and the responsibility of overseeing such unions. Consequently, distinctions of birth order within generations are terminologically stressed with separate terms for elder brother (*i-mana,* "male speaking"; *i-wuri,* "female speaking"), elder sister (*i-tuie,* "both sexes"), but a single category for "younger sibling" (*i-wie*).

It would be preferable, however, in terms of adequately expressing Bororo views on the point, to substitute a "more-less" idiom for the "elder-younger" distinction, since age differences are taken only as general indexes to more substantial and critical differences. That is, the older brother is assumed to have more experience, more knowledge (especially of traditional lore), more material possessions, and greater status in the clan and the village than any of his younger siblings. For these reasons, he is qualified to assume responsibility and authority for their conduct. In precisely the same way, the first-ranked name-set is sometimes termed the "eldest brother" of the other name-sets, on the grounds that it is demonstrably "richer" and "wiser."[15] The Bororo readily admit that the correlation between greater age and more wisdom/ wealth/ability does not invariably occur, and there are many cases in which a younger brother has gained ascendancy over an older one. Certain persons may even recognize this terminologically, but more often proper names or nicknames are used to resolve the contradiction between principle and actuality.

The distinction of relative age establishes an age heirarchy which extends throughout the clan. A man has authority over his younger uterine siblings first of all, but he must answer for their and his own conduct to an "elder brother" in his name-set, while the senior male of a generation has responsibility for all his real and classificatory siblings within the subclan or clan. His status as clan chief is expressed through his occupancy of the prestigious ceremonial roles connected with the first- and second-ranked name-set. In practice, the system emphasizes relative age over actual birth order and genealogical generation, for there are no external generational markers, such as would be provided by an age-set system. I believe, in fact, that the Bororo stress on age differentials within the corporate unit is comparable to the age-sets among the Central Gê, especially since the differentials tend to apply within the moiety and to the collectivity of young bachelors (*i-pare;* cf. Crocker 1969b), which most resembles the junior age-set among the Shavante.

But in the Bororo case, the system is infinitely flexible, admitting not only of resolutions between actual ability and absolute age, but also of changes through time and external events. One of the features of the Bororo domestic group cycle is the shifting of relationship terminology as the group and its component individuals develop, and especially as children are born within it. Thus I would be likely to term as *i-edaga* (mother's brother) the jural superior of my own elder brother (my *i-mana*'s *i-mana*) while I was a child and as a young bachelor. But as I grow older, have children, and begin to exercise political power, the *i-edaga* may well become an *i-mana:* that is, his authority comes to be expressed directly to me, rather than through my brother. As time goes on, he may slip back into the *i-edaga* category as an old man.

Social contexts, shifts in village politics and events, such as the arrival of fellow clansmen in the village, all affect the age hierarchy and the terminological usages which express it. In a general sense, the flexibility of the system decreases as consanguinity increases. The *i-mana* who is one's uterine elder brother is very much there to stay, and the only way to escape his authority is to exceed him in ritual ability, deny the relationship altogether (usually with total lack of success), transmute it through ceremony, or move from the village.

As this indicates, actual relationships between male clan members of roughly the same generation are fraught with tension and conflict. Every case of homicide I recorded among the Bororo (a total of five) involved clan brothers, of every degree of relationship, including uterine; fights, quarrels, and other disruptions of the moral order nearly always involve fraternal relationships. I have dealt with the structural reasons for this elsewhere (Crocker 1969a), but, basically, fraternal conflict reflects the fact that brothers are competitors for the same scarce goods: women, the clan's intangible valuables, political status, and ritual honor. It might seem that especially these days there would be enough ceremonial prestige to go around, but the Bororo clan system is based on the premise that there can be only one head for every social unit. Rivalry is especially intense between the leaders of the subclans, who must demonstrate to the community at large their effective control of the younger individuals in their groups along with their ritual abilities. These are indeed correlated, in that the only real power a brother has is moral coercion through the legitimacy of traditional knowledge and his own reputation for responsible conduct.

As a consequence, and in startling contrast to practice among the Central Gê and Northern Kayapó, the political process among the Bororo is conducted publicly in highly stylized and even mannered ways. The tensions emerge at the level of gossip within the domestic group, and it is symptomatic of the Bororo that, for men, the unit of trusted supporters is an affinal one. Appropriately, the most valued elements of prestige are prestations from the other moiety: invitations to represent a clan spirit, to fulfill critical roles in initiation and funeral ceremonies, and, above all, to represent a dead Bororo. It would not be correct to say that the community as a totality determines relative rank within the clan, for no one honors a man who does not have the respect and obedience of his siblings, real and classificatory. But the other moiety does cast the deciding vote.[16]

In brief, instead of placing conflict between generations, the Bororo have focused it within generations. The elaborate systems of corporate property, name-set rankings, birth orders, and so on, are ways of restraining the expression of this conflict, which they do remarkably well. Ultimately, too, it is to everyone's mutual advantage to foster clan solidarity, for it is essential to the life of the community that every clan fulfill its categorical responsibilities as one of the eightfold divisions of the cosmos. But none of this could be accomplished, in my view, without the unique Bororo avuncular and paternal relationships. As recounted in an earlier section, the essence of cross-generational bonds in the clan is contained within the relationship between the name-giver and the name-receiver, *i-edaga* and *i-wagedu*. The basic character of this dyad is expressed in the former's obligation to instruct the latter in all the esoteric details of ceremonial property, name-set composition and ranking, especially those pertaining to their common clan. All ceremonial and much political authority depend on this guarded knowledge, so the young man is eager to court the favor of his uncle. Senior men, especially "chiefs," are constrained to pass on their learning to a junior clansmen, but they are also free to choose the most able candidate, who very often is not the actual name-receiver or sister's son. Old men consequently are able to wield influence through their students, mature men active in political affairs. Both parties have much to gain through the relationship, and not surprisingly it is extremely solidary.

It would be most incorrect to assimilate the Bororo *i-edaga* with the traditional anthropological image of a mother's brother in a matrilineal society. The former's role is much closer to that of a grandfather in societies which emphasize intimacy between alternate generations. In fact, as mentioned earlier, the actual, consanguineal, mother's brother is often termed and treated as an elder brother (*i-mana*), even if he was actually the name-giver, while a mother's mother's brother, uterine or classificatory, complies with the obligations of the *i-edaga*. To phrase it another, and perhaps more accurate way, there is always *at least* one generation between the *i-edaga* and *i-wagedu*, whatever the genealogical relation might be.

Another dimension of this relationship is contained in the obligatory usage of the terms between wife's father (or wife's mother's husband) and daughter's husband. Over time, this relationship tends to reduplicate the spirit as well as the letter of the clan-based bond, although it is not particularly common for the two ties to overlap, for a senior clansman to be the wife's father. The economic and social integration of the domestic group as well as the solidarity of the clan depends almost as much on the enduring character of this relationship as it does on the even more powerful bond between a mother and her daughter. Finally, the interests of the *i-edaga* (whether mother's brother, wife's father, or name-giver) nicely complement those of the father. As will be seen in a later section, affines normally enjoy mutually supportive relationships partly because they can assist one another in their mutual struggles within their own clans. Brothers must compete for the attentions of both men, a situation senior Bororo find quite delightful. Very often they share a division of labor, with the father imparting pragmatic skills such as hunting and fishing knowledge, and the mother's brother, the esoteric lore. One critical dimension of the cross-generation relationship is that the *i-edaga* very seldom attempts to exercise any control over a group of brothers, including here the entire junior generation in the clan. If the senior member of that group cannot resolve matters himself, the father (either real or the most senior affine in the clan) arbitrates the issue. The only time when his intervention fails, and that happens quite often, is when sisters and mothers/wives are involved.

The domestic group and the clan are very different matters when viewed from a female rather than a male perspective. A woman, until at least fairly late in life, has little involvement or concern with the details of ceremonial roles and bits of ornaments. Her relations with her clan sisters tend to be poor but not as bad as her brother's with his clan siblings. Unlike men, women do not compete with other members of their clan for name-set ranks or the titles and privileges associated with them. The authority of a mother, including here any senior woman of the clan, owes as much to her control of household resources as to her position within the clan.

But the interests of sisters are so sharply opposed that, as we saw earlier, they seldom coreside for any length of time as married adults. The major reason for this is that they must compete for the attentions of men, both husbands and brothers. According to masculine jokes and anecdotes, unmarried women regard their sisters' husbands as fair game. Further, the Bororo, both male and female, found my accounts of sororal polygyny ludicrously impractical. The presence of a mother or father in the household does again exert some control over this dimension of sisterly regard, at least for a time.

Finally, little can be done to offset the endemic problem of women in regard to their brothers. The males in any generation are morally obligated to support any clanswomen of that generation, including her dependent children, if her husband is unable, remiss, or not present to do so. The last condition is very common. I have never seen any exception to compliance with this rule in practice, although usually the burden was shared among the clan brothers resident in the village, and the other members of the woman's household contributed generously to her and her children's sustenance. This meant that, in one village, slightly under half of the mature men were attempting to provide for two families, their own and their (often categorical) sisters'. Wives tend to find such situations highly undesirable, and they are never under any circumstances on very good terms with their husbands' female relatives. Sisters compete bitterly for their brothers' assistance, and attempt to involve them in adjudicating disputes with their malingering or divorced husbands. Much of Bororo politics is conducted through these trivial and nagging domestic maneuvers, since public opinion stresses that a man must honor his clanswomen to achieve any status in his clan. Consequently, sisters are able to play off brothers through gossip and slander, quite effective though covert sanctions.

There are, of course, positive elements in the sororal/fraternal bond, but these derive from the sister's assumption of the maternal role. The relationship between mother and son is usually mutually supportive. However, in the absence of any mother, the elder sister (*i-tuie*) is obliged to act the supportive, nurturant role for her younger bachelor brothers. This is quite literally true in practice, with the sister and her husband providing all daily meals, clothing, and even some manufactured items for her unmarried siblings. This practice allows the Bororo male to delay his marriage and provides him with virtually a guaranteed source of support, or at least female services (except, obviously, sexual ones), whenever he is unmarried. Men in these situations do incur a debt to their sisters, which can be redeemed at a later time through compliance with the obligations of clan support of unmarried women. It would not do, though, to overemphasize the *quid pro quo* element in cross-sex sibling relations. Perhaps thus related share common interests, not the least of which is the welfare of the juvenile members of the clan, the sister's children, both real and categorical. Just as a man is bound to protect his brother's children, so too, a woman is committed to her sister's descendants. The parallel is not an idle one. I know of two cases in which a man married his dead brother's wife's elder sister with the ostensible public motive of caring for the children of the union, the mother having abandoned them. In both cases, the parties were much commended in public for their ethical behavior; in private, women's gossip accused the elder sisters of driving away the childrens' mothers. As this indicates, if the sisterly relation among the Bororo precludes that of cowife, it is predicated on the comother bond, and whatever solidarity it possesses derives from that.

Far from stressing the cross-sex sibling bond, Bororo ideology and practice emphasize the highly distinct and even opposed interests of brother and sister within their corporate group. This extends much beyond the issue of material support and jural authority. A man finds that his relations with the opposite moiety as a collectivity are absolutely critical to his social maturation, but a woman discovers that the females in that group, whether husband's sisters or brothers' wives, are her implacable enemies. A mature male is committed to his clan as a corporate, ceremonial right-holding collectivity, while a woman is concerned with the future of her own narrow portion of that corporate identity, the household/name-set. She sees the interests of her own children as opposed to those of her brother's descendants, at least while they are young.

Since the Bororo do not utilize marriage to relate corporate groups (cf. Crocker 1969b and below), a woman's brothers have no vested interests in preserving her marriage. They are hardly indifferent to the character of their brother-in-law, and are obliged to intervene if he treats her cruelly, but they must relie on *his* elder brother for influence over his treatment of their sister. Only in middle age, after she becomes involved in the system of ritual representatives of the dead, does a woman come to have some sort of identity of interests with her brothers. These ritual roles emphasize her status as "mother of the clan." One receives the impression that for most Bororo males, sisters are a liability, and become assets only in their capacity to fulfill the maternal role either in respect to them or as the genetrix of later generations of clan members. It is little wonder that the men, caught between the demands of their sisters and of their wives, choose to spend most of their time in the transitional "middle ground" of the men's house, which is categorically forbidden to all women.[17] For the sake of clarity, I should add that a man's conflict of loyalties between his natal and conjugal households does not extend to the descending generation male members of those residences. That is, a man finds that his sons' and sisters' sons interests are not at all identical with those of their mothers, for reasons just outlined.

And, of course, after initiation none of these male relatives is resident in those households.

As this last fact suggests, one critical factor in the dynamics of the relationships within the household and clan is the uxorilocal rule of residence. This requirement, which permits the localization of the matrilineal group at a fixed point in the village circle, has certain aspects which relate to the character of relations in the family. The Bororo appear to express a conviction that a man should not procreate and rear children in his own natal dwelling. For example, the explicit motive for initiation is that after a son reaches puberty and commences active sexuality, his parents are deeply shamed for him to continue sleeping in their house. The implication is that he might witness sexual intercourse between them. After initiation, as the Bororo say, no man should sleep in his mother's house.

I feel that the problem of the parent's and child's mutual recognition of each other's sexuality is not the main difficulty here, for the Bororo find no bar to the daughter's continued presence in the household. Rather, the prohibition on virilocal residence has to do with the character of male sexuality, which is to procreate children who are categorically different from oneself. As I discuss in the next section, the implications of the agnatic relation among the Bororo are radically different from those of the maternal relation. One aspect of this difference is conveyed in the highly ambiguous relationship between a woman and her brothers' or sons' children, which alternates between informal joking and formal avoidance. Further, some Bororo express a preference for patrilateral cross-cousin marriage, "for then the *i-edaga* [mother's mother's brother] is also the father's father." There is, then, some feeling that generative male sexuality should oscillate every generation between two categories of women. These aspects of uxorilocality tend to substantiate Terence Turner's claim that for Gê males, the families of origin and of procreation must be kept rigidly distinct for a plethora of psychological, sociological, and cosmological reasons. I discuss the implications of his argument in the conclusion of this paper; its ultimate relevance to Bororo structure reflects material yet to be presented.

One final aspect of relationships within the household and clan needs to be clarified. This concerns the relevance of consanguinity to personal transactions and the maintenance of the group through time. In the preceding descriptions I have made a distinction between real and classificatory clan relatives. This principle of ordering personal transactions is less important than relative age and sex, but the Bororo do base many of their actions upon their perception of the importance of consanguineal bonds. Generally, the obligations of clanship operate with the most stringency when such relatives are involved, and tend to diminish as knowledge of common ancestry decreases. Conflicts are most intense when between full siblings. But parents and other senior relatives correspondingly feel a greater obligation to mediate such problems, owing to the normative injunction for complete sibling solidarity. It is when these persons die or move away that disputes between brothers or sisters become the most acute.

Overall, the performative dimension of kinship bonds is highly stressed; the Bororo would agree with the Italian maxim quoted by Radcliffe-Brown, "I call father the man who gives me bread" (1950:4). It is just because persons tend to comply with the formal obligations of biologically derived relationships rather than corporately determined ones that the former have any sociological significance at all among the Bororo. The relationship categories derived from the family are applied throughout the society, and each individual is quite willing to transform his or her terminological usage to express the facts of daily life. There are no terminological categories which distinguish between real and classificatory clan relatives. The only terminological way to express a genealogical bond is to describe it. As I have said before, contrasts between classificatory and blood relatives are usually expressed through terms based on residence and name-set affiliation. Finally, relations within the clan are constantly modified by ritual events, above all those concerning funerals and the symbolic representation of deceased Bororo. The Bororo, in short, transmute their personal experiences of gestation and parturition into a social framework which emphasizes the personal, symbolic influences over the interactive destiny of these "facts." Once again, genealogy is one mode among many others used to express the attributes of corporate membership.

After such grim documentation of sibling discord, it may be wondered that the Bororo corporation survives as a viable sociological entity under any conditions.

Its property is not limited by natural events or circumstances, as in the case of lineage land or herds, so its members have no obviously pragmatic, utilitarian motives for collaboration. The very principles which dictate its existence seem designed to cast sibling against sibling as a precondition of their social and private existences. Yet the Bororo clan constitutes the most elemental ground of metaphors in which both self and alter can be defined. It provides the only icons in which personal acts can be expressed in any lasting, sociological, and cosmological way. As the categorical precondition of all human activity, it is more comparable to the caste as discussed by Lévi-Strauss (1963b) than to Morgan's gens, since it defines the person in terms of transcendent, cosmological attributes rather than through an idiom of genetic substance.

Most of all, the Bororo corporate group is the only lasting social unit which carries out exchanges on behalf of ego with other comparable units. Just as the clan is defined through its ceremonial participation in transactions involving spirit representations, so too the individual is related to persons in other groups through his inclusion in one of the "representing" or "represented" collectivities. Relations based on personal consanguineal ties are not relevant to these contexts. Fundamentally, any Bororo individual can be replaced by a clan sibling of the same sex, as far as other clans are concerned. Members of the clan are the same kind of logical thing, from the status of the exchanging nonmember. The Bororo clan's attribute as a condition of Bororo existence has little to do with any consanguineal definitions of individual or group relationships, but depends on its ritual and jural singularity as an essential component in all social transactions. The only way its domination of personal identity can be mitigated is through the other moiety.

Agnatic Relations and Cross-Moiety Transactions

The relationship between father and son among the Bororo is extremely complex, since it serves as the basis for the majority of cross-moiety exchanges and for nearly all contacts between men and the *aroe* spirits. The agnatic bond even penetrates into relations between members of the same clan and moiety, transforming completely the categorical shape and content of these. The total effect of all this is to invert the entire Bororo social system, so that on many ritual occasions that system appears, in a great many crucial ways, to be a patrilineal one. I regard this process of dialectical inversions as perhaps the most fundamental attribute of Bororo social structure. This section describes its character and scope.

A Bororo calls his or her father and father's brothers (that is, senior male members of the father's name-set) *i-ogwa*. The term can also be applied in address or polite reference to any senior male of the opposite moiety, and a man nearly always categorizes his father's clan as *i-ogwa wobe*. The correct reciprocal for children deemed to be one's own offspring (including adopted ones) is *i-tunarigedu*, which is also used by mothers in the same restricted way. Men tend to use this term more than women to differentiate referentially true children from classificatory sons and daughters (*i-medu* and *aredu*), those fathered by the male members of ego's own clan or moiety. The agnatic relation in its most intense and pervasive personal form is limited to behavior between a man, his consanguines, and his agnatic descendants. The normative requirements for all such relations call for unquestioned, diffuse, and continuous mutual support in all areas, a general "categorical obligation," as da Matta phrases it.

Although these obligations are nearly always fulfilled in actual transactions between a man and his immediate paternal relatives, their moral force tends to dissipate rapidly once outside the limited area of known agnatic genealogical connections. A man still looks to a classificatory patrilateral parallel cousin or a senior man in the father's clan as one of his first sources of aid, but with less realistic expectations that their support will be automatic. But the categorical imperatives of the bond remain fundamental to interaction with the other moiety, even if one has had a negligent pater and absent paternal kin. These imperatives involve elements of what Terence Turner calls "symbolic fatherhood" or "substitute fathers" in the Kayapó context (1971:367). One of the issues addressed in the following pages is precisely the sense in which these relations might be regarded as "symbolic" or "substitute."

Throughout childhood, Bororo boys are encouraged to maintain active relations with their genitor/pater and his matrilineal relatives, even though their current mother's husband may be a different man. The expectation is considerably diminished in the case of daughters, with idiosyncratic elements much affecting the amount of actual interaction. A father will take his young son "home" (to the boy's father's sister's or father's mother's house) on ceremonial occasions which require his presence there. The father's brothers will often play with the boy and, as he grows older, may take some interest in his education, particularly if they are childless themselves (or interested in his mother). Most Bororo fathers are exceedingly affectionate with their children, leaving it to the mother and elder siblings to perform disciplinary actions. Early in life, a son (or daughter) is often symbolically identified with the father in an important manner. A father can delegate his young son to receive a valuable body painting being given to the father in exchange for some ritual service by members of the opposite moiety. A sister's son or daughter's son (and, less frequently, daughters) may also be substituted, but it is universally accepted as highly ethical for a man to choose his son, in preference to other relatives, to represent him in receiving these honors.[18] It may be remembered that such paintings are given as compensation for a "revenge" upon nature, both transactions being across moiety lines. Consequently, the son is painted by members of his own moiety, in his capacity as substitute for his father. Such a "boomerang effect" is a basic attribute of Bororo ceremonial life, and the use of paternal relations to mediate those within the moiety is essential to their political as well as social existence.

At initiation, these informal contacts between a boy and his agnatic relatives are institutionalized in the status of the *i-orubadari*. This is the boy's "special friend," who must sustain the initiate through the various trials of the ceremony and who has formal responsibility for his conduct during it, replacing both father and maternal relatives. It is he who, at the conclusion of initiation, sponsors the boy's introduction into the world of mature men, sexuality, and the *aroe* spirits. The bond between *i-orubadari* (the term is reciprocal) can never be superseded by subsequent events (such as marriage) and remains in effect throughout the lives of the partners, who are expected to epitomize the unquestioning loyalty characteristic of agnatic relatives. The essence of the *i-orubadari* bond lies in the survivor's duty to represent his deceased's friend's soul during his funeral and during subsequent rituals, until his own death. Now, the initiate's *i-orubadari* must always be a member of his father's clan, and should preferably be a recently initiated younger uterine brother of the father. Needless to say, such a relative is rare in modern Bororo communities, and some effort must be made just to secure a reasonably young representative of the paternal clan. However, in every case observed by me and noted in the genealogies, these efforts were always successful. Precisely the same actual situation obtains for the parallel injunction, that the ceremonial representative be the deceased's *i-orubadari* or at least classificatory male agnate. This was carried out in practice in every recorded funeral.

Finally, it is considered exceedingly correct that *i-orubadari-mage* (that is, the special friend of initiation and the initiate himself) marry each other's sisters, or for one of them to do so. This amounts to a formal preference for marriage with either type of cross-cousin, with a certain emphasis on the patrilateral side. According to informants, unions with the true father's sister's daughter/mother's brother's daughter rarely occur nowadays, and never in my records. Marriage with the father's clan does occur, but not any more often than marriage with other clans of the opposite moiety. However, I was assured that in the past compliance with the preference in strict genealogical terms was not uncommon, although it was never a matter of wide practice owing to discrepancies in age, personal idiosyncrasies, and so forth. Some informants opined that it might even be somewhat risky to marry any member of the father's clan, since poor relations with the wife might endanger other agnatic relations. I feel that there are few if any strategic advantages or structural imperatives to either form of unilateral cross-cousin marriage in the Bororo situation, and understand the formal preference as a partly metaphorical statement of the ideal intimacy between a man and his father's group.

As recent theoretical disputes have shown (Needham 1969:xix; Lévi-Strauss 1969:xxx–xxxv), the statistical and normative aspects of an institution do not exhaust its theoretical significance. The term *i-orubadari* literally means "my possessor of the fireplace" (cf. derivation in Albisetti and Venturelli 1962:572). "Fire," *eru*, has the connotations both of domestic hearth and of sexual passion among the Bororo. It is the *i-orubadari* who bestows a penis sheath upon the initiate, an object which is associated with categorical rights over the sexuality of women in the other moiety (Lévi-Strauss 1970:45–47; Crocker 1969b). He is also personally responsible for mediating the relation between the boy and the forces of the *aroe* spirits in their most powerful guises (see below). In view of this set of attributes, the *i-orubadari* does not seem to be a "kind of substitute father" because it is not the bond of some common physical substance that links him with the initiate, but rather some general categorical relation of logical complementarity, such as that found in affinity.

The previous data indicate the reasoning behind the Bororo assumption that sexual relations with a consanguineal father's daughter are equivalent to those with a uterine sister: both are completely incestuous. There is no question that the Bororo express a critical aspect of the paternal relation through a "biological" idiom. But if this consanguineal thought were followed out completely, the father's uterine siblings and the children of these, above all the father's sister's daughter, would be regarded as blood relatives. This would hardly be congruent with the normative preference for marriage with this type of relative. In the Bororo case, at least, the argument that all "agnatic relatives" are "sorts of fathers" is too literal, and raises again the image of "complementary filiation." As I argued earlier, this position does not recognize the distinction between procreative beliefs *per se* and the symbolic interpretation of their characteristics, which always must reflect the sociological categories governing interpersonal transactions. Nor is it any solution to speak of a "patrifiliative link" connecting distinct corporations. The varied obligatory relations with the father's clan are not most usually seen as cause and effect, for they all must express the same set of paradigmatic assumptions. These concern the view that ego's relations with all that is dangerous, including sexuality, *must* be mediated through members and groups of the moiety opposite to his own.

To put the matter in a more conventional way, the male privilege of engendering life in that "other" group entails a further series of obligations to sustain and continue that life. In this sense, the Bororo understanding of male, procreative reciprocity would have to be couched in terms of "life-givers" and "life-receivers."[19] Thus, the father's clan sustains and protects the life of ego through providing him with a sponsor during his initiation into the world of spirits, the *i-orubadari;* with "safe," rule-bound sexuality, in the provision of a proper sexual partner and mother to his children; and with continuing social life after his physical death, through the ceremonial representative *(aroe maiwu)* .

In view of these considerations, to label the *i-orubadari* a "substitute" or "symbolic" father is appropriate only if we recognize as symbolic a transition from a direct, personal relation to a categorical one involving corporate units and emphasizing metaphysical aspects of the bond. But, as I have tried to show, the Bororo understanding and institutionalization of "biological" relations is itself eminently symbolic. The *i-orubadari* certainly does not replace the father, except in the sense of standing in for him and extending his sphere of responsibility into highly potent ritual areas. The Salesians' gloss of the term *i-orubadari* as "padrinho" (godfather, "spirit father") is by no means inaccurate (Albisetti and Venturelli 1962:572) .

This problem cannot be fully resolved without some consideration of the most important ritual relationship involving agnatic bonds, that of the *aroe maiwu,* the deceased's representative, or "new soul." This person is chosen or confirmed by the men's council, which gives particular consideration to the wishes of the head of the deceased's clan and his or her immediate uterine relatives, such as a mother or sister. In the absence of the *i-orubadari* gained during initiation, which is now a nearly universal condition,[20] a vigorous, ethical male member of the deceased's father's clan, and preferably his subclan, is chosen. As will be seen, there are reasons to suspect that the actual selection is heavily influenced by political considerations. The men's council further selects a close female relative of the deceased, along with her husband, to be the custodians of his soul *(aroe)* . Here, as with the representative himself, the council expressly desires persons who, owing to their general probity, skill in hunting and gardening, and fondness for (or obligation toward) the deceased, will be punctilious in carrying out their extensive and lengthy duties.

Normatively, it is assumed that the dead man's own mother and father, and the *i-orubadari* of initiation,[21] have had the requisite intimate commitment to the deceased to assure such fulfillment of the ceremonial requirements. But since these individuals have very probably predeceased the dead man, substitutions are made on the basis of criteria derived from the preceding assumption. Thus, on the grounds that the closer the "blood tie," the more congruent with expectation actual behavior, the elder uterine sister of the deceased may be substituted for their dead mother. In her absence, a uterine sister, parallel cousin, or any female member of the deceased's subclan may assume the role of the ritual "mother." In all cases, the husband of the woman selected becomes the representative's ritual "father." The implications of these terms are correct: the ritual replacement (*areo maiwu*) becomes and remains a "son" (*i-tunarigedu,* the term otherwise reserved for one's own children) to the ritual "father" and "mother" in nearly every sense characteristic of the "true" filial relationship.

These three persons form what I have termed the Bororo ritual triad. The representative does, in principle, assume certain aspects of the deceased's social personality for the latter's entire clan; clan members should address him, for example, with the same category they used for the deceased and behave appropriately. Except during a four to six month period immediately after the funeral, few persons bother with these requirements.[22] But the relations between the members of the triad are taken very seriously indeed: as informants constantly put it, "The spirit mother and the spirit father must be treated as if they were actually one's own parents, but much better." In addition to the extensive set of ceremonial duties outlined below, persons related in this way must observe great politeness and dignity in all their actions toward one another. An *aroe* father and son must on no account quarrel, or even publicly disagree; they are even very circumspect about the company and circumstances in which they gossip about each other. A spirit son and his mother are so formal in their behavior that their relation might be regarded as one approaching avoidance. This bond is inalienable throughout both their lives, and the Bororo regarded as reprehensible the suggestion that it should ever be colored by sexual overtones. The paradox here, of course, is that prior to the funeral the *aroe* mother would have been an *aredu,* a classificatory mother's brother's daughter, to the future representative and, as such, a potential spouse.

The *aroe* father is, of course, a member of ego's moiety, even a clan brother or uterine brother. But the same perpetuity does not characterize the spirit father–son relation, which depends upon the continuation of the marriage of the "father" to the "mother." If he at any time divorces the mother, all aspects of his ritual relationship with the representative cease. Such a break is regarded as most unfortunate, and may even anger the ancestral spirits, the collectivity of *aroe,* who punish gross breaches of proper behavior between members of the ritual triad. For this reason, custodianship of the soul is not usually given to young women, whose marriages are notoriously unstable. But young men can be and frequently are chosen as the representative, so there is often a considerable age discrepancy between the ritual parents and their son. Bororo men seldom take a sexual interest in women very much their senior, and, as we have seen, the greater an age contrast between same-sex members of one moiety, the less their conflict. No doubt these factors contribute to the extent to which nearly all persons succeed in fulfilling the norms of this sacred relationship.

The formal duties of the members of the spirit family toward each other are bound up in ceremonial events, particularly the ritual hunting and fishing expeditions, which occur nearly every week in the traditional villages. These are collective enterprises in which every able-bodied spirit representative and "father" should join, and usually do. During the evening before the expedition, the council decides which spirit relations are to be operative the next day, since nearly all adult males are involved in anywhere from six to a dozen "active" triads. After killing game, each ritual "son" delivers it to his "father," who in turn gives the meat to any one of his actual sons (*i-medu*), real or classificatory, or in their absence, to a younger brother-in-law, who carries it back to the village.[23] There the food is delivered to the spirit "mother," who immediately gives her husband a large plate of cooked vegtable food or a bowl of sweetened water (substances relished by the spirits). He takes the item to the men's house and gives it to his ritual "son," who shares the food or water among the members of his *own* moiety. But all of them, or nearly so, are, of course, representing deceased members of the other moiety. Therefore, what are in fact exchanges between the moieties (from women of one to the men of another) are in Bororo ritual theory merely prestations within the moiety: "mothers" giving food to their "sons" through the agent of the "father."

While the feasting and intermittent singing proceed in the men's house, where the *aroe* spirits are said to be present at this time, the spirit "mother" prepares the game. She retains some of the finished dish, but the bulk of it is taken out again to the hunters by her husband. By this time, the *aroe* spirits have left, and the men have reassembled in the dance plaza. Each "son" shares some of the cooked meat among his wife and children, and other members of his conjugal household. If the kill has been reasonably good, there is enough food left over for him to give to his actual parents and his matrilineal kin, beginning with his unmarried sisters.

A "son" may deliver game he has killed outside of ritual contexts to his "father" to be prepared and distributed in the same fashion. Further, during every public ceremony, all of which involve the active participation of the *aroe,* every "mother" is required to prepare appropriate food and drink for her spirit "sons." During the months between the first and second interment of the funeral cycle, food passes in these manners almost daily between the members of the ritual triad. Although this flow dimishes with the years, it never approaches complete cessation. When all the ritual triads current in the villages are active, as they are following some unusually successful hunting or fishing expedition, the prestations and counterprestations occur with bewildering variety and rapidity and last for most of the day. At these moments, the paths which mutely testify to the extent of interaction between Bororo households, both of different and identical moieties, are well trodden; the *utawara* (the ritual "roads" linking different name-sets in ceremonial tradition) are a physical fact.

As I have mentioned, the political dimensions of the ritual triad are critical to the distribution of power and its institutionalization among the Bororo. First, there appears to be a marked tendency for the council to place brothers who have reached a phase of active political competition in a ritual relation of "father" and "son." I know of no traditional community in which the leaders of subclans are *not* thus related. This fact is not as impressive as it might seem, since only a minority of the clans present in any village are so extensive as to boast two factions. At Korugedu Paru, all clan brothers who had attained stable positions of importance in large domestic units and who played important roles of any sort in their own clans were "father" and "son" to one another. In a case involving two uterine brothers in their early thirties who had had a very severe falling-out, I heard the council deliberate for a week as to whether it should "give the *powari*" (the gourd whistle symbolizing the deceased's soul) to the wife of one of the brothers, and make the other brother the ritual representative. The plan was ultimately rejected on the grounds that the marriage was quite recent and was already showing signs of strain. Further, the brother nominated as representative was extremely reluctant to assume the role, partly because, as it later developed, he had designs on his brother's wife. However, I do know of two cases of actual uterine brothers of more advanced years and greater status who are related as ritual "father" and "son."

One very important objective criterion employed by the council in these decisions is that "the *powari* should not stay in one house," that is, the three persons in the ritual triad can never be coresidents. In practice, this means that a wife's father and daughter's husband (*i-edaga* and *i-wagedu*) are never also ritual "father" and "son." I well understand the informants who implied that the figure of a mother-in-law who is also a ritual "mother" is simply inadmissible as a condition of daily household life. Aside from the logical problems, it might be argued that such a move would be superfluous. The domestic group is already well integrated, at least in terms of persons of different generations, and one feature of the ritual triad is to provide a context for prestations between domestic units of the same moiety. Most ritual "mothers" in fact live next door to their "son's" wife's house, or at most two or three houses away in the village circle. Although women supposedly believe that the soul of the deceased actually does return to kill game and participate in ceremonies, they are quite aware of the actual facts, and the sharing of a common husband–ritual "son" is one of the few things that mitigate the mutual tension between the women of adjacent households.

The rule does preclude the possibility of relating coresident men married to sisters in this ceremonial fashion. Perhaps this is one reason why stable instances of this arrangement are rare to the point of nonexistence in Bororo domestic groups, with married sisters maintaining separate households. When this last arrangement occurs in a village, there is no bar to sisters' husbands' assuming complementary roles in the ritual triad, and I know of one case in which this has occurred, with apparently beneficial results. Generally, there is nothing to preclude a man from representing a deceased member of his wife's clan, as long as the ritual "mother" is residentially segregated from his wife and himself. It is not at all uncommon for older men with long-established marriages to be thus related to their wife's clan. Finally, it should be mentioned that often the ritual triad extends outside the village, owing to one or the other of its members opting for residence in a new community. Although this obviously diminishes the flow of goods and services within the settlement, it does afford another matrix for intervillage cooperation and articulation,[24] and another demonstration of the social validity of a single organizational model.

As I have maintained from the beginning, the extension of the *aroe maiwu* institution throughout Bororo social relations lends that society a curious upside-down quality. Consider only the most obvious deductions from the terminological usages in themselves. A male ego's clan and moiety brothers become his ritual "fathers" and his "sons"; his potential wives (FZ, FZD, BD, and MBD), along with any bilateral cross-cousins who happen to turn up in the other moiety, become his "mother." Moreover, a man could conceivably represent his own father if the father's father was also a mother's mother's brother, which, of course, would be the case if his father had married any categorical patrilateral cross-cousin. To the degree that the representative acquires rights in the deceased's clan,[25] the Bororo would thus even satisfy that ideology found in some patrilineal societies, that a son replace his father. The extent to which he might assume the father's social personality is, of course, quite limited, as it is for all *aroe maiwu*. The derived rights of such a replacement clearly do not, and cannot in all logic, extend to assumption of the deceased's categorical privileges with regard to the sexuality of females in the other moiety (Crocker 1969b). The Bororo could be accurately characterized as patrilineal if only some brief moments in their ritual activities were considered. Nonetheless, the Bororo must be recognized as "patrilineal" only in the same sense, if not in a comparable degree, that they are said to be "matrilineal." The pervasive influence of the inversions wrought by the "new soul" render absurd any application of "complementary filiation," or any scheme based on some biologically derived "givens," such as that of "substitute fatherhood."

The issues here, like those pertaining to the Gê in general, involve rethinking some of the basic assumptions of social anthropology. Such effort involves the obligation to consider the institutions and beliefs of any society as a totality, not as a piecemeal aggregation of jurally defined "rights and duties" portioned out among a series of dyadic relationships; not as some compound in which meaning must be distinguished from action as a basic procedure in analysis. In the Bororo case, the traditional understanding of "lineality" clearly becomes an obstacle to the comprehension of their social dynamics. Even any presumed disjunction between the "natal household" and the "conjugal household" falls away, or at least is transformed in its implications, when we consider that the phenomenological ground of ego's relations with each group is utterly different. This holds, if not for the Shavante and Northern Kayapó, then certainly for the Bororo, the Krahó, and the Northern Gê generally. It is my thesis here that Bororo perception of this difference provides one basic generative force in their social dialectics. In brief, they contrast the conditions of social "being," as determined by the corporate group and the associated perpetual categories of universal order, and those of social "becoming," as set forth in the reciprocally inverting ritual requirements for the personal representation of these enduring categories. In other words, a Bororo ego is and has only that which he can never be but must give away, so that both his enduring identity and his occasional transcendence of it are accomplished through highly differentiated alters. These are, respectively, his mother and his brothers, and his father/son and wife. The consequence, then, of Bororo ritual inversions is to collapse these theses upon themselves to produce the synthesis of death.

Conclusion: Bororo and Gê

Such romantic, if not mystical phrasing is not likely to appeal to my more empirically minded colleagues, but it is the only adequate way I have found to communicate an understanding of Bororo society in a manner at once expressive of ethnographic reality and potentially useful in cross-cultural comparison. This final section considers some of the more obvious issues raised by the Bororo material in terms of its relationship to Gê systems. First, it seems clear that the dialectics of all these societies concern oppositions between male and female which are partly phrased in terms of corporate recruitment. Thus Maybury-Lewis has shown that the Shavante have imposed patriliny upon an ideology otherwise neutral on this point to effect groupings of related males. Bororo "matriliny" might be said to create common interests among unrelated units of maternally defined household groups, while at the same time separating definitely any agnatically defined collectivities of "blood," of common physical substance as traced through paternal lines. To my mind, such "descent" terminology is irrelevant to all the Gê as well as to the Bororo, which seem to organize themselves on very different principles of "shared substance." At the most, these societies can be said to recruit personnel to social groups on a basis of "unilateral affiliation." Nontheless, the "matrilineal" complexion of the Bororo clan, as distinct from the name-sets/matrilineages, requires further investigation.

When I first began to inquire into the issue of "why matriliny?"

among the Bororo, informants usually responded that "there is nothing for the child in his [or her] father's clan," which I took to be a strictly jural interpretation emphasizing the importance of the nominative capacity of the maternal group, with its integrated icons and cosmological orderings. When later, pursuing the matter, I received a very standardized reference to a myth, I was at first inclined to accept an indigenous *de facto* attitude of acceptance of tradition and its incomprehensible dictates. But the myth proved consistently to be the one used by Lévi-Strauss as his "reference myth" within the *Mythologiques* series, the one presented as the opening theme of *Le cru et le cuit* (1970:35–65). This myth recounts a patricide occasioned by the son's supposed intercourse with a father's wife and his father's ultimately disastrous efforts to avenge himself. Informants' repeated references to it as a justification for matriliny now seem to me to express a view that only such a principle insures that father and son should not be competitors for the same resources, and institute a state of social arrangements in which they can indeed be cooperative and mutually complementary statuses. Unfortunately, I have no evidence that this deduction is expressed by the Bororo through any other collective representation, and must be cautious in applying this interpretation in any extensive way. But it does indicate the character of the reasoning with which the Bororo regard their own institutions.

In my opinion, the final answer as to why the Bororo have opted for matriliny as the basic condition for social being is ultimately unobtainable. Much more important, in the Gê context, are the precise "hows" and consequences of this condition. Like the Gê, the Bororo institutionalize in both residential and ceremonial practices some total opposition between male and female states of being. Not only are males identified with the village center, and females with the periphery, but rituals constantly represent this division as fundamental to social life. Most spectacularly, during the ritual representation of the Aije, the great water *aroe* which appear as the climax of all Bororo funerals and initiations, the women are obliged to barricade themselves inside their huts while the actors personifying the Aije spirits through paint and the whirling of bullroarers "attack" the village with balls of white clay and obscene shouts. The bullroarers and clay pellets are explicitly said to represent the power of the male principle as against the female. If, for example, a woman should chance to see any aspect of the Aije representation, including the bullroarers themselves in their detumescent state, when they are hidden away between ceremonies, then "the Spirits [*aroe* as a totality] cause her belly to swell up until she dies."

If men and women are conceptualized as radically different and antithetical states of being, to the degree that contrasts between wife-daughter and mother-sister disappear, it is only consistent that corporate categories as well as daily residential life should reflect this antithesis. Men are always associated with the permanence of categories, with the "plantonic ideals" embodied in the clan totems and the ceremonies which represent them, with the entire system of *aroe* spirits: with, in short, order. But this order in itself is sterile, a set of categories which classify reality. Women, by contrast, are the vehicles of change, transformation, and renewal; they are intimately associated with the *bope*, who are responsible for all processes of growth and destruction. Instead of basing their social system on notions of descent, on the idea of biological continuity through time, the Bororo relate their institutions to a complex set of beliefs concerning female fecundity and male sterility. Why, then, should they accentuate the paradox by placing the transforming female as the origin of cosmological order? Where else is she to be placed? By permanently embedding the women in the village circle, so to speak, as originators and fixed perpetual references of social divisions, their dangerous power of fecund transformation is at least limited to categorical boundaries (Crocker 1977). Each is limited to perpetuating her own logical species. Perhaps this accounts for the final "arbitrariness" of the entities (name-sets, *aroe* totems, ceremonial property, and so on) grouped under the same corporate heading: all of this represents the power of categorization to set arbitrary limits on natural proliferation.

The preceding is only a rough outline of a sexual dichotomy which seems fundamental to all the Gê systems as well as to the Bororo. Clearly, the contrasting ways it is institutionalized by these systems are the critical elements for comparative analysis. Among the Krĩkatí, Apinayé, and perhaps Ramkokamekra, men and women seem to form distinct moieties, based on logical principles not unlike those of parallel descent and related through the cross-sex sibling bond. The antithesis between the public ceremonial life in which these moieties are active and the private affairs of the domestic group and village periphery, also appears to be correlated with the presence of a cognatic kindred which orders economic and political relationships between households. The Bororo domestic household sometimes approaches that level of integration characterized by the exclusiveness of shared common substance and absolute "categorical obligation" which is the hall-mark of Apinayé residential units. But of course in the Bororo case the pervasiveness of the name-set divisions and a man's identity with his natal corporate group constantly challenge this integration and make the public-private dichotomy much less relevant to this society than to the Gê.

Further, another dimension of the sexual dichotomy critical for pan-Gê-Bororo comparison is the different ways paternity is ritually transmogrified. Among the Kayapó, Shavante, and Bororo, such transformations of the paternal relationship seem to be the basis for reciprocity between dyadically ordered social divisions. At least the Bororo institutions of the *i-orubadari* and *aroe-maiwu* are structurally analogous to the transforming roles of the substitute father among the Kayapó and the affinal *ĩ-amõ* of initiation among the Shavante. The total inversions of social categories that result from the paternal transformations appear unique to the Bororo case. But the total exclusion of women from these transformations, from the dimension of masculinity that is expressed through representations of the *aroe,* has parallels in Shavante, Kayapó, and even Ramkokamekra practices. It seems as if the Central Gê, Kayapó, and Bororo have elaborated, in quite different ways, idioms of paternal relationship that stress an absolute dichotomy between relations founded on these and those based on ties through women. The conflict between these principles thus serves as the generative force behind the dialectical processes in these societies. But the Northern Gê, as hypothesized earlier, utilize the sexual dichotomy to transform both men and women.

Whatever the worth of these speculations, one theoretical perspective in anthropology seems completely inappropriate to these materials. In none of these societies are blood ties, bonds of common genealogical substance, the *fundamental* means whereby individuals are recruited or related to social units or categories. None of them, with the possible exception of the Shavante, is descent based in the sense of traditional anthropological understandings of that term. "Unilineality" seems quite a foreign concept in the highlands of Central Brazil.

As Durkheim pointed out lucidly so long ago, the greatest impetus to reciprocity is social differentiation. It is precisely the incredible elaboration of this principle within a basically common structural framework that provides the Gê and Bororo with their dialectical complexity. Differentiation can proceed on the basis of distinctions founded on descent, or "blood," but, as Lévi-Strauss has made clear (1969), only in restricted circumstances does one descent line logically imply others. Categories founded on other sources of distinctions between groups can possess precisely the same inexorable implications for social interaction which must express a logical model as the most rigidly prescriptive "elementary structure." Whether these distinctions relate to symbolic attributes of paternity and maternity, to the classificatory logic of names, or to the processual dynamics of power, the Gê and the Bororo employ such contrasts in the elaboration of structures which are clearly "elementary," even if they lack "unilineal descent" as a ground of differentiation. Now, these principles of social classification ultimately relate to the process whereby individuals acquire, modify, and transform their own sense of personal identity. This understanding is the basis of all transactions, and ultimately of the dialectic as Hegel conceived it (Kaufman 1966). This paper has emphasized the assumptions and symbols from which the Bororo derive sexual identity and nominative character. A complete account would have to include the Bororo view of the moral personality as itself bifurcate in terms of the forces represented as *aroe* and *bope* (Crocker 1977) in relation to these two definitional grounds. Consequently, I feel that one profitable comparative analysis of the Bororo-Gê could be couched in terms of the institutionalized, rhetorical means which confer and maintain individual identity.

In this regard, however, there remains the task of summarizing the factors behind the Bororo distinctiveness in the Gê context at the level of those obvious contrasts described at the beginning of this paper. As I said at that point, Bororo "matriliny" permits that society to express a pan-Gê ideological complex through a precise village plan. Although the Bororo commitment to the virtues of this model is a powerful integrative factor in their society, this in itself does not explain why there is so little divisive conflict between social units, whether within or between communities. As we have learned from Simmel, sharing a commitment to one normative system does not inhibit the expression of social antagonisms. In the Bororo case, there seems to be operative a complex variant of that old theoretical maxim that if each set of personal interests is countered by another equally strong set, maximum social solidarity results. The precise conditions which generate this state appear to be fivefold.

First, the "scarce resources" which serve to define the Bororo corporate group are *not* personally available to the members of this group for their own usage. Further, these resources are totally nonutilitarian, so that competition for them does not involve extrasocial or ecological limitations. Simultaneously, the warranties of prestige, which can only be conveyed by the "other side," do not confer rights over any "instruments of production," including women. The Bororo corporate group is totally dependent upon other such units for the expression and affirmation of its own existence.

Second, the social consequences of inversion extend to ego's own moiety in addition to transforming his relations with the other moiety. In effect, the Bororo have been able to counter matriliny with patriliny, making brothers into fathers and sons, and wives into mothers. To be sure, the benefits of this paradox extend only marginally to women, but, as I have tried to show throughout the paper, they present a problem the Bororo have only defined and not resolved.

Third, the moieties themselves relate in a twofold and opposing manner, first as affines in an almost classic expression of dual organization, and then as paternal derivatives each of the other. Although I have not been able to elaborate this point previously, there is much evidence to confirm the importance of a certain antagonism between Bororo moieties (Crocker 1969a). They compete in various ceremonial contexts in a quite explicit fashion, and gossips, male or female, constantly find fault with the other moiety as a totality, blaming "them" for failures in hunting, epidemics, and all manner of afflictions. Males are severely inhibited from the overt expression of such dyadic hostility, simply because the "other men" are at once fathers, sons, and brothers-in-law. Women, again, are not similarly restrained by these ambiguities, which operate in their case with much less force. Husband or father, mother-in-law or brother's daughter, the "others" have few interests in common with a female ego.

Fourth, all domestic households are integrated into a corporate system which articulates their differences in a highly restrictive way. No matter how bitter the conflicts between units representing subclans, they are each necessary to the other in the ritual contexts which establish individual and corporate prestige. Further, men are not able to translate directly their positions within the conjugal household into political, economic, or symbolic personal benefits. No matter how many sons he has, no matter how long established his marriage or esteemed his services as an affine, a man is essentially a stranger to his domestic unit. Further, his interests in his own clan are limited to its ceremonial-social manifestations as a collectivity, and to his own position within the name-set hierarchy. He has only a formal position in his sister's household. He must consider her husband's character as a father/son/wife-giver, and assess her sons' positions as political rivals (younger brothers) or true successors (*i-wagedu*). Although all the Gê seem to construct barriers to a man's identification with any residential unit, whether through rules of uxorilocality or ones inhibiting any marked unilineal transference of authority, the Bororo are far the most excessive in this regard. After puberty, regardless of where his domicile might be located, a Bororo man lives in the men's house. Here he transacts meaningfully with other men, and here his identity is determined. I suggest that these factors are instrumental in the complete contrast between the social and analytical significance of men's houses among the Bororo and their significance among the Shavante and Kayapó. That is, it is not the institution of the men's house *per se* which is important to comparison, but the character of a man's relations with various domestic, corporate, and categorical entities, for which the men's house merely serves as an arena of expression (see Maybury-Lewis 1967: 306–309 for the relevant counterargument).

Fifth, the principles underlying Bororo dyadic order, and the dialectics which result from their conjunction, are not founded on logical antitheses alone, but on the complex juxtaposition of these symmetrical oppositions with complementary or asymmetric polar forces. I have made this point before (Crocker 1969a, 1969b, 1971, 1973, 1977), and it still seems to me the basis of Bororo structural processes. As I remarked at the beginning of this paper, the Bororo are what Lévi-Strauss felicitously termed a "harmonic society," in that their "rule of residence," in traditional anthropological categories, is congruent with their "rule of descent." That is, they are at once "matrilineal" and "uxorilocal." Throughout this paper, I have tried to document the indigenous reasoning behind these institutions, so as to reveal it as consistent and "reasonable." One aspect of the polarities which thus emerged has not been elaborated here, since I have discussed the matter at some length in other publications. This involves the nature of nearly all Bororo polarities as mutually essential and implicatory (Lloyd 1967). Whichever Bororo dyad is considered, whether male-female, younger-older, being-becoming, village center–village periphery, domestic unit–corporate group, father-son, *aroe-bope,* or self-alter, the two poles do not basically oppose each other in a symmetrical, like-against-like fashion, but relate as logical complements, essential to each other's categorical attributes. This is not to say that in various contexts or in respect of certain of those attributes the dyads are not symmetrically related and mutually antagonistic. This tends to be true, as we have seen, of the relationships between brothers, of those between brother and sister, and even of those between the moieties. But Bororo structure rests, it seems to me, on the fundamental "unlikeness" of the dyads which generate its dialectical processes. Since Bateson proposed the attributes of asymmetric relations some time ago (1936), my usage of his insight in this context is hardly innovative. However, it may be relevant to point out that in the Bororo context, it is this asymmetry which is basic to many features of their dual organization, not some "triadic" scheme. I might further suggest that in my Bororo-derived perspective, the Northern Gê groups are just as profoundly asymmetric, while the Central Gê and Kayapó are models of symmetrical schismogenesis. The documentation of this argument must wait, but it may prove a useful mode of inquiry into "comparative dialectics."

Conclusion: Kinship, Ideology, and Culture

David Maybury-Lewis

SINCE THE PIONEERING STUDIES of Nimuendajú and the Salesians we have known that the Gê and the Bororo invested an enormous amount of energy in a rich and elaborate ceremonial life. They had in fact developed such an array of social groupings to which people were assigned for different purposes that ethnographers had a hard time keeping track of them. One was led to suspect that the Indians themselves might have had difficulty sorting out their multiplex and partially conflicting allegiances. Yet there was a common theme running through this welter of groups. Each society had at least one and often several moiety systems, and it was this pervasive dualism which led the Gê and the Bororo to be considered classic examples of "dual organization."

The cultures of Central Brazil are thus intricate and perhaps difficult to analyze, but there is nothing particularly mysterious about them. On the contrary, the supposed anomalies and puzzles of the Central Brazilian material have more often than not been in the minds of the analysts. There is therefore no need for extraordinary efforts to demystify these systems by attributing them to Incaic survivals or Amazonian invaders. Such explanations are more bizarre and considerably less well evidenced than the puzzles they are supposed to solve.

The Central Brazilian cultures have provoked bewilderment in some quarters because it was assumed that no peoples would choose to live on the *cerrados* (sometimes loosely called the savannahs) of Central Brazil in preference to the more productive forests. Therefore, either the peoples on the *cerrados* must be prehorticultural hunters and gatherers who had not taken up agriculture to any great extent, or they had been driven out of the forests by more powerful neighbors who had seized the better lands. If, then, the Central Brazilians were either weak or backward or both, how, it was thought, could they have developed such sophisticated institutions? From there is was but a step to arguing that the institutions were either diffused to them from peoples who had developed them elsewhere, or had been developed by the Gê and Bororo themselves before they were exiled to the *cerrados*.

The Indians were, until recently at any rate, unaware of the theories according to which they should, if they could, have occupied the jungles and river banks rather than remain on their inhospitable savannahs. Many of them spoke eloquently of their love for the comparatively open country of their homeland and their scorn for other Indians who "lived in the jungle like monkeys."[1] They seem to have considered their own habitat a particularly favorable one and to have prized the seminomadic existence it afforded them.[2] They had no particular difficulty in living the way they wanted to out on the savannah, and their complex institutional arrangements were supported by what they considered to be a bountiful environment. It is therefore not surprising that they have not, as far as we know, made any attempt to conquer (or reconquer) the forested lands from which some theorists suppose them to have been expelled.

In fact it is quite wrong to maintain that the Gê and the Bororo were somehow trapped on inhospitable savannahs. Bamberger showed (1967) that the Kayapó and other Gê peoples exploited a varied and bountiful environment. Most of the Central Brazilian peoples, as Turner has argued in this volume, enjoy the benefits of considerable ecological variety. All the evidence indicates that the Gê and Bororo have been living comfortably in Central Brazil since time immemorial. But in that case are not their large villages and complex social institutions still anomalous?

We lack reliable historical evidence on the size of Central Brazilian villages. The Indians did not make censuses. The chroniclers and travelers who visited them usually translated accounts of "many Indians" in a given place into arbitrary and probably exaggerated figures. Yet even if we discount these exaggerations, it is clear that the villages[3] of the Central Brazilian peoples were on the average larger than those of the tropical forest tribes. But this piece of evidence could just as well indicate that these were relatively secure societies, living in a plentiful environment which provided them with a wide variety of resources.

Furthermore, the traditional view of these Central Brazilian societies as "marginal" ones, depending primarily on hunting and gathering with little or no agriculture, is an inaccurate generalization. Nimuendajú's work early cast doubt on it. Our own results have shown that all Central Brazilian societies practice some agriculture and that some of them do a great deal of it. Yet it was possible for societies to manage on the *cerrados* with the barest minimum of agriculture. During the year I spent observing one Shavante village in 1958–1959, its inhabitants spent about three weeks working in their gardens, the produce of which could not have sustained the community for more than two months at the outside. Among the Shavante, then, hunting and gathering were the basic subsistence activities, with agriculture providing a bonus. This could very well have been the traditional way of life of the Central Brazilian peoples on the *cerrados,* and it could easily support villages of between 100 and 400 people.

The only "mystery" in Central Brazil is that people who could manage very well on the *cerrados* with comparatively little agriculture and who had a relatively backward material culture should have developed such complex social institutions. This problem, however, only looms large for those who still try to see the world through the blinkers of an evolutionary typology which assumes that levels of technological achievement must correspond to levels of sociological sophistication in given cultures. Such an assumption ought to have been discarded in the face of our knowledge that the technologically "backward" Australian aborigines developed highly elaborate social and philosophical systems. The Central Brazilian material confirms that such a feat is not unique to Australia.

Although there is nothing anomalous about the cultures of Central Brazil, their analysis does pose some special problems. Certain ordinary anthropological concepts prove inadequate. Previous anthropological theories do not quite work. All of which is fascinating for the students of the Gê and the Bororo, but it also has implications which transcend Central Brazil.

The first difficulty is with the interpretation of the Indians' descent systems. The Northern Gê and the Bororo were originally reported to have matrilineal institutions, in contrast to those of the Central Gê, which were patrilineal.[4] This raised the question of how and why such a difference should have come about. We were clearly dealing with a "culture area" of some sort. If all these societies were closely related historically and linguistically, how could they differ on such a fundamental point? Or were matriliny and patriliny perhaps not so diametrically opposed? Were they perhaps relatively insignificant? Finally, how could one understand the curious system of "parallel descent" so tantalizingly sketched for the Apinayé by Nimuendajú (1939) and on which some authors (for example, Lévi-Strauss 1952) had laid such theoretical weight?

I am pleased, on both intellectual and personal grounds, that the "Apinayé anomaly" has now been cleared up by Roberto da Matta.[5] It is gratifying to have confirmation of my original idea (Maybury-Lewis 1960) that the parallelism of Apinayé succession was anomalous as a "descent system" and could not, in any case, have been the major "descent system" of the tribe. Nor am I distressed that my alternative suggestion as to how the Apinayé system did work proved to be quite incorrect, for that suggestion was based on an attempted formal analysis of the Apinayé kinship terminology of a kind which I now believe to be misguided.

The resolution of this apparent anomaly has an important bearing on the question of matriliny versus patriliny in Central Brazil, for it focuses attention on the unsatisfactory way in which the term *descent* has all too frequently been used. Our analyses showed that not only is there nothing which can usefully be called parallel descent among the Apinayé, but there is nothing either which can usefully be called matrilineal descent among any of the Northern Gê peoples. All the Central Brazilian societies practice uxorilocal residence, with the result that they contain extended families or households or even household clusters grouped around lines of interrelated females. These are not, except among the Bororo, given any institutional recognition and are not, save again among the Bororo, used to form matrilineages. The supposed matriliny of the Northern Gê is thus a misinterpretation based on the cumulative effects of uxorilocality.

This finding alters the nature of the problem. There are not diametrically opposed principles vying with each other among the peoples of Central Brazil. They share a common set of cultural parameters, within which differences of emphasis produce Timbira, Kayapó, Shavante, or Bororo, as the case may be.

One of the basic features of this complex is the rule of uxorilocal residence after marriage. We know now not only that this is common to the Gê and Bororo, but that it is the rule in many societies of lowland South America. Indeed, more and more cases are being discovered of uxorilocality combined with patriliny,[6] a pattern which was still regarded as highly anomalous when I was writing up my Shavante data (Murdock 1949: 217–218). Terence Turner suggests that the uxorilocal rule is explicable as a mechanism for enabling men to exercise control by retaining their daughters under their authority. It is debatable whether the data from the Gê and the Bororo consistently support this hypothesis. Even if uxorilocality is used as a means of control, however, one must look to the total system of which it forms a part to understand why that particular means was selected. Uxorilocality does not "mean" the same thing everywhere,[7] and it is precisely its meaning for the Gê and the Bororo which other contributors to this volume have stressed.

While uxorilocality proved to be fundamental, the notion of *descent* was unhelpful in trying to understand or even to describe the variations in these Central Brazilian systems. Our conclusions add therefore to the growing literature of dissatisfaction surrounding the concept of *descent,* which used to be regarded as a standard and relatively unproblematic anthropological term. The ambiguities of definition and application which make the term difficult to use with any precision have now been pointed out by a number of writers.[8] The word obviously refers to the transmission of rights from one generation to the next, but which rights, how they are allocated and whether automatically, probabilistically, residually, and so forth, is frequently unspecified or a matter for debate. Needham was clearly correct in arguing (1971:8–13) that we should unravel the concept and thus entertain as a matter of course the idea that a society may at a given moment have various formally distinct ways of transmitting rights between generations. I would go further. Our Central Brazilian data show that there are yet more variables which should be included in even a formal discussion of descent rules. It seems, in short, that the term *descent* does little more than indicate an area of analytical interest. In our discussion of Central Brazil, we have had to break it down in order to develop a language precise enough to analyse the Gê and the Bororo.

All these societies make a sharp distinction between the public and the private domains, between the forum, where the ceremonial life of the society is conducted, and the household, to which everyday affairs are relegated. Among the Northern Gê, it is further held that each individual has a dual nature. He has a social persona acquired through names which are passed on through certain categories of relatives and which allocate him to appropriate ceremonial groups. But he acquires his physical substance from both of his parents, and this physical persona has its corresponding role in the domestic sphere. Not all of the Central Brazilian societies make this distinction so clearly, but it does provide the terms of a dialectic which is common to all of them. The statuses of an individual are thus allocated to different categories, according to principles which have much to do with relationships between kin but which cannot usefully be lumped together as *descent*. Moreover, these categories are not always corporate groups. They are frequently little more than social fields from which groups can be recruited when the occasion demands it.

Even those societies which are said to have unilineal descent systems (the Sherente, the Shavante, and the Bororo) differ markedly from one another in the nature of what is implied by *descent*. Furthermore, descent is only one among the major structuring principles of their social systems.

Analyses of the Gê and the Bororo in terms of unilineal descent and corporate group formation are thus not very helpful. But attempts to treat them as alliance systems have been little more illuminating. Yet it was inevitable that, as examples of "dual organization," they should be included in the debates concerning elementary structures of kinship and exogamous moiety systems. Lévi-Strauss included the Apinayé and the Bororo as elementary structures in his impressive work on the topic (1949), but he seems to have felt from the start that the Central Brazilian peoples did not fit very well into this category. He therefore devoted a paper to them a few years later (1952), arguing that there was more to these societies than exogamous moiety systems and suggesting alternative ways of looking at them. He followed this up with another paper (1956) in which he argued that the symmetry of Central Brazilian societies was illusory and that they were really asymmetrical systems. It need only be said here that I disagree with Lévi-Strauss where he argues that the dualism of the Gê and the Bororo is some sort of ideological smoke screen, masking a different and asymmetric reality. I agree with Lévi-Strauss, however, where he separates the whole concept of dual organization from that of alliance.

It might seem perfectly reasonable to treat at least the Bororo, the Shavante, and the Sherente as alliance systems, since we know that these societies have exogamous moieties or have had them in the past. But to consider them as alliance systems means stressing the primary importance in them of the communication of women[9] through marriage, and it is precisely this primacy which our analyses do not confirm. The Sherente have retained much of their binary organization, although they have now abandoned moiety exogamy. The Shavante had moiety exogamy in only part of their society and everywhere spoke of the we-they opposition as a categorical and political matter in which marriage was a minor mechanism. Christopher Crocker's paper in this volume shows similarly that the marriage relationship was not the dominant one in the complex web of connections between Bororo moieties. While it is thus possible to treat these societies as instances of prescriptive alliance in a purely formal sense, there seems little point in doing so, for such a classification actually obscures rather than elucidates the fundamental features of their organization. This classification would make an unhelpful distinction between the Northern Gê, who do not have alliance systems, and the Central Gê and the Bororo, who do or did. Since we have shown that we are dealing with a common set of cultural parameters for the Gê and the Bororo, the effect of such a classification would be simply to reduce the significance of alliance systems. This would run counter to the notion that alliance is a major ordering principle where it is found[10] and thus deprive the classification of the Bororo and Central Gê as *alliance systems* of much of its force.

Another debate over a possible alliance system in South America concerns the Siriono. I refer to that debate here because it is directly relevant to the arguments expressed in this book and because Scheffler and Lounsbury have suggested that it offers a different kind of solution to the problems raised by the Northern Gê material.

The Siriono are a small tribe in eastern Bolivia who lived in the jungles between the affluents of the Guaporé River, which in those latitudes forms the boundary between Bolivia and Brazil. They were originally studied by Holmberg (1948, 1950). Needham reanalyzed Holmberg's material and concluded that the Siriono were a matrilineal instance of asymmetric prescriptive alliance (1961, 1964). Later Scheffler and Lounsbury published an extended study of the Siriono kinship system (1971) in which they rejected Needham's characterization of the society and proposed an alternative analysis which they suggested could be extended to some of the Northern Gê systems.

The "matrilineality" of the Siriono is taken first of all from Holmberg's report that they had "matrilineal extended families" (1948:458). They were subsequently characterized as having matrilineal *descent* by Murdock (1951:44), Needham (1961:231), and, with some misgivings, Eyde and Postal (1961:769). Needham later insisted that Siriono *society* was matrilineal (1964:232) at a time when the matter was specifically being debated and when Holmberg was claiming that he had not gone beyond the statement that the Siriono had matrilocal extended families (Needham 1964:232). It appears that Holmberg became increasingly confused by the whole issue, for he is reported in a different place to have said that he might after all have overlooked the existence of lineages among the Siriono (Murdock 1962:133). This barely perceptible matriliny which was being ascribed to the Siriono derived from a confusion similar to the one which led to the postulation of matriliny among the Northern Gê. We know that the

Sirionó practiced uxorilocal residence after marriage, and they do not seem to have had any clear rule of unilineal descent. As Lounsbury and Scheffler point out (1971:161), this is a fairly common arrangement in South America. As the Northern Gê systems show, it is not an arrangement which is usefully described in terms of unilineal descent.

Needham's contention that the Sirionó have an asymmetric alliance system also raises some difficulties. The major evidence for this argument is taken from the Sirionó kinship terminology, which Needham sets out (1961:244) on a chart to demonstrate its properties. However, the terms on the chart do not discriminate between descent lines or between husband-giving and husband-receiving categories.[11] All they show is that the system is consistent with the assumption that a man must marry a woman from the kinship category *yande,* glossed as mother's brother's daughter. We do know that this is the Sirionó rule, though the precise nature of the rule and therefore of the gloss which would best characterize it is a matter for debate (see Scheffler and Lounsbury 1971:163–171). If, however, this is a rule prescribing marriage with the mother's brother's daughter, as Needham believed, then it does not have the systematic consequences in Sirionó culture and society which are supposed to follow from such a prescription.[12] In effect, the Sirionó, if they are to be classed as having an asymmetric alliance system, pose a problem for the theory of such systems. If a prescriptive rule of marriage with the mother's brother's daughter is sufficient to class theirs as an asymmetric alliance system, then it remains to be explained why this particular system (and perhaps others like it) institutionalize marriage with the mother's brother's daughter without this entailing the other categorical and social consequences which are supposed to be established on the basis of such a prescription.

I therefore share Scheffler and Lounsbury's view that it is unhelpful to view the Sirionó system as matrilineal or as an asymmetric alliance system. Yet our own research in Central Brazil lends little support to the alternative analysis of the Sirionó system which Scheffler and Lounsbury propose. They suggest that the Sirionó kinship terminology can be elucidated if we assume that it operates on a strictly genealogical basis. They then claim to show that the systematic application of certain rules generates the genealogically defined kinship classifications of the Sirionó. Finally, they discuss the social implications of those rules and the comparative implications of their study, which lead them to suggest that the Sirionó system is basically of the same type as others in South America, including various Northern Gê systems (Apinayé, Ramkokamekra, Kayapó) .

The most distinctive principle of this type of system is a parallel-transmission rule, according to which a kinsman succeeds to the kin-class status of his father and a kinswoman to that of her mother.[13] It is thus suggested that this is an important principle in the Northern Gê terminologies, which are of the same type. Scheffler and Lounsbury did not claim to make a thorough analysis of these systems, nor could they have done so, since much of the data was still unpublished at the time they wrote. Nevertheless, they made a number of suggestions concerning the Northern Gê. Aside from the importance of the parallel-transmission rule, they argued that there must have been some sort of parallelism operating in the system which produced the Apinayé moieties, even though Nimuendajú misinterpreted it in his account. They also noted the cross-sex principle governing the transmission of names in Northern Gê societies and pointed out that the Crow-Omaha oscillations of the kinship terminology appeared to be contingent features (1971:179–190) .

Yet an accumulation of such insights does not culminate in the sort of understanding of Central Brazilian systems which we have tried to communicate in this volume. On the contrary, Scheffler and Lounsbury's method is likely to lead to the conclusion that the Northern Gê systems, like that of the Sirionó, contain a core of terms which can be accurately translated by the English words *father, mother, grandfather, grandmother,* and so on.[14] A series of additional rules, of which the most important is the parallel-transmission rule, would then generate the full range of the terminology from these core meanings.

Such an analysis would distort rather than elucidate the meaning of Northern Gê kinship systems. It would miss the distinction between the public and private domains and the corresponding distinction between the social and physical aspects of the individual, which are fundamental principles of Northern Gê ideology and are expressed in their kinship systems. It would focus on the parallel transmission of kin-class status rather than on the complementarity between social transmission and physical transmission of status, and so on. One can state these omissions in a hypothetical analysis with a fair degree of certainty, since none of these points was made in Scheffler and Lounsbury's study of the Sirionó system, which they claim is of the same type. This in turn gives reasonable grounds for wondering whether similar considerations might not be at work among the Sirionó. If so Scheffler and Lounsbury's study of that system is inadequate, and inadequate in the way in which genealogically based analyses of kinship are bound to be inadequate. Such analyses focus on the terminology of kinship and its presumed genealogical referents. In other words, they select certain aspects of the use of each term (its genealogical denotata) while excluding everything else. Yet a terminology cannot be properly understood without a full consideration of its use and of the ideas behind its use. Attempts to analyze terminologies on genealogical principles tell us little or nothing about the ideology or the sociology of the people studied.

The limitations of the genealogical approach become all too clear when one considers the Central Brazilian material. In fact, we have shown that a number of traditional approaches and theories did not work in Central Brazil. But the result has not been entirely negative, for we have developed an alternative approach which does work. The key to this approach lies in its emphasis on ideology. Its prime assumptions are that kinship systems are ideological matrices and that their integrative or linking functions are so important that they cannot profitably be analyzed on their own. This has, of course, been previously recognized to some extent, as the debates over whether kinship has any content go to show. Yet many analysts admit that "kinship" may refer to all sorts of things but then return to what they either implicitly or explicitly believe it *really* deals with, and concentrate on that domain. We have tried instead to follow through from our own initial assumptions and treat kinship analysis systematically as part of a wider investigation of cultural categories. We are not, of course, the first scholars to attempt this. Our work grows out of a tradition which dates back at least to Durkheim, but it is a tradition which has been fitfully developed and only spasmodically applied. That is why Schneider (1968, 1972) still needed to advocate such an approach and why there are still relatively few studies which put it into effect.

The implications of all this should by now be clear. The Central Brazilian systems show up the inadequacy of some of the previous concepts and classifications used in the study of "kinship," but they also provide us with some useful lessons. They have forced us to go back to first principles and therefore to break down the systems we were dealing with into what appeared to be their constituent elements in order to rethink them.[15] The results are a series of componential analyses. But these componential analyses do not simply deal with distinctions of the sort which were originally outlined by Kroeber in his classic paper (1909) and which have guided the practice of componential analysis ever since. They show instead how basic notions of nature and culture, individual and society, male and female, ceremonial and instrumental, public and private, and so on, fit together in these Central Brazilian cultures to form coherent patterns of thought and guides to action.

The acting out of these ideologies is, of course, far from mechanical. The neatness of anthropological models derives from the analyses rather than from the action systems being analyzed. The Gê and Bororo show yet again, if any further demonstration of this point is needed, that kinship systems which order complex and intricate societies do not need to be used with a rigid or automatic precision. Flexibility does not lead to confusion. On the contrary, these people use their systems with a high degree of flexibility, and yet the systems are informed by ideologies which can be precisely and if necessary formally represented.

That is why we have attached such importance to the natives' theories of their own cultures, for it is through these that we have tried to understand the logic of their classifications and the meaning and use of their kinship systems. The enterprise has enabled us to clear up many of the supposed anomalies of Central Brazilian ethnography and to develop a framework for the intensive comparative analyses of these societies. It has also led my colleagues to develop their analyses of naming systems, which I consider to be one of the most significant advances to come out of our work, and, as a corollary, led them to a fresh understanding of the way in which kinship systems can be used by societies to link domains which are otherwise considered separate.

Nimuendajú long ago reported the critical importance of naming among the Timbira, but confessed that he had been unable to understand how it worked (1946:77–82). When my colleagues came to try to unravel the systems, they discovered that, in a welter of anthropological references to names and their significance, there were few comprehensive treatments of the topic to which they could turn for help. So the papers by Lave, Melatti, da Matta, and Crocker are important contributions to a somewhat neglected topic.

Furthermore, it was this inquiry into the ideology and practice of naming which enabled us to understand the basic premises of Central Brazilian social theory. Nor was this all. We saw that naming was as effective a means of setting up social categories, organizing groups, and allocating new people to them as descent or filiation. In fact, the Central Brazilian peoples used naming and filiation through kinship as alternative principles of social organization. They could be used to reinforce each other, as they are reported to have done among the Sherente in times past (Nimuendajú 1942:42–46, 52–54), or they could be used to counterbalance each other, as they still do among the Northern Gê. Melatti makes this point well when he says that Krahó men see their names as continuing in the households, while they themselves move across to their wives' households to be physically continued there.

This theme of balance and complementarity is a fundamental preoccupation of the Gê and the Bororo. It informs their theory of the individual just as it does their theory of society. They order their cultural classifications in accordance with it, and it regulates their social organization and their social action. It is in this sense that they can be viewed as "dual organizations." Thus I disagree with Terence Turner where he derives this whole ideology from the control exercised by men over their daughters, uxorilocality, and a resulting generation of moiety and age-set systems which serve as models of and regulating mechanisms for the passage of men from their natal to their affinal families. This view seems to me to be overinfluenced by the special circumstances of the Kayapó, a limiting case where dual organization has been all but exploded by political factionalism.

I take a rather different view of these Central Brazilian systems. All societies attempt to live out their own view of the world, and there are many which believe that the universe is an organization of antithetical principles. The remarkable thing about the societies of Central Brazil is that until comparatively recently they seemed to be in a position to live out a social theory of this sort with a minimum of external constraint. They were relatively unaffected by pressures from other peoples or by environmental limitations. Their own societies were homogenous, unstratified, and egalitarian both in theory and in practice, since there were no means easily available for groups of indviduals to establish control over others. Their wars and their feuds often resulted in the breakup of their communities, but not in the erosion of the system which the villages represented. Like the Australians described by Meggitt (1972), they were remote enough to perfect their own dreamtime. But the dreamtime of Central Brazil was interwoven with the profane flow of day-to-day activities in the villages. The Gê and the Bororo could literally live their dream. In such societies, individuals could go about their daily business of hunting and gathering, fighting and making love, and at the same time be playing roles in the drama of opposition and resolution, of antithesis and harmony, which made up their view of the world.

References
Notes
Index

References

Introduction

Barlaeus, C. 1647. *Rerum per octennium in Brasilia et alibi nuper gestarum, sub praefectura Mauritii Nassoviae comitis, etc. Historia.* Amsterdam.

Baro, R. 1651. *Relation du voyage de Rovlox Baro, interprète et ambassadeur ordinaire de la Compagnie des Indes d'Occident, de la part des illustrissmes seigneurs des provinces unies au pays des Tapuies dans la terre ferme du Brésil* (1647). Paris.

Coelho dos Santos, Silvio. 1973. *Indios e brancos no sul do Brasil.* Florianópolis, Brazil: EDEME.

Colbacchini, A., and C. Albisetti. 1942. *Os Boróros orientais orarimogodógue do planalto oriental de Mato Grosso.* São Paulo: Companhia editora nacional.

Haeckel, J. 1939. Zweiklassensystem, Männerhaus und Totemismus in Südamerika. *Zeitschrift für Ethnologie* 70:426–454.

Lévi-Strauss, C. 1944. On dual organization in South America. *América Indígena* 4:37–47.

Marcgrav, J. 1648. *Historia naturalis Brasiliae.* Amsterdam.

Maybury-Lewis, D. 1960. Parallel descent and the Apinayé anomaly. *Southwestern Journal of Anthropology* 16:191–216.

———. 1965. Some crucial distinctions in Central Brazilian ethnology. *Anthropos* 60:340–358.

———. 1971. Recent research in Central Brazil. *Proceedings of the 38th International Congress of Americanists* (Stuttgart-Munich, 1968) 3:333–391.

Meggitt, M. 1972. Understanding Australian aboriginal society: kinship systems or cultural categories? In *Kinship studies in the Morgan centennial year,* ed. P. Reining. Washington, D.C.: Anthropological Society of Washington, D.C.

Nimuendajú, C. 1939. *The Apinayé.* Washington, D.C.: Catholic University of America.

———. 1942. *The Šerente.* F. W. Hodge Anniversary Publication Fund. Los Angeles: The Southwest Museum.

———. 1946. *The Eastern Timbira.* Berkeley: University of California Press.

315

Steward, J. 1946. *Handbook of South American Indians,* vol. 1, bulletin 143. Washington, D.C.: Smithsonian Institution.

Urban, Gregory P. 1978. A model of Shokleng social reality. Ph.D. diss., Department of Anthropology, University of Chicago.

Von Martius, Carl. 1867. *Beiträge zur Ethnographie und Sprachenkunde Amerika's zumal Brasiliens.* Leipzig.

1. Cycles and Trends in Krikatí Naming Practices

Crocker, William H. 1966. Ramkokamekra-Canella factionalism. Working paper, Harvard Gê Seminar.

Lave, Jean. 1972. "Some suggestions for the interpretation of residence, descent, and exogamy among the Eastern Timbira." *Proceedings of the 38th International Congress of Americanists* 3:341–345.

————. 1975. Inter-moiety-system systems: a structural explanation of the proliferation of Ramkokamekra ceremonial associations. Social Sciences Working Papers 69a and 69b, University of California, Irvine.

————. 1976. Eastern Timbira moiety systems in time and space: a complex structure. *Actes du XLII Congrès International des Américanistes* (Paris) 2:309–321.

Lounsbury, F. G. 1964. A formal account of the Crow- and Omaha-type kinship terminologies. In *Explorations in Cultural Anthropology: Essays in honor of George Peter Murdock,* ed. Ward H. Goodenough. New York: McGraw-Hill.

Nimuendajú, Curt, 1946. *The Eastern Timbira.* Berkeley: University of California Press.

2. The Relationship System of the Krahó

Câmara Cascudo, Luis da. 1962. *Dicionário do folclore brasileiro,* 2nd ed. Rio de Janeiro: Instituto Nacional do Livro.

Carneiro da Cunha, Manuela. 1978. *Os mortos e os outros: uma análise do sistema funerário e da noção de pessôa entre os índios Krahó.* São Paulo: HUCITEC.

Da Matta, Roberto. 1967. Mito e autoridade doméstica: uma tentativa de análise de um mito Timbira em suas relações com a estrutura social. *Revista do Instituto de Ciências Sociais,* 4 (1):93–141.

Lounsbury, Floyd G. 1964. A formal account of the Crow- and Omaha-type kinship terminologies. *In Explorations in Cultural Anthropology: Essays in honor of George Peter Murdock,* ed. Ward H. Goodenough. New York: McGraw-Hill.

Maybury-Lewis, David. 1967. *Akwẽ-Shavante society.* Oxford: Clarendon Press.

Melatti, Julio Cezar. 1967. *Indios e criadores: a situação dos Krahó na area pastoril do Tocantins.* Rio de Janeiro: UFRJ.

Murdock, George Peter. 1949. *Social structure.* New York: Macmillan.

Nimuendajú, Curt. 1946. *The Eastern Timbira.* Berkeley: University of California Press.

Radcliffe-Brown, A. R. 1965. *Structure and function in primitive society.* New York: The Free Press.

3. The Apinayé Relationship System

Da Matta, R. 1970. Apinayé social structure. Ph.D. diss., Harvard University.

————. 1973. A reconsideration of Apinayé social morphology. In *Peoples and cultures of native South America*, ed. D. R. Gross. New York: Doubleday/ Natural History Press.

Douglas, M. 1968. The relevance of tribal studies. *Journal of Psychosomatic Research*, vol. 2.

Dumont, L. 1970. *Homo hierarchicus: the caste system and its implications.* Chicago: University of Chicago Press.

Fox, R. 1967a. *Kinship and marriage.* Baltimore: Penguin Books.

————. 1967b. *The Keresan bridge: a problem in Pueblo ethnology.* London: Athlone Press.

Harris, M. 1968. *The rise of anthropological theory.* New York: Thomas Crowell.

Henry, Jules. 1940. Review of *The Apinayé* by Curt Nimuendajú. *American Anthropologist* 42:337–338.

Holmberg, A. 1960. *Nomads of the long bow: the Sirionó of Eastern Bolivia.* Chicago: University of Chicago Press.

Kroeber, A. L. 1917. *Zuñi kin and clan.* Anthropological Papers of the American Museum of Natural History, vol. 18, part II. New York.

————. 1942. The societies of primitive man. *Biological Symposia* 8:205–216.

Lave, J. C. 1967. Social taxonomy among the Krĩkatí (Gê) of Central Brazil. Ph.D. diss., Harvard University.

Lévi-Strauss, C. 1949. *Les structures élémentaires de la parenté.* Paris: Presses Universitaires de France.

————. 1962. *La pensée sauvage.* Paris: Plon.

————. 1963. *Structural anthropology.* Garden City, N.Y.: Doubleday.

Lounsbury, F., and H. Scheffler. 1971. *A study in structural semantics: the Sirionó kinship system.* Englewood Cliffs, N.J.: Prentice-Hall.

Lowie, Robert H. 1940. American culture history. *American Anthropologist* 42:409–428.

Maybury-Lewis, D. 1960. Parallel descent and the Apinayé anomaly. *Southwestern Journal of Anthropology* 16:191–216.

————. 1967. *Akwẽ-Shavante society.* Oxford: Clarendon Press.

Melatti, Julio Cezar. 1967. *Índios e criadores: a situação dos Krahó na área pastoril do Tocantins.* Monografias do Instituto de Ciências Sociais. Rio de Janeiro.

————. 1970. O sistema social Krahó. Ph.D. diss., University of São Paulo.

Murdock, G. P. 1949. *Social structure.* New York: Macmillan.

Nimuendajú, C. 1939. *The Apinayé.* Washington, D.C.: Catholic University of America.

————. 1956. *Os Apinayé.* Bulletin of the Museu Paraense Emilio Goeldi, vol. 12. Belém do Para, Brazil.

Nimuendajú, C., and R. H. Lowie. 1937. The dual organization of the Ramkokamekra (Canella) of Northern Brazil. *American Anthropologist* 39:565–582.

Rivière, P. G. 1974. The couvade: a problem reborn. *Man* n.s. 9 (3) :423–435.

Rose, F. G. G. 1960. *Classification of kin, age structure and marriage amongst the Groote Eylandt aborigines.* Berlin: Akademie-Verlag.

Scheffler, H. W. 1966. Ancestor worship in anthropology, or observations on descent and descent groups. *Current Anthropology* 7:541–551.

———. 1969. Comments on social organization of the Central Brazilian tribes. Mimeo.

Schneider, D., and John Roberts. 1956. Zuni kin terms. Notebook 3, Laboratory of Anthropology, The University of Nebraska.

Tax, S. 1937. Some problems of social organization. In *Social anthropology of North American tribes,* ed. F. Eggan. Chicago: University of Chicago Press.

Turner, T. 1966. Social structure and political organization among the Northern Kayapó. Ph.D. diss., Harvard University.

Turner, V. 1968. *The drums of affliction: a study of religious processes among the Ndembu of Zambia.* Oxford: Clarendon Press and the International African Institute.

———. 1969. *The ritual process: structure and anti-structure.* Chicago: Aldine.

Zuidema, R. T. 1969. Hierarchy in symmetric alliance systems. *Bijdragen tot de Taal-, Land-en Volkenkunde* 125:134–139.

4. Exit and Voice in Central Brazil

Audrin, José M. 1947. *Entre Sertanejos e índios do norte.* Rio de Janeiro: Pugil Limitada.

Bamberger, Joan. 1971. The adequacy of Kayapó ecological adjustment. *Proceedings of the 38th Congress of Americanists* (Stuttgart-Munich 1968) 3:373–379.

———. 1974. Naming and the transmission of status in a Central Brazilian society. *Ethnology* 13:363–378.

Carneiro, Robert L. 1961. Slash-and-burn cultivation among the Kuikuru and its implications for cultural development in the Amazon basin. In *The evolution of horticultural systems in native South America: causes and consequences—a symposium,* ed. J. Wilbert (*Antropologica,* Supplement 2). Caracas: Editorial Sucre.

Coudreau, Henri. 1897. *Voyage au Tocantins-Araguaya.* Paris: A. Lanure.

Hirschman, Albert O. 1970. *Exit, voice, and loyalty: responses to decline in firms, organizations, and states.* Cambridge, Mass.: Harvard University Press.

———. 1974. Exit, voice, and loyalty: further reflections and a survey of recent contributions. *Social Science Information* 13:7–26.

———. 1978. Exit, voice, and the state. *World Politics* 31:90–107.

Krause, Fritz. 1911. *In den Wildnissen Brasiliens; Bericht und Ergebnisse der Leipziger Araguaya-Expedition 1908.* Leipzig: R. Voigtlander.

Lévi-Strauss, Claude. 1955. *Tristes tropiques.* Paris: Plon.

Lowie, Robert H. 1948. Some aspects of political organization among the American aborigines. *Journal of the Royal Anthropological Institute* 78 (1–2):11–24.

Meggers, Betty J. 1954. Environmental limitation on the development of culture. *American Anthropologist* n.s. 56:801–824.

————. 1971. *Amazonia: man and culture in a counterfeit paradise.* Chicago: Aldine-Atherton.

Murdock, George P., ed. 1960. *Social structure in Southeast Asia.* Viking Fund Publications in Anthropology, no. 29: New York: Viking Press.

5. The Gê and Bororo Societies as Dialectical Systems

Bamberger, J. 1967. Environment and cultural classification: A study of the Northern Kayapó. Ph.D. diss., Harvard University.

————. 1971. The adequacy of Kayapó ecological adjustment. In *Verhandlungen des XXXVIII Internationalen Amerikanisten-kongresses* (Munich), 3:373–380.

Bateson, G. 1968. *Naven.* Stanford: Stanford University Press.

————. 1972. *Steps to an ecology of mind.* New York: Ballantine Books.

Carneiro, R. L. 1960. Slash-and-burn agriculture: a closer look at its implications for settlement patterns. *Men and cultures,* ed. A. F. C. Wallace, 229–234.

Cooper, J. M. 1942. The South American marginal cultures. *Proceedings of the 8th American Scientific Congress* 2: 147–160.

Coudreau, H. 1897. *Voyage au Tocantins-Araguaya.* Paris: A. Lanure.

Crocker, C. 1967. The social organization of the Eastern Bororo. Ph.D. diss., Harvard University.

————. n.d. Working notes on the Bororo,2:ecology and economics. Unpublished ms., University of Virginia.

Goldman, I. 1963. *The Cubeo.* Illinois Studies in Anthropology, no. 2. Urbana: University of Illinois Press.

Haeckel, J. 1952–53. Neue Beiträge zur Kulturschichtung Brasiliens. *Anthropos* 47:963–991 and 48:105–157.

Hugh-Jones, C. Working paper on Barasana (Tukano) social organization. Unpublished ms., Cambridge University.

Lathrap, D. 1968. The "hunting" economies of the tropical forest zone of South America. In *Man the hunter,* ed. R. B. Lee and I. DeVore. Chicago: Aldine.

Lave, J. 1967. Social taxonomy among the Krĩkatí (Gê) of Central Brazil. Ph.D. diss., Harvard University.

Lévi-Strauss, C. 1944. On dual organization in South America. *America Indigena* 4:37–47.

————. 1952. Les structures sociales dans le Brésil central et oriental. In *Selected Papers of the 29th International Congress of Americanists* (New York), ed. Sol Tax. Chicago: University of Chicago Press.

————. 1956. Les organisations dualistes existent-elles? *Bijdragen tot de Taal-, Land-, en Volkenkunde* 112:99–128.

————. 1958. La notion d'archaisme en ethnologie. *Cahiers Internationaux de Sociologie* 12:32–35.

Lowie, R. 1952. The heterogeneity of marginal cultures. In *Indian tribes of aboriginal America: selected papers of the 29th International Congress of Americanists,* ed. S. Tax. Chicago: University of Chicago Press.

Marx, K. 1958. *Capital,* trans. Samuel Moore and Edward Aveling, vol. I. New York: International Publishers.

————. 1967. *The German Ideology*. In *Writings of the young Marx on philosophy and society*, ed. L. Easton and K. Guddat, part I. New York: Doubleday.

Maybury-Lewis, D. 1967. *Akwē-Shavante society*. Oxford: Clarendon Press.

————. n.d. Sherente. Unpublished working paper.

Melatti, J. 1970. *O sistema social Krahó* Ph.D. Diss., University of São Paulo.

Nimuendajú, C. 1939. *The Apinayé*. Catholic University of America Anthropology Series, no. 8. Catholic University Press: Washington, D.C.

————. 1942. *The Šerente*. F. W. Hodge Anniversary Publication Fund. Los Angeles: The Southwest Museum.

————. 1946. *The Eastern Timbira*. University of California Publications in American Archaeology and Ethnology, vol. 41. Berkeley: University of California Press.

Ollman, B. 1971. *Alienation: Marx's conception of man in capitalist society*. Cambridge: Cambridge University Press.

Piaget, J. 1970. *Structuralism*. New York: Basic Books.

Seeger, A. 1974. Nature and culture and their transformations in the cosmology and social organization of the Suyá. Ph.D. diss., University of Chicago.

Steward, J., and L. Faron. 1959. *Native peoples of South America*. McGraw-Hill: New York.

6. Kinship, Household, and Community Structure among the Kayapó

Bamberger, J. 1974. Naming and the transmission of status in a Central Brazilian society. *Ethnology* 13 (4) :363:378.

Fortes, Meyer. 1958. Introduction. In *The developmental cycle in domestic groups*, ed. Jack Goody. Cambridge Papers in Social Anthropology, no. 1. Cambridge: Cambridge University Press.

Goody, Jack. 1958. The fission of domestic groups among the LoDagaba. In *The developmental cycle in domestic groups*, ed. Jack Goody. Cambridge Papers in Social Anthropology, no. 1, Cambridge: Cambridge University Press.

Leach, E. R. 1958. Concerning Trobriand clans and the kinship category *tabu*. In *The developmental cycle in domestic groups*, ed. Jack Goody. Cambridge Papers in Social Anthropology, no. 1. Cambridge: Cambridge University Press.

7. Cultural Categories of the Central Gê

Barnes, J. A. 1962. African models in the New Guinea Highlands. *Man* 62:5–9.

Cook, W. A. 1909. *Through the wilderness of Brazil, by horse, canoe and float*. New York: American Tract Society.

Dumont, L. 1953. The Dravidian kinship terminology as an expression of marriage. *Man* 54:34–39.

Homans, G. C., and D. Schneider. 1955. *Marriage, authority, and final causes*. Glencoe, Ill.: The Free Press.

Keesing, R. 1970. Shrines, ancestors, and cognatic descent: the Kwaio and the Tallensi. *American Anthropologist* 72:755–775.

Kroeber, A. A. 1942. Societies of primitive man. *Biological Symposia* 8:205–216.

———. 1948. *Anthropology*. New York: Harcourt, Brace.

Lévi-Strauss, C. 1952. Les structures sociales dans le Brésil central et oriental. In *Indian tribes of aboriginal America,* ed. S. Tax. Chicago: University of Chicago Press.

———. 1958. L'analyse structurale en linguistique et en anthropologie. In Lévi-Strauss, *Anthropologie structurale*. Paris: Plon.

Maybury-Lewis, D. 1958. Kinship and social organization in Central Brazil. *Proceedings of the 32nd International Congress of Americanists* (Copenhagen), pp. 123–136.

———. 1965a. Prescriptive marriage systems. *Southwestern Journal of Anthropology* 21:207–230.

———. 1965b. *The savage and the innocent*. London: Evans.

———. 1965c. Some crucial distinctions in Central Brazilian ethnology. *Anthropos* 60:340–358.

———. 1967. *Akwẽ-Shavante society*. Oxford: Clarendon Press.

———. 1971. Recent research in Central Brazil. *Proceedings of the 38th International Congress of Americanists* (Stuttgart-Munich, 1968) 3:333–391.

Murdock, G. P. 1949. *Social structure*. New York: Macmillan.

Needham, R. 1958. The formal analysis of prescriptive patrilateral cross-cousin marriage. *Southwestern Journal of Anthropology* 14:199–219.

———. 1962. *Structure and sentiment*. Chicago: University of Chicago Press.

———. 1967. *Rethinking kinship and marriage*. London: Tavistock.

Nimuendajú, C. 1942. *The Šerente*. F. W. Hodge Anniversary Publication Fund. Los Angeles: The Southwest Museum.

———. 1946. *The Eastern Timbira*. University of California Publications in American Archaeology and Ethnology, vol. 41. Berkeley: University of California Press.

Radcliffe-Brown, A. R. 1952. The mother's brother in South Africa. In Radcliffe-Brown, *Structure and function in primitive society*. London: Cohen and West.

———. 1950. Introduction. In *African systems of kinship and marriage,* ed. Radcliffe-Brown and D. Forde. London: Oxford University Press.

Robertson Smith, W. 1885. *Kinship and marriage in early Arabia*. London.

8. Selves and Alters among the Eastern Bororo

Albisetti, C., and A. J. Venturelli. 1962. *Enciclopédia Bororo,* vol. I. Campo Grande, Brazil: Museu Regional Dom Bosco.

Colbacchini, A., and C. Albisetti. 1942. *Os Boróros orientais orarimogodógue do planalto oriental de Mato Grosso*. São Paulo: Companhia editora nacional.

Crocker, J. A. 1967. Social organization of the Eastern Bororo. Ph.D. diss., Harvard University.

————. 1969a. Reciprocity and hierarchy among the Eastern Bororo. *Man* 4:44–48.

————. 1969b. Men's house associates among the Eastern Bororo. *Southwestern Journal of Anthropology* 25:236–260.

————. 1970. Bororo. *The Encyclopaedia Britannica.*

————. 1971. The dialectics of Bororo social reciprocity. *Proceedings of the 38th International Congress of Americanists* (Stuttgart-Munich, 1956) 3:387–391.

————. 1972. Lineal equations in a two-section system: Bororo relationship terminology. Unpublished ms.

————. 1973. Ritual and social structure. In *The roots of ritual,* ed. J. Shaugnessy. Grand Rapids: Erdman's.

————. 1977. My brother the parrot. In *The social use of metaphor,* ed. J. D. Sapir and J. C. Crocker. Philadelphia: University of Pennsylvania Press.

Greenberg, J. H. 1960. The general classification of Central and South American languages. In *Selected papers of the fifth international congress of anthropological and ethnological sciences* (1956), ed. A. Wallace. Philadelphia: University of Pennsylvania Press.

Kaufmann, W. A. 1966. *Hegel: a reinterpretation.* Garden City, N.Y.: Doubleday.

Lévi-Strauss, C. 1936. Contribution a l'étude d'organisation sociale des Indiens Bororo. *Journal de la Société des Américanistes* 28:269–304.

————. 1955. *Tristes tropiques.* Paris: Plon.

————. 1958. *Anthropologie structurale.* Paris: Plon.

————. 1960. On manipulated sociological models. *Bijdragen tot de Taal-, Land- en Volkenkunde* 116:45–52.

————. 1963a. *Totemism.* Boston: Beacon Press.

————. 1963b. The bear and the barber. *Journal of the Royal Anthropological Institute* 93: 1–11.

————. 1964. *Mythologiques: le cru et le cuit.* Paris: Plon.

————. 1969. *The elementary structures of kinship.* London: Eyre and Spottiswoode.

————. 1970. *The raw and the cooked.* New York: Harper & Row.

Lloyd, G. E. R. 1966. *Polarity and analogy: two types of argumentation in Greek thought.* Cambridge: Cambridge University Press.

Maybury-Lewis, D. 1960. The analysis of dual organizations: a methodological critique. *Bijdragen tot de Taal-, Land- en Volkenkunde* 116:17–44.

————. 1967. *Akwē-Shavante Society.* Oxford: Clarendon Press.

Montenegro, O. P. 1958. Conservadorismo e mudança na cultura bororo. Plano de Pesquisa. Rio de Janeiro. CAPES.

Needham, R. 1969. Preface. In Lévi-Strauss, *Elementary structures of kinship.* London: Eyre and Spottiswoode.

Petrullo, V. M. Primitive peoples of Mato Grosso, Brazil. *The Museum Journal* 23:83–173.

Radcliffe-Brown, A. R. 1950. Introduction. In *African systems of kinship and marriage,* ed. A. R. Radcliffe-Brown and D. Forde. London: Oxford University Press.

Steinen, K. von den. 1940. *Entre os aborígenes do Brasil Central* (Portuguese translation by Egon Schaden of *Unter den Naturvölkern Zentral-Brasiliens*) . São Paulo.

Turner, T. 1971. Northern Kayapó social structure. *Proceedings of the 38th International Congress of Americanists* (Stuttgart-Munich, 1968) 3:365–371.

Turner, V. 1967. *The forest of symbols*. Ithaca: Cornell University Press.

Worsley, P. M. 1956. The kinship system of the Tallensi: a reevaluation. *Journal of the Royal Anthropological Institute* 86:37–75.

Conclusion

Bamberger, Joan. 1967. Environment and cultural classification; a study of the Northern Kayapó. Ph.D. diss., Harvard University.

Barth, F. 1973. Descent and marriage reconsidered. In *The character of kinship*, ed. J. R. Goody. Cambridge: Cambridge University Press.

Colbacchini, A., and C. Albisetti. 1942. *Os Boróros orientais orarimogodógue do planalto oriental de Mato Grosso*. São Paulo: Companhia editora nacional.

Eyde, D., and P. Postal. 1961. Avunculocality and incest: the development of unilateral cross-cousin marriage and Crow-Omaha kinship systems. *American Anthropologist* 63:747–771.

Holmberg, A. 1948. The Sirionó. In *Handbook of South American Indians*, vol. III, ed. J. Steward. Bureau of American Ethnology Bulletin no. 143 Washington, D.C.: Smithsonian Institution.

———. 1950. *Nomads of the long bow*. Institute of Social Anthropology Publications, no. 10. Washington, D.C.: Smithsonian Institution.

Kensinger, K. n.d. Fact and fiction in Cashinahua marriage. In *Marriage practices in lowland South America*, ed. K. Kensinger. Forthcoming.

Kracke, W. 1976. Uxorilocality in patriliny: Kagwahiv filial separation. *Ethos* 4:295–310.

Kroeber, A. L. 1909. Classificatory systems of relationship. *Journal of the Royal Anthropological Institute* 39:77–84.

Leach, E. 1961a. *Pul Eliya*. Cambridge: Cambridge University Press.

———. 1961b. *Rethinking anthropology*. London: University of London Press.

Lévi-Strauss, C. 1949. *Les structures élémentaires de la parenté*. Paris: Presses Universitaires de France.

———. 1952. Les structures sociales dans le Brésil central et oriental. In *Indian tribes of aboriginal America*, ed. S. Tax. Chicago: University of Chicago Press.

———. 1956. Les organisations dualistes, existent-elles? *Bijdragen tot de Taal-, Land- en Volkenkunde* 112:99–128.

Lewis, I. M. 1965. Problems in the comparative study of unilineal descent. In *The relevance of models for social anthropology*, ed. M. Banton. London: Tavistock Press.

Lowie, R. H. 1943. A note on the social life of the Northern Kayapó. *American Anthropologist* 45:633–636.

Da Matta, R. 1971. Uma breve reconsideração da morfologia social Apinayé. *Proceedings of the 38th International Congress of Americanists* (Stuttgart-Munich, 1968) 3:355–364.

———. 1976. *Um mundo dividido*. Petropolis: Editora Vozes.

Maybury-Lewis, D. 1960. Parallel descent and the Apinayé anomaly. *Southwestern Journal of Anthropology* 16:191–216.

———. 1965. Some crucial distinctions in Central Brazilian ethnology. *Anthropos* 60:340–358.

Meggitt, M. 1972. Understanding Australian aboriginal society: kinship systems or cultural categories? In *Kinship studies in the Morgan centennial year*, ed. P. Reining. Washington, D.C.: Anthropological Society of Washington, D.C.

Murdock, G. P. 1949. *Social structure*. New York: Macmillan.

———. 1951. *Outline of South American cultures*. New Haven: Human Relations Area Files.

———. 1962. Ethnographic atlas. *Ethnology* 1:113–134.

Murphy, R. F. 1960. *Headhunter's heritage*. Berkeley: University of California Press.

Needham, R. 1961. An analytical note on the structure of Sirionó society. *Southwestern Journal of Anthropology* 18:239–255.

———. 1964. Descent, category, and alliance in Sirionó society. *Southwestern Journal of Anthropology* 20:229–240.

———. 1971. Remarks on the analysis of kinship and marriage. In *Rethinking kinship and marriage*, ed. Needham. London: Tavistock.

———. 1973. Prescription. *Oceania* 43:166–181.

———. 1974. *Remarks and inventions: skeptical essays about kinship*. London: Tavistock.

Nimuendajú, C. 1939. *The Apinayé*. Washington, D.C.: Catholic University of America.

———. 1942. *The Šerente*. F. W. Hodge Anniversary Publication Fund. Los Angeles: The Southwest Museum.

———. 1946. *The Eastern Timbira*. Berkeley: University of California Press.

Scheffler, H., and F. Lounsbury. 1971. *A study in structural semantics: the Sirionó kinship system*. Englewood Cliffs, N.J.: Prentice-Hall.

Schneider, D. 1968. *American kinship: a cultural account*. Englewood Cliffs, N.J.: Prentice-Hall.

———. 1972. What is kinship all about? In *Kinship studies in the Morgan centennial year*, ed. P. Reining. Washington, D.C.: Anthropological Society of Washington, D.C.

Siskind, J. 1973. *To hunt in the morning*. New York: Oxford University Press.

Notes

Introduction

1. For a discussion of the relationship between the historical Tapuya and the modern Gê, see Maybury-Lewis 1965.

2. The most convenient place to look for a general statement of our ethnographic reinterpretations is in my account of the Symposium on Recent Research in Central Brazil (Maybury-Lewis 1971).

1. Cycles and Trends in Krīkatí Naming Practices

1. The end of the bathing sessions also marks the end of the prohibition on sexual relations for the child's parents.

2. Although the analysis here is concerned with interpersonal relations, the association of names with marginal positions can be extended to the level of community-wide organizations. Names are used as recruiting devices for ceremonial organizations, kin relationships as recruiting devices in domestic life. In the sense that ceremonial occasions represent a break in the even flow of life, a crisis situation, a contact with natural or supernatural dangers, it is consistent that the ceremonial system is organized as a system of named positions, just like the other marginal classes described above.

3. Of the enormous body of work Nimuendajú produced on the Gê, the Krīkatí are discussed only in *The Eastern Timbira* (1946). Most of the fieldwork on which his monograph is based was carried out among the Ramkokamekra and Apanyekra, who live about fifty miles away from the Krīkatí; all speak mutually intelligible languages. On linguistic grounds, Nimuendajú includes all three of these groups in a single subdivision, the southern group of the Eastern Timbira. But it is clear that in his judgment these groups share far more than close linguistic affinity. He describes the habitat and history of contact with Brazilians for the Timbira as a whole, emphasizing the similarities across groups. He visited the Krīkatí, and by inference from the title of his book, it may be concluded that he felt the general outlines of Ramkokamekra/Apanyekra culture to be valid for all of the Eastern Timbira.

4. Nimuendajú is ambiguous on the timing of the official establishment of a new age-set in the plaza. A new age-set probably assumed its meeting place in the plaza as it began initiation, not at the end of the ceremony. It should

be noted that the groups he designates by the term "age class" were in fact age-sets.

5. Linguistic evidence confirms this. The terms are either borrowings from related tribes that still use them (*ikamtele* and *ikachui* are Apinayé terms), or compounds built from existing kin terms (*inchigrunto, inchungrunto*), or words with other meanings used analogically in this context (*comaiyront,* sometimes with old suffixes (*comaiyront-muhum, comaiyront-menche*).

6. He does report terms for formal friends, *hupin/pemchui,* and the term for another type of ceremonial friend, *kwu'nõ.*

2. The Relationship System of the Krahó

1. This research was carried out over a number of years with six periods of fieldwork. It was originally undertaken as part of two overall research projects under the direction of Roberto Cardoso de Oliveira, namely, A Comparative Study of Indian Societies in Brazil and A Study of Areas of Interethnic Friction in Brazil. In its later stages, the research came to be carried out also in collaboration with the Harvard Central Brazil Research Project, under the direction of David Maybury-Lewis of Harvard University. The major sponsor for the work was the Sub-Reitoria de Ensino para Graduados e Pesquisa of the Federal University of Rio de Janeiro. The Fundação de Amparo à Pesquisa of the state of São Paulo and the University of Brasília each financed one of my field trips.

2. Here I am following David Maybury-Lewis's criteria for dual organization (see Maybury-Lewis 1967: 298–300).

3. I would like to take this opportunity to point out that the distribution of these groups was incorrectly described in a previous work (Melatti 1967). Both in the text and in the table on page 66 there are unfortunate typographical errors which were not corrected in proof. The correct arrangement of these groups is as follows: in the Khoirumpekëtxë moiety, on the eastern side of the central plaza of the village, from north to south—*pã, autxet, txon,* and *krẽ;* in the Hararumpekëtxë moiety on the western side of the central plaza, also from north to south, *txó, hëk, khedré,* and *kupẽ.*

4. In a previous work (Melatti 1967: 69–69), I unfortunately subsumed the domestic group and the residential segment under the single denomination of *extended family.*

5. The Gaviões Indians, a Timbira group in the state of Pará which I visited in 1961 as research assistant for Roberto da Matta, do not use the terms *itamtxua* and *iwawï* for the living, but use them only for the dead.

6. For a discussion of the cognate terms *kwu̧'nó* and *hǫpin* (feminine *pinčwei*), see Nimuendajú 1946:100 and 104.

7. In a recent work (1978) Carneiro da Cunha takes up the analysis of the idea of the person among the Krahó and sheds new light on the relations between *ikhïonõ* and between *hõpin.*

3. The Apinayé Relationship System

1. This article is based on fieldwork carried out for varying periods in the years 1962, 1966, 1966–67, 1970, and 1972. I would like to thank the follow-

ing institutions for contributing to the support of my work: the Conselho de Pesquisas of the Federal University of Rio de Janeiro, the Brazilian Conselho Nacional de Pesquisas, the Ford Foundation, and the Department of Anthropology of the National Museum in Rio de Janeiro. I also received funds from the Harvard Central Brazil Research Project.

I would like to thank Dr. Peter Rivière for his careful reading of an earlier draft of this paper and for his useful suggestions. Various graduate students in the Programa de Pos-Graduação em Antropologia Social at the National Museum in Rio de Janeiro discussed this paper during seminars, and I am grateful to them for suggestions and criticisms which have improved and clarified parts of my arguments. However, I accept entire responsibility for any errors or misinterpretations which remain.

2. As will be remembered, in this same article Nimuendajú and Lowie presented a classification of the Gê tribes and divided the Timbira into Western and Eastern groups, according to their position relative to the Tocantins River (see Nimuendajú and Lowie 1937:565). Such a classification was later elaborated by Nimuendajú (1946:6).

3. From July to October 1970, inspired by Rose (1960) I photographed all the inhabitants of an Apinayé village (São José, the most populous and important). Later I showed these photographs to a selected sample of sixteen Apinayé individuals, noting the following data: how that individual called the photographed person (if terms or names were used), why he called him thus, what such a person was to him. I managed to get some informants to arrange the photographs on a table, taking as a reference point the informant's own picture. It was curious, among other things, to notice that the Apinayé always placed the old people on the lower part of the "genealogical tree," since they are the "root" or "foot" of the village. My sample was made by considering the age of the informant, his position in the factional structure of the village, whether he was an outsider, and his sex and status in the community. A conversation with Warren Shapiro in a plane after the meetings of the American Anthropological Association in New Orleans in 1969 was very useful for the development of this technique, since Dr. Shapiro had also used similar materials.

4. The Apinayé do not consider a cut or a wound an illness, inasmuch as the person affected continues to execute his normal social activities. To be *me-o,* then, is to be in a marginal state in relation to society.

5. Some authors translate *mekaron* as soul. I prefer "image" because this seems to me to be closer to Apinayé thought, since for them everything has a *mekaron.* It so happens, though, that the "image" of real and concrete things is weak.

6. Lévi-Strauss and Mary Douglas develop similar points in connection with the same phenomenon (Lévi-Strauss 1962:258 and Douglas 1968). See also Rivière 1974.

7. When one observes that this is an inversion, since the Ipognotxoine ought to be related to the serious and regular things, like men, sun, and so on, the Apinayé say that this is correct, but that sun and moon, the two major creators of social rules, left things thus for men. It seems that the idea is that the "Ipog people" can afford to be nasty and irregular because they are superior

to the rules of behavior that control the conduct of normal persons. The inversion observed, therefore, has perhaps also an idea of transcendence, that is to say: Ipog people transcend normal and regular behavior.

8. Maybury-Lewis presented this idea during the defense of Julio Cezar Melatti's thesis and in personal communications.

9. It is curious that Fox seizes upon precisely this distinction to analyze the Cochiti social system (Fox 1967).

4. Exit and Voice in Central Brazil

1. An early version of this paper was presented in May 1975 at the Conference on Anthropological Research in Amazonia, sponsored by the Anthropology Department of Queens College, CUNY. I am grateful to Albert O. Hirschman and David Maybury-Lewis for their comments on earlier drafts.

2. Such an incident almost occurred during my fieldwork at Gorotire in 1963. Intervention by the Indian Protection Service saved the village from an all-out battle between the disputing factions.

3. There is no female institution analogous to the men's house, although the uxorilocal household itself might be viewed as a female counterpart.

4. Ceremonial sexual access to each other's spouses, although sanctioned by custom, is a frequent cause for intragroup distress.

5. The Kayapó say that they marry only *mẽbaitebm* and never *ombikwa*, although it can be discovered that the rule is not always followed.

6. Although Hirschman's examples come predominantly from Western society, he is cognizant of the applicability of his theory to so-called primitive societies (1978).

7. I do not wish to imply by these comments my endorsement of the present government in Brazil or its Indian policy. My remark would be applicable to any government whose action promotes a positive effect, whether intended or not.

5. The Gê and Bororo Societies as Dialectical Systems

1. This is obviously a rule subject to the *ceteris paribus* qualification. It will, I suggest, tend to hold without qualification in systems in which kinship, in the sense of the relations of human production or socialization as the term is defined here, is the dominant form of production. In more economically developed systems, other things are no longer equal, the family and kinship system become subsumed into other, more complex relations of production and reproduction, and the rules of conservation as formulated here for the kinship system as a self-regulating and self-reproducing structure cease to apply.

6. Kinship, Household, and Community Structure among the Kayapó

1. I am very grateful to Professor Jean Lave for her close reading and incisive criticism of a draft of this paper, and to Professor David M. Schneider for many helpful comments.

2. There are a few additional relations included in the terminological categories of marginal relations owing to the Omaha cousin terminology and the subsumption of affines in the ascending generations into the categories of

their linking spouses, but these terminological additions do not affect the basic structure of marginal relations as discussed here.

3. These rituals and myths cannot, however, be assumed to reflect tensions peculiar to single-moiety villages, since they presumably were performed and told in two-moiety villages.

7. Cultural Categories of the Central Gê

1. Nimuendajú called it patrilocal. The importance of distinguishing between patrilocal and virilocal is discussed below.

2. To facilitate comparison with the Shavante terminology in Maybury-Lewis 1967:216–217, I shall give each Sherente term the same number as its corresponding Shavante term. Since there are fewer Sherente terms than Shavante terms, some numbers will be missing from the list presented here.

3. In a previous publication (Maybury-Lewis, 1965a:222) women of the opposite moiety in a generation older than ego's were inexplicably stated to be in the category *ĩ-tbe*. I wish here to rectify that slip and to emphasize this contrast between *ĩ-tbe* (own moiety) and *awasni* (opposite moiety).

4. See Maybury-Lewis, 1965b:chap. 6.

5. The modern Shavante use this word to refer to the two meeting places at the fulcrum of the village and reserved for the councils of mature men and young (initiated) men, respectively. The Sherente use the word to designate a men's house which, according to informants, used to be constructed somewhere in the middle of the village (see Figure 1). Nimuendajú stated that the *warã* used to be a bachelors' hut (1942:17), but I am led to doubt this. The only eyewitness description of an olden-day Sherente village which I have been able to find does not resolve the question. It indicated instead that, even at the turn of the century, the semicircular village layout was obsolete. It does, however, mention that a Sherente village had a central house occupied by older people. It also had a bachelors' hut built at some distance from the village (Cook 1909:143). This supports my belief that traditionally the Sherente, like the Shavante, had a central forum, or *warã*, for older people which was distinct from the bachelors' hut, located at a short distance from the village proper.

6. I use quite arbitrarily for standardization and convenience the roots of the Timbira terms given in Nimuendajú 1946:105.

7. These terms correspond to *ked, tui,* and *tamchwę* in fig. 4.

8. Corresponding to *ked, che,* and *tamchwę* in fig. 4.

9. These conclusions amply bear out Needham's contention that labels such as Crow and Omaha do not identify discriminable systems and should therefore be abandoned (1967:15–17).

10. See, for example, Barnes 1962 and particularly Keesing 1970.

11. See, for example, Radcliffe-Brown 1950; also in formulations derived from learning theory, as in Murdock 1949.

8. Selves and Alters among the Eastern Bororo

1. The research on which this paper reports was supported by N.I.M.H. Grant No. MH06185 and by a grant from the Duke University Committee for International Research. I am also grateful to the Duke University Re-

search Council for several Faculty Research Grants which have facilitated the analysis and preparation of this material for publication. My intellectual debts are to Claude Lévi-Strauss, Victor Turner, Thomas O. Beidelman, and, above all, David Maybury-Lewis. I also owe a great deal to several of my students who, over the years, have criticized the various drafts of this paper with much vigor and subtle perception. I particularly wish to thank Messrs. Richard Huntington, Joseph Woodside, Peter Huber, Robin Carter, Fred Damon, and Miss Patricia Beaver.

2. The major contributions to Bororo ethnography include Steinen 1940, Colbacchini and Albisetti 1942, Albisetti and Venturelli 1962, Montenegro 1958, Crocker 1967, and, of course, Lévi-Strauss 1936, 1955, 1958, and 1964.

3. I do have the impression that, in comparison with the Gê, relatively few Bororo have thus left their society, or rather their village.

4. See, for example, Albisetti and Venturelli 1962:429–445; Lévi-Strauss 1958:142–144, 156–158; Lévi-Strauss 1955:229–231; Lévi-Strauss 1960:48–49; and Maybury-Lewis 1960:23–27.

5. There is not the slightest indication of bellicosity between contemporary Bororo villages, and according to informants this has always been the case. There are no reliable historical records on this topic, but Albisetti and Venturelli (1962), and Montenegro (1958:passim) cite circumstantial evidence supporting this contention. I hope soon to publish an account of Bororo history which may clarify some of the economic, political, and historical factors which heavily contributed to the tribal harmony.

6. I have discussed the details of this model in Crocker 1967, 1969a, 1971, 1973, and 1977. In essence, the Bororo maintain that in the world of the dead, or the domain of the *aroe*, there are two villages of the dead sited far to the east and the west, respectively, of modern Bororo land. The rivers in this world all run from east to west, and all topographical spaces within it are populated according to the eightfold social division of the cosmos.

7. Here I have in mind the village of Pobore, sited a few kilometers outside the thriving boom town of Rondonópolis and scorned by other Bororo as the habitation of "thieves, alcoholics, and incestuous ones," who have completely lapsed from Bororo ways, and the Bororo settlements at Sangradouro and Merure, the two Salesian mission stations. As a general rule, the closer the Brazilian population, the more depressed and nontraditional the Bororo village, owing to the influence of wage work and, consequently, alcohol.

8. I wish to thank Professor Maybury-Lewis both for the sense of this insight and the specific formulation of it.

9. Bororo theory holds that every man who has intercourse with a woman during the period between the birth of one of her children and the next are genitors of the latter child. That is, they do not recognize any temporal limitation on gestation. If the time between parturitions is lengthy, and a woman's life turbulent, as tends to be the case, her child might recognize as many as a dozen genitors. The ritual acknowledgement of paternity becomes, in these common instances, rather more than an acquiescence to traditional practices.

10. The *i-maruga* ornaments the infant with duckdown and other items,

and holds it during the ceremony. The importance of this bond is attested in the usual mode of reference to one's clan *aroe* as both *i-edaga aroe,* and *i-maruga aroe.* The odd thing is that *i-maruga* is emphatically an agnatic-affinal category, applied to the FM, FMM, FZ, FZD, WM, WeZ, and so forth. However, the "naming *i-maruga*" is always that older woman who assisted the mother at childbirth, and who had the obligation to kill the infant if the ritual auspices at birth were bad. Normatively, the father's *i-maruga* (FFM, FFZ, and so on) should undertake this role. But nearly all women prefer that their own mother assist them, so that the "naming *i-maruga*" is usually a true MM. Given either prescriptive bilateral or patrilateral cross-cousin marriage, the MM would be the FFZ. The point is that the "naming *i-maruga*" is the only member of her moiety to whom ego applies this category in any strict and regular way. She appears in many myths and ritual statements as a highly ambiguous figure, always coresident with a masculine ego before his initiation. This obvious problem has confused many commentators on the Bororo scene.

11. Some aspects of a clan's property are transferable. Men of the opposite moiety may receive clan property as compensation for ritual acts, but they only have rights of usufruct over a certain number of ornaments, and these rights terminate on their death.

12. I am aware that such translocations are a common mode of lineage fission in both matrilineal and patrilineal societies, whatever the attendant motives or ideological interpretations (Worsley 1956). However, the immediacy and inconsequential character of Bororo practices would seem to distinguish them from such patterns. That is, there are no historical consequences of Bororo movements away from a "hiving" lineage: the new unit does not found a distinct group, and it may be reincorporated (and often is) into the "parental" unit at any time.

13. "Adoption" is a frequent event within the clan, and occurs within the moiety from time to time. The most usual motives are either the obligatory assumption of parental responsibilities toward an orphan or a desire to replace a unit which has died out. In all cases a name is again bestowed, from the adoptor's name-set. Although consanguineal and clan relations nearly always employ the category, and adopt the behavior, that such adoption implies, it rarely "takes" for any extended period. As the Bororo say, "Everyone knows where the person was born, and the first name is the right name."

14. I use "cultural" here to mean an abstraction of the symbolic modes utilized to express the nature of the relationship. I do not find any heuristic value whatsoever in a sharp distinction between culture and society.

15. The unwary might leap to the conclusion, as I initially did, that this formulation represents the presumption of some (hypothetical) genealogical relation among the founders of the clan's name-sets, such as the birth order among a set of uterine sons of someone's mother. Nothing could be further from the Bororo understanding of the situation. Their analogic model is drawn not from a historically projected understanding of descent, but from the contemporary dilemma of actual brothers, who view primacy of birth as conferring a very real advantage.

16. Bororo politics are so complex, so bound up with domestic affairs and

ritual honors, that only a very lengthy account can do justice to the subtlety of the system that regulates the individual's strivings for power. Further, as Maybury-Lewis pointed out to me some years ago, the Bororo find there is very little actual "power" for which to contend, thanks to the Brazilian usurpation of all real jural control. Nonetheless, such power as there is derives from the various judgements of the opposite moiety.

17. The men's house is open to certain women who enjoy the status of *aredu baito,* or "men's house prostitutes," and to other women at certain specified ritual moments (Crocker 1969b). However, the admission of the first category was strictly regulated, and it is my impression that traditionally they were permitted access only at night, during those times when a ritual was not in progress.

18. A father may thus substitute for his son until initiation. After this rite, it is felt, the son must gain his own honors; that is, after initiation a man becomes ritually and jurally autonomous and responsible for his own actions.

19. I have some reason to believe that Bororo women, appropriately enough, do perceive the relation between the moieties as precisely that of exchanging husbands, and, as noted earlier, the men often characterize the other moiety as "our fathers." A careful interpretation would have to emphasize the close association between fathers and the privilege of *aroe* representation, for this is the subject of Bororo ceremonial transcendental "life."

20. It is of course axiomatic that women lack an *i-orubadari,* for they do not participate in initiation. In theory, a woman should be represented at death by one of her brother's *i-orubadari,* but in practice, her *aroe maiwu* is simply a member of her father's clan.

21. There is a problem here which the Bororo explicitly recognize, that a man's father and mother are rarely alive at the time of his own death. However, children who have received a name are also given a representative in the event of death. Their actual parents will then often carry over their roles into the ritual triad. In these cases, the representative simply is a member of the father's clan. I know of several cases in which one or the other parent made toys or prepared the dead child's favorite dishes for the *aroe maiwu,* who received these prestations with respectful and appropriate behavior.

22. They are, however, reflected in the elaborate and flowery terms of Bororo formal speech. For example, in most public contexts adult men commonly address and refer to the senior women of the other moiety as *pa-xe aroe,* "our spirit mothers," or even as simply *pa-xe.* Such usages make the study of Bororo relationship terminology highly confusing to the novice.

23. The importance of this service should not be minimized, since lugging a thirty- or forty-pound deer ten miles through jungle in the middle of a tropical day is not a pleasant task. The Bororo assumption here is that the carrier is always a member of the dead man's clan.

24. During major ceremonies, when it is not uncommon for half a village to visit the sponsoring community, ceremonial hunts are held as often as possible for economic and ritual motives. I was also told that the dry season treks, which are no longer performed, were occasions upon which the triads could be reactivated as the trekkers visited one community after another.

25. These include the right to make and wear any property belonging to

the deceased's name-set, but not the right to dispose of these to a third party except an uninitiated relative. Representatives are nearly always termed *i-adu* by most members of the deceased's clan, this category replacing all others except those of direct genealogical connection (for example, father, father's brother).

Conclusion

1. See, for example, Nimuendajú 1946:1–2 and Maybury-Lewis 1965:343.

2. The Shavante were quite explicit about this when I was working with them in 1959. When asked why they did not cultivate bitter manioc, since they were so fond of *farinha* (manioc flour), they replied that it required too much attention and that it would prevent their going out on trek.

3. Or rather the base villages. Most of the Central Brazilian peoples were transhumant, living much of the year on trek in relatively small bands and coming together for only part of the year in the base village.

4. This information was taken from Nimuendajú's accounts of the Eastern Timbira (1946) and the Kayapó (Lowie 1943) for the Northern Gê, and of the Sherente (1942) for the Central Gê. The characterization of the Bororo comes from Colbacchini and Albisetti 1942. The anomalous descent system of the Apinayé is discussed below.

5. See da Matta, this volume, and da Matta 1971 and 1976.

6. For example, the Sharanahua (Siskind 1973), the Kashinawa (Kensinger forthcoming), the Mundurucú (Murphy 1960), and the Kagwahiv or Parintintin (Kracke 1976).

7. See Leach (1961a:11) for a similar argument concerning unilineal descent.

8. See, for example, Leach 1961b; Lewis 1965; Needham 1971; Barth 1973.

9. Or men, among the matrilineal Bororo.

10. See, for example, Needham 1973 and 1974:107.

11. Needham argued that the Sirionó were matrilineal. If they had an alliance system, then, husbands would be communicated in marriage.

12. See Lévi-Strauss 1949 for an extended discussion of the implications of marriage with the mother's brother's daughter and Needham 1973 for a more recent and different view of the entailments of prescription.

13. See Scheffler and Lounsbury 1971:179 for a discussion of the "type" (their quotation marks) and 1971:110 for a description of the rule.

14. See their rendering of the Sirionó kinship system (1971:145).

15. A similar approach was advocated by a number of contributors to Needham, ed., *Rethinking kinship and marriage* (1971).

Index

Abortion, 58
Affinity, *see* Kinship
Age: classes, 11, 118; grades, 9, 10, 11,
134–135, 153, 179, 205–206, 213, 235;
moieties, 26, 47, 236; sets, xiv, 9, 17,
33–44, 47, 171, 176, 178, 219, 236, 249,
251, 275, 312, (contrasted with
names) 17, 33–37
Agriculture, xii, 15, 33, 35, 40, 41, 45,
48, 49, 51, 81, 129, 130, 147, 149–152,
156–157, 175–178, 215, 216, 219, 248,
269, 301–303
Akwẽ, xiv, 3
Albisetti, Cesar, 1, 253, 258, 262, 286, 287,
330, 333
Amazon: invaders of, 301; lowland
Amazonian society, 164, 165, 174–176;
region, xi, xii, xiii, 174–176; Trans-
Amazon Highway, 81, 129, 145, 146
Apaniekra, xi, xiii, 4, 5, 7, 15, 45
Apinayé, xi, xiv, 1, 4, 9, 10, 15, 45, 81–
127, 234, 235, 239, 240, 241, 295, 296,
306; anomaly, 9, 10, 84, 85, 112, 303–
304, 309
Araguaia River, 129, 216, 247
Arawak, ix, 165
Associations, *see* Societies
Asymmetry, social, 300, 306
Australians, 12, 84, 303, 312

Bachelors' hut, *see* Men's house
Baldus, Herbert, xi, 2
Barlaeus, C., 1
Barnes, J. A., 329

Baro, Rovlox, 1
Barth, Fredrik, 333
Bateson, Gregory, 300
Bathonga, 126
Beidelman, Thomas O., 330
Belém-Brasília Highway, 15, 216
Belief, *see* Ideology
Benedict, Ruth, xii
Birth, 58, 101–106, 185, 188
Boas, Franz, xii
Boats, xii
Bolivia, 307
Bororo, xiii, xiv, 1, 2, 3, 4, 5, 7, 9, 11, 12,
13, 17, 84, 85, 147–178, 179, 216, 233,
234, 236, 237, 239, 240, 241, 242, 247–
300, 301, 302, 304, 305, 306, 307, 311,
312; Eastern and Western, 247
Bullroarers, 294
Bunzel, Ruth, xii

Câmara, Cascudo, Luis de, 76
Canela, xi, 33, 51, 116
Cardoso de Oliveira, Roberto, xiii, 326
Carib, ix, 165
Carneiro, Robert, 132, 149, 176
Carneiro da Cunha, M., 326
Caste, 283
Cattle, 15, 45, 81, 216
Central Gê, 4, 5, 9, 11, 17, 215–246, 254,
276, 296, 300, 303, 307
Ceremonial: communal, 150, 152, 160,
168, (contrasted with consanguinity)
107, 112, 113–115, 120, 123, 124,
(contrasted with domestic) 9, 10, 29,

335